Love Letters
A NATION AT WAR

MARCIE MCGUIRE

WITH
ELLIOTT CRANFILL & ELMA BEATTY

Matthew Sleadd
A Small press family

Copyright © 2022 by Marcie McGuire

All rights reserved.

No part of this book may be reproduced in any form or by any electronic or mechanical means, including information storage and retrieval systems, without written permission from the author.

All brand names and product names used in this book are trade names, service marks, trademarks, and registered trademarks of their respective owners.

Although every effort has been made to verify the information contained in this work of non-fiction, the author and publisher make no guarantees of its accuracy.

No claim is made to works that exist in the public domain. These items are used in compliance with United States Copyright with attribution provided.

Contents

Preface — vii
Introduction — xiii

PART ONE
1917

1. June - August, 1917 — 3
2. December, 1917 — 17

PART TWO
1918

3. June, 1918 — 27
4. July, 1918 — 69
5. August, 1918 — 111
6. September, 1918 — 163
7. October, 1918 — 207
8. November, 1918 — 277
9. December, 1918 — 325

   Before Texting — 347
   Epilogue — 353

Lexicon — 355
Dramatis Personae — 357
Notes — 377
Works Cited — 385
Bibliography — 391
Marcie McGuire — 401

*To Elliott Cranfill and Elma Beatty;
your love is our inspiration.*

Preface

While going through my mother's house after she died, I came across a box of nearly 250 letters that my grandparents wrote in college from 1917 to 1920. The letters were in their original envelopes, in small bundles tied with ribbon or held together with rubber bands. I was surprised they had survived all those years and curious to see what was in them. Our family moved many times over the years. Still, my grandparents valued this box of letters enough to carry them along on every move — from Kentucky in the 1910s and 1920s, to Mississippi in the 1930s, to Texas in the 1940s, back to Kentucky in the 1950s, and finally to Florida in the 1960s. I don't know whether they reread their letters or moved the box from place to place unopened. By the time my grandfather died at age 89, after letting go of everything else in his life, he still had these letters in his room at the nursing home.

Remarkably, both correspondents saved most, if not all, the letters they wrote during their courtship. I was shocked that my grandfather held on to all the ones he received from my grandmother. I don't know how many young men would have done that. This meant that while he was in the Navy, he must have carried her letters in his ditty box every time he moved. I was less surprised that grandmother saved the letters she received. She also held onto scrapbooks and yearbooks and always talked about her college days as the happiest time of her life.

I knew I wanted to preserve these letters for the family, but I also thought they might have broader appeal because of the time and place they were written. I love everything about them — from the high-quality paper with a simple gold edge or embossed college seal to the elegant Palmer-style handwriting, a simplified style intended for business writing.

I love the spark of recognition when I read things that remind me of the grandparents I knew as older adults — grandaddy's simple sense of humor, seriousness, and interest in politics, grandmother's love of social entertainment and her tendency to exaggerate and dramatize. I love hearing the day-to-day details about life in the nineteen-teens. I love hearing about their friends, their classes, the things they thought about, and their hopes, fears, and beliefs.

I love the sense of time that opens up when I think about how they wrote to each other three or four nights a week, long detailed letters of 1500-2000 words. Of course, if grandaddy had not spent the fall of 1918 at the naval training station, these letters would not exist. If both of them had remained at school, there would be no reason to write about their activities because they would have just talked in person. As it was, they felt the need to stay connected through letters. Phone calls would have been possible but expensive.

I wonder how different they were from young people today. In some ways, they seem similar—at the stage of life where they seek their path, explore their beliefs, connect more with friends than family, and try to figure out how they fit into a rapidly changing world. But in other ways, they seem more grounded, more optimistic about the future, more goal-oriented, and more mature. They work harder and believe they can make a difference in the world.

In these letters, grandmother seems susceptible to fads and concerned about the impression she is making. She probably would have loved Facebook. Her talk about how she loves to sew and her statements about housework made me laugh. She never did housework that I know of and must have been trying to impress grandaddy with her vast knowledge of "domestic science." Grandaddy did most, if not all, of the

PREFACE

cooking and house cleaning when I knew them. It also made me laugh when I read a program for the Zeta literary society in which she participated in a debate over whether men should be required to take two full years of domestic science to earn their BS degree.

I feel very fortunate to have so many well-preserved artifacts from 100 years ago — letters representing both sides of the conversation, photos, news clippings, songbooks, and yearbooks (except for 1918, because the college did not produce a yearbook during the war). I am also fortunate to have several well-made scrapbooks of their college days. The carefully labeled photos help identify people mentioned in the letters, and the mementos add context to some of the references. For example, when grandmother talks about a banquet they attended, I have the menu, the place cards, and the program. Do young people still attend banquets these days? Surprisingly, even grandaddy kept a scrapbook during college. Was that typical for men? His, of course, has more photos of sporting events than grandmother's.

The letters are well-written and beautifully legible. The Palmer method of handwriting — a simplified style of the more florid Spencerian method — was in vogue at the time. It was characterized by its legibility, rapidity, and beauty and was considered suitable for business writing. Elma and Elliott must have learned this style well, for they apparently could write letters of 1500 to 2000 words in ink with very few cross-outs or blots. Most letters were written with a fountain pen on quality paper, so they are in excellent shape, considering they are over one hundred years old. A few of grandaddy's letters from Great Lakes Naval Training Station were written in pencil on wood-pulp paper, so those required special handling. The letters also reflect the classical education that Elliott and Elma received in high school and college. They follow standard grammar, syntax, and punctuation rules, with occasional sprinkles of foreign terms, slang, or "countrified" diction for variety. They often mention current events and politics, books they were reading, classes they were taking, and social customs, in addition to more personal reflections and gossip about people they knew.

PREFACE

It was such a treat for me to read these letters from the past and to recognize in them the spirits of my grandparents. By the time I knew my grandparents well, they were in their sixties, but their personalities were not that different from what is reflected in these letters. Grandmother always enjoyed being around people, and she looked forward to getting letters from friends and family all her life. If no letters arrived and no one was around to entertain her, she became pretty "blue." Grandaddy was more introverted and could engage himself better. He enjoyed reading, gardening, and fishing and had a dry sense of humor. Generally, if both were in the room together, grandaddy remained quiet and let grandmother have the stage. Both were effective public speakers; they taught college and were active in their church. They kept well informed about current events. They valued education and kept in touch with their college classmates for their entire lifetime. They held to the Christian virtues of faith, hope, and charity and believed in service to God and their fellow humans.

Elma's letters can be frustrating in their lack of particular kinds of detail. For example, she might say she saw "a real good war show" but not mention the title. Or she might talk about "visiting various places of interest" but not say where they were or what she found interesting. Or she will talk about going to a friend's house to listen to the Victrola but won't say what music they listened to. However, her vivid descriptions and storytelling style present a good view of what life was like for a sociable young woman living in a small town in Kentucky in 1918. Occasionally, she includes some information I can verify, such as when she mentions the June 1918 eclipse. I also found historic postcards of many of the places she mentions in Bowling Green. Elma's college yearbooks and scrapbooks, of course, were invaluable resources.

Elliott's letters tend to be more informative and less designed to entertain, so many of the names, dates, and events he mentions can be verified in historical records. Still, there are things that I wish I could find out more about. For example, in a couple of letters, he talks about lawn parties in Anderson County, Kentucky. He mentions electric lights and an orchestra and some system involving tickets, which was apparently how he knew how many girls were at the party. At one of these parties, he says that truckloads of people showed up from towns as far as

PREFACE

forty miles away, but he doesn't describe what went on at the parties. His references to family and friends from home can also be frustratingly vague, as when he talks about "my brother" (although he had three brothers) or "my cousin" (without providing a name) or refers to "a high school friend."

Still, I'm not complaining. These letters contain a fantastic amount of information about my grandparents' lives during a time that was incredibly important to them both. I am lucky to have had this chance to get to know my grandparents as they were in college — idealistic young people figuring out who they were and what they wanted to be at a time of intense social and political change. In letter after letter, I am privileged to hear little dramas of daily life, cameos of friends, snatches of gossip, and earnest questions about love and life as they explore their thoughts and feelings about the world and each other. The letters chronicle the story of two bright young people coming of age at the beginning of the last century, a hundred years ago. In some ways, their concerns feel very familiar. They remind me of things I've forgotten, values we have lost sight of. I hope that by publishing these letters, I can pass some of these values on to my children and grandchildren.

These letters by Elliott Cranfill and Elma Beatty are currently located at my home in Columbia, Missouri. I have tried to follow standard archival principles to preserve and protect them while they are in my care, but at some point, I will seek to donate them to a library or archives where they can be cared for and made available to a broader audience. The total collection consists of 230 letters written from 1917 to 1920. Elliott and Elma were students at Georgetown College in Georgetown, Kentucky, and at first, they mainly wrote during summer and Christmas breaks from school. However, in July 1918, Elliott enlisted in the Navy and headed to Great Lakes Training Station, and they were separated until after the war ended. During their separation, they wrote 88 letters detailing their daily lives and exploring their "ideas and ideals," allowing a glimpse into what college and military life were like in 1918. The earliest letters are somewhat formal, but after Elma and Elliott got to

PREFACE

know each other better, many of their letters read almost like journals, written in real-time, with breaks for dinner or to respond to other interruptions. Their separation allowed them to reflect on serious issues and express their views candidly. It also led to occasional misunderstandings, which they thought would not have happened if they had communicated in person.

This volume includes all their letters from June 1917 to December 1918. I have transcribed the letters as written and have not edited them for spelling or punctuation. I made scans of each letter and proofread each transcription against the original.

The chapter headings are taken from the titles of popular songs during the era. Although there is no way to know whether Elliott and Elma listened to these particular songs, the lyrics reflect the sentiments expressed in their letters, and it is easy to imagine that Elma might have listened to some of these songs on friends' Victrolas or purchased sheet music to play on her piano. Elliott mentioned songs the sailors sang, and he attended concerts and shows during his time in the Navy.

I have included introductions and footnotes, where needed, to provide additional context. A complete list of the individuals mentioned in the letters is provided at the end of the book. Elma and Elliott often use abbreviations in their letters, such as G.C. for Georgetown College, S.S. for Sunday School, and B.G. for Bowling Green. In addition, they sometimes use a shorthand very similar to today's texting, for example, when they write "C" for "See?" or "See." A list of abbreviations can be found in the appendix.

Marcie McGuire

Introduction

Elliott Cranfill was born September 18, 1896, and was raised on a farm in Anderson County, Kentucky, near the village of Sinai. The youngest of five sons, he was the first in his family to attend high school. His father, a contractor and farmer, had a good-sized farm, where he and his sons raised wheat, corn, and tobacco; raised cattle, pigs, and chickens; and grew enough vegetables to feed the family. He also worked in construction and built furniture. When Elliott was a young teenager, he took time off school to help his father and his older brothers build a county road, after which his father agreed to let him go to high school. This was likely a major turning point in Elliott's life. He drove his horse and buggy more than ten miles each way to Lawrenceburg, Kentucky, where he attended high school and played sports under the colorful principal Mrs. Rhoda Kavanaugh, a stern disciplinarian and basketball enthusiast. In addition to teaching the "day students" like Elliott, Mrs. Kavanaugh also coached numerous students in preparation for entrance exams to West Point and Annapolis. Elliott greatly admired Mrs. Kavanauagh. He did well in classes, participated on the debate team, set the high jump record in track, played basketball, and was inspired to continue his education past high school. After college, he returned to teach at Mrs. Kavanaugh's school for a year.

He was twenty when he arrived on campus at Georgetown College, somewhat older than most students and grateful for the privilege of going to college. His freshman photo in the 1917 college yearbook shows him wearing a dark suit with wide lapels; a white shirt with a tall, stiff, rounded collar; and a solid necktie. His dark hair is longer than that of the other boys, parted on the left side, with a long curly shock combed back on the right side. Introverted, serious, and hardworking, but with a folksy sense of humor, he became a proud member of the Tau Theta Kappa (T.Θ.K.) literary society, which engaged in competition with the Ciceronians in debate and oratory. Both literary clubs regularly presented programs and organized receptions to entertain the girls of Rucker Hall. He took classes in history, German, Greek, physics, and English. He also played sports in college.

On breaks from school, Elliott boarded the train to Lawrenceburg, where he would catch a ride in a Lizzie automobile from one of his brothers or a neighbor the rest of the way to the farm. During winter breaks he attended basketball games and receptions at his old high school. During summer breaks he changed back into his overalls and straw hat and headed out to the fields to work. He said his family lived so far out in the country that you couldn't see the sun unless it was straight overhead, but he liked it that way because no one could hear him singing in the fields.

INTRODUCTION

Elma Beatty was born January 1, 1898, and grew up in Simpson County, Kentucky, near the Tennessee border. She was essentially raised as an only child, although her parents had had three children; Elma's older sister Mary died of typhoid fever at age 18 when Elma was 5; a brother died in infancy before Elma was born. After Elma's sister died, the family moved into town, and the father gave up farming. At some point, he was also a rural mail carrier. It is not clear whether the family suffered financial problems that made them give up the farm, or they decided to move so Elma would be closer to school. Perhaps the farm simply held too many sad memories for the family to stay there. Elma mostly remembered having to leave her puppy behind.

Although they were not rich by any standards, Elma's parents doted on her and made sure she got a good education. Somehow they scraped together the resources to give her piano lessons and send her to Miss Maude's private grade school, then to the Franklin Female Academy for high school, and ultimately to Georgetown College. Her church also helped by providing scholarship money for college, and Elma worked in the business office at college to pay for room and board. Elma loved school and always enjoyed spending time with friends. But it must have been very hard on her parents to send their only living child 200 miles away for school, especially at a time when only about 16%[1] of the U.S. population graduated from high school.

Her college yearbook shows Elma Beatty stylishly dressed in a long skirt and middy blouse, with her auburn hair piled up on her head in a way that made her look quite elegant. Popular and vivacious, smart and hardworking, she loved everything about college. She took a full load of courses each semester, including English, French, German, and piano, in addition to working in the business office. But she also left plenty of time to socialize with her many friends and participate in the Zeta literary society.

On school breaks, she would return home by train to Franklin, Kentucky, often in the company of other schoolmates, and they would sing songs and tell jokes and party as the train traveled across the state,

INTRODUCTION

dropping people off at various stations along the way. During longer layovers in Louisville, she would walk downtown with friends to get a bite to eat or catch a movie. When she arrived in Franklin, after a full day of travel, she walked into the arms of her best friend Delma and her dear father and mother. Back at home, she helped her parents around the house, caught up with old friends from the Franklin Female Academy, attended church and Sunday school, led programs for the Baptist Young People's Union, entertained her parents with renditions on the piano, and wrote long chatty letters to her college friends. Years later, she continued to think of college as the best time of her life.

Elliott Cranfill and Elma Beatty met during their freshman year at Georgetown College,[2] in the fall of 1916, when he was 20 and she was 18. Most of the 280 students enrolled that fall, like Elliott and Elma, came from small towns and rural areas of Kentucky.

There is no record of their first meeting, but they most likely took classes together and attended many of the same school activities. Georgetown followed a "modified classical curriculum" at the time, and students were required to take core courses in English, Latin, mathematics, and German during their first year of college. Intercollegiate athletics were popular, and Georgetown competed in football, basketball, baseball, and track. Elma probably did not play sports herself, but she likely attended college athletic events and may have noticed Elliott on the sports field.

Both Elliott and Elma regularly participated in literary societies, which emphasized public speaking and held lively competitions and socials in their respective halls. The Opera House downtown provided additional entertainment, including vaudeville groups, plays, minstrels, and silent movies, with the bill changing every three days. Although Elma and Elliott occasionally mention movies in their letters, they apparently did not care much for them, and such entertainments were not a big part of their social life. There would have been no dancing or alcohol at Georgetown, a Baptist college. Students were more likely to participate in activities and programs at church or Sunday school. They

INTRODUCTION

may very well have been part of the Student Prohibition League organized to help make the nation "high and dry forever."[3]

By the end of their freshman year, Elliott obviously felt confident enough in their friendship to initiate their correspondence and to send a poem he wrote for Elma on the train ride home. In his first letter, he refers to the enjoyable evenings they spent together before school was out. He surely would have been pleased to hear how "dreadful glad" she was to get his letter and to read about how she began to "quiver and quake" whenever she thought about their last Sunday together. Their personalities shine through these letters: Elliott, the introverted farm boy with a keen sense of humor and a quiet determination, and Elma, the fun-loving girl who enjoys socializing with friends and entertaining others. Elliott and Elma were both raised in Christian families and shared many of the same beliefs and moral standards. They were devoted to their families and valued their education. They were dedicated to providing service to others. Both were skilled correspondents. They took care with their writing and apologized when they thought the letters might be too long or too short, or if there were disorganized thoughts or blots.

During that first summer, they wrote three letters each, in which they tentatively explored ideas and beliefs and got to know each other a little better. In some cases, the letters appear to continue discussions that were started while at college. They talk about what they were working on while at home and say they object to the "common belief" that college folks don't know how to work. They share news about people back home and people they both knew from college. They report on what grades they received. They request photos of each other. They flirt and tease each other. They talk about lawn parties and picnics and parades and revivals and driving around in the Lizzy. They express their opinions on social and political events of the time. Elliott talks about girls and says that Elma seems different from other girls. They talk about county politics and woman's suffrage. And Elliott expresses concern that he might not be able to return to campus in the fall if his brother is drafted because he would then need to stay home to help on the farm.

When Elliott and Elma sat down at their respective desks to write to each other during school breaks, their sense of distance and separation

INTRODUCTION

and time would have differed greatly from today. Telephones were available, but not everyone owned one, and calls were expensive. They were mostly for business or emergencies, not just to tell your girlfriend how much you missed her. There was of course no email, no Facebook, Twitter, Snapchat, or Instagram, no text messaging, and no instantaneous responses to questions or concerns. When they sent a letter, they had to wait several days for a response, which sometimes led to misunderstandings. By today's standards, they did not live far from each other — a couple of hours by car — but in 1917, it was not so easy to travel the distance between Elliott's family farm in Anderson County and Elma's home in Franklin.

Their earliest letters describe their trips home, and the contrast between the two writers is quite striking. They start out riding the train together from Georgetown, but Elliott gets off in Frankfort, where he catches a Ford truck on to Lawrenceburg and then has to wait all evening for his brother to take him the rest of the way to their farm. In the meantime, Elma and several other schoolmates continue on toward Louisville, laughing and singing and carrying on. During the layover, they check their bags and walk to town for lunch. When Elma arrives in her hometown of Franklin, several friends and her parents are there at the station to meet her.

As early as the summer of 1917, specific themes start to emerge in the letters. Elliott eventually went on to teach economics, and he enjoyed reading biographies, histories, and political science all his life. So it's interesting to read his early impressions of local county politics, as well as national events that affected him even on the farm and in the villages in Anderson County. For much of her career, Elma taught sociology, which also fits with her early interest in people and relationships. Her favorite course to teach was Courtship and Marriage, which no doubt allowed her to relive some of the best times of her life.

By the time Elma and Elliott complete their sophomore year of college in 1918, they had become quite close. By then, they had apparently spent many "calling nights" together during the school year, and

INTRODUCTION

their "good nights" had taken on special significance. Whether they hugged or kissed when they said their good nights is not clear, but the letters written during the summer of 1918 are longer than previous letters and are signed "with love." Elliott makes indirect references to curfew at Rucker Hall dormitory, and Elma refers to "calling day" and mentions several items that Elliott had given her, including a cup, a book, and a pin with his literary society Greek letters on it. She says her mother is beginning to suspect something.

As Elliott feared, he did not get to return to college in the fall of 1918. Rather than wait to be drafted into the Army, he decided to enlist in the Navy. He felt that he would be considered a slacker if he did not serve his country. He spent that summer helping his family on the farm as much as he could before he left for boot camp at the Great Lakes Training Center. Elma enrolled at the Business University in Bowling Green, where she took courses in typing, shorthand, and penmanship. Throughout the summer and fall, they wrote two to three times per week, long, expressive letters in which they shared thoughts and feelings about their relationship and about many important issues of the time.

After Elliott gets out of the Navy and returns to college in early December 1918, there are no more letters until they go home for Christmas break. Unfortunately, there are no written descriptions of what they did when Elliott returned to campus and no descriptions of their senior year together. Since they were both on campus at that point, there was no reason to write to each other. However, there are a few short notes likely written in early 1919, when both of them were sick and confined to their rooms. During this time, they sent letters several times a day "postmarked" from the library or the chapel or the office, and delivered by mutual friends. After that, they wrote several letters in late spring 1920, after they left campus and before they married on June 15. These tell about many practical details, including getting their marriage license and shopping for wedding clothes, among other things.

PART ONE
1917

CHAPTER 1
June – August, 1917

The Sunshine of Your Smile[1]

Verse 1:
Dear face that holds so sweet a smile for me.
Were you not mine, how dark this world would be.
I know no light above that could replace
Love's radiant sunshine in your dear face.

Verse 2:
Shadows may fall across the land and sea.
Sunshine from all the world may hidden be.
But I shall see no clouds across the sun.
Your smile shall light my life till life is done.

Chorus:
Give me a smile, the love-light in your eyes.
Life could not hold a sweeter paradise.
Give me the right to love you all the while.
My world forever, the sunshine of your smile.

JUNE 6, 1917

Shortly after arriving home for the summer at the end of his freshman year in college, Elliott took the initiative to write to his classmate Elma.

Dear Miss Beatty:

Hello, how is home? But I know you are having a nice time. You ought to see me with my overalls on, and my big straw hat. You would never think by seeing me now, that I had ever been inside of a college. I look like I had been a farm hand all my days, but perhaps you thought that even while I was at G.C. [Georgetown College].

Well, how was the "Devil's" play Tuesday, and the rest of the commencement exercises? Did you have any more adventures before you left? I am trying to find out what lucky fellow had the opportunity of sitting in the swing with you until Miss Howard came in after I left. I sure did enjoy that little evening with you, Elma, and also Monday night. I did not have time to tell you really how much I did enjoy being with you, for it was so late. Indeed I had many things I would like to have said to you but — Miss Howard[2] came in the first evening, and I was afraid you were too sick to listen to it the last evening. (I do hope you did not feel any bad effects of the banquet, for I was really afraid that you were too sick to go, and yet I was too selfish to even mention such a thing as you not going for I felt that I couldn't miss having your company that night.) I hope you enjoyed all of it.

Say, I am rather lonesome now, but I hope it will not last. I do not imagine you will be lonesome at all when you get home, for that fellow you left last fall will look very nice to you this summer. Say, I wish you would send me your picture (and his too). It will be so long before I will see you again. But if you would rather keep his, would you please just send me one of yours? Really, I do not especially care for him anyway, (as I would not know him anyway). You see I try to keep my promises.

Your friend,
"Sam the T.Ø.K"

P.S. If you can't read this just send me word and I will come down to your place and read it to you. S.E.C.
P.P.S. I am sending a bit of rhyming prose that I wrote as I came home on the train just to let you know that I was thinking of you. Tot[3]

∼

JUNE 12, 1917

Elma's chatty response confirms that she was quite pleased to correspond with Elliott.

Dear "Tham"[4] (the T.Ø.K):

I was dreadful glad to get your interesting letter and to find out that you were a real sure enough poet. Honest, you are equal if not superior to Reinhardt. I believe you are going to be the poet of the class of 1920, that is if you are not Valedictorian, which I am expecting you to be.

I reached home safely Thurs. night and it seemed that all Franklin[5] was out to meet us. They pretended they were dreadful glad to see us, but I don't think they really were. My thoughts were back at old G.C. until I got within twenty miles of home, then I began to get excited and Blanche [Hall] said she was truly glad she could get off at Woodburn[6] and not see me land in Franklin a raving maniac. But I have about subsided now and am almost ready to come back to the bluegrass region. When I think of that Sunday night I begin to quiver and quake. I wasn't a bit scared at the time, but I sure wouldn't try it again. It was nothing short of a miracle that Miss Howard didn't tell.

Oh, yes, I went to the plays and they were very good, however not quite as good as I had expected. Instead of the "League of Youth,"[7] they gave the "School of Scandal"[8] and no one liked it very much. The rest of Commencement was great and I wasn't at all sorry I made up my mind to stay. I wouldn't have missed the banquet for anything. I enjoyed every minute of it and entirely forgot that I was sick.

I just wish I could see you in your overalls and big straw hat. I know you make a dandy good farmer. But don't think you are the only one who is working. I have been washing, ironing, cooking, and keeping house since I came home. Mother has turned everything over to me and I am taking a thorough course in domestic science. I really believe it is better than our friend Miss Howard could give. Talk about college folks not knowing how to work — I say it is all nonsense. Don't you? I think it is heaps of fun after nine months of studying. You said something about a picture — well, let me suggest something. You send me one of yours, then I'll send you mine. Don't you think that would be right nice? I just want it awful bad. Honest, I do. By the way, I got my annual [the Georgetown College yearbook, *Belle of the Blue*] (is that the way you spell it?) Wednesday afternoon before I left. I suppose you have gotten yours by now. I think they are much better this year than they were last.

Please forgive me for writing a regular newspaper the first time. I never know when to stop when I get started. If you will answer immediately, forthwith, if not sooner, and also send that picture, I'll promise not to tire you so anymore (I mean with such a long letter).

Your Sincerest Friend,
Elma

P.S. Thanks awfully for the little poem. Give me another one sometime.

JUNE 25, 1917

Elliott's sweet disposition and folksy, self-deprecating humor come through in his second letter.

Dear Miss Beatty:

I was glad to hear that you got home o.k. and that all of your friends were at the train to give you a hearty welcome. I felt rather deserted and lonesome when I got off the train, no one to meet me (except [my] brother)[9] see? But I have been having a real nice time since I got home. I got to the station [at] about 8:45. I got home [at] about 1:30 p.m. You all [k]now about how far out in the sticks I live. We had a "Lizzi"[10] too, but my brother had to stop and register.[11] The preacher at church today, when speaking of the time to begin service, said he would begin by sun time for "we are nearer the sun than the railroad."

Well, I didn't think about you making fun of a fellow's poetry by telling him that it was good. Thank you just the same.

You said you never expected to spend another Sunday night as you did one. Every girl I ever went with has said the same thing. They all regret ever having been guilty of going with me. I knew that you would also. I did certainly enjoy that short evening (if you didn't).

I got my annual about a week ago. I thought it was very nice, but it couldn't have been otherwise for look whose pictures were in it. I got my grades too. I got two 95s and a 94. I felt like "shoutin" for I was at a sanctified meeting when I opened the letter — and a woman preacher but — she was a "Frau." 92 was my second lowest grade for the semester. I got 86 in Latin. I guess you got four hundreds and one 99?

Oh yes, about that picture. I haven't any pictures of myself. I can't find a photographer who will risk his camera on me. I have tried to get a picture all of my life and I haven't got one yet. I believe you knew that fact and that is the reason why you suggested the thing that you did. If I could ever get a picture made, and if I knew that you would really have one of them, I would send it immediately. I mean after I got it made. Elma, I think you could send me one of your pictures for I can't help it that I am so unfortunately ugly. I promise to send you one (if you will actually have it) just as soon as I can invent a camera that won't break, or just as soon as I can find a man that will risk his machine. Be kind and send me one of yours won't you please. "Bitte bitte fraulein."

A long letter, did you say you ever wrote a long letter? I never write long letters, but I do enjoy reading short ones like yours was. That letter you wrote me was about the nicest letter I ever got. I did enjoy it very much. I did not expect you to ever answer my letter. The girls have fooled me so often. But from the very first of school, I thought you were different from other girls. (For none of the other girls that I ever knew would go with me.) Most all the girls around here are flirts. You might be one for all that I know about you, but I have never taken you for that kind of girl. Of course, you have never made a pretense that you even like me except that you gave me your company once or twice. I guess you could tell by my actions that I liked you better than any other girl in college. I am not trying to compliment you merely for compliments' sake, but you did impress me as being one of the nicest girls that I ever knew. I guess I had better stop right here or I will begin on another poem. I do not believe in giving compliments just to be talking, but if anyone does really believe in a person it is good to tell them so, for I know by past experience confidence that has been shown by friends in me has always encouraged and helped me. Of course, I have done nothing yet, but if I ever amount to anything I will attribute a great part of it to words of confidence that have been spoken to me by friends.

Well, you will think I am trying to write phylosophy [sic], or a sermon, or something. I do not know what it is myself. I have often had folks tell me that I take things too seriously. Perhaps I do. You know about how serious I usually am.

I guess I had better stop. I guess you take a newspaper or two, as you said something about one to me in your letter. But perhaps you have never read such a mixed up [sic] lot of news as you will find in this.

Your friend

Elliott Cranfill

P.S. My pen doesn't always write just what I want it to and I can't teach it to spell. Remember me by sending me one of your pictures, but not in that way only, please. E.C.

JULY 8, 1917

Elliott and Elma continued to exchange letters throughout the summer, averaging about one letter per month. While Elliott was serious and rather reserved, Elma was a virtual social butterfly who greatly enjoyed her time back home with long-time friends.

My dear Mr. Cranfill:

It is almost too hot to work so I will try writing. Have been having quite an exciting time for the last few days. Last Tuesday evening our B.Y.P.U.[12] had a picnic supper on the College[13] (my Alma Mater) campus. We had all kinds of good things to eat and played games. It made me feel almost as if I were a child again. [At] about 8:30 we disbanded and John Conn came home with me. We had a real nice time talking [about] Georgetown. We had only been home a short time when Ira and Beulah Porter and Blanche Hall drove up in a "Lizzy" and informed me that I was going to Woodburn, Ky[14] for a few days. Without hesitation, I packed my suitcase and started. You can imagine what a time we had, especially Blanche and Ira. Of course, Beulah and I enjoyed teasing them. We spent the Fourth of July in Bowling Green,[15] which is about eleven miles from Woodburn. It was quite a large day in the city and everybody and his dog was on parade. We visited the Western Kentucky State Normal Reservoir Park and various places of interest. We reached Blanche's home at 7 o'clock and after eating supper started for Franklin. The road is wonderful between Woodburn and Franklin and we made some speed even with "Lizzy." However, on our way back we had a "blow out" and didn't get in until eleven o'clock. Beulah and Ira started home at 4 o'clock the next morning. They live about sixty miles from here. I stayed several days longer and got home last night. I'm going to be good a while now and stay at home "mit mein mutter."

Prof. J. L. Hill was in Franklin a few days ago canvassing for G.C. The prospect is good for a large crowd from here next year — here's hoping — Really I am getting anxious to go back. How is this for next year's course? Physics — History — Latin 3-4 — English 3-4 — German 3-4 and French 1-2. It means a lot of work but I am willing to undertake it. I haven't decided yet whether I will take piano or not.

Yes, I have received my grades. Made 90 and above in everything except Latin and I passed all right in that, which is better than I expected. Can you realize that we are no longer "green little Freshies?" I can say one thing — my ideas about many things have changed considerably. I suppose it is natural for College to make you look at life in a different attitude. Perhaps I am a bit more serious than I used to be. Anyway, I think it is well to be serious occasionally. By the way, I like your phylosophy [sic] (if that is what you call it). I really believe you would make a good preacher. I always did like preachers, you know.

Please do not accuse me of being a flirt. I would rather you would call me most anything else. I hope I have never given you cause to think I was insincere.

In regard to the picture, if you do not want it bad enough to send me yours, I am afraid you will have to do "mit" out it.

Sincerely,
Elma Beatty

~

JULY 22, 1917

Elliott ventures a step toward more intimacy, opening his third letter with "My dear Elma." He expresses concern that the war will prevent him from returning to college in the fall, then goes on to talk about other things: political speeches, a joke played by his cousin, parties, and picnics, and a revival meeting.

My dear Elma:

I was glad to hear that you have been having such a nice time at home, or rather away from home — but I mean not at college. I guess you have been rather lonesome since your visit to Woodbourne, especially after being with Blanche Hall and Ira Porter. But perhaps you never get lonesome. (Say, do you ever have the blues?), but I will say no more about the blues. I am sure I will forget them when I get back to G.C. I would like to see some of the old G.C. students again. Just any of them would look good to me. Of course, some of them would look better than others. I am anxious to go back in September. I am afraid that I will have a poor show to get back to college. Chances that I get to come back look blue. If my brother should be drafted for the army I am most sure I can never get a college education until after the war at least. I would give ten years of my life for a college training and I will have it if any chance whatever presents itself.

I believe you are expecting to do some work next year. I guess I will try the same course, if I get back, except French. I think now that I shall take Greek instead of French. I will take expression too. I feel like now that I could almost do two years work in one. I guess when I get back the less work the better pleased I'll be.

I went the other night to hear the Honorable W.J. Bryan[16] speak. I stood in the middle of the street and listened to him for two hours. His subject was Prohibition. He certainly was some speaker. We get a "Wet" and "Dry" election in this county October the first. I guess I will get to cast my first vote then. A fellow asked me last night if I would make some dry speeches between now and Oct. the first. I told him I would if he wasn't afraid I would injure the cause. I do not know now whether or not he will want me to speak. I guess he "won't."

Elma, my cousin played a joke on me the other day. She said she was to have a Bishop visit her and asked me to come over and help her to entertain. She sent me word that the Bishop had come. I went over on Sunday afternoon to see him for my own personal benefit and instruction, but behold when I got there it was "Miss Bishop," and so you see she had put one over on the bashful little boy. That was the first time I ever went to call on a girl (except one night at Georgetown Ky, when I saw Miss Howard.)

Well, I am sending you the only picture of the Hon. S.E. that I have. Honestly, I didn't know that I had it. I "straightened" up my trunk the other day and found that picture, and so I am sending it to you. I know you don't want it, but you can burn it up if you want to, but now I see no excuse why you can't send me a picture of "Fraulein" Beatty. If you don't send me one, I fear that I will wear my annual out looking at a Freshman's — beg pardon — a Sophomore's picture. See if you recognize the street and background of that picture, especially the little house on the right.

I was out upon the road the other day and a big car passed me with a young lady in it. She looked very much like Miss Hart. If it wasn't her it must have been her twin sister.

Tell John Conn he is about the most lucky fellow I ever heard of, especially after the B.Y.P.U. supper at Franklin.

I have attended three lawn parties and a Sunday school picnic since I got home.

My old High School chum "Jeff" (I used to be "Mut") came to see me last night. We started to a party. We got about eight miles from home and about halfway to the party, to a little village, and we didn't get any farther. There was a candidate speaking there, right in the middle of the road. Of course, it was blockaded and so we had to sit there until about eleven o'clock, while the candidates abused each other. I think there were about forty "office seekers" present and all of them must have spoken from the time it took then. The party was over when we got there, and the night too when we got home — one o'clock. (It wasn't a banquet either).

A revival meeting began at my home church, "Friendship,"[17] to-day. It continues [for] two weeks. I ought to be a good little boy by the time it is over don't you think so. It is a former G.C. student who is carrying on the meeting.

"Sei ein gutes kleines Madchen, und bleiben Sie zu Hause mit deiner Mutter." ["Be a good little girl, and stay home with your mother."]

Your friend,
Elliott C.

LOVE LETTERS

AUGUST 6, 1917

Elma follows conventions of letter writing as she responds to Elliott's comments about the war and elections and prohibition, but her writing is most animated when she tells about going places with friends.

Dear Mr. Cranfill:

How are your blues by this time? Entirely faded away, I hope. Yes, I will have to confess I have them sometimes. I think everyone does, but just so we don't let them get the best of us, it isn't so bad. I am hoping you get back to College all right, for I know if you want a College education half as bad as I do, it will be a very great sacrifice to lose even one year. If you really want to get back pray to that end.

I was talking with "Jake" this morning. As you know, he was expecting to sail for China [on] the 16th of this month, but he has not yet been released by "Uncle Sam." Having received his appointment from the Mission Board[18], I should think it would be quite a disappointment to miss going.

I wrote Laura Learned a great long steamer letter to-day. She sails at the same time and "Jake" was to meet her in Cincinnati. I imagine she is quite excited. Just think — going to China to meet her husband-to-be.

I saw Blanche a few minutes yesterday afternoon at the Band Concert. She told me she was expecting Ira and Beulah down again next Saturday. Also Hal and Ava Washburn. Hal graduated from the Dental College in Louisville last year and is coming to Franklin to see about locating her. Ava, his sister went to G.C. last year. Perhaps you met her. I think Ira has a dreadful good excuse to get back to see Blanche. If he can't find one, he will another. Last time he brought his sister and brother-in-law down to Bowling Green to visit relatives. See?

You were speaking of the election. I am wondering if you have made any prohibition speeches yet. Honest, I believe you would help the cause a great deal instead of injuring it. We had a primary election last Saturday. A woman was nominated for county superintendent.[19] But I'll have to say she bought the place from a man who never used a cent of money. One of my neighbors came over and asked me if I had been to vote. I told her not much. Oh if I had only been two years older I might have gone down and sold my vote to Miss Adams. Ha! ha! Yes, yes, clean politics when women vote..........

Please excuse me for getting off on Woman Suffrage, but it just came in so nice, I couldn't resist the temptation.

I have been real real good since I wrote to you last. Haven't been out of town but once and then I was attending the Simpson County Baptist Association. It met two days and we had dinner on the ground both days. Good things to eat — my! my! It makes me hungry to think of them. Then, too, we had some splendid talks. For instance by Dr. Powell of Louisville, the State Mission Secretary. I guess you must be awful good after attending the revival. A meeting is in progress at "Providence," my home church in the country, but I haven't been [to] any yet. You didn't know I used to live in the country, did you? Well, I did and I liked it too.

I certainly appreciated the picture and I'm awful sorry to tell you but I haven't a single Kodak[20] picture of me and myself by ourselves but just as soon as my chum succeeds in getting a good one of me and myself I'll send it "immejetly." I have a very good one made with June but I'm not going to send that 'cause I'm skeered you might like June's better than mine. I am sure you will not be very muchly disappointed because you have to wait a little while. Only four more weeks after this, and I hope to be back in old Georgetown. It will be quite changed, probably, nevertheless, I am anxious to get back. Please don't get blue anymore.

Your friend,
Elma Beatty

AUGUST 27, 1917

In this letter, Elliott says he guesses he will get to go back to college since none of his brothers have been drafted yet. Otherwise, Elliott would have to stay home to help his father on the farm. He responds to Elma's earlier comments about woman suffrage.

My dear Elma:

How are you now, as school time draws near? I am getting real anxious about coming back to old G.C. again. Dr. Mitchell came over to Anderson last Thursday and stayed with me all day. He telephoned me to meet him at Lawrenceburg, and when I got there, he told me that he was very much surprised to know that it was Fair day in our town. But I think he enjoyed our county fair very much. He said we would have as large a Freshman class as ever in the history of the college. That sounded good to me. He also said that Rucker Hall [21] was full [of] all but three rooms, and not an Academy[22] girl was assigned to [the] room there. I believe we will have a large crowd of girls anyway.

I guess I will get to come back O.K., until mid-year at least. Neither of my two brothers at home have been called yet and my other brother has been exempted on account of weight. I am at my brothers [sic] now. I have been here since Saturday evening and do not know when I will go home. I have been going to church since I have been down here. I saw only two people that I knew (Tham and Tot[23]) and had to have a mirror then.

I went to Lawrenceburg a Sunday or two ago and I saw Mr. Eddings. I thought perhaps you would be interested to hear that he is still living and that he looks as well as ever. He always seemed to be so interested in you, but perhaps you have already heard from him. I saw several others from G.C. during our Fair, Jack Morris[24] for one. He says he is going to room at the Logan house this year. I wonder if I will get to sit in the swing down there any this year, but if I should Miss Howard would not be so much interested about it I guess.

I believe you said something in your last letter about woman's suffrage. I saw an example of it in our county this last election. It would not be quite so hard now to convince me that women would not reform politics simply by the right to vote. I knew how much you liked woman suffrage, but I didn't expect you would be so much in with it as to sell your vote the first time as they did here with us.

Some of the women here voted for the candidate who would haul them to the election in an automobile, a rather cheap sale I think.

Well, I have written a long letter, and yet haven't written anything. So I guess I had better close for this time. I will see you soon, and that picture you promised me shall not have done me any good during the whole vacation of '17.

Your friend,
Elliott Cranfill

CHAPTER 2
December, 1917

Ring Out the Bells for Christmas[1]

> Verse 1:
> *Ring out the bells for Christmas,*
> *The happy, happy day,*
> *In winter wild, the Holy Child*
> *Within the cradle lay.*
> *O wonderful! The Saviour*
> *Is in a manger lone;*
> *His palace is a stable,*
> *And Mary's arm His throne.*

Verse 2:
On Bethlehem's quiet hillside,
In ages long gone by,
In angel notes the glory floats,
"Glory to God on high!"
Yet wakes the sun as joyous
As when the Lord was born,
And still He comes to greet you
On every Christmas morn.

Verse 3:
Where'er His sweet lambs gather
Within this gentle fold,
The Saviour dear is waiting near,
As in the days of old.
In each young heart you see Him,
In every guileless face,
You see the Holy Jesus,
Who grew in truth and grace.

Verse 4:
In many a darksome cottage,
In many a crowded street,
In winter bleak, with shivering cheek,
The homeless child you meet.
Gaze upon the pale, wan features,
The feet with wandering sore.
You see the souls He loveth,
The Christ-child at the door.

Verse 5:
Then sing your gladsome carols,
And hail the new-born sun.
For Christmas light is passing bright,
It smiles on everyone.
And feast Christ's little children,
His poor, his orphans call.
For He Who chose the manger,
He loveth one and all.

Chorus:
Ring out the bells for Christmas,
The merry, merry Christmas,
Ring out the bells for Christmas,
The happy, happy day.

DECEMBER 19, 1917

By Christmas, Elliott and Elma are much more comfortable with each other, and there are increasing signs of intimacy. Even during their short Christmas break, they managed to send two letters and one gift to each other.

Wednesday night
Dear Elliott,

Home once more, but I can't say that I am having a very large time 'cause I've been sick with a cold all day. We arrived in Franklin about 9:30 Monday night. I intended to slip in on the folks but when we got to Louisville we found that our train was 2 hrs. 10 min late so I called father and told him to meet me.

You missed all the fun by not being with us from Frankfort to Louisville. There were about twenty-five Georgetonians in the bunch and we sang, yelled, etc. until the passengers looked as if they would like to throw us out of the window. A bunch of the boys gave fifteen Rahs for [Ira] Porter, then fifteen Rahs for widow Porter.[2] I thought that was real mean in them for it is going hard enough with that old girl without teasing her about it.

When we got to Louisville and found we had four hours to wait, Herr Acton, Mary Eliza, Blanche, and I decided to go uptown and try to find a picture show. After a good deal of walking, we found the one we were looking for, and the time was passed without any troubles.

I rec'd my grades this afternoon. They happened to be one A, two Bs, and three Cs. Dad and mother were very well satisfied so I guess I ought to be too. Dr. Adams sent a little letter with my grades explaining why I was sent home. His explanation was a little more satisfactory than mine because I told them I had been sent home on account of flunking in German.

I wondered last night if you thought about it being calling night. I don't imagine it ever crossed your mind. Fess up. Since I haven't heard from you yet and am feeling a little bit tough I guess I had better stop.

As ever,
Elma

[P.S.] Excuse the pen. It has a bad case of indigestion.[3]

DECEMBER 24, 1917

While Elma was singing and giving "15 Rahs" with fellow students on the train ride to Louisville, Elliott was bumming a ride from the station to the farm and then trudging a mile through snow, only to find out that his folks were sick.

Dear Elma:

How are you enjoying your Christmas? I hope you are having a fine time. But I forgot, it is only Xmas eve now. I haven't seen any Christmas yet, but I am going to hang up my sox tonight. I have tried to be a good little boy this year. Perhaps Santa will come to see me to-night. I haven't been away from home yet since I have been home. I may go to town[4] to-morrow if it does not rain to-night. If it rains I will have to bulk tobacco to-morrow. Just think have to work on Christmas day.

I have joined the Hospital Corps since I got home, I think. Every one of the folks here were sick when I got home. My brother had not been out of the house for six weeks. Dad and my other brother went to bed on the next day after I got home. So you see I just got home in time. I thought I was sick but when I saw the rest of them here I knew I did not have time to be sick and so I have been wading [in] the snow ever since. They are all better now and I never felt better in my life (except on Tuesday nights for the last two or three months).

Did you give your folks a nice surprise? I did mine. I came walking in through the snow. They asked me if I had walked from town. I told them yes. It is just twelve miles out. They believed me (for I am always truthful, nicht) when really I had only walked about a mile. I had bummed[5] a ride with a neighbor whom I happened to find in town as it was county court day. I think they were really glad to see me for once. Something unusual though, but I guess your folks are always glad to see you. They don't like me because I make so much noise when I get back from school. I even try to sing sometimes when I get back on the farm, for you know nobody can hear me out here. I am twelve miles from nowhere and I never see the sun except at twelve o'clock in the day on account of the hills, and yet it is the best place in the world. It is the garden spot of the world in fact to me, for "there's no place like home[6]."

I said I might go to town to-morrow. I am going to see my old High School[7] play basket ball [sic]. They play Frankfort high school. Don't you think I am loyal?

I guess you are getting anxious to be back to old G.C. by this time? I mean to tackle Physics with a new Vigor after the holidays, if ….well… perhaps. Of course, it depends on how I feel on the New Year.

I hope Santa comes to see you and brings you lots of good things — a whistle, a doll, a ….. etc. A Merry Christmas and a jolly good time for your vacation are my best wishes. Hope to see you some Tuesday night.

Your friend,
Elliott

P.S. Perhaps you thought you won't be bothered with me during Xmas but guess you will have to open this old letter at least unless you recognize the handwriting on the outside. I hope you will take time to think once of your Georgetown S.E.C. friend and not think all the time of that one at Franklin. E.C.

∽

DECEMBER 27, 1917

Elliott and Elma sent each other the same gift for Christmas.

Dear Elma:

I was very much surprised to get the nice present you sent me. I thank you very much indeed. I hope you took a good look at the present you sent me or else you might think I had just returned it to you. I did not by any means (if perchance you did not look at them very closely) for I would not trade with you at all. I was sorry I had sent you the handkerchiefs after I got yours, but it was too late then. I sent mine on Xmas day and that night I got yours. I never did get to go to town and those two handkerchieves was all I could find at the little country store (except a little doll and a tin horn). So you see I did not have a very great variety to choose from. I had no idea what to get for a girl anyway. I did not know then or now whether you would accept a handkerchief for a present or not, but nothing could have suited me better for a present. You see I never had any experience buying for a girl. I kept waiting to go to town until I guess it was most New Year before you got it anyway.

I went hunting yesterday and took Christmas right, but didn't get any game.

Thanking you again for your present. I am your friend,
Elliott C

LOVE LETTERS

∼

DECEMBER 29, 1917

Elma thanks Elliott for her gift and reports that she had a good Christmas, with several dinners and a "theatre" party held in her honor.

Dear Elliott:

I sure was surprised when I got home Thurs. afternoon and found a letter and package from you. The handkerchiefs certainly were pretty and I appreciated them just a whole heaps. You remember the old saying: "Great minds run in the same channel"... that explains why we both happened to decide on the same thing. "C."

I have been having some Christmas! Had a big dinner at home [on] Xmas Day. Went out to dinner Thursday and also Fri. Went to a "theatre" party which was given in my honor Thurs. night. There happened to be a real good war show on that night and I found it quite instructive as well as entertaining. Had an awful good time but I might have had better if...You don't believe that do you? Well, do as you like about it.

I met Jake down in town this morning and he at once began teasing me. It was the first time I had been teased since I came home and I told him so. He immediately said he should take it upon himself to enlighten people around here a bit. I just dared him to tell any tales out [of] School.

Santa was powerful good to me but I'm sure it wasn't because I deserved it. He brought me a dandy good looking coat and new dress and handkerchieves etc. etc. and oh! I was about to forget — two more days vacation — He haw — wasn't that funny. When I got the card from Dr. M. B.[8] I danced all over the place grabbed mama around the neck and almost took her breath away — Oh. I'm a piece when I get happy. Yes. I've read two of Shakespeare's Plays and part of George Eliot's Mill on the Floss. Can you beat it? Let me thank you again for the lovely handkerchieves and assure you that you could not have sent anything I needed worse. Farewell, till Thurs. Jan 3 5:10 o'clock p.m. You may not recognize me next time you see me cause I am going to be [paper torn][9]

    Your College Friend,
    Elma

PART TWO
1918

CHAPTER 3
June, 1918

Love's Garden of Roses[1]

    Verse 1:
    Come dearest heart mid the flowers of June,
    Come out in my garden so gay.
    I've roses, bright roses, of every hue
    And sunshine for the whole day.
    There is laughter and song in my garden
    And a spell over all the land.
    Ah! never a fairer world could be
    To wander hand in hand.

Verse 2:
Come dearest heart where the flowers enfold
A dream that is tender and true.
Tis here we may find in a rose's heart
A message glad for me and you.
There is laughter and song in my garden
And such bliss that our hearts can tell.
In the world we walk together
Where love alone doth dwell.

Chorus:
Come to my garden of roses.
Winds whisper low.
Ne'er was so sweet a garden
With love aglow.
Laughter and love in the sunshine,
Joys all divine,
Come oh come to my garden,
Dearest heart of mine.

JUNE 7, 1918

After arriving home for summer break, Elma begins her first letter with "Dearest Elliott" and then proceeds to give a "raving" description of her trip home.

Friday Afternoon
Dearest Elliott:

I am home again and mama and papa have most talked my head off. I wasn't expecting anyone to meet me but them and when I walked off the train right into Delma's arms, I was quite surprised because you know I had not written at all. There were several other girls along too besides mama and papa. We started off and I rec'd another shock when one of the girls placed me in her car and said she would take me home.

[Maybe] you think I didn't feel fine but I did. The trunks and all landed safely with me. Now I guess I had better tell you about my trip from Frankfort on. I settled down as comfortably as possible and started "Over the Top"[2] 'cause you see that old man had swiped my paper and when he got through Adams borrowed it. However, I finally got to peruse it a little bit! But as I was about to say I read two chapters in my book when along came Keller and seated himself. He asked me where I was bound for. I says Franklin. Then a wild grin spread over his countenance and he says — I'm going to Nashville. So we breezed on the rest of the trip together. Poor boy! he sure was feeling blue about Hough beating his time. He poured out his troubles to me and I tried to lend an attentive ear and console him as best I could. We carried on a rather serious conversation 'till we got to Louisville. On reaching there he had our baggage checked and we found that we didn't have but 2½ hrs to wait. We then went up town and got a lunch, after which he took me around to the Herald[3] office and introduced me to one of his friends, a Mr. Townsend and by the time we had talked to him awhile it was time to go back to the station. Didn't have time to take in the show. We were sailing down Broadway at about the rate we were coming from Old Sem[4] Wednesday night when my hat blew off. Well you should have seen old Keller chasing it down the street. I almost got tickled but of course it wasn't the proper place to laugh. He, at last, captured it and we were off again. Just then it began to rain but as we were near the station, a few long steps put us under shelter. I was some hot! I was just about to get cooled off when who should dash up to us but "Tubby" Brown, saying he was on his way to Bowling Green. Well since he was an old Georgetown fellow we condescended to talk to him a wee bit and he kept us company off and on all the way to B.G., with his hot air. We passed off the time by observing the beauties of nature. Keller was mighty nice and took good care of me all the way to Franklin, but oh! how I wished it was you. Please believe me when I say that I am sincere in all I say to you. You may think that I forgot you when you have read this raving description of my trip home, but no sir. I didn't forget you I don't believe for one minute. Already to-day I am beginning to be dreadful lonesome without you. When I think that it might be three whole months before I can see you again, I can hardly stand it, but I'll be true no matter how long it is. I believe mother suspects something already but she hasn't said one word against you. She thinks the cup is beautiful. It is right funny — she has asked where I got various little things like the T.ø.K. pin and bar pin etc and a little while ago she asked whose book "Over the Top" was. When I told her, she just laughed and said from now on she would take for granted that all strange things belonged to you.

I am wondering if I shall get a letter from you to-morrow. I don't much imagine I shall – might do well to get one by Monday or Tuesday. I wish Sinai wasn't quite so far away. Please don't be afraid to write long letters, that is if you have time. I think it is a sure thing that I will go to B.G.[5] a week from next Monday. I can hardly wait to get to doing something. Time passes so much faster when one is busy. Idleness doesn't agree with me much — can't be contented. Had a card from Blanche to-day and she said the view from the porch of Robt. E Lee Hall was worth the trip. She seems to be having the time of her life. Dear, don't let what I said the other night keep you from going if you feel that you can. You might never have another opportunity. I may have written too much for the first letter but I just couldn't help it, honest I couldn't. Let me thank you again for the lovely time you have showed to me. I don't think you left a single think [sic] undone that was for my comfort and pleasure. I do hope I will not have to wait long for a letter. Be good and don't work too hard. That is all I have to ask of you.

With Love from Elma

∽

JUNE 7, 1918

Elliott's trip home and his experiences once he arrived were quite different from Elma's. In this letter, he says he feels very much like a farmer and is tired but not too tired to write to her.

Dear Elma:

How are you feeling to-day? I am feeling very much like a farmer to-day. I have really been at work once more it seems. You know I did not do anything while I was at Georgetown. You ought to see me in my overalls setting tobacco[6] — that has been my job to-day and really I am tired but not too tired to write to you. I think I would be to [sic] tired to write to anyone else.

I got home last night at the early hour of twelve. I stayed in Frankfort till two thirty. Then caught the Bus (I mean the automobile) for Lawrenceburg. I got there about 4 P.M. The bus was a Ford Truck, and believe me it made some speed — about fifteen miles an hour was my rate of speed. I was going along with the Ford at about five miles an hour up, and down at about ten miles per hour. So you see I was going some. Then I had to wait at Lawrenceburg until six o'clock for my brother. It was the night for my high school commencement exercises and so I stayed for that as my big brother was there and had a date with my old girl I told you about — Miss Crossfield.[7] I could not very well come home till he saw fit to come along and he did not hurry in the least. The exercises were over about eleven. Then another hour and I was "home again" with a nice headache, hungry, and a little sleepy. Just in condition to enjoy my rest. You know tobacco setting is a rush season, and so I was out at it by five this morning. I stopped at eight and now I am writing. This is really the only time to-day that I have felt rested. Really I don't feel tired at all. My little nephew[8] is telling me all that has happened, is happening, and will happen at the rate of about two hundred words per minute. He wants me to write for him. He can ask more questions than I can. He cried at dinner because I went back to work and wouldn't stay with him. You see how much he thinks of his "Uncle Tot." I am afraid he won't think so much of me when he finds me out. Most folks are that way by me. I asked him to-day what he was good for, and he said "to carry in cooking wood." Then I asked him if he did not [want] me to go cut some for him to carry and he said no. So you see he is like me in one respect in that he likes to work.

I guess you were about dead when you got home? (Say, you will have to excuse all these blots. My pen stammers to-night.) I know you had a tiresome wait in Louisville unless you were fortunate enough to find someone whom you knew. I thought after I left you, that perhaps some of the folks that were on the train would be in Louisville too and that perhaps you might have company after all.

The seniors of my high school are giving a reception to-morrow night at Lawrenceburg. I got an invitation but I am undecided as yet whether or not I shall go. You know I like receptions when I go to the train instead. There is nobody leaving to-morrow night and no "little girlie" to break rules and go with me to the depot. So you see I am not so crazy to go. I really don't think now that I will go, although I saw Nina last night and she even asked me to come up and stay all night and really said I could take her and I did not ask her if I might do it either. If there is a reception in Franklin, however, and you will send me word I might come. I know I would like to much better than to go to-morrow night. They have my horse loaned out and they have torn up my buggy, so I really don't expect I could go if I wanted to ever so much.

Did you have any trouble with your baggage or suitcase after I left you? I mean except carrying that suitcase. I know you had trouble doing that. I know you enjoyed carrying it very much.

Did Professor Martin go on any farther than Frankfort? If he did I know you did not get very lonesome.

I guess your folks were very glad to see their "little girl" coming home again. I bet they haven't stopped loving you yet, and I do not blame them. I have not either, although I have in the sense I meant the first statement. I have not forgotten you yet. I guess you were not expecting me to think that long were you?

By the way I forgot to tell you how I spent the time in Frankfort. I went to the pool room first and had several very interesting games with (I've forgotten his name) then I went in and took a few drinks and a smoke and finally I went to the show and saw most all of a "wild west" or a "Buffalo Bill" or something I don't know what as I had to leave before I saw all and . . . . well, I guess now you will know why I came to have [a] headache when I got home. Well, "little girlie" it is most bed time for little farmer boy and so I guess I better say good night, but this good night isn't like the handclasp and the . . . . you gave me at Rucker Hall last time. I wish I could come to see you to tell you good night, but I can't to-night. So I just remember the last good night at old G.C. and use this war time substitute the pen till again I see you.

Good night it is nine thirty, but the bell hasn't rung yet.[9] I'm leaving early so miss (or is it Mrs?) MC won't see us while arranging the rug.

Be good and don't forget me,
Elliott

~

JUNE 11, 1918

While Elliott worked on the farm, Elma attended church functions, entertained her parents, visited friends, and looked for a place to stay in Bowling Green during summer school at the Business University. Her narrative is filled with details about what life was like for small-town teenagers in 1918.

Tuesday afternoon
Dear "Tot:"

I rec'd your letter this morning and I think it was awful sweet of you to write to me when you had been working all day and were so tired. I can't tell you how much I appreciated it.

I have been doing so many things since I last wrote that I scarcely know what to tell first. Saturday I was very, very good. In fact I didn't do anything Saturday afternoon but read and watch the eclipse[10] of the sun. Were you so far back in the hills that you didn't see it, or did you get a good view of it? Well Sat. night I entertained mother and father with a free concert. I acted my part in the play — all about Theophilus you know — banged on the piano a little etc etc. There was a vaudeville show in town, but I decided I was show enough and therefore proceded [sic] to furnish the amusement until 10 o'clock.

Sunday morning, I went to S.S. [Sunday School] and after Sunday School my chum, Delma, and I took a little paper called *Kind Words*[11] around to an old crippled woman. She can't get out at all and seems to be the most appreciative old soul I ever saw. After we had performed this little act of charity we went to the Methodist Church 'cause you see we haven't any pastor here yet. Now I am beginning to get to the part of confession. I reckon you would call it confession — yet you said I could do it. It is dreadful, worse than anything you did in Frankfort. I can scarcely make up my mind to tell you but it must be done — So here goes — I was just eating my dinner Sunday, when Delma came breezing in and said she had something very important to say to me. Of course, I was all ears and she imparted the following news: said her fiancee [sic] (is that what you call 'em) was coming up that afternoon and his cousin Thomas Meador, the little preacher who has been going to Bethel College[12] and to whom I wrote that crazy letter — wanted to come in and see me — Well I thoughts to myself I wasn't a caring about seeing him or anybody else 'cept you and I didn't know whether I had any business to let him come or not. But after much consideration and due deliberation I decided you wouldn't mind me letting him come just to see how it felt to have company and not have any rules hanging over my head. So I told her to tell Oral to fetch him along. Delma and I got together and about 3 o'clock they came rambling up in a little Ford (it wasn't named Sallie[13] however). We sat around and argued about which was best Bethel or G.C. for awhile [sic], then we boarded "Lizzie" and drove out to Green Lawn Cemetery where there was a big decoration, fine program etc. Delma had to give a reading and as soon as she had performed we went out to Oral's house, about 5 mi. from town, to hear a new Victrola. He wanted Delma to help select some records "C." I think they would have already been married but he too had to register June 5[14] and she hasn't made up her mind to marry under those circumstances. After we had played the Victrola for awhile they brought out a freezer of the best cream I ever devoured. I ate all I wanted for once. At 20 minutes to 7 we started home. Delma and I were both scheduled to be on B.Y.P.U. program at 7 o'clock. We touched the road in a very few places only and Thomas and I almost tickled them to death. You see we weren't used to riding in automobiles. I mean Fords and we acted as silly as possible. You know what that means for me and Thomas is about such a case as John Browning. Does that give you any idea? Well we got to B.Y. almost on time. What do you think of them putting me on program the very first Sunday I was home? We had a great service anyway because one of the girls who is about the best worker in the church said she had been called to be a missionary and was going to enter the Training School in the fall. It certainly was a surprise to most of the folks, but I knew she had been trying to decide for some time. The program was rather long and we did not get out in time to go to church so we just drove around a little while then went home and they left at 9:30 because they had to begin cutting wheat Monday morning. Thus ended my first Sunday at "home sweet home."

I spent yesterday in Bowling Green looking for a boarding place and at last found a lovely place with two other Franklin girls. They were already rooming together and I got a room with a little girl from Florida who is taking music. There isn't a man on the place — just us 4 girls, three old maids and a dear old lady who has charge of the house. I think that is all that stay there. I'll tell you more about the place after I get there. Am going up to stay next Monday.

I'll bet your little nephew is cute. I wonder if he would like me as well as Ira's little nephew likes Blanche. ha! ha! I had a 15-page letter from Blanche yesterday. She sure is having a time but hasn't heard from Ira in about 3 weeks. Isn't that awful?

I haven't had much rest since I got home. Haven't slept later than six any morning and ironed all morning this morning. Mother begged me most every breath to stop and rest but I knew she would do it if I didn't so I just worked on.

I hope you won't mind these samples of paper 'cause I am short on stationery. I can't tell you what my address in B.G. is but will let you know as soon as I get there. Oh, I believe I miss you more every day. Won't you please hurry up and come to see me? Give Nina my regards. I haven't but one more thing to ask of you and that is don't do anything that you wouldn't want me to do. From the same,

"Little Girl"

JUNE 13, 1918

In this sweet, rather sentimental letter, Elliott tells Elma how much he loves and trusts her and how different she is from other girls he has known. He somewhat reluctantly broaches the subject of the war. He expects to be drafted at some point and is trying to decide whether to try to join the Navy first, if he can, or wait and be drafted into the Army.

Dear Elma,

Well, you are the sweetest girl yet, to write to me so soon, really I did not expect to hear from you until you had received my letter. I was glad to hear that you got home so nicely and that you had the good fortune to have good company all the way. I know both Keller and you enjoyed it. I am sure you do not wish it had been me with you instead of Keller any more than I wish it might have been me. Really, I hoped after I had left you that someone else would be on the train and I am glad it was so. If I can't be with you I hope you will have a good time with somebody else if you can. I have been going with you so long now that I do not care about going anywhere since I got home, just because I know that you will not be there. I haven't been anywhere yet, except I went fishing yesterday. My brother [Calvin] went to Taylorsville to his farm — a distance of about 40 miles. I went with him and we went fishing while there and then got home again before dark. We started at one o'clock. I did not go to the reception I was telling you about. I was sick. I have had a light attack of tonsillitis since I got home. In fact, I was taking it when I left Georgetown. I did not know exactly what was the matter with me. I knew I was feeling terribly bad. I thought it was all because I was leaving you. I am about well now. I worked a little yesterday morning. That was the first I had done for a day or so. I am feeling fine to-day and my throat isn't sore hardly any at all.

You said I might think you had forgotten me already by your raving and you asked me to believe all you have told me. Truly, if I hadn't believed all you have said to me I would never have said all I have said to you. If I did not have all confidence in you that it is possible to have, I would never have told you what I have told you, and I think you know that I have said what I have said in earnest. Elma, I would trust you with anything, and I would feel safer of your word than I could be of my own. That sounds like egotism on my part. I don't mean it that way at all. I mean that I know myself better than I know anybody else but that I would rather risk your word for sincerity even than my own intentions. One statement in your letter means more to me, Elma, than all you have said to me before, if you really mean it. That is when you said you will be true to me no matter how long it is till you see me again. I have told you that for myself already or at least I have tried to, and I know that I feel that way, and if there is any honesty in me I have told you that "I love you" honestly. I don't believe I would ever forget you no matter what you should do (or say to me) yet I will never have occasion to forget you because of any wrong you should do. I am sure of that. "Little girl," when I was with you I never feared but one thing and that was that you would never love me but some other fellow, for I know how much I like [sic] of being good enough for a girl like you. I am really acquainted with more girls perhaps than you would think from what you have seen of me. To be true with you I was about disgusted with most all that I knew. I wouldn't say that to everybody, but it is true. I had about decided I did not want to keep company with girls if they were like most all that I knew, before I met you. That is not very nice to say about the girls and I guess I ought not say it. Perhaps it was just the type I looked for, but if it was my intentions fooled me. I love to think of women as pure, and true, but I am sorry to say that that is not true about the majority of girls with whom I have associated. Elma, you have no idea what a contrast I see between you and them, and you have little idea how much I wish I could feel that I was worthy of the love I hope you can give me, and that I know you will give to the man you love truly and whom you marry. Honestly, I don't think I ever had an impure thought when I was with you and I couldn't say that truthfully about anybody else that I ever saw. That is why I love you. I would be the happiest man in the world to know that you really love me as I believe you are capable of loving. I do not say this doubting anything you have ever told me, but I mean, to know for sure that time will prove that you are not honestly mistaken or that I am not in what I have said to you. My greatest hope is that I am able in the future to love you and prove that I do love you as much as I feel that I do now. I believe folks might decide too quickly and honestly be mistaken. I don't feel like now especially since I got home from G.C. that I could be mistaken. Well, I guess Prof Daniel would think this too sentimental. I hope you don't. Really I do not want to seem more silly to you than I am, but I do mean all that I am saying and I do not think I am crazy. I hope you do not think so either. If this is too much, say so, when you write me again, and I will try to do better. I am afraid I can't if you let me write at all.

Well, if you go to Bowling Green do you want me to address your letters there or to your home? I do not know how often I can write to you or what times. I would love to be writing to you all [the] time when I do not see you or when I am not reading from you. I am going to write when I can and as often as I can (and do not worry about the length). I will write as long as I can find time. I guess you won't ask for long letters [anymore] after you read, or try to read, this jumble of penmanship and spelling. I hope you like B.G. if you go.

Elma, I have a subject I have kept till toward the last of this letter because I hate to talk or think about it — the war. I do not mean I hate to think about it because I personally dread the war so much. I just hate to think about not seeing you for —. Well, I don't know how long. I am going to-morrow to town to see if I can get any idea about when I may have to go. My brother [Ike] goes 26. He is talking of joining the navy next week. There are only thirty more in Class I[15] in this county besides the newly registered ones of June 5. So if I should be among the first of those I might have to go this month too. I have thought all the time that I would rather be in the navy than army. I have said all the time I would join the navy. So that might mean that I join next week. I don't think I ever asked you which you would rather see me in the army or navy. If you should have any objections to my joining the navy in preference to the army I wish you would say so. I know so little about either. It doesn't make so much difference to me. If you would rather see me in the army I will not think of joining the navy any more. I wish you would tell me next time you write. If I should decide to go to the navy I might want to come to see you if you want me to, if the call is not too rushing.

I would also like to have your phone number[16] in B.G. and at home if you have no objections. I might want to call you if I should suddenly decide to come or that I couldn't come if I am forced to rush.

Well, you asked about two things of me in your letter, "Be good and not work too hard." Don't worry about the last. No danger. I pray daily that I may be good and partly for your sake. You can help me be good. You have already and always will.

Elma, whatever I say or may not have said I think, "I love you."
Elliott

P.S. I mean by the last sentence that that is my one and only thought. E.C.
P.P.S. I hope your mother doesn't say too much to you. I know if she could see me she would think lots — of bad things. E.C.

JUNE 15, 1918

Elma thanks Elliott for his sweet letter and lets him know where she will be staying and taking her meals when she gets to Bowling Green. She urges him to follow his conscience regarding enlisting in the Navy.

Saturday Eve.
Dear Elliott:
Just a little note in reply to your sweet letter which I rec'd this morning. I will write more when I reach B.G. I go to-morrow afternoon and I can't tell you my address exactly until I get there. Anyway my room is with Mrs. Charlie Potter, on the corner of High and Broadway and I take my meals at a Mrs. Allen's Boarding House. No, I haven't said much about your going to war, but it was only because I wanted you to do just as your conscience guided you. And now since you have so nearly decided I will say that I had much rather see you join the navy

than wait and go in the army as a private. Of course it will be hard to see you go but we all want to do our part toward "Making the World Safe for Democracy."

Dear, I feel perfectly sure that I know my feelings now. You know I told you as we came back from the Old Mill on Wednesday evening that I thought after we were separated for awhile we could tell and oh! These few days certainly have brought the truth to light. I knew I thought more of you than anyone else I had ever been with but I really didn't know I could love one person so much.

I will be expecting you anytime and will be more than delighted to see you. I'll write to you as soon as I get there and find out just where I am located but if you start before you get the letter just keep hunting' till you find me. If it is in the daytime you had better come to the Business University, if at [mealtime] look up my boarding place and if at night go to Mrs. Charlie Potter at the corner of High and Broadway. The streetcar will bring you directly from the station to the door. I am praying that you will be led to do whatever is best with regard to enlisting. With a loving goodnight. I am your own Little Girl. Elma. Am awful sorry you've been sick. Feel like I was to blame for it.

JUNE 16, 1918

Elliott covers many topics in this long, chatty letter. He tells her he will try to write on Sundays from now on, if she doesn't think it's wrong to write on the Sabbath.

Dear Elma:

I will break the Sabbath by writing you a letter. I am so hot I can't be satisfied doing anything else. I have been hotter this evening than — I was when we went to the play. I did finally make up my mind to go to Sunday School this afternoon and that is all I have done to-day — except read a little, and eat. Lo and behold, when I got to S.S. the supt. had gone a-visiting and I was called upon to lead. I said I couldn't, of course, but I did. Don't you know we had some S.S.?

Well, I am feeling very well now. My throat is quite well only just can't talk much yet I am so hoarse. Of course I never could talk but now I am worse than usual. They (the home folks) think I am "playing off" on them. They say they're going to put me to work to-morrow. They say I am pretending to be sick. You don't think I would do that do you? I mean to keep out of work? They are going to put me to use a cradle. Say, do not misunderstand what I am going to do. The cradle I am to use (to-morrow) is an instrument to cut wheat with and not ... It is really a scythe and cradle.

Well, you certainly did make me jealous to tell me about what a good time you have been having already with your old beaux. Just to think of you going all the way home with Keller, then the first Sunday at home to do all that you were telling me, with a preacher. I would never have thought you would let a preacher lead you away so soon into the gay world. But the worse of all was that you came back at me by "kidding" me about Nina. Of course that would be all right only she is engaged, they tell me, to a boy who goes to the war soon. I guess you (or the preacher one) by this time hold to the old maxim "Absence makes the heart grow fonder"?

By the way the war has just come into my mind again. I went to find out what to do and I found out that I can't join the navy now. I have to wait till I have been classified. I guess it will not be long, however. Then I may not have a chance to enlist in the navy. It all depends. The board doesn't seem to know anything about what I can or cannot do. They just say it depends. My brother [Ike] was expecting to have to go on the 24. It happened that they just got to him and didn't take him this month. He is first one for next time unless something should happen yet. He is expecting to be home till next month now. There are just seven more after him in Class I in this county. Then they begin on the new registrants I guess. So it depends again as to where my call number comes as to when I will have to go. They are talking of a re-classification. If they do have it, I might not have to go before school begins. So that is all I know about it and more than anybody else knows. A part is imagination, intuition, or something. I don't know what on my part perhaps.

Well, Elma, I am about the "lonesomest little boy they is." I haven't been anywhere, because I didn't want to go, and 'cause I was partly sick, but anyway I have just felt lost. One thing has kept me company a little and that is your lovely letters. You can just about write the best letters I ever read. I read them over sometimes two or three times per day (all except where you were with another feller.) I think I shall start out next Saturday night if nothing prevents. There is to be a big lawn party about three miles from home. I got an invitation to-day. (Two of my old high school chums were to see me to-day for a little bit. They invited me.) So I think I shall go. See they are inviting everybody, and that's why I'm going. I guess I will not know anybody, however. It has been so long since I have been to a party. Say, don't get scared I am not going to take a girl. You see I can't find one to go with me. My brother [Ike] has beaten my time with the only one [Grace Crossfield] who would ever go with me here at home. You are about the only girl who would ever go with me much, and that is why I like you so I reckon. The last time I went to a party at this place there were 120 girls there, and I wouldn't try to count the boys. It was like the fair. How I came to know the girls present was that I was late and my ticket was 118. I was about last you see. None of the girls would take me till they had to. "C." The reason I like to go to parties is that I can talk to the girls a little bit whether they want me to or not. I had an invitation to two other parties this week but I did not go. My little cousin what came to see me at G.C. (you heard about her I guess) came home yesterday. Somebody said she had a little party. If she did she didn't even invite me. Now what do you think of that? I am insulted badly, wouldn't you be?

Do you want me to write to you at Bowling Green or at home? I think from now on I will try to write you on Sundays, (if you don't think it is wrong to write on Sunday) and then perhaps along in the week too if I have time. I am expecting to be tolerable busy in the week from now on, (unless I can play off sick again) for about a month at least. Then really if things work out as I think and if honestly and truly you want me to, I might come to see you. You do not know how much I wish I might see you even just as often as I used to. I believe you would look good to me about now. If I keep on thinking of you as much as I have since I got home I know I will have to see you before the summer is over, whether I go to the army or not. Of course that also depends on how badly you decide you want to see me. I know already how I shall be. It also depends, I guess, on how often you and the preacher are together. Say, Elma, do not take seriously what I say and have said about the preacher. Go with him or anybody else you want to, and as much as you want to. I have said this to you before and I really was in earnest. Your word is all I want. I think you are honest enough to tell me when you decide you do not want to talk to me [anymore]. I could not possibly have a right to ask you not to go with other fellows when there is no possible chance for me to be with you myself, and especially when you write to me about it and confess it all. I don't think you would tell me about it if you were aiming to deceive me especially when there is no chance for me to know anything about your actions except you write it to me yourself. Now if I was close enough that I could come to see you and then you were going with another fellow, I would think I would have a right to act. I could have no right to say anything even then as I see it. I guess I would feel like talking some (I expect I would act) but then I would not feel that I had any right to blame you. A girl I go with I give her a right to do as she pleases (so far as I am concerned) then if her actions do not suit me I reserve the right to do as I please. You see I am liberal in my convictions and opinions because if folks are like I am I guess they keep company with whom they like best provided the two parties of the company are willing. If a girl thinks more of another fellow than of me I expect her to go with the other fellow. And if she was talking to me and thought more of another fellow I would be glad if she would go with him. If I think anything of a girl and want her, I would like to be sure that I was the only fellow she loved. That is why I have talked to you or anybody else that I ever went with as I have. If a girl and boy are near enough together to be together and if they really think anything of each other, neither is apt to keep company with somebody else. If folks are so far apart as you and I, I say keep company with anybody you like as much as you like and as soon as you find out whether or not you love me as I hope you can and do I would appreciate it if you tell me. If you can honestly say you do I am the happiest man there is. If you can't say you do I've got no right to be mad at you and I only wish you can be as happy as I believe I could be with you. I have no objections to anything you have ever done to me. If I ever have any objections I expect you will find it out, by my actions if not words. With love, Tot

P.S. Say, I only wish I could promise you that I wouldn't do anything that I wouldn't want you to do. I will try my best and I believe I can for you, and you can help me, if you will, to do it. E.C.

∼

JUNE 17, 1918

Elma wrote this letter from Bowling Green, where she lived in a boarding house while taking courses at the Business University.

Monday 9:30 A.M.
Dear Elliott:

Am all fixed up and feeling very much at home. At present I am sitting in a porch swing, enjoying a nice cool breeze and doing something I really enjoy. The place has a big yard with a lawn swing and settee in it and the porch is all fixed up with chairs and a porch swing. It faces the street that the car line comes up so there will be no trouble finding the place if you get on the right route and all you would have to do would be take a car at the station and tell them to put you off at the corner of High and Broadway and you are right at the door.

Delma brought me through yesterday afternoon, in her new Buic. Wasn't that nice? I can't say the trip was very pleasant because it was so fearfully hot. Oral came with us and also another girl who lives close to home and is boarding here at the same place. I found out after I got here that I didn't have to start in school until Tuesday because the B.U. doesn't teach on Monday and the course I am going to take doesn't take but about half a day and that way you see I'll get plenty of rest. I am just delighted with my rooming place and my roommate is the dearest little girl from Florida. Then there are 3 other Franklin girls in the house. I almost missed breakfast this, the very first morning. Got up at 10 min. of 7, dressed and got to the boarding place which is 5 or 6 blocks away at 5 min. after 7. Don't you think I am a sure enough fast lady????

I went to church and B.Y.P.U. last night. The church is perfectly beautiful. It was built in 1913 and they say it is one of the finest Baptist Churches in the South. I have to pass it going to my meals. I wonder if you really care about hearing all this. When I get to writing I just somehow tell everything, then I wonder if it interests anybody. Am I wrong when I dare to think you are interested in whatever I am? You see, I am interested in whatever interests you and I thought perhaps you felt the same way. I just hope you can come at the end of the week so I can be with you most all the time. If you can come at the last of the week we are going on down home. Mama and Papa are anxious to meet you and the girls are too, especially Delma. You'll have to be prepared to be stared at on all sides, for those other Georgetonians have published all kinds of news about us. We don't mind, do we? John [Conn] was still in Franklin yesterday, but he is expecting to leave for Alabama at any time. He has been asking about you quite often. Oh I mean he has been asking about Theophilus.[17]

We came through Woodburn yesterday afternoon and they said they were expecting Blanche home last night. I am getting a little anxious to see the old girl as well as somebody else. Can you guess who that somebody is? The postman is coming. Must stop.

With Love,
Elma

~

JUNE 19, 1918

Elliott urges Elma not to work too hard at summer school, then describes the difference between mental work and physical work. He talks again about registering for the Army and says he wants to come see her soon.

Dear Elma:

I got both your letters to-day at the same time. You dare ask me in one of them if I am interested in what you write. I am interested in you, in anything you do, or in anything you tell me. You write the sweetest letters of anybody in the world. I am interested in anything you are because I know you are not interested in anything a girl should not be interested in, and I am also interested in you because you really always seemed interested in the same things I was.

Elma, I am glad you are satisfied at your new place and that you do not have to work all day. Really, I did not much like to see you go to school for the summer, because I thought you needed rest. I didn't say anything about it much, because I thought you perhaps knew best. I knew you had really worked hard enough at school to need a rest, but I guess from what you say you will not have to work so hard as you did at G.C. Don't work too hard. Doing mental work isn't like doing physical work. One dosn't [sic] know so well when he gets tired. I saw you several times when you were too tired to work as hard as you were working about the time school was out, and I did not like to see you look tired.

I got a letter from my "Roomie Steve" the other day. He says he has a lazy man's job in the radio work[18] and for that reason it would just suit me. Isn't that like him to accuse me of being lazy? He says it is easy and he wants me to join what he is in. I think, however, if I ever get another chance I will join the Navy. I may not get another chance, however. But in fact I haven't had a chance since I registered. I guess I will have before I have to go to the Army but I might not.

Elma, it was just like you to just leave it all to me about going to the Army or Navy and just like me never to say anything to you about it. Really if you would rather see me in one service than another I would try my best to get into it. It makes little difference to me. I would rather you see me in that service you prefer than be anywhere else. It is settled that I will have to go into the service somewhere I am sure and every other young man. They are beginning to put the young married men of Class IV back in Class I now in this county. There are only seven more in Class I as it was originally.

Elma, that friend of yours (I mean Delma) must be a very nice girl. I know already I would like her because she is so good to you and because you like her so well.

If I come to see you I guess I had better come on the first of the week, for it would be best for me not to go to your home. If your father and mother should see me once I am afraid it would be "All off" with me unless I could steal you. I really am afraid they could know too much about me just by seeing me. "C." Of course I would like to meet them and your friends, but if they have a very strong influence over you I am afraid they might advise you to not talk to me any more, and then I would wish I hadn't come at all. That is if you should listen to them. My folks said to-day that you must like me pretty well by my getting two letters at once. My brother went to the box and he could tell that it was the same writing. They say I am crazy about something and they have said that I am in love is what is the matter with me. If being in love with you is being crazy, the only thing I am sorry about is that I haven't been crazy longer.

Well, I can't write a very long letter to-night. It is beginning to be late bedtime for a farmer. It is most ten o'clock. I have been cutting wheat all day. When I started to work in the harvest Monday they said I couldn't stand to make a hand as I had been sick and in school too, but I have been keeping up O.K. I heard my brother say to-night that he was tireder than he had been this year. So I guess he thinks now I can keep up. I am not so tired (while I am writing at least). I was so sore this morning I could hardly walk when I first got up, but I soon forgot it. I felt like I did next morning after the track meet.

You ought to see me about Saturday night or the last of the week, with my beard a week old and my old dirty harvest clothes. You would think I was a tramp. I believe you like a mustache, don't you? I don't think I will shave it off anymore till I come to see you. I will stop this time. Be good. With love, Elliott

P.S. Are you going to go home each week end as you said you thought you would?

JUNE 21, 1918

Elma's more serious side is evident in this letter, the first in which she expresses her deeper feelings and doesn't just talk about running around with friends to picnics and parties. She reports that she is pleased with her schedule of classes in the morning and office work in the afternoons.

Thursday Night
Dear Elliott:

I rec'd your letter which was written Sunday, this afternoon. It went home and they forwarded it. I'm all worried 'cause I believe you really think I did wrong to let Thomas come. Honest, we never did go together at all. He just ran with our crowd and we were good friends. That is the only time I have been with him or anyone else since I came home. What hurts me so is — I am afraid you haven't got the confidence in me that I want you to have. I am perfectly honest when I say that I would not have gone with him for the world if I had thought you would care. But I know how it is, when folks are separated doubts will arise. Sometimes I wonder if you really do care for me very much, and such a thing as that never entered my mind when we were together. Oh, how I wish I could be with you to-night and tell you I am really in earnest about all that I say. Somehow, it is so much easier to understand one another when face to face. Don't you think so?

Elliott, I am coming from a state of darkness to the light with regard to conditions in the world. Since I have been in this place I have seen enough to open my eyes and I can understand now what you meant when you said you had almost lost confidence in girls. Great crowds of students take their meals at the same place I do, and I am thoroughly disgusted every day with the way the boys and girls carry on. My roommate is a very sweet little girl but she is a society belle and has gone out to a big dance to-night. I believe I am strong enough not to be affected by any of these things but I had lots rather have remained ignorant of the ways of the world.

I am getting along real well with my work. Have all my schedule arranged so I get through by 12 o'clock. Then I work in the office in the afternoon. The very first day I started in, Mr. Dickey, the president, called me in his office and asked me if I would like to work in the office. Of course, I jumped at the chance and have been working at odd times ever since. I was very much surprised when he asked me and said there were other girls who wanted the place, but he thought I would suit best. Can't account for it unless it was because of the experience I had had in Georgetown. I sometimes feel like I am the most lucky girl in the world and I know I would feel that way if you should not have to go to war, and could come to see me real real soon. Surely you know I want you to come, just about as bad as anyone could. Not a single day passes that I do not wish I could see you. Maybe Prof Daniels wouldn't like this letter either but I'll bet he has been over the same road and it's just natural.

I've been more homesick since I have been here than I was the whole time I was in Georgetown. I believe it is because I am away from you and the home folks too. Don't you dess [guess] that is what the trouble is? I would just love to get a letter from you every day but of course that is impossible and I am going to try to be satisfied with the number you can find time to write. It is now after 11 o'clock and as I have to walk 5 blocks to my breakfast and be there at 7 o'clock — I guess I had better try to get a little sleep, although I had much rather write to you. Once more, I plead with you to have confidence in me and believe me always sincere in whatever I tell you. I don't believe I am mistaken in my feelings and if not I know, I love you.

Elma

JUNE 23, 1918

> *Elliott has been put on a committee to sell war savings stamps (W.S.S.) for the county and says he is getting to be a "big bug" since he got home — making speeches, putting up notices, visiting the chair of the W.S.S. meeting, and talking with the county attorney. He thinks it will be a good thing when the county goes dry.*

Dear Elma:

Another Sunday has at last rolled round and I am still living. I am writing to you again on Sunday before I hear whether or not you think it is wrong for me to write to you on the Sabbath day. I certainly have been busy to-day. I have been put on the W.S.S.'s committee for this county. I drove about twelve miles to a church this afternoon in order to make a speech which had been arranged for me that I did not know anything about until day before yesterday. I had to get up something this morning to say for this afternoon and so I did not go to church. I got back from the speaking about 4:30 P.M. I then went out to tack up some notices of the W.S.S. meeting in my school district, and also to see the chairman of the meeting for 28th. I got in from that trip about 8:30; ate my supper and now I am writing to you for my recreation. Say, "little girl" really and honestly I do enjoy writing to you. It is the only letter writing I ever enjoyed. I had the honour of speaking this afternoon with the county attorney of Anderson County. See I am getting to be a "big bug" since I got home. They had the speaking advertised in the county paper and on bills all over the county. Just think my name among all the other preachers and politicians of the county. Believe me I made some speech. Just about ten minutes long, but I am sure that was long enough to those listening. The school district I am to work over is supposed to subscribe $2,000[19] they told me. I was very much afraid I couldn't get it. I have better hopes now my big brother said he would take 100 stamps and my dad says he thinks he might take 200. So that makes $1500 worth and they are the only two I have seen. That is pretty good I think if they don't back down before 28th. I guess I will perhaps get my quota now.

Well, Elma, I went to the party last night that I was telling you about. I looked all over the crowd for you. I thought perhaps you would be there as everybody most else was there. I never saw such a crowd at a party in my life. There was a big truckload there from Springfield and Bardstown. It is about forty miles to either place. I was just three miles from home and I did not know half of the folks there. It wasn't a bit like Rucker Hall receptions, not near so good. That party was out in the yard. They had some very pretty lights. They also had quite an orchestra. It was  a swell affair, but I got stuck and had to stay with the same girl about an hour. I finally got up and left. I never was so tired in my life. I never did a trick like that before in my life. I asked her to let me trade her off and she wouldn't do it. So I then asked to be excused and I left. I didn't wait to see whether or not she would excuse me. I don't think she would ever have answered me anyway. She hadn't said three words the whole time I was with her. They had an ice cream supper at another place before the party. I did not go to that, however. After the supper was over two boys started to the party. They were drunk and they had more whiskey than gasoline. So they filled up their gasoline tank with whiskey and started. I guess the machine got drunk, at any rate they were, and it turned over and killed one boy and almost another. The boy who got killed was a high school classmate of mine. He was always "tough" and so now I guess he has paid for his "good times" as he used to call them. He married about a year ago. I guess perhaps I ought not say it but I think if he had been at home with his wife where he ought to have been he would not have been killed. One good thing this old county goes dry, as they say, about the first of next month. It was voted out last fall but they got a decision in court allowing them to sell on till their lisenses [sic] run out.

In your last letter, you said the other Franklin folks had been telling on us. I really feel sorry for you, but there is one consolation. They really don't know how bad it is on you as most of the folks down there have never seen me. As far as I am concerned myself I wouldn't care who knew what we have done and all we've done. And folks don't worry me any be [sic] joking me about you. I really enjoy it. So as far as I am concerned if they tell nothing but the truth I do not care how much they tell, but really I don't like to think that you have to stand it all and me not get my share. You see there is no one here to tell on me or to joke me. I put your picture in my watch. I put it right on the front so I could see you every time I looked to see the time. One fellow saw it the other day and he seemed very much surprised to see me carrying such a good looking picture. Of course he wanted to know what I had been doing at G.C. Well, I thought I could tell him some of it so I did but some things I had been doing I thought were my own affairs, and so I ommitted [sic] them. (Perhaps you can guess what I ommitted.) I told him about football and track etc, etc, but that did not seem to interest him and therefore he had to have his curiosity unsatisfied.

One of my girl friends at the party the other night asked me the time and when I opened my watch, she seemed to forget all about the hour and to have a sudden interest in the picture. She asked "who"? I told her that was "my sweetheart," (do you object to me calling you that, if you do I will try not to any more) and that you are the sweetest girl in the state. Really you don't believe I told a girl that do you? But I did and I believe it too. By the way, you said my watch would stop if I put that picture in it. It hasn't. You know my watch used to be too slow. Now it runs too fast. Can you tell me why? (Oh, I beg your pardon. I had forgotten what you said about yourself when you liked [sic] to have missed your breakfast.) If you are so fast as you said you were don't worry you won't miss your breakfast if you really try to get there. I guess you won't want to answer this letter and I don't blame you. You needn't too if you don't want to, provided you will just write to me. I don't care whether you answer any of these or not if you don't like them, just burn them up and tell me what you want me to write and I will try to please you. I would do anything you want me to (provided it suits me). Do you remember saying that to me? That was about the best thing you ever said to me, except when you ended your last letter by saying "your own little girl." I would rather think that than anything I know.

I guess you will think I am asleep and writing from the looks of this letter but I guess you have found out by now that I can't write a nice letter.

Elma, if you know John Conn's address I wish you would send it to me that is if he has gone from Franklin yet. I want to write to him on a little business, see?

It is about sleeping time and I must say goodnight.

With love, Elliott

~

JUNE 23, 1918

This chatty, upbeat, affectionate letter is typical of Elma's letters. She invites Elliott to come to see her and insists that he stay for the weekend to meet her parents, but she tells him he can leave "his little mustache" at home.

Sunday night

Dear Elliott:

I have just gotten home from church and am just a wee bit sleepy but I think I shall soon get over that altho' I may have to prop my eyelids up with tooth picks. It wasn't the preacher who made me sleepy, because he was splendid. It was a Mr. Tupper from some city out West and he seemed to have a wonderful education. You know B.G. is without a pastor as well as Franklin, that is until the 1st of Sept. They have called a man from Austin, Texas, who comes at that time.

I was exceedingly smart this morning. Got up at 10 o'clock. Oh, yes. I went to church alright even if I did miss Sunday School. We were a little late getting there and I went stroling [sic] in, took my seat, glanced around and whom should I see sitting on the same bench but Thomas Meador. Well I believe I should have fallen over if you had just been there to catch me. I didn't know he was within 25 mi. of B.G. and consequently I was somewhat surprised. However my curiosity was satisfied after services when he breezed up and informed me that he was on his way home from the Assembly at Russellville and was just spending the day here with his cousin who lives just across the street from where I room. Then he goes on to say that a bunch of them had planned to go walking in the afternoon and he was to go with me. Well, there I was again and I am so in the habit of saying "yes" to everything you ask me that it just slipped out before I knew it — and — I went. Please now dearie, don't be jealous again — that's a nice little boy — 'cause you see, it was just a happen so and honest to goodness I would go with Thomas everyday and we would never be anything more than friends and I am sure he feels the same way about it. My going with him doesn't make me think one bit the less of you and surely by this time you know that I wouldn't go with another soul if you were here. Really, do you think, deep down in your heart, that I would have done and said the things I have when with you, if I had not thought of you in a way that I have never thought of anyone else in all my life?

Now I am perfectly willing to give up anything you say for me to and if you would honestly rather I would not go with other boys, I will not any more. I leave it entirely with you. You are the first boy I ever told that but I hasten to say that it isn't with any regret whatever. It just makes me feel good to tell you that.

You asked me if I was going home every week. No. Only every two weeks, but it certainly isn't because I don't want to — cause this sure is a homesick little girl most all the time. It is 'es dreadful to be separated from you and the folks too at the same time. And by the way I am going to see how it feels to be with you both at the same time, so you had just as well make up your mind that you are going down home. You said in your letter that I got Saturday, that you were coming at the 1st of the week and that's all right but you are going to stay until the last and go down home. Understand? And as for the little mustache, you can just leave that at home 'cause I might not love you so good if you fetch it along with you. I hate for you to work so hard but I guess you don't mind it much. I rather believe you like farming anyway. I know I do, especially when that is your occupation. You said I wrote interesting letters. I only wish I did but I fear everybody wouldn't think so. It is nice of you to say it anyway and I certainly can say the same about yours. You don't know how much I look forward to getting them. It is almost like looking forward to calling night. Letters are really just little one sided chats anyway, aren't they. It is now 11 o'clock again and I must say goodnight. Let's play like it is a good night like the last one I gave you in Rucker Hall. What do you say?

With lots of Love, Elma.

JUNE 26, 1918

Elma and Elliott tended to write letters to each other on the same day. As a result, their letters often crossed in the mail, leading to misunderstandings. Here Elliott blames the misunderstanding on his inability to express himself clearly in letters.

Dear Elma:

I got a letter from you Monday and one again this afternoon. Really I was surprised that you took what I said about you going with Thomas as you did. I have been unfortunate always when I write letters, in that I am always misunderstood. I was never farther from being jealous or angry in my life than when I got the letter that you went with him or when I wrote to you. I was honest in what I said, and in earnest, when I said that if you want to go with another boy it is alright with me. The only thing I ever feared was that you honestly couldn't love me as I hoped that you could. I really would feel hurt if I thought in any way I had deprived you of any pleasure whatever or any good time whatever that you might have. You have told me that you care nothing for him except as a friend and that you do love me and as I have always told you, I believe every word you ever told me when you pretended to be in earnest at all. I have had and have no occasion whatever to not believe you now. I tell you again with all earnestness your word is all I want and

I trust you forever. If you really care for another fellow there is no reason why I should be angry, and I believe you are honest enough and true enough to tell me. If we were together you would know I am not in the least angry or jealous and that I am truly in earnest in what I say. It is true one will have doubts when he cannot see the one he loves. But when you tell me anything really I do not doubt you. I couldn't say that, absolutely, about any other person I know. Perhaps you think I doubt you because of what I said about not having confidence in girls. You are an exception to all others in my opinion and I guess every other girl is too to the fellow who loves her, but truly I never knew any other girl that I would have had so much confidence in as I did in you even before I ever thought that you could ever mean more to me than a friend. You always seemed different to me from the very first. And when I said that about girls perhaps it was unjust and I ought not to have said it. I really meant folks in general rather than girls especially. I guess I have noticed it more in girls than in boys.

You said you were lucky in that you always got good things as in your work now. Elma it is not luck. Truly it is you. Just you. You are a superior type of girl and it is plainly written on your face. That is what gives you luck. I am not trying to flatter you at all. I know it will not give you the "Big head" or I would not say it. Anyone who has studied folks at all can see something good in you and that is why you are lucky. But really don't you work too hard if you are expecting to go back to school next Sept. Don't forget that you are doing hard work and that you are really not taking vacation when studying and working in a business college. I was awful glad you got the work if it isn't too much for you.

I was very sorry to hear that you are so homesick. I certainly wish I could be there with you if that would keep you from being so. I might "be to see you" most anytime again. You will be thinking soon that I am not meaning any of it, but really I am coming as soon as I can. I have been waiting to see whether or not I am going to the navy. I got my questionaire [sic] to-day. And when I get it filled out I will know whether or not I can join the navy, I guess. If I get another chance I am going to enlist. So when I go to get it fixed up, if I can join the navy, I am going to do so immediately. Then I am coming to see you before I go. If I don't go to the navy (I mean if I can't) I am coming to see you anyway before the summer is over. I am sure now that I will not be back to school next year.

That Mr. Tupper you heard I guess was the fellow who spoke at the woman's meeting at G.C. during commencement, don't you guess?

It was awful sweet of you to say you would give up anything I asked you to, I believe you were in earnest and I believe you are true. Then after you saying that and as I believe in you as I do, I hope I will never be guilty of asking you to give up anything that is any pleasure whatever to you. And I hope you don't ask me to pass my judgement on anything you are expecting to do or want to do if it is any pleasure to you. Honest, I love you, and I trust you forever. And don't ask me if you can do anything if you feel like you want to do it or that you ought to do it. Let me tell you once more I won't be angry or jealous as long as you tell me that you love me.

You said you liked to get my letters. Letters are not like talking in my estimation, I assure you, or I wouldn't be trying to explain in this letter what I meant in my other one, but it certainly is a pleasure to get a letter from you and also for me to try to write to you. Letters are better than nothing but how I wish I could be with you again. I wish it every day. I love to play like I am telling you good night like I did at Rucker Hall every night, but it's not real. I sure hope those good nights have meant as much to you as they have to me.

"Little girl," I must stop. I have been setting tobacco yesterday and to-day, all of both days. It is getting late. I have to set tobacco again to-morrow. I will begin at daylight. So I must go to bed.

Say, now don't think I care for you going with whom you want to or doing what you want to. Your word that you love me is all I want — except you. So, as long as you love me I don't care what you do, that you want to, for I know you don't want to do anything wrong.

With the most of love and hoping you understand me this time, I play good night with you, anytime you wish. Elliott

JUNE 26, 1918

This letter seems to be a good representation of what Elma was like in person and how her mind leaped from topic to topic. The overall arrangement appears rather random and includes such transitions as "Oh, listen," "I've had a little intermission," and "I think I told you about..."

Wednesday P.M.
    Almost 9 o'clock
Dear Elliott:

Your letter of the Sabbath rec'd and must say it was exceedingly welcome. I suppose you will conclude when you receive my letter written on Sunday that I have no scruples about such a task and I haven't. In fact, I don't call writing to you, work at all. [Therefore] I do not think I am breaking any of the commandments. "C" My! but I sure am proud of you — I always knew you would be great and I claim you are making a nice beginning right in your home county. Just keep it up and make a big drive for W.S.S. I believe you can make it $3,000 instead of $2,000. Wish I had a little to invest but my bank acc't isn't increasing very rapidly on 10¢[20] an hour. That is the salary I boast of at present.

    I am sure you have enjoyed the parties but did you say you got stuck? Poor boy! Dat wuz awful. You see I haven't been to any parties since I came home and so haven't had any chance to get stuck, which I do not regret enough to mention. There is some excitement on for Saturday night however. Had a letter from Delma this afternoon saying our crowd was planning a picnic on Drake's Creek for Sat. night or rather evening. Some of the girls have visitors and of course they want to show them a good time. She wanted me to come down on the 7 o'clock train as I had already planned to do and said a gentleman would be waiting for me there and "Ford" me out to the selected spot. Now that would be sure enough thrilling if you were just the one to meet me. I really mean that! Guess I will have a fairly good time but oh! there is always something lacking about everything down here. If you were just going to the B.U. too, we could be together all we pleased. However, I suppose fate did not will it so.

This morning the whole student body of B.G.B.U. marched down town and joined in a "farewell party" held for the eighty boys who left for camp to-day. It was the first time I had witnessed anything of the kind and it certainly was heartrending. We didn't follow them to the train and of course I guess it was worse up there. They informed us before we left school that we were to return just as soon as the program ended down town. I tried to obey orders but when I got back to the building and found out what hour it was, the penmanship classroom door was locked and I was marked absent. Don't know what the consequences will be but guess I shall find out tomorrow. Of course I wasn't by myself for several others were in the same predicament.

Oh listen, I have something dreadful to tell you — just awful. It is a matter of life and death, and I am sure you will be horrified when I tell you. 'Tis this! I gained 2 pounds last week and think I have gained an equal am't this week. Could anything be more calamitous?? There is only one consolation and that is that I lost four more lbs while at home. Got down to 114. Franklin just naturally doesn't agree with me because mother gave me lots of good things to eat — fried chicken every meal.

～

10:45 o'clock

I have had a little intermission. One of the Franklin girls, and by the way she is one of my pals, has been in my room for about an hour talking over the problems of life. I have told her a little bit about you and she said tell you that you had a real staunch friend although she had not yet met you. I will describe her and when you come you will probably recognize her. She is 5 ft. 7 in tall, rather stout, has dark hair and blue eyes and is really very good looking. We have found a new spot in which to study. Yesterday afternoon we took our books and went up to Reservoir Park to improve our intellects. On the way we stopped at a little country like store and got some candy[21] as we were both famished for some. We spent a very delightful afternoon and I learned enough shorthand to last me two days. That is how I happen to have so much time to write to-night. When I get real hungry for excitement, I just read a little in "Pendennis[22]." Undoubtedly that is the most disgusting book I ever read. I suppose that is where I show my ignorance of high class literature.

I believe I told you about my roommate going to a dance the other night. She got in at 4:30 a.m. Tonight a sailor boy with whom she had never gone called her at 9 o'clock and wanted to come up for awhile as he was leaving town in the morning. She let him come and it is now after 11 and she hasn't come up yet. I believe she is a straight girl but she certainly believes in having a good time. Of all tough places Bowling Green is the toughest I have "abode" in yet according to my belief but some say it isn't as bad as Franklin. I am rapidly coming to the conclusion that the world isn't as good as it might. If the heathen Chinese are any worse than some folks I have seen in B.G. I think we had better take the 1st steamer across. I'll bet you are saying I am extremely pessimistic to-night but no, I was just looking at one side of life and that happened to be a dark side. When my memory turns back to old G.C. and especially to a little walk from the "Old Mill" three weeks ago to-night, things look much brighter and I feel much happier. Wouldn't it be lovely if all life was as bright as that? Dare I hope that it will be someday?

With Love,
Elma

JUNE 30, 1918

In this long chatty letter, which Elma refers to as a "courier journal,"[23] *her personality and storytelling abilities shine through.*

Sunday Afternoon
  Dear Elliott:
Home again for a little while. But I just am here for I waited and waited for the "Crackerbox" (streetcar) to come along 'cause I live fully a mile from the station. It was 6:10 and still, it did not come. I knew the train left at 6:40 so I pulled out in my own automobile — carrying a heavy suitcase. I kept thinking the —— dear little thing would overtake me, but no such good luck. I'll tell you my practice in hiking came in handy. I made the entire distance in 20 minutes and was in mortal agony the whole time for fear the train would pull out just as I got in sight. It was a close race and I dropped into the seat hot and panting, only a few minutes before it started. "Never again" will I wait so long for the little "cracker box." Think I shall start from my rooming place about 5 o'clock next time. Honest to goodness I believe I would have died if I had missed it. Was most dying to see mama and papa, then the picnic

was on hand too. Daddy met me at the train and said the crowd was waiting up home for me. Thomas had been working in wheat harvest all day and couldn't get in in time to meet the train. I found a letter that was so fat it had to have six cents on it and a post card waiting for me. The card was from Harold Snuggs. He is in Elizabeth, N.J., in some kind of chemical school. He said tell Theophilus hello for him so there it is. Said he was enjoying his work fine altho the other night they got gassed with NO_2 and his hands were all burned with nitric acid. But he said that just relieved the monotony. That's about all he said. I had just finished the card and had opened the letter when the boys drove up. Another girl, the one who stays with me up at B.G., her name's Alma Johnson, was at home and she and another boy and Thomas and I "Forded"out. It was out on the creek about 5 miles from town with a dandy pike[24] all the way. The rest of the crowd had preceded us and supper was all ready when we arrived. Sandwiches good gracious. I know I must have eaten about twice as many as I did out at the Old Mill[25] — you can calculate how many that would be — and if you'll believe me they had ice tea and a big freezer of peach ice cream. I ate till I was almost foundered. Then the fun began. The boys tried to make all us girls walk across the mill dam — after dark — if you please. Well they didn't succeed but I sure did wish for you to help me out. Delma and I got off to ourselves and made love[26] to each other a little while but Oral soon found us and of course I had to give her up. She sure is a cute little girlie and I know you will like her. We have been chums for about ten years now and have never had a real sure enough falling out. I don't fuss with folks I love, do I?

Well, back to my narrative. We didn't start back to town until a little after 10 o'clock. It didn't take long to come in and we all stopped at the Alexander girls', who were the hostesses, for a little while, had some music and then came home at 11:30. There was no Lady Mac to scold and rave neither. Mother never says a word about me staying out late. She too tells me she can trust me and oh I do pray that I may never do anything to cause either of you to lose confidence in me.

I suppose I had as good a time as it is possible for me to have with anyone other than you. Thomas certainly is nice to me and yet I maintain that he is only a friend. If he should ever get the least bit serious I would never let him come again because I have said before and will say again that I would not for anything in the world lead a boy on to caring for me if I could not return his love. That is from my heart and I do believe that you have confidence in me. I rec'd your letter yesterday morning and I honestly don't believe any body in the world could have written so dear a letter, but you. You don't know how sorry I am that I misunderstood but I really didn't feel like you meant it as I seemed to take it. Anyway everything is alright, only I want to see you just awful, awful bad. I am sitting in the parlor now and everything is so nice and clean just like mother had prepared it for you. As I came down on the train I was wishing all the time that you were with me. That was the only thing that kept me from being supremely happy.

 I didn't get to read my long long letter until this morning. It was a chain letter that the Y.W. Cabinet is writing. Beulah Rusk started it from Blue Ridge, sent it to Katherine Anderson who lives in South Carolina. She sent it to Mary Anna [Beard?] and then Mary Anna to me. I added a folder and will send it to Gladys Bryson. They are awfully interesting and I guess those who get it last will have a regular book. I have not seen Blanche since she came home. If I ever get my hands on her we'll have one of our old time fights. She was here mama said last Saturday but of course I wasn't at home.

 I will go back to B.G. either to-morrow afternoon or Delma and Oral and Thomas will take me through to-morrow night. I am so glad Thomas didn't ask to come this afternoon for I had so much rather write to you than talk to him. Then if they take me back it would have been too much anyway, don't you think so? I didn't go to S.S. or church this morning. Just stayed at home and talked to mama and played for her some. Guess I'll go to B.Y.P.U. and church to-night.

 Got my grades this week + passed alright in everything — even Latin but I had 2 unexcused absences. One was that crazy thing of Ichie's and I can't account for the other. I wrote to Patty this morning and am going to investigate the matter. I haven't any credits to "frow[27]" away. No, sir. I should say not. Before I forget it. John left day before yesterday and Mrs. Conn said his address was Muscle Shoals, Ala. I asked her last night as I came from the train. Told her somebody wanted to know it and his little brother immediately piped up and said: "I'll bet I know who wants it" and Mrs. Conn says, "oh yes. When did you hear from him?" I says says I this morning. Please don't worry about me because I don't mind what folks say one bit — no not one bit. I believe I can almost sympathize with you when you have to work so hard. I am so sore to-day from catching the train yesterday that I can scarcely wiggle. Have a big bruised spot on my arm about the size of a dollar and can't imagine how it got there. You would probably think Blanche had pinched me. "I don't half like for you to work so hard." I think you had better take a rest and come down right soon. Won't you? Please sir, do. I want to see you mighty bad. Oh I forgot. You might think I'm like Nina, begging so hard. But I just can't help it cause I do want to see you. If I didn't I wouldn't be writing all this courier-journal. I never did before write so long a letter and I 'spect you'll wish I hadn't this time, but it is just as easy for me to write to you and tell you everything as it is for me to sleep and that's pretty easy.

I'm not a bit sleepy this afternoon altho I didn't get to bed 'till after 12 last night. I dess it's because I'm writing to you and when I stop I'll just about keel over. Hope I haven't written enough to tire you too much. Maybe I won't punish you so next time. Even if I do write long tiresome letters I love you just the same and am all the time wishing for you.

Love, Elma

~

JUNE 30, 1918

Elliott reveals more of his thoughts and feelings in this letter than previously. He includes his thoughts about going to war. He has decided to enlist in the Navy if he can and will come to see Elma soon. His brother Ike has already received orders to report to the Army, so they are trying to help their dad on the farm as much as they can before they must go.

Dear Elma:

The company is about all gone and so I will try to write you a little letter. We've been having company the last two Sundays — about ten here last Sunday and about fifteen to-day. There were about six kids here this afternoon and of all noisies [noisy children]. I never heard so many since I was a kid myself. They were running tricycles, wagons, and tongues — isn't that a combination?

Well, I got through with my W.S.S. work O.K. I had to do some pretty hard work and I met some disappointments. I lacked five dollars making my quota of $2000. My district is composed of very poor folks. Most everybody pledged some but many only bought one and so you can see that doesn't count very fast. Perhaps I can go "over the top"[28] yet. My neighboring district which had the same quota as mine only got $600 pledged. Many others fell short too. I am afraid folks got a wrong idea in many places that they were about to be forced to buy "Whether or not" and many just bought one to say they had bought.

Say, Elma, I sure wish I could be in the B.U. with you, or out in the park studying shorthand, or in the country store eating candy, or — or just any old place. I wouldn't care where just so I could be with you.

That calamity which has happened to you sure is terrible. I am sure if you have gained so much I would never know you, you would be so terribly large. You are hardly able to get about since you have gained so much are you? You must go to work, quit work, eat more, or eat less, 'or something,' or else I might not love you so well. You know I do not like fat women and that much gain surely has made you terribly fat. Well, what I mean when I say I don't like fat women is that I don't want a girl so large that I — I — I can't reach round her waist — oh — oh — I mean her neck — well you see I (to tell the truth) just like my "own little girl," see. But perhaps I will still know you if you don't go on and gain two more pounds before the end of the week.

Elma, I am sure I will like the girl you wrote me about if she and you are good friends. She sure knows a good person to go to, to talk over life problems if she goes to you. Life certainly is full of problems. I have been up against the hardest I have ever had, in the last few weeks. That is to know exactly best about going to the war. I guess now I have fully decided. I am going to-morrow to Georgetown, and am coming back by

Lexington to enlist in the navy. I had my questionnaire filled out yesterday. The board told me they really had no right to give me a permit to go to the navy, but I have a good friend on the board, an old high school prof. of mine, and he said they would give it to me anyway. He said he thought I would be apt to have to go in July anyway and so I feel that I would personally rather be in the navy and as you have said you would rather see me in it than the infantry I am going if I can pass the examination. The board said the navy might be full and that they might not take me, but they (the board) thought I could get into it. So I am going to enlist to-morrow if I can. My bad eye may keep me out. I am a little afraid it will. I know I would be taken in the army, for I passed one examination while at G.C. I think I told you about it. My brother [Ike] goes to camp next Friday 5 of July. I think he will go to Ft. Thomas. And, Elma, if I get into the navy you needn't be too much surprised to see a little "stranger" boy in B.G. most any day or time. If I am not told definitely when to report, but that it will be soon, I think I will do as you asked me and come on the last of this week perhaps on Friday night or Saturday morning. Don't be disappointed if I should not come until later and don't be surprised if I should arrive a wee bit sooner. I am aiming to come just as near before the time I go as possible. I know if I should come to see you and then got to stay at home a month, then I would want to come back to see you again and I know you couldn't "put up" with me so often as that. Really, I am trying to help Dad and my brother get the crop up so they can tend it after my other brother and I are gone. They will have a very large crop when we go, and every day I put in now will make it that much easier on Dad. He is too old to work as he is expecting to have to work when we leave. He is 65 years old and is aiming to do the work of a young man this year. Nobody can get help these days or at least it is that way here. Farmers are offering $5 per day for work hands and can't get them at all. This right now is the busiest time of the whole year. Say, you said you liked farming because I do. I do like to work on the farm truly, but I do not expect to make farming my life's work. Or at least I was not expecting to while in school. I like it better than any other work I have ever done, but I always felt like there were other occupations at which one could do more good than at farming and that is my reason for giving it up as I did. It seems the freest and easiest life to me that is, if one just considers self and ease as his highest ambitions. Really "little girl," I believe your life is centered on being a missionary. That is the greatest work in the world, and oh how I would love to be a missionary too, if I could always just have you to help me live and work as I should. Elma, my only ambitions now in life are, to make you happy if you can trust me and love me, and to serve my God and my fellow men. And Elma, I believe one reason why I can love you so much is because you always seemed to me to have the same ideal of service as I have always felt. Really I have never done anything of service in my life, but I have always had that first at heart till I knew you and knew that I love you. Since then I have felt that I could do or give up anything for you if you asked me. I don't know what I could do best but I just sure would love to use every bit of talent that I have, in any kind of service that I could do best. My motto of life has always been: "Whatever I ought and can that I must." I have never lived up to it but have always felt it as my ideal. Somehow I just feel that the navy is offering me an opportunity of decision for my life's work and Elma I just know that, if you really love me, or if you don't, your acquaintance or your advise [sic] can mean more for a decision for me than any one thing I know.

This is the way I feel about going into the Army service. Since I have always lived with this idea of service at heart, I feel that I am offering all I've got in the greatest field of service there is at present, as it is service to my country, to my God, and to my fellow men. (And Elma you are now the greatest active human force in my life to keep me true to all of these that I know.) I feel that if this is the greatest service my life can be, I freely give it. If it is all the service I can render all is well. If there is more service I can render after the war, there is one to protect me in danger and to prepare me for it. I feel that if I enter this war of service conscientiously and prayerfully and that if I have other services to perform after the war, I will be rewarded for my faithfulness. And Elma I have dared to hope that reward will be your love. I can think of no greater earthly reward for me. If I am not true to my convictions and conscience, I am not in the least worthy of your love, of my country, or of my God. And that is why I can even joyfully go into this terrible field of war which will win a new world for Democracy, but which democracy must be bought with human blood. I am not saying these things to make you sad, for I hope you really won't pity me and feel sorry that I go but that you feel proud I can go. I don't mean that I can tell you goodbye without feeling sad. I couldn't leave you just for one week without feeling a little sad that I couldn't see you for even a few days. When I go of course I do not know how often I will see you or even how often I can write to you. But I believe I can always be as true as I am now and if I could say all this to you you would know I mean it. You know folks are in different moods at times. I felt like saying these things this evening. And rather than wait to say them to you face to face I wanted to say them now. If we really love each other, as I believe we both honestly think we do we will be true to each other no matter how long we are separated. And if we are true to each other, to our God and to others whom we meet and know we will receive the greatest reward on earth and in heaven.

Elma, I do not know exactly what you will think of this letter. If you don't like it, you really don't like me. I never came as near putting my secret feelings into a letter before. I know I haven't even imitated by living what I have written in this letter but when really true to myself I have felt it. Hope I will see you real soon.

Elliott

P.S. Got my Semester grades 4 B's, one C. Also, got a card from H. Snuggs. He's in N.J.: likes fine; called me "Clarissa"[29] on the card. E.C.

CHAPTER 4
July, 1918

Au Revoir, But Not Good Bye (Soldier Boy)[1]

Verse 1:
So you're leaving me today, Soldier boy
And you're going far away, Soldier boy.
There's a tear drop in your eye
For it's hard to say "Goodbye"
But you're out to do or die, Soldier boy.
All the things we planned to do
I am sure will all come true
And I'll watch and wait for you, Soldier boy.

Verse 2:
I am proud to see you go, Soldier boy.
And it makes me love you so, Soldier boy.
There's your mother old and gray,
I will cheer her up each day
And will always hope and pray, Soldier boy.
When your fighting days are through
For the old Red White and Blue
We'll be here to welcome you, Soldier boy.

Chorus:
"Au revoir" but not "Good-Bye," Soldier boy.
Wipe that tear drop from your eye, Soldier boy.
When you're on the deep blue sea,
Will you sometimes think of me?
I'll be waiting anxiously, Soldier boy.
Though we're many miles apart, Soldier boy,
Keep my picture near your heart, Soldier boy.
When you've won your victory, God will bring you back to me.
"Au revoir" but not "Good-Bye," Soldier boy.

JULY 9, 1918

After Elliott enlisted in the Navy, he visited Elma before reporting to training camp. Elma's serious, self-reflective letter provides few details about how they spent their last days together, but it describes very well her feelings as they faced "the future which is entirely unknown."

Tuesday Afternoon
Dearest Elliott:

I haven't yet realized that you are really gone. It seems like a dream that you have been here, but yet I have been feeling dreadfully lonesome to-day. I would have liked to say more last night but I just couldn't. And I am not sure that I am going to be able to write much either. I'm afraid I am not as brave as I ought to be. Please don't worry about me 'cause I'm sure I am as strong as others who have said good bye. All we can do is be true to each other and pray that we may not be separated long. I believe things will work out right bye and bye. At any rate we must submit to God's will — whatever that may be.

I worked as hard as ever I could all morning but they didn't need me in the office this afternoon and all I have to do is think of you. That is the reason I am writing and eating the candy you brought me. I have just been in and given Miss Mai and Mrs. Potter some. They seemed to enjoy it very much, but not as much as I am.

I am afraid I didn't show you as nice a time as I might have but for my part the past two days were the happiest of my life so far. I couldn't ask to be any happier than I was yesterday and Sunday. I believe you know I am honest in that. Of course there was a tinge of sadness last night for I could not help dreading the parting. I do not believe you will have any doubt now about my caring for you. I know I haven't about you. I "dess" [guess] this will be the last letter I can write you till you get located and send me your address. After that I will write real often whether I hear from you or not. I am afraid you will feel a wee bit blue at first — especially while you are in the "detention[2]" camp — that is if they put you in that. I will do all I can to make it easy for you. Remember "I believe in you" and don't forget to be brave and strong at all times and come back to me as pure and true as you left me last night. We must ever keep before us our ideals and try hard to live up to them. If we do this I believe we shall please God and that should be our chief aim at all times. It is very very hard to be contented with the routine of everyday life, especially in a time like this but by doing well each little duty in its turn, we are prepared for greater and bigger things when they come. For that reason I shall work hard in the B.U. this summer and perhaps I shall see the day when I can use what I have gotten in helping you in some way. It is taking about all the courage I have to go straight through two years without any vacation scarcely at all. However I believe I am equal to it and if I can just work on through college and you can get out of the navy in time to take the other two years —won't it be glorious. Patience and endurance are the things we must both have and mixed with these there must be a great deal of faith. Having these, I have no fears as we face the future which is entirely unknown.

I am just as proud of you as I can be and have always been ever since I have been going with you. I don't believe you will ever give me cause to be otherwise.

Don't forget to send my mail to Franklin after this week and let me have your address just as soon as you can. With truest love, from

your <u>own</u> "Little Girl."

Elma

JULY 10, 1918

Elliott thanks Elma for a wonderful visit and says he feels "more lonesome" than ever since he left her in Bowling Green. He says he may not be able to make her any happier than she is now with her family and friends, but he would love to spend his life trying.

Wednesday night

Dear Elma:

I am at home again, and am feeling more lonesome than I ever did in my life. I guess I am not <u>homesick</u> but I feel like it. Elma, really, I have felt lonesome ever since I left Bowling Green Tuesday morning. I feel like I would give more to see you again and to be with you again tonight than ever before in my life. I haven't anything new to tell you, but how I just love to be with you!

I got home O.K. about eleven o'clock this morning. I wrote you the card in the P.O. and just as soon as I stepped out on the street I saw a boy from my home neighborhood driving by in a "Lizzy." I followed him to the Garage and he told me he would be glad to bring me out as only his mother and sister were with him. So I had a real pleasant way out, and got home much earlier than I was expecting. The folks seemed <u>really glad</u> to see me. Said they had decided that I liked other parts of Ky. better than Anderson and that they had decided I wasn't coming home any more. They didn't have to ask me if I had had a good time. They could tell by looking at me that I had seen a good time. I read your nice letter and really enjoyed it more than I can tell, although you had already told me little parts of it. I had double pleasure in those parts of having heard you tell me yourself then of reading them too. Say, "little girlie" please don't ever think you are writing too much to me in your letters. I certainly will find time to read all you can write me, and more than one time too. I always have. And I always enjoy reading every word of it every time that I read it. Really you can't know how much pleasure I do have reading your letters and in writing to you. Every thing that happens the first thing I think of is, "Oh, I'll write that to Elma." Then I more often than not know that you couldn't possibly care anything about hearing it and so I forget it, but not you. I truthfully don't believe there are five minutes day or night, when I am awake, that I don't think of you. Everything I ever think about or dream about for the future I want to do it for you, and I want to be with you all the time. I just want you and that's all I can think about. Well, well, here I go again just telling you the same thing over and over that I love you, and I always tell it in a sillier way. I know you get tired of it and disgusted but I just can't help it.

    Say, I want you to tell your mother and father that I really did appreciate their kindness while I was there. I know they thought I didn't, but it's just my way. I never could thank anybody for a kindness in a way to seem in earnest, and I could never show that I appreciated what folks did for me. But I do really appreciate hospitality and you and they certainly treated me nicely. You know that I appreciated it all, but perhaps they don't know it. Elma I never spent days more happily in my life than those two I spent with you in your home. I certainly know you are happy there and I just now begin to realize how much I am asking or hoping when I hope that you may ever think of leaving it for me. I do know you are happy and I don't know whether I could ever make you happier but I do also know I would love to spend my life trying. Elma, I believe you really know how to appreciate your splendid home and those good friends of yours. I think you are sure lucky to have such associates as those whom I met while there especially Delma and Miss Johnson. I liked them both especially because they seemed to like you so well especially Delma. And I think Miss Johnson is as pleasant and charming girl as I ever met (excepting you of course, for you know they do not seem anything like you do to me). And Blanche. You certainly are fortunate in having a friend like her. Of course I know her better than your other friends, and really the more I know of her the better I like her.

Well, it's getting late and I had better go to bed I guess. I will write you again Sunday I guess and then I don't know when you may expect a letter from me, but as soon as I can get a chance to write you.

I will stop this time. Tell your mother, father, and friends how much I appreciate what they did to show me a good time. And "little girl," I can't begin to thank you for all you did to make me happy. Truly I was happy while with you and I will always be true to you.

Elliott

JULY 16, 1918

This rather disjointed letter was postmarked from Georgetown, where Elma was working in the office while a Chautauqua[3] was in progress on campus. It's not clear whether her classes at the Business School in Bowling Green were over, or if she was just on a break.

Tuesday night
8:30 o'clock
Dearest Elliott:

I have been so lonesome since Sunday night. Nothing whatever doing. Mrs. Kenneth R. Patterson (nee Miss Lillian Lowe) came home yesterday and she has been staying here at Rucker Hall with me at nights while everybody else goes to the Chautauqua. She attended the same things while she was in Lebanon and she doesn't care to go to it again. Robin D. has left me strictly alone since he got back from Corinth. He has had very little to say to me and has been rushing Eula Daniels' visitor franticly [sic]. Last night I walked over in front of the tent with Lillian so she could fall in with Mrs. Lowe and Lelia. When I started back Mr. Browning, seeing that I was alone, stepped up to my side and came over to R.H. with me. On the way over Robin D. fell in behind us and this morning he siezed [sic] the opportunity to tease me. He said, among other things, that I had better be careful or you would be getting jealous of <u>him</u>. I told him he needn't worry about anything like that. Lillian Holmes has been begging me to go home with her after the Chautauqua to-night but Mrs. Patterson is here with me and I want to go to bed real early so I think as how I'll remain to home.

Wednesday morning - 7 o'clock -

Well, dearie, Lillian got to telling me her love story last night and I didn't get to finish this so will do it now although my little eyes are just barely open. A mosquito bit me on my left eye lid and it isn't quite normal so you can imagine what a peach I look. I guess my little boy has been at work for a long time and here I am just waking up. I would feel real lazy if I didn't imagine I was up later than you. I have stayed up 'till 11 both nights since I told you good-bye but I'm hoping that hour will not find me up to-night. I want to get a little better preparation for my journey to-morrow. I haven't quite finished packing my trunk so I think I'll get up and do that before I go to work this morning. Strange to say I'm not half so excited over going home as I was this time last week, but I know mother and daddy are spinning around on their eyebrows and when I think of that I feel happy to think that I can give them a little pleasure. I hope to write more often and more newsy letters when I get settled at home, although I doubt if there is much to tell except — the same old story. I've had a thought. Suppose sometime that we mention five things that we remember most distinctly in our period of courtship. I have my five in mind already but I won't have time to tell you about them this morning.

My! but I wish you were going to make that trip with me tomorrow! It will be a rather lonesome journey unless I meet up with someone I know on the train. Please don't work so hard as you have been cause I don't want you to kill yourself.

Yours with lots of Love, Elma

∼

JULY 16, 1918

This letter expresses some of the excitement and apprehension Elliott felt upon arrival at the U.S. Naval Training Camp[4] in Great Lake in Great Lakes, Illinois.

Co 397 8th regiment
BHS 851 West
Camp Decatur
U.S. Naval Training Camp
Great Lakes, Ill.

Dear Elma:

I am at last in camp and am feeling fine. It is about "chow" time. That is supper, dinner, or breakfast. I am on duty after supper to mop the floor. Good start you see. I will be in detention camp 21 days they say. I will not be allowed outside tent in that time. Everybody in uniform that we've met to-day says "You'll like it" and I guess we will. I think I will. I get to bunk with L.C. Ray whom I was telling you about. He is an old G.C. student. I have my bed all fixed up O.K. Fixed it myself see? Everything is clean spick and span. They took everything away from us to-day and I say they will take the rest to-morrow. I think I have the proper address at the beginning in full. They say we are moved every day or two. I will try to send it each time. I can't write much but will write again when I get time. I got here about one o'clock P.M., had "chow" and have been marching and walking all evening. There are about 20 fellows writing at the table I am at and all are very lively.

I guess you will excuse this pencil as it is all I have. "Little girl," know that I am thinking of you always and am expecting to see you again whenever I get a chance. Write to me when you can. I may not always get your letters, but guess I will.

As ever with love
Elliott

P.S. This letter may not read like the others I have been writing to you but [missing text]

JULY 19, 1918

This letter provides considerable detail about Elliott's early experiences in "detention" at Camp Decatur, where new recruits were sent upon arrival. He says he now knows the seriousness of war and can tell by the constant noise of cannons, airplanes, commands, and drills that the United States means business.

Company 397 8th Regiment
Bks 857 Camp Decatur
U.S. Naval Training Station
Great Lakes, Ill
Dear Elma:

At last I am about fixed up ready for drill. Our Co. had its first drill to-day. I was on guard and did not have drill. I have had an arm that was sore from the first "shot." It is about well now however. I have had headache a little this afternoon, but otherwise I am feeling good. Detention is not so bad as I had expected. They say it is much worse than the other camps. The officer said we would "Catch H__" in detention but we would be "Little Gods" when we get out of it. So I am looking forward to that time. You know I am not used to anything like that. I have seen so much since I got up here I hardly know what to write to you. I have been to Y.M.C.A. entertainments every night. I have to do about six hours regular work then whatever special duties fall upon me such as guarding, scrubbing, serving "chow," etc etc. We had to scrub the barracks all over this morning. We have to mop the floor three times each day. I think I will be a good "housekeeper" by the time I get out of the navy. Especially at scrubbing, sewing, washing etc.

I had to get up last night at 2 a.m. and stand guard till four. Everything was quiet for the first time (when I've been awake) since I've been here. From 5 a.m. till 9 p.m. you hear nothing but the band, orders, aroplanes and cannon. The Victoria at night in Louisville is quiet beside this camp in day time. But it is really quiet at night. It was the stillest place I ever saw to be so many buildings. Those two hours last night were the most pleasant I have had since I've been here. I had nothing to do except stand at the door of our Barracks and keep awake. I just stood there and dreamed and thought of you. Really the first time since here that I've had nothing to do but think of you, and I was happy. I really will enjoy standing guard at night for I will be free then to dream of you (and may I say our happiness when I come back?) and think of the many pleasant times I've had with you. I sure will be happy when I get to see you again. Don't think I'm homesick. I don't have time to be. I couldn't see you anyway if I were at home. So don't think I am homesick when I tell you I have been thinking of you. When I think of you I am happiest. I love to be alone and think (what little I am capable of thinking). I think of you all the time. And I am happy because I am doing my duty.

You know we were talking about my coming back clean. The greatest danger I see in the navy is forming the habit of rough, unclean language. That has never been much temptation to me, I mean swearing mostly. I must say I have not always used the best language but I was never guilty of swearing in my life. If one is not very careful he will become rougher in that respect. A man in the navy cannot get alcohol under any consideration. I can assure you now that I will not form the cigarette habit in the navy or the tobacco habit of any form as to that matter. While in detention no man can smoke a cigarette. If navy men go with impure women and it is found out it is a court-martial offense.

LOVE LETTERS

So you see many temptations at home are barred from navy men. I am so glad I got in to the navy on that account. Men naturally become more hard and selfish in the navy or at least that is my first impression. I mean one will have to be on his guard if he doesn't. I had a wrong impression of the navy that there would be a lack of religion. I find already that the navy stands for religion. I believe there are more religious boys to the same number in the navy than any place I've been. Of course I do not know any except my own Barracks. There are about 140 in our company. These boys come from all over the U.S. The navy stands for clean morals, clean speech, and religion. That is evident by the rules and commands that are enforced.

So don't worry about me. I won't be very much worse when I get home than I was when I left. I know I will try hard. They are to have a vaudeville[5] in Y.M.C.A. to-night. So I really don't care for it much and I am taking all the time to write to you. "C?" We have to go to some of the entertainments but not to-night. I don't think I shall go <u>every</u> show for sometimes I would rather write to you, in fact every time. Most nights I have extra duties but not to-night. When we have no extra duties we get off at three o'clock. We can't write except from 6 to 9 p.m. in this camp. It may be changed in other camps. Detention is harder in many ways, privileges, eating, everything I guess.

I went to a musical concert night before last and they sang twice "It's a Long Long Trail." I guess you know what and whom that made me think of, and of the last time I was with you? I do love that song. Next Tues. night we have a world famous symphony orchestra of 50 pieces and a vocal concert. I hope I get to hear that. I know it will be great. All Y.M.C.A. entertainments are free. The singers the other night were women, the first I have seen since I got in camp. The theater is made out in a deep ravine. Seats are fixed into each side of the hill under the shade of the trees. The stage is a bridge across the stream in the center. It is a pretty nice arrangement. It has to be large to accommodate all the folks. There are two whole camps[6] to be accommodated. There are 16 camps in the whole station, counting some say about 40,000, others say 75,000. I do not know which is right. I do know there are <u>some</u> people here.

I never knew the real seriousness of the war until I got here.

When one hears the cannon roar all day and the aroplanes [sic] continually whirring above him and hears the sternness of the commands, and sees the seriousness of the drill he sure knows the U.S. means business. One gets the spirit too of the nation when he hears the young men from the many different states talk and show their earnestness in their duties. I have never heard one fellow grumble because he has to scrub or sweep and if you know <u>men</u> at all you have heard at least how they hate such work. I have never talked to one yet who has joined the navy for any purpose except to whip the Kaiser. Everyone wants to go as soon as possible so as to go back home as soon as possible. No one wants to stay at home or seems to be hunting the easy place. I believe that is the spirit that will win the war too.

Well, the climate is quite different up here. The days are terribly hot, as hot as in Ky. The nights are cool enough to wear an overcoat. One really gets cold without a coat on before nine o'clock at evening.

I have tried to tell you a little bit of many things. I just wanted to tell you one thing that is I love you. I know you get tired of the same old story over and over. You know how much I think of you already and so I will always try to tell you all that I think would be permitted to be written and what I can pick out in the time I have to write. If any of it is tiresome and bores you to read it tell me and I will try to do better. By the way I think they will let me have a pen when detention is over. I am awfully glad I sent mine to you. Someone would have swiped it up here if I had brought it. I am going to get a cheap one to use in the navy. So don't think I mentioned the pen as a hint. I only mean that you won't have quite so hard time reading my scribbling when I get hold of a pen again. I know it is bad enough anyway.

Mr. Ray the G.C. fellow is seated by me writing a long letter to his wife. There are three other fellows out of 36 in my Barrack who married within ten days before they came up here.

I told you about seeing Ramises [sic] in Louisville. He went to New Port R.I., as an electrician. He said he had been sick all summer. Do you reckon Blanche had anything to do with it? But he didn't say it was heart trouble.

Well I must stop. You will never get this read now. Be a good Little

Girlie and write to me real soon. I know you haven't had time yet. My letter laid in the Barrack for a day or so before they got it after I wrote it.

Always know I love you.

Elliott

~

JULY 18, 1918

Elma began writing to Elliott as soon as he left for basic training, using stationary with flags and "U.S.A" printed across the top and placing American flag stickers on the envelopes. She also began buying patriotic songs to play on the piano and sing. Apparently, this was new behavior for her, as her mother teased her about becoming "dreadfully patriotic." This letter covers many topics and a range of emotions.

Dearest Elliott:

I haven't yet rec'd your address but I decided I would just write anyway so I would have it ready to start as soon as it comes. It seems like ages since the last time I wrote to you — over a week — and in that time I have gotten two letters, a card and the pen which I am using now. I got your last letter just as I was starting to the train Tuesday morning and read it while on the train. I was all by myself and it was just so sweet I had to cry dess [just] a little bit. It wasn't because I regretted your going so much but just because I love you so. Each day I feel that I am drawn closer to you and I think of you almost constantly. I know now that you occupy the second highest place in my life. Of course God comes first and it must always be so, but you come next. I love mother and father dearly but not in the same way I do you. I don't believe any parents ever did more for a child or made more sacrifices than they have for me. I <u>must</u> in some measure try to repay them and this will be my task while waiting for you.

I am all disturbed about my work just now. After coming home I have found that I cannot get a student ticket [for riding the trains] because I am over 18 years of age and besides they will not sell them only at the 1st of the month. However I can get a business ticket for just a little more and I may do that at the 1st of August. I came down to Blanche's night before last and on down home last night. Father decided for me to stay at home the remainder of this week and during that time decide on the best plan. If I go back to B.G. I will have to get another room because the one I left has already been taken. Altogether I am somewhat upset. But I guess it will all work out all right bye and bye. At any rate I am enjoying being at home these three days. It is just an ideal morning to write to you — real cool — all quiet save for the pity pat of the rain gently falling (descriptive).

I was so glad to hear you were going to have company on the way up. I imagine it is heaps easier when you have somebody else along who doesn't know any more than you do. In other words misery likes company. But when you told me that Mr. Ray was married I almost fell over. Surprising things will happen.

I wished for you when I went down to Woodburn Tuesday night. Had such a nice time. Blanche is keeping house this week while her mother is away taking a rest. We got through with supper about 9 o'clock, got to bed at 12 and to sleep at 2. As a natural consequence I went to sleep in shorthand class yesterday morning. I don't think I shall try keeping such late hours anymore soon, but you see we hadn't been together in so long that we just had to talk and talk. She had a letter from Ira yesterday morning. He hasn't any hopes of getting out of the school any time soon. I had a letter from Lelia Harris this week and she said that she, Faith [Snuggs], Roland [Snuggs] and Prof. Ragland made up the office force [at Georgetown College] just now. I imagine they need me, don't you?

I got me five new patriotic songs the other day. Mama says I am getting dreadful patriotic all of a sudden. But I have always been that way, haven't I? If I hadn't I could not have given you up so cheerfully. [Small question marks surround the word "cheerfully."] Last night I wasn't very hungry when I got home and papa said, "What's the trouble — grieving so that you have lost your appetite." I says yes that's it.

LOVE LETTERS

I came across the following little verse the other day and it struck me so that I put it away in one corner of my little cranium:

> *What if he comes not back? you say,*
> *Oh well, my sky would be more gray.*
> *But through the clouds the sun should shine*
> *And golden memories be mine.*
> *God's test of manhood is, I know,*
> *Not will he come, but did he go?*

I wish some time when you gets real lonesome and "doesn't" have anything to do that you would write a little more poetry for me. I always did like poetry and yours especially.

Well, I have had dinner now and am ready to start all over again but I'm like you — haven't but one thing to tell you and have already said that over and over. I would not mind if you should tell me a thousand times a day cause it gets sweeter each time. I never think your letters are silly. How could I if I loved you in the least. Please always say just what you feel like saying and be assured that I will be vitally interested in all that you do or say. If you get blue, tell me about it. If you have any little problems to solve and I can help you out it would make me very very happy if you would only call on me. The only real genuine pleasure I find is in thinking of you. To make you happy is my sincere desire. Life is so different since I have learned that I really love you. Now, there is something big and bright in the future and for that I can work, hope and pray. I love to think and plan for the time when we can be happy together. Of course there is a long space intervening but there are many many things to be done and perhaps the time will slip by more quickly than we are expecting. I haven't been with any boy since I told you good bye. I haven't yet decided whether I shall or not. One thing I know is that I do not care for anybody else's company and if I do go with anyone it will be for only one purpose. That is to keep young. I have a horror of getting old and "sot" in my ways and I fear if I don't run around with young folks a little I might do that very thing. I wish I could be just as young at 25 as I am now. I would love to be a "little girl" all my life. Sure enough I have lost 1/2 lb. since you left. Am afraid I will lose some more if I don't hurry up and get "settled down." I find that worry isn't very good on the constitution. I'm hoping the postman will bring me a letter this afternoon. If he does I may write another folder later.

༄

JULY 20, 1918

While waiting to receive Elliott's address, Elma continued writing, and she saved up all her letters to send at once in one large packet.

Second Edition
    Saturday morning
    Well, I rec'd your letter this morning. It seemed like a dreadful long time coming but I waited patiently. I was just ready to begin mopping the floors and after I read your letter, oh! how I wished for you to help me and after I read part of your letter to mama and papa — mama said she wished you were here. What do you think of that? I believe you made a hit while here. I'm awful glad you are liking [sic] so well. Hope it will continue so. I think it is real nice to have a real live Georgetonian around you all the time. Maybe you will meet some more after you have been there awhile. I'm wishing you the best o' luck, while in the detention camp. Wish I could happen around occasionally to cheer you up a bit but since I can't — will just send this "little" journal in my place. Listen, whatever you do don't get too fat. 200 lbs is the limit so be careful how much you eat!
    Delma came in just then and started to write you a little bit but decided she didn't know what to say and didn't do it. She came by and took me out driving yesterday afternoon and I went to the band concert last night. There was a big man from Louisville made a stirring patriotic speech. I think his name was Major MarmaDuke Bowen — or something like that. He has rec'd his appointment to a Captaincy as soon as there is a vacancy.
    I'm going back to B.G. Monday to stay. Oh agony unspeakable! As

soon as I find a place to hang out I will send you my address. In the meantime mother will forward my mail to you. It's hard to tell which of us moves around the most. I would write some more but I am afraid this may never reach you and just think how much paper and ink would be wasted. Anyway I'll be writing all along whether you get them or not.

With heaps of love,
Elma

∼

JULY 22, 1918

Elma has returned to Bowling Green and settled into her new boarding house that she says has "all conveniences." The war is very much on her mind, and she describes "a dreadful crowd" of people at the train station saying goodbye to the boys leaving for war. She thinks it is "terrible" the way some folks "weep and wail," and she considers them selfish for carrying on so. The news in the papers has been encouraging, though, and she dares to hope that the war will be over by fall and Elliott can come back to college.

Dear Elliott:

Once more I am "settled down" and have me a room and a roommate. I came up this morning and struck this place the first one. It is real nice and has all conveniences. I think I am going to like it very much. Haven't been with my roommate but about five minutes but she seems to be a very sensible kind of girl. You know I can't say that about all the girls in B.G.

The woman with whom I am rooming lost a son in France. He was with the first American troops that went across and died of pneumonia soon after he arrived. His grandmother told me all about his death the first think [sic] after I got here and it sure was a sad story.

Eighteen boys from home left on the same train that I came up on and I thought there was a dreadful crowd at the train for I could hardly get on, but when I got up here I decided I hadn't seen any crowd at all. About 50 were leaving from here and there must have been a million people in town. The station was packed and jammed. I finally made my way out to the car track, caught a cracker box [trolley] up town. All the way from the square to the depot, people were swarming and they couldn't be missed down in town. It is County Court Day anyway. Some man is auctioneering about half a block down the way and I never heard quite so much noise. It is the 1st performance like that I have ever heard. I'm just one block up the street from the Y.M.C.A. building. Perhaps you'll remember. It is on the corner of Chestnut and 11th. I like it because it is so much nearer my boarding place. Just two blocks.

I intended to write to you yesterday afternoon but I took dinner with a girl friend, one you didn't meet, a Miss Gossett. Didn't get home until time to go to the Band Concert. It was about the same performance as usual so I soon got tired, went home and ate supper (chow) then back to B.Y.P.U. What did they do but put me to work playing [piano]. That has been my job every Sunday night almost that I've been home. I'm going down home Wednesday night to hear Bro. Lovelace preach. He is coming down to the Association and is to preach in Franklin that night. I can hardly wait I am so anxious to see him. I had rather see him than anybody I know of except you.

Landsakes! I never have heard or seen so much excitement as there is around here just now. All that yelling, a great throng of people up the street and some man has just fainted and was brought in here. I might go down and see about him but I think he has enough nurses for the present. If it was only you I'd be there mighty quick. You bet I would.

I'm still loving you just as much, if not more than ever. The news in the papers the last few days has looked so encouraging that I have dared to hope that you'll get to come back and finish college — maybe with the class of '20. Wouldn't that be great??

Oh! if we could only win the war by fall, there would be many a happy person. It was terrible to see how the people wept and wailed over the boys who left this morning. I think folks are downright selfish when they take on so. If they were thinking of the boys they would bear up for their sakes. That is the way I look at it. I do wish I could do something for you while you are in detention. If you are not allowed outside of your tent, it must be dreadful lonesome for you. I know from experience that as long as one is busy time passes rapidly. I'm going to try my very best to be satisfied this time. I think I can be contented most anywhere if I will just make up my mind to be. The trouble has been I couldn't make up my mind. "C."

I haven't seen Thomas since you were down here, thank goodness. But I heard that he was in love with me and another girl and didn't know which he liked best. I might tell him to bestow all his affections on the other lady 'cause I haven't got any at all for him. I think probably he has already found that out.

Listen, please don't forget to have your picture made just as soon as you can. I can hardly wait to see how you look in the uniform. And don't be afraid to have one made that is big enough to be seen.

There are four girls in here, all talking at once and you can imagine just how rapidly my thoughts are flowing. I believe I'll stop for this time. Don't fall so desperately in love with the navy that you forget the "little girl" back in Kentuck [sic].

Wif Love,
Elma

JULY 23, 1918

Elma admits she is quite blue, but she believes this separation will make them appreciate each other more when they get back together. She tells Elliott about the bell that rings each day at twelve o'clock for everyone to stop wherever they are and say a prayer for the boys, which always makes her think of him.

---

3 o'clock P.M.

Dearest Elliott:

I have been so lonesome for you this afternoon I could hardly stand it. When I feel like this I always re-read your dear letters. They mean so much to me and especially since you are so far away and I know it is impossible to see you for a long long time. I have just read the one you wrote the day before you left. It made me almost feel like I was with you again. In that letter you promised to be true to me and I <u>know</u> you will. I could not ask for more because I believe you do love me as I love you. I have only had one letter from you since you reached camp, the one in which you sent your address. Of course I have looked forward to another and perhaps one has gone down home, but anyway I know you will write just as often as you possibly can.

They have graduating exercises at the Business University once every year and that came off last night. They had prepared to have it on the lawn of the B.U. But it began raining about the time for it to begin so we had to go to the Baptist Church. There were about forty graduates and an enormous crowd. Dr. Willett of Chicago University delivered the address which was on the war of course. He said the danger now was, that we would stop before a complete victory was won and that would take at least three or four more years. He certainly was a brilliant man but I got so sleepy before he got through that I almost fell over. Didn't get home until after 11. I'll bet you don't keep such late hours, do you? I was oh so sleepy this morning but had to get up just the same.

I perhaps should not have written this afternoon for my letter may be a little bit blue. If it is, don't let it worry you for it is only because I feel so lonesome for you. I believe this separation is going to make us appreciate each other more when we do get to be together. At least that is the way I feel about it now. Each day at twelve o'clock they ring a bell here and everyone stops wherever he may be and offers a prayer for our boys. I appreciate that opportunity to offer a little prayer for you each day, so now when it is 12 o'clock you can know just what I am doing. I thought perhaps it would make us feel a little nearer if I told you that. I wish it were possible for you to keep up the B.Y.P.U. Bible Reading for they are so interesting now, then too we would be reading the same chapter each day, but of course that will perhaps be impossible.

I have been thinking over the happy times we have had together, this afternoon. We used to think two weeks was a dreadful long time but we really didn't know how fortunate we were. Honest to goodness I haven't hardly any respect for boys who are not in service now. Of course, some poor fellows can't get in but there are some who dread to go. You know we were talking about our B.Y.P.U. president when you were down home. He is about the most miserable looking specimen I have seen in a long time. He seems to have a perfect horror of going and almost crys [sic] when anyone mentions it. Gee! I wish I were a man. I'd be right up there with you in the navy. Don't believe it, do you? Anyway it is the truth. They think Blanche and I are both crazy when we talk like that!

Oh, I must tell you about the fine man I am eating by now. He is real fat and has the daintiest little lady hands. In fact he is downright sissy. However he stirred up a little conversation with me at dinner and I gathered the following information. He is from Helen Saunders' home town and knows all that bunch of G.C. Folks who went down there and gave the Red Cross programs. Sis Mullins included in the bunch, you know. This fellow said he thought about going to Georgetown next year, but had decided to go to State and take an agricultural course. I thoughts to myself, dear brother, what do you expect to do on a farm with those pretty little white hands?

Well dear, I must close and go mail this. Think I shall try to persuade the Postmaster to give me a letter whether there is any there or not. I'm about to get over my "blues" now and am going to try to keep from getting them anymore soon.

With heaps of love,
Elma

～

JULY 24, 1918

Elliott provides details about his life at camp and says that if his letters seem different, it is because of all the noise and commotion in the room where he is allowed to write. He thanks Elma for being so true and brave and for making it easier for him to do his duty to Uncle Sam.

Great Lakes, Ill

Dear Elma:

I just got a letter from you about half hour ago. I got your first letter Monday. Both of them made me feel terribly good. I have never felt happier in my life than when reading those letters, except when I was with you. You can have no idea how good it makes a fellow feel, that is in the navy, and knows his "Little Girl" is far away and he has no idea when he will get to see her, as it does when he gets such a sweet letter as those you wrote me. Then I was sick too. I tell you these inoculations and vaccinations make one feel terribly bad. I had just had my second shot Monday morning. My head was just bursting. Every bone and muscle in my body was aching. Oh gee I was feeling tough when the company clerk came in and yelled "Mail!" And there was a letter from you! I entirely forgot that I was feeling bad. I tell you I've been feeling so much better ever since but still I have felt bad physically. The tough part about it is we can't lie down in day time unless we are sick enough to go to the sick bay. I hated to go to the hospital but I felt like it. I have just got one more shot now and then I guess I am through. I was going to write to you last night but I had to do extra duty yesterday and did not get through untill three o'clock this morning. I was working in the laundry with eight other men from our company. I just got two hours sleep last night. You know we have to be up at five a.m. no matter what happens. I am feeling good now, however, although I have been drilling all day in the hot sun. One of the fellows in our unlucky bunch of yesterday went out to drill and fainted and fell over. He had to be carried to the sick bay. The way I and the rest of us got on that job was due to the fault of some other guy in our barracks. The commander came in for inspection and found that someone had spit in the garbage can (which had been cleaned). He asked who did it. Nobody would own up and so the whole barrack got an extra duty. Of course I got the hardest job. I don't kick about doing my part but I do hate to be punished for the lack of some other guy's manhood and honesty. If he had owned up, he would probably have gotten a little extra duty, but the rest would have been free. That is what a little bit of dishonesty in the navy will do. About the hardest part about it was I did not get to write to you when I was expecting "C."

Well, I have got all my things packed to move from this camp, either to-night or to-morrow. I think I must have made a mistake when I wrote to you before. I did not mean that I can't get out of my tent. I can go all over the camp. It is quite a town of itself. I haven't been over near all of it yet, and I can't go to any other camp except as I am transferred from one detention camp to another. This whole station is some big place. It is a big city almost, over 40,000. There are about 4,000 in this one camp where I am I guess. So you see it is not so bad as I made it appear in my other letter. It was a mistake. I do not have time hardly ever to read over what I have written, (I doubt if I could read it if I had time). I know you have a time reading this.

You asked me not to forget to have a picture made. I will have one made as soon as possible. I don't draw any pay for three months. So if you know me, you know I will be scarce of money until then. I might get a furlough at the end of the three months and then come home. Would you rather see me or the picture? I won't forget you or the picture either. I will have one made as soon as I get a chance.

I went last night for an hour and a half to see some famous Russian dancer (I got off that long from the laundry. I worked from 7 a.m. till 3 a.m. next day.) It was put on by the Y.M.C.A. They say it always cost from $5 to $10 per seat to see it. It was said to be classic. It must have been classic. It failed to appeal to me. I never saw anything more rotten. The Great Lakes Orchestra played. That was fine. The sailors sang, "It's a Long Long Trail." That was good. You see there are other fellows here who love that song. If I have room in my letter for it, I will send you a little leaflet with a part of the songs on it which the sailors are taught to sing here. I will send it right away if not this time. I thought perhaps you would like to read them over. I guess you have heard most of them already.

I am glad you have gone back to B.G. and that you are settled again. Don't worry if you can help it. These are hard times for any of us to stick to our post or to keep at any one thing. The war news sure is looking better of late. My, I sure would be glad if I could be back at old G.C. this fall and graduate with the class of '20. I do not want to leave the navy till the war is settled and I am no longer needed to serve my country. But if it is over don't worry about me being enough in love with it (navy) to stay or forget "my little girl in Ky." Just as soon as Uncle Sam says he can do without me, I'll hit that "Long, Long Trail" to Ky. There is talk that our company might go to sea within a month. I wish we would. I do not like camp much, if it is all like what we are having now.

As soon as I find out where I am to be moved I will send you my new address. I think they will send our mail on to us O.K. I hope so at least. I hope I do not miss one letter that you write me. "Little Girl" you are so true and brave. You write so cheerfully. You have the spirit that encourages the fellows who have to go. If you had cried and acted as though you hated to see me go it would have been much harder for me all the time I am away. I know you love me and hate to be away from me as much as any girl does and whom she loves yet you never said one word to keep me from going. I knew I would have to go anyway and it was much easier for me when you took the right spirit and seemed glad that I could have my part in this great cause.

In one of your letters you said you had something to look forward to. That's the greatest pleasure I have now and helps me to pass many otherwise lonesome hours thinking of you and the future.

You said you wanted to keep young. I sure want you to. I want you to be as much like you are now as possible when I come back. Then I know there will be many times you will want company and I want you to have just as much as you want. I know you are true to me. The only way I would ever think you should not keep company is that you should not go with any one fellow too long unless you expect to return his love, for he will love you. Men do not go with girls of your type unless they expect to love them. When men talk to girls and want to love them they look for girls of your type. I am saying this simply for the sake of the other fellow.

You may think my letters are different since I got up here. If they are it is due to the noise. I just can't hardly write at all for there are 36 men all in the room together during the only times that one can write at all. I guess you can imagine how much noise there is. Perhaps it may be different when I get out of detention. So we can go to the Y.M.C.A. Headquarters to write. Here we have to write within our barracks. There are about a dozen [singing] in here all the time. We have no time to write except between 4 and 9 P.M. Many times I start to write something and forget it entirely. When I write to you I just love to be all alone. Then I can imagine I am just with you and write [how] I would like to talk. Don't think I have changed in feeling for I would just give anything I posess [sic] to be alone with you again. Really, I believe I could "Be Good" for a little while — if you wanted me to, and when somebody else was 'round or coming near. I will write you a card or letter just as soon as I move. 'Twill be to-morrow I guess. It is now 7 o'clock.

You said I made a hit. I sure do hope your mother and father think well of me. Not boasting, but really I believe I am better liked when better known (if ever known). Must stop. Out of paper and it is raining so can't go after any. With Love, Elliott

∼

JULY 25, 1918

Elma's interest in people and her desire to tell entertaining stories are apparent in this letter.

Dear Elliott:

Your nice long letter of the 19th reached me yesterday and I enjoyed every single word of it. Of course it went to Franklin first and that made it so much longer getting to me. But that made it all the dearer when I did get it. I was so glad to hear you were getting along so well and that the conditions were so desirable. I had no fears for you but I was glad for the sake of other boys who are less strong. I think it is so nice that you have so many Y.M.C.A. entertainments. I imagine they have the very best artists.

We had a speaker in chapel yesterday morning from New York City and he certainly made an inspiring address. All the students went wild over him and prevailed on having him again this morning, but I missed this one by going home last night. Went down with Bro. Lovelace and nearly talked him to death. Nearly all the Baptist Church was at the depot to meet him and his Sunday School Class in a body. I was so afraid I wasn't going to get to go when it began to rain about 4 o'clock. Then I called and asked about the train — 30 minutes late — was the old old story. Of course I had plenty of time to go to supper and by the time supper was over it had stopped raining, much to my joy. Dad was at the train with all the rest of the Baptists and we went right on to church. I heard a sure enough good sermon once more. It wasn't before I needed it either I don't guess.

A bunch of little boys passed below my window then and of all the language. I think they surely have been up there taking lessons. Believe me, this is some place anyway. There is a girl that lives here who married when she was eighteen, lived with her husband three years and now is divorced and having a gay time, while her mother is taking care of her little girl. That is the way such cases generally turn out. I think it is so much nicer to wait until you learn some sense and know what you are doing.

Bro. Lovelace told me an amusing little story about a woman who is a member of his church. He said she came up to him with the longest face and said she was so distressed because the war was taking all the boys and there wouldn't be anybody left for her daughter to marry. He said he almost laughed in her face but that she was perfectly serious about it. I have a picture of mama saying anything like that right now. Oh! Listen I had the queerest dream the other night. It was about you and mama, and believe me! You were having war. I guess that is a good sign she likes you for you know you must always take a dream backward. Guess I will most die this weekend because I'm not going home anymore until Saturday week and then Blanche is going down with me. I'll ask her if she has been writing to "Rameses" very often to cause him heart trouble. I know she has written a few times anyway.

My roommate is talking of going home at the end of this week. Guess I was too much for her. Her home is in Miss. And she has been up here since April. Another girl who rooms here is talking of leaving Sunday. Seems like I am running them all off. It's just awful to be so hateful that nobody can stay in the house with you.

Oh! I'm about to get up a case with that dainty little sister that I eat by. He's a peach and I laugh right in his face but he talks on just the same. He smiled so sweetly at me clear across the typewriting room this morning. Then at dinner in that charming little voice, he started up a conversation by saying, "My! You were playing some on that old typewriter this morning!" I said Oh yes, I was just trying to pass off a little time. And yes, I forgot to tell you that he had red hair, and more pretty little freckles on his face. Well, I must <u>not</u> talk about him anymore cause mama says it isn't nice.

The man that looks so much like you happened to [have] an accident the other day. He fell in the swimming pool at the Y.M. and cut his head so badly that they had to take 5 stitches. Weren't that awful!! 'Spect you'll think I've got the men on the brain but you're mistaken. I have only one in mind and that one is "U." I don't love nobody a tall but you and I don't want to see nobody a tall but you. That's the whole story told in just a few words. However much I may rave, I don't mean any harm, and I'm loving you all the time just as hard and as much as I did the last night I was with you.

Yours as ever,
Elma

∼

JULY 27, 1918

Elma referred to this letter as a "Chinese puzzle," due to the way the pages were arranged. The content is similarly jumbled, as she jumps from topic to topic.

Saturday afternoon
Dearest Elliott:
I believe you have been having a real taste of detention camp. I thought it was awful when I was vaccinated for typhoid fever and mother treating me like an infant all the time too.[7] That was two years ago but I haven't forgotten how badly I felt. It must have been fierce to

take so many inoculations at once, but thank goodness you'll soon be through with it.

I would have been dreadfully disappointed if I hadn't heard from you this morning. When I went over to dinner one of the girls handed me two letters, one containing your nice long letter and the other the songs which I think are quite fetching and I like your favorites very very much. The only thing I regret is that I can't hear you sing them.

I'm not going home this week end and I just know I shall pass off. I haven't spent but one week end up here and that was the time Thomas happened around. I am quite sure nothing like that is going to come to pass tomorrow. I'd lots rather spend the time writing to you anyway.

I heard that Mr. Spillman from New York speak again yesterday morning. His subject was "My Country" this time and it was great. He delivered three addresses while here, in the following order: "My Ships," "My Friends," and "My Country." I missed the second one when I took my little trip home.

You can imagine how surprised I was when I walked out of chapel yesterday morning and found myself face to face with Dr. Leigh. He was just as surprised to see me because he did not know I was in school up here. We were dee-lighted to see each other. You have no idea how much better he looked to me then than he used to in Chemistry class where I was so often minus knowledge. He said he had been out to sea since school closed, trying the smoke screen. Said it was wonderfully successful, surrounding the ship for a circuit of three miles. At least that is what I understood him to say. My! But I feels awfully proud of my teacher. Then I heard the other day that a boy, with whom I have gone a few times, was on the San Diego[8] when it was sunk and played the part of a hero by saving the flag. Now when you do some notoriously daring deed I'll be quite puffed up. But, dear, I'm not so anxious for you to put yourself on a sinking ship just to snatch a flag. No, no, I think you are being heroic enough when you work from 5 one morning to 3 the next and all because of someone else's meanness. Maybe when the Huns have been thoroughly beaten such conditions won't exist. You asked me which I had rather see, you or your picture. Well of all the questions. If I only could believe that you would get a furlough in three months I would be as happy as if I had good sense. But about the time I was rejoicing so gayly [sic] over that statement you came along and said you might go to sea within a month. Now that was pretty — to get my hopes up so high, then let them come down with such a dull thud. But that's alright. It matters not when I see you I'll love you all the time just the same. Of course not a single day passes without a deep longing to see you. It could not be otherwise when I love you as I do. But even when I want you most, I would not take you from Uncle Sam's service, if I could. I love to think of you as big and strong — both mentally and physically — standing ready to do whatever falls to your lot. I know you will be brave. A person like you could not be otherwise. We are all longing and praying for the war to end but of course no one knows how much longer the struggle will last. At any rate I shall wait for you just as patiently and bravely as I possibly can.

I went over to school last night to hear some negroes sing. There were five of them and when they all sang it was real good, but there was one old fellow all dressed up in his "pam beach" and white shoes, who insisted on singing solos and they were truly so lows. One thing that they sang was "It's not my sister, but it's me Oh Lord."[9] They sang three or four on that order and they sounded like real sure enough "niggers."[10]

This morning Mr. Mumford of the Gregg Shorthand School in Chicago gave a short address. I wasn't paying much attention — in fact I was dreaming a wee bit, but all at once I was forced to prick up my ears for I heard him say something about the Great Lakes Naval Training Sta. When I listened more closely I learned that he taught a Sunday School Class out there every Sunday. And he told about what a fine lot of fellows there was there. Maybe you'll happen in his S.S. Class sometime.

I've been having more fun paddling around in the rain for the last two or three days. Nothing like rain for drooping spirits but we really did need it. I can't realize that I have only six more weeks here. Oh but they can't pass too quickly for me. I am anxious to get back to Georgetown. I will at least be surrounded by pleasant memories there.

While looking at the calendar a few minutes ago I read this: "There is but one failure, and that is not to be true to the best one knows." I thought it sounded like you but I noticed it was from Canon Farrar.

Guess this letter will be like a Chinese puzzle but I did not intentionally arrange it so complexly. Must stop so I can mail it before supper. With lots of love and — Elma

~

JULY 28, 1918

By this time Elliott had moved from Camp Decatur to Camp Perry.[11] *In this letter he introduces Elma to some Navy terms that were new to him, including "shake it up," "on the double," "hit the deck," "fall out," and "pipe down." Although his writing was interrupted for YMCA Bible class, church, doctor's inspection, and chow, his letter is quite cohesive and filled with details about life at camp and his reactions to it.*

Sunday morning

Dear Elma:

I am all dressed up in my white suit and no place to go. It is a suit that I washed myself. So you know it is <u>some</u> clean. We all have to do our own washing now. Each fellow has to take care of himself and his clothing in the navy. He has to keep clean too. We are supposed to wash as much as one white suit each day. We have from four to eight o'clock in the afternoon for washing (if we have nothing else to do). When I was in Camp Decatur I thought I would have plenty of time to write but I have been in this camp three days and this morning is the first time I have had one minute to spare. Everything we start to do the officers are yelling "Shake it up" or "On the double." (These terms mean <u>hurry</u> and <u>hit the run</u>.) And believe me we are running most of the time. <u>We</u> have a certain time and a certain number of hours or minutes for everything. Just at five o'clock in the morning we are yelled at "to hit the deck" and there is some hurrying then to get our beds up off the floor and get dressed. Only fifteen minutes for all of it including a shower bath. Just an hour to have the whole barracks swept and scrubbed besides dressing.

Then it's rush, rush, rush, till nine o'clock in the evening. Then it is "Pipe down" in other words no more talking. Things are quiet then till five again. Nothing is quiet in the day time. We have to sleep on a sack of straw on the floor. We are supposed to have hammocks but haven't gotten them yet as there are so many men here and as they are coming in so fast.

Well, I was just now ordered to "fall out," that is line up in marching column for church. (I may bore you with explanation of these terms. They were all new to me and I take for granted they are to you). When I got out it was for Jews and Catholics only. So I am back to my writing. I will have to go to the Protestant service. I do not know when or where but every man in the navy has to go to one service of some kind on Sunday. I went last Sunday in Camp Decatur. It sure was a good sermon too. One of the best I ever heard. I think that is one good feature of the navy. I think I would go anyway but as it is I know I will go. I try to read my testament daily. Sometimes I do not have time however. I haven't seen one other fellow reading since I have been in this camp. It is so noisy round here it is hard to get much out of a reading and as soon as the men get quiet the lights are out.

As I came into this camp I met Roy Martin. I hear he is not far from my barracks. We were in ranks and I did not get to speak to him. I saw Fred Amerson this morning when I went to chow. He is stationed just across the street from me. He's an officer now, a company commander I think. (I thought perhaps you would be glad to hear from him.) He looks natural. And he looks better in his sailor suit than in his civilian clothes. Gee, I look terrible in a sailor suit. I look like a regular slouch. I doubt if I ever let you see me again till I get in my civilian clothes again.

Just now interrupted for a Y.M.C.A. Bible Class. The fellow who had charge sure made a fine talk. He was discussing the Beatitudes. I will have to go to church soon. I guess I will have all the evening off however and so I will have plenty of time to finish.

I got my third "shot" yesterday and I am feeling rather tough to-day. I have the headache and my arm is so sore I can't lift it up. It doesn't hurt much to write.

Again I have been interrupted for church, doctor's inspection, and chow. It is now afternoon. The church service was good only it was terribly hot. We had to stand up in the sun and I tell you it was hot. It was a stirring sermon too. The main appeal in every service I have heard yet is for the men to keep clean. Purity is the thing stressed most. They all ask us to go back to those who are depending upon us as pure and straight as we were when we left home. There are the same temptations here that there are at home only they are stronger. I think I can meet the temptations here just as well as I could at home. Many fellows who are here think they can just do as they please and nobody will ever know it. I don't look at it in that way. I want to be a <u>man</u> just for what manhood is and not for reputation only. "Little girl," you have little idea how much I appreciate that you remember me in your prayers. I sure believe in prayer and I try not to neglect it. Yesterday and to-day both I have felt different just at twelve o'clock. I have remembered what you said and it will make it much easier for me to do right and live right just to know that you are praying for me. I never forget you either in my prayers. I begin to pray each night just as the lights go out at nine o'clock. So you may know too that I am thinking of you. I have never said my prayers since I have been going with you that I do not thank God that I have known you and have been permitted to have your company. Now I feel that I have greater reason to be thankful since I know you love me as you do. It requires as much courage for those at home as it does for those in the service. Both those in the army and those at home need to pray in these times and I do not think we should be ashamed for folks to know that we pray. I believe prayer will win the war in the end for right.

You were saying you hardly respect those able men who are not in the army. I have the same feeling myself. I had stayed out of the army myself until I felt almost like a slacker. I did not stay out because I was afraid to go. I never told you before but I stayed out on purpose to find out whether or not you loved me. I would have joined last fall only I knew I loved you and I wanted to stay near you until I found out whether or not you loved me. When school was out I was sure, and so I enlisted just as soon as I could after I got home. I sometimes thought I was perhaps doing wrong to stay and get you in love with me knowing I would leave as soon as I knew you did. I just felt that I could not leave without knowing. I knew I loved you almost a year ago. I think men will know whether or not they should go. I couldn't have stayed out any longer and felt like a man at all. I believe all real men who pretend to have an ideal feel the same way. I must confess that I did not have an easy conscience one day for the past year till since [sic] I got to the navy camp. I know I am doing my duty and I feel good. So don't forget to continue your prayers for me. I need them and certainly appreciate that you told me. I felt that you were praying for me all the time.

One half of the barracks I am in got quarantined to-day for German measles. It is for 14 days. I sure am glad I was not in that end. We may get it too. When quarantined the fellows are not allowed to be outside the building except on drill. That is tough. We are apt to get it too. Mr. Ray is in the quarantine. I won't get to be with him for 14 days anyway.

I am sorry you haven't been getting my letters. I have already gotten three from you. I think I have written four letters and two cards since here. Mail lays in the box here sometimes for a day or so. I am going to write just as often as I can. I expect I will not have so much time as I thought I would.

To-day is visiting day. There is a large crowd of folks here. The first time I have seen any women hardly at all since I have been here. I see boys walking round with their mothers, sisters, and sweethearts. It makes me think of you and wish we could be together again. When I get out of detention I get twelve hours leave each week. I don't know where I will go or how I will spend my liberties. Guess I will go to Chicago and Milwaukee and other towns round here and see the country if I ever get any pay. I heard some fellows talking to-day. Said they had seen posters to advertise the navy which read "Join the navy. Learn a trade and save your money." They said the trade we learned was to wash clothes, and that the government saved the money. I guess that is about right too.

I wrote to my brother [Isaac] this morning. He is in the army. He left on the next day after I did. He was sent to Camp Meade in Maryland.

I got three letters yesterday. One from home, one from Bill Bauer, and another from a cousin of mine at home. I have been lucky. I have gotten about 8 letters since here. A fellow appreciates them too when he is away. I am expecting another letter from you about to-morrow. I sure appreciate your letters. I read them over and over almost every day. I just love to read your letters than lay at night and think of you when everything is still. I think every day of all the pleasant times we have had together. That is the happiest times I ever have now, is just thinking of you.

You asked me to write you some poetry. Really do you love to read the stuff I write? I have about all I have written at home. If I ever go home again I will send it all to you, or bring it, I guess if you will let me. It is so noisy round here a fellow can't think much. I would love to do anything I could that you enjoy. I love to write anyway and so I will be glad to write if I can.

I guess I had better stop this time. I am afraid you will never get this all read.

My arm is feeling a little better now but is awful sore. I can't hardly salute my commander at all. Our commander seems like an awful fine fellow. His name is Schonfelt. It is real interesting just to look at the folks here and study them. One sure sees every type of person here.

I see so much but it is hard for me to decide what to tell you or when to stop.

I have been learning a new code of signals. It is how to send messages with flags.

I will stop. I hope you get all the letters I write and that I get all you write to me.

With the most of love,
I am,
Lovingly yours, Elliott

JULY 29, 1918

In this letter, Elma complains about three grass widows[12] who live in the boarding house where she is rooming and are always "beating" on their child and quarreling among themselves. She describes an incident where she had to "play the part of a hero" and "snatch a razor[13] from the hands of that kiddo that is always into something," but she says she hopes to learn a lesson from them, never to be guilty of saying a cross word.

Monday Afternoon
10 o'clock

Dearest Elliott:

    Have just gotten back from dinner and found your card here for me. I was so glad 'cause I was dreadfully scared I wasn't going to get to write to you this afternoon. I started a letter Sat. afternoon to the old address. Hope they send it on to you, although there wasn't anything so important in it. I am glad your new camp is a change for the better, hope you left your dishonest cousin back in the other camp so you won't have to do extra duty when you don't deserve it. I imagine you rather enjoy a change of any kind. Think I should. In fact, I think I would like to change my rooming place but I guess I'll stick it out here the rest of the time. I'll tell you why I dislike the place. There are three grass-widows — mother, daughter and grandmother. The daughter has a little girl just three years old who is undoubtedly the most terrific little peace [sic] I have ever seen. They beat on her from morning till night and it doesn't help her one bit. I think I'll be a nervous wreck by the time I stay here six more weeks and hear nothing but beating and quarreling. I guess it must run in the family not to be able to get along, judging from the number of divorces. I hope I will learn such a lesson here that I will never be guilty of speaking a cross word.

    I had a letter from mama and papa this afternoon and they were telling me how much they missed me yesterday. It sure did make me homesick. If I had only known it I could have waited until the week end instead of going down Wed night for Bro Lovelace stayed over and preached down there yesterday. We went to town Sat night and bummed around until rather late and I didn't get to sleep until 12 o'clock. Then we got up at 4:30 to go to the train with one of the girls who was going home. When we got to the station we found that the train was 1 hr 20 min late. To pass off the time I read a little story in the Pictorial Review[14] entitled "Will True Love Last" or something to that effect. It sure was sweet and when I had finished I was of the same opinion that I was at first — that true love does last as long as life does. I do not believe anything could cause one that loves in the right way to forget.

We got back from the train just in time for breakfast. Then I got ready and went to S.S. and church. Dr. McGlothlin who preached the commencement sermon preached here yesterday. It wasn't quite so good as that one was, or rather I didn't enjoy it so much. It might have been because I was so tired and sleepy.

Immediately after dinner I went to sleep and slept untill [sic] the family got into a fuss and I was rudely awakened. It poured down rain so late yesterday afternoon and last night that I did not get to go to B.Y.P.U. and church so I wrote some letters to the girls. I enjoy getting letters so much but of course none of them can compare to yours. I look forward to getting your letters just like I used to [look forward] to calling night. I often think of those times and the jokes the girls used to play on us. I wrote to Willie Lindley last night and told her how you had been down to see me and what a nice time we had without anyone to dope us or throw ink bottles at us. Even such stunts as those would be jolly now, wouldn't they? It seems like a year since I told you good-bye, but I reckon it was only three weeks ago to-night. Backward turn backward oh time in your flight. Give us again just such a night. My! That's poetry dat is but it would take a genius to discover it. Ain't that what you say?

I've been studying hard to-day. Didn't wake up until five minutes of 7 — got to breakfast at 5 after 7 — Now that's the truth. Then after breakfast I went home with a girl who is in my class and we studied shorthand as hard as ever we could till dinner. That brings me up to the time I started this letter but I had just written a page when I had to stop and play the part of a hero —that is snatch a razor from the hands of that kiddo that is always into something. When her grandmother found out what had happened she received one of her semi-hourly beatings accompanied by the usual squaling [sic]. It was naturally some time before I could collect my thoughts enough to resume your letter. I do believe the roar of cannons would be pleasant compared to such encounters. I'll bet you are tired of hearing me rave about my trials and tribulations and it is selfish in me when you probably have to endure things a thousand times more annoying. Please forgive me and I won't do it anymore. I mean I'll try not to do it anymore.

I can hardly wait for a letter telling me all about your new situation and not only that but telling me you still love and think of me real often. You may think I grow tired of hearing it but I do not, and I never expect to.

With lots of love,
From "your little girl,"
Elma

JULY 31, 1918

Elliott is still training hard but says he has never felt better in his life and loves being strong physically because it makes it easier to be strong mentally and spiritually.

Wednesday
Dear Elma:
I got your letter of 25th at noon. It sure helped me to go through the afternoon's work. The regimental commander took charge this afternoon. He sure put us over the road too. We began at one P.M. and just now stopped. It is 4:30 now. We did not stop once even for a minute. If you believe me, one will get tired in that time if he keeps stepping as we

did. When they train like that it looks like going to sea in a short time. It is the report in camp that 14,000 men are wanted real soon from this station to guard the Panama Canal. If I do not get transferred to the radio or something else it is very likely that I will be among those that go. There is a chance anyway. I just have one more week of detention. Then I will know whether or not I can get transferred. I am not caring much whether I get changed [to a different position] or not. I think the navy needs second class seamen more than any other branch of workers. Many tell me it is better than the radio. Not many fellows here seem to be struck on the radio much. We trained yesterday with guns. I carried the gun so long that my shoulder is so sore to-day I can't hardly use my arm. I will be glad when we have gotten used to all the drill so that I will not get so sore. It won't be so bad after I get used to it. I know I will like the drill when I get on to it. It sure will make one strong physically. I would love to be strong physically and then it would be easier to be strong mentally and spiritually. This life up here is healthy. I never felt better in my life.

We all dressed up in our "blues" yesterday and day before and went over to the main camp to have our pictures made in a waving flag. You are apt to see me sometime and not know it (if you are a picture show goer). You see I am a movie actor already. Oh Ain't I great? The main camp is real pretty. The radio towers are there. They look to be about five or six hundred feet high. Wouldn't you like to see me on top of it? I saw some painters up there. One of them was standing on his head. He seemed to be very much at home. The aviation camp is near-by also. We could see several at a time. The lake is near-by too. I have never seen the lake yet.

I am about well now from my third "shot." I think I am due one more and then I am through for a while at least.

Gee! But I wish I had been that preacher with whom you went home. I've been over the road once and I know how he enjoyed it. You talk some but I'll bet he didn't even get tired much less you talking him to death. If you can talk anybody to death I hope it will be me, for then I know I would die happy.

You were talking about the divorced girl who married too soon. I agree with you that folks ought to know what they are doing before they marry. Some folks are older however at eighteen than others at twenty-five. I mean in knowing what they ought to do. I really think if a couple know they love each other and after learning each other, then they ought to marry. If folks really love each other they ought to be happy in marriage. I think happiness should be considered first. It is often parents and friends who fix up unhappy marriages that lead to divorce. Folks sure ought to be certain they know what they are doing before they marry. That is a step that can't be retraced or blotted out. It lasts as long as the couple lives whether happy or unhappy. But I don't love to talk about marriage now. It makes me think how long I am tied up, and who knows what will happen in that time, or afterwards? The future now can be but a dream and even that is not too clear. I love to think of the future, and yet how puzzling and how one's imagination can play. Nothing definitely sure to look forward to. But I have faith enough to believe the right will prevail and all will work out for the best. I love to think of this terrible war as being directed by the hand of God and I love to look forward with my greatest hope that the war will awaken the world that it may see God in a new light and that true religion of Christ may at last have its place in the hearts of men. Profanity is the great sin in the navy. I don't believe there is a minute in the day that one doesn't hear someone use an oath. I never dreamed there was so much profanity among young men. You can never have an idea how it is. I can't tell you so you could know. It seems to me that everybody swears in this camp. The boys from the north and east are much worse than the Ky boys. I sure feel proud of old Ky, since I am here. Perhaps I am judging wrong. The fellows here may not be fair representatives. I hope not. Pardon, I did not mean to preach a sermon myself, but really I feel like it sometimes.

That was a joke about the lady's poor daughter. Tell her to send the sweet little thing up to this station (if you should see the fine mother). I expect she could find a husband for her daughter. I am sure there are fellows here. Not joking. That lady has about as much sense as half of the mothers. And mothers like that need daughters to rear about as badly as the Devil needs a powder house, if you will excuse the expression. No, I can't imagine your mother saying a thing like that just from knowing you. That lady's idea [is] a good example of why there are unhappy marriages.

Well, I guess you think I am a warrior, but your dream — well — I can't imagine such trouble yet. A fight with — with — my — my — mother-in-law!! Did you say?

Well, I always knew you were awful hateful (nicht) but I never dreamed that you would run all the folks out of Ky. That's (you mean) the reason why I left. If you aren't careful you will have to live by yourself. It looks like you might be better by this time judging from the company you've been keeping. Take my advice and follow your associates to ... Great Lakes Ill.

And now you are telling me about flirting with a pretty red-headed freckled-faced sissy. Well, well! That's O.K. I'll be telling you about some "little" blue-eyed girl that I've seen, and even fallen in love with, if you aren't careful about that red-headed fellow. (But that girl lives back in old Ky, in Franklin). Say, don't take me seriously when I'm joking, and take me seriously when I'm in earnest. It is "chow" time and mail time. So I will stop.

As ever,
With lots of love,
Elliott

P.S. Will write as soon as I can. Sunday I guess.

∼

JULY 31, 1918

Elma says she enjoys getting letters so much that she cuts chapel nearly every day to check whether the postman brought her any. She confirms that she never paid much attention to world events until recently, but now she pores over magazines and newspapers as she used to over "thrilling novels."

Wednesday P.M.
   3:30 o'clock
   Dearest Elliott:
Have just gotten in from school and I nearly always write to you at this time. I find it the best time because none of the other girls get in until late and everything is quiet as long as there is peace in the family below.

I rec'd your nice long letter which was written Sunday, this morning. I was so disappointed because I did not get it yesterday that I almost cried but it was so sweet when it did get here that I felt real mean for becoming so impatient. You see I don't have half enough work to keep me busy and therefore I can't possibly make myself contented. I'll be dreadfully glad when time comes to go back to dear old G.C. I'm sure five subjects and Office work will keep me out of mischief. I know I will miss you terribly but I believe I shall be better satisfied there than I am here. I had a letter from Patty this morning and she said the prospect was awfully good for next year. Almost all of Rucker Hall has already been reserved.

I was real lucky this morning, got three letters. Had one from June [Corbin] — my first husband — and she said her man had already reached France. I agree with you when you say it is good to get letters. I cut chapel nearly every morning just to see whether the postman is going to bring me any mail or not. And when I think about it I find that yours is really the one I am watching and waiting for. When it fails to come I usually betake myself up stairs and re-read some of your old letters. I say old but they really <u>never</u> grow old to me. I have never read a book the second time because I could never find them interesting after I had once read them but it isn't that way with your letters. I enjoy them almost as much the second, third or fourth time I read them as the first. I have already read the one I got this morning three times so you see somebody else's letters are appreciated. I will be so glad when they get through with that "shooting" business. I don't think they are a bit nice to keep your arm sore all the time. I know it must hurt you to use it to write. It is awfully sweet of you to write me such a nice long letter under those conditions.

Do you get anything to eat? You haven't said much about your "eats" so I judge they don't make a very great impression on you. I'm glad you have found some of the Georgetown fellows for I know you are in good company when you are with them — even "<u>Commander</u>" Amerson. That little bit of news strikes me as being funny. I am sure it was through Dr. Leigh that he got the place for I heard him dictate a letter last spring recommending him for some kind of place. Why don't you get in touch with Dr. Leigh? Perhaps he could help you along some.

Another girl from Franklin entered the B.U. yesterday. She married about a year ago and her husband was already in the army. He has recently been sent to France and she has decided to take a Business Course. I think that it is nice for us girls to be able to do something worth while, while you all are fighting so bravely for us. If we could only keep the World Vision[15] before us, we would not feel so badly about having to be seperated [sic]. It is only when we begin to think in selfish terms that fate seems cruel and our skies become cloudy. How I long to be able to look upon life in a sane intelligent manner and extend my views beyond the small sphere in which I move. Not until recently did I try in any way to keep up with the activities across the waters, but now I pour [sic] over the papers and magazines like I used to over a thrilling novel. People certainly do change as well as the times.

I truly believe God has a purpose in our lives which he will work out in due time. Because of this belief I feel that He <u>will bring you back to me</u> in every way prepared to perform the task He has planned for us. If He should see fit to take you while in the service of Our Country, I know he would give me strength to perform my mission alone. Forgive me if I cause you to feel sad. I do not want to. I only wanted to express my inmost feelings to you as you have to me. I shall continue to hope and pray for your safe keeping — all the time keeping before me <u>our</u> ideals and trying hard to live up to them.

Yours in love and service,
Elma

CHAPTER 5

August, 1918

There's a Long Long Trail A'Winding[1]

    Verse 1:
    Nights are growing very lonely,
    Days are very long.
    I'm a-growing weary only
    Listening for your song.
    Old remembrances are thronging
    Through my memory,
    Till it seems the world is full of dreams
    Just to call you back to me.

Verse 2:
All night long I hear you calling,
Calling sweet and low,
Seem to hear your footsteps falling
Ev'rywhere I go.
Though the road between us stretches
Many a weary mile,
I forget that you're not with me yet
When I think I see you smile.

Chorus:
There's a long, long trail a-winding
Into the land of my dreams,
Where the nightingales are singing
And a white moon beams.
There's a long, long night of waiting
Until my dreams all come true
Till the day when I'll be going down
That long, long trail with you.

AUGUST 1, 1918

In this rather spirited letter, Elma recounts an incident at the place where she takes her meals. She claims she has thrown her dignity aside and contaminated her end of the table at the boarding house, leading to chair tipping and water tossing and bawling out. She also reports that a new girl is moving into the boarding house and wishes they could "initiate" her but says her roommate is too dignified.

Thurs. Afternoon
    4 o'clock

LOVE LETTERS

Dearest Elliott:

I have a superfluous hour before me and can't think of anything more exciting to do than write to U. Then when I think about it, I get "kinder" "skeered" for fear you will get a wee bit tired of hearing from me so dreadfully often, especially since they are all so much alike. I do wish I knew how to write real nice entertaining letters. You see nothing much happens here and there you see and hear so much that I sometimes feel like nothing I could say would be of very much interest. However, nevertheless, notwithstanding, I am just going on and write to you as often as I have time, regardless of whether I have anything to say or not and all because I love you so. You may think I'm rather extravagant on the line of stationary but it's like this. I've been trading a little as usual. You know I always did like to swap around in everything. So now don't think I'm too unpatriotic if I use a different kind of stationary every now and then.

I spent the night with one of the Franklin girls last night. Not Alma [Johnson] — 'cause she has gone home. I've been so lonesome since she left last Friday that I have almost died. Oh listen, I don't believe I had ever told you that "Fine Day"[2] has moved over next to me but even he doesn't keep me optimistic all the time. But you just ought to see me at my meals. I throw all my dignity aside and act like I used to up at old G.C. In fact I have gotten our end of the table contaminated. I always did have a bad influence over people. Why really you used to be real civilized until you got to associating with me so much. Well as I was about to say, the girl who eats second from me — perhaps I had better say woman 'cause she is somewhat ancient — anyway she had one of my mean spells and when the boy, who sits at the table back of us, almost turns her chair over, she bapsoused[3] him with a glass of water. War was at once declared and a girl who is in love with this boy proceded [sic] to fly off the handle and bawl the other girl out. My! Things were hot for a little while. I felt it my duty to make my exit, thus I escaped with my life. Gee! That was some thrilling. I'll bet you don't experience anything like it in the navy. Oh! I have a new nickname — "Zip" — That old boy that eats by me donated it to me. He calls me "his friend" and is dreadfully attentive. In fact he most pesters me to death. I most faint and fall over sometimes. Was about to forget to explain why he calls me "Zip." Well it's because I eat so much of it. Honest to goodness I'm about to get fat again. Weigh 120 — ain't it awful?

A new girl is coming here to-night. I wish we could initiate[4] her but lawsy! My roommate is too dignified. She's dignity personified and I have to be so dreadful good that I almost feel like I was rooming with Lady Mac. Well, dear, I must calm myself for she has just entered. Be lots better than I am and I'll keep on loving you a whole heaps.

From Your wicked Little Girl Elma

AUGUST 2, 1918

Elma says she feels "kinder bum" today and observes that their occupations are at two extremes, where Elliott has to drill all the time and she has to sit still. She says it always did get on her nerves to be still for very long. She is thinking of leaving the Business University early and going home for a break before starting back to college in the fall.

Friday Afternoon

Dearest Elliott:

I rec'd your letter of July 31 this afternoon and I believe you were in just about such a mood as I was when I wrote yesterday afternoon. In other words feeling a little giddy.

I feel "kinder" bum to-day. I imagine it is like you feel after you have had a "shot." Have the headache, pain in my shoulder, etc. Guess I've been working too hard to-day. Can you conceive of anything like that? I had three hours typewriting straight. Our occupations seem to be two extremes. You have to drill all the time and I have to be still. You know it always did get on my nerves to be still very long at a time.

If you want to go to sea I sure do hope you will get to go. It seems that guarding the Canal would be much less dangerous than some other places to which you might be sent. Of course I know absolutely nothing about the naval positions. All I can say is that I hope you land in the safest place.

Oh! I'll be going to the picture show all the time now since you've gotten to be a prominent actor. I think I told you about seeing "Pershing's Crusaders"[5] Monday night. Got a little insight into the navy, for example, saw the boys washing their clothes. They are going to show "Over the Top"[6] here Monday night next but I'll be home. They may put it on again Tues. Night, if so I'll be right there to see it. I may not get to write to you any more until Tues. afternoon as Blanche will be down home with me. But I'll be thinking of you all the time just the same. I can't hardly wait 'till to-morrow night to board No. 7 for Franklin. I only wish you were going to be with me.

You know what I have about decided to do is go down home for a week before going back to G.C. regardless of how much shorthand I know. I won't get in my full three months that way but I feel like I almost have to have a wee bit of rest. I may have come to that conclusion just because I was feeling a little "badly" to-day but I think I shall stick to it anyway. I'm awfully sorry you are finding the drills so hard. Hope things will be easier for you when you get out of detention. I've been counting up to see just how long it was before the 21 days were up. I nearly always get your letter in the morning but this time it didn't come until afternoon. I was about to conclude that you had been quarantined and couldn't write. Am awful glad it wasn't that way.

Well, dear, I will have to cut this epistle a little short and try to recuperate enough to review shorthand for a test. Test — did you get that word? What does it make you think of? Don't let them work you to death for I wouldn't have my little "Tot" to love if they did.

Lovingly yours,
Elma

AUGUST 3, 1918

Elliott is happy to report that he has at last gotten "a pen and some nice green ink," after several trips to the ship store and negotiations with a fellow at camp. He then proceeds to write a long, chatty letter. He says he considers them engaged although he never directly asked her and hopes he hasn't taken too much for granted. He offers to send money to help with Elma's expenses if she will accept it.

Dear Elma,

I have at last gotten me a pen and some nice green ink. The ink just suits me I guess. If you would rather I would write with some other color just know that this is all I could get. I had a hard time getting this. I went to the ship store yesterday and got a bottle of ink. I seated myself to write a card home and when I opened the box the ink bottle was empty. Not a drop in it. I took it back to them to-day. They finally gave me another bottle, but they did not want to. They said they knew they never sold such a bottle as that. You see my word doesn't always go everywhere. I got the ink O.K. I had a hard time getting a pen. I got points at the store but couldn't get a holder. I happened upon a fellow to-day who sold me a holder. So I am equipped. I hope you can read this a little better than what I have been writing. I don't know whether you can or not. I did all my washing yesterday and have written home this afternoon. I will have nothing to do to-morrow, but go to church. I got a book from the "Y" and so I think I shall read. It is The Prince of the House of David,[7] a story of the Christ. I think it is fine. I have read about 100 pages of it. I will have to hurry on it or I may have to leave before I finish it. It is reported that we leave this camp next Wednesday for Camp Ross.[8] Ross is the last camp we will be in before we leave this station. Our detention is out on Tuesday. If we go to Ross it means we will go East or to Sea this next week. Of course we will have to have more training somewhere. I do not care if they do move us. I saw Harry Rankley yesterday. He is in camp Ross already and is expecting to ship out any time. They never stay in Camp Ross more than 72 hours. I also saw Jack Morris and Slaughter of G.C. They say Geo Mitchell is in this same camp as I. I haven't seen him yet. I guess you have heard it already. George is married. He married during commencement. I heard he was married but thought it was only a joke. They say he is going to bring his wife up here near the camp.

Prof. Martin, Ogden, and Macklin are up here at Ft. Sheridan about ten miles from this station learning of military drill so as to give instruction at Georgetown next year. I may go out to see our friend Prof Martin if I ever get a chance. I know he would love to see me. There are lots of folks round here that I know if I could only find them.

I got two nice long letters from you. One day before yesterday and another to-day. I just know you are the sweetest girl in the world to write to me so often. I know I would think that about you if you just wouldn't go and say you are afraid I will think you write too often. I would love to get a letter from you every day if you could write them. And you keep saying that your letters are no good. If you knew how much I read them you would know how I appreciate them. Your letters are about all I get. I don't have time to write much and so I write to you and home all the time I have for writing. I try to write home once each week. I have only gotten one letter from home since here. Dad pretends he can't write and my brothers won't. My sister-in-law[9] wrote once. So you see I would get terribly blue for a letter if it were not for you. You and the folks at home are all I care especially to hear from anyway and you most of all. So you really can't know how much I do appreciate your letters. It's really all the real pleasure I've had since here just to read your letters. So don't fear that they won't be appreciated when you write no matter how often I get them. The oftener I hear from you the better I will like it. I don't think you are extravagant either in your letter paper, especially when it is coming to me.

Well, I have at last gotten all my "shots"[10] and am well. I never felt better physically in my life than to-day and yesterday. My arm is entirely well. It is healthy up here. We get plenty of exercise and most always enough sleep. I have to get up at three in the morning and do guard duty until five. I will loose [sic] about two hours sleep, but to-morrow is Sunday and I will have it easy. I haven't been on guard since I came to this camp. I have been real lucky. You said the eats here surely didn't make much impression upon me. Eats always make an impression on me, but since I've been here they've left a de-pression most always. No, really we have plenty of good food and we are always hungry enough to eat it. I never have been fed like you fed me when I came to see you. I have never had any fried chicken yet, but I get plenty of everything except bread. We had plenty of that until yesterday. We've only gotten one small slice of light bread each meal since yesterday noon. The great objection I have to the eats is everything is all mixed up to-gether. Then we get nothing to drink except coffee and very strong tea. I never did like coffee and the tea is so strong it is bitter. It also has very little sugar in it. I have had a terrible time drinking either the tea or coffee. They say you can't be a sailor unless you drink coffee and tea. So I am learning. There is no danger of me starving, but I really don't enjoy the eats any too well. I am glad to-morrow is Sunday for we have pie on Sunday. I expect I will get fat on the feed they give us even though it is not very tasty. We don't even have Zip[11] up here. We get very little sweet.

Well, I don't know what you will be saying to me next. You even so much as say I am uncivilized. It was real nice of you to excuse me for it by saying you were the cause of it. I admit you have influenced me considerably but I won't consent to you saying that your influence has been uncivilizing upon me. As to your dignity I have failed to ever see it if you had any dignity since I've been going with you. You surely have just begun to think you have been dignified in the past because of your present associations with your roommate. Well I don't know about your roommate but I have an idea you are not any too crazy about her.

I say you did have some experience when that girl threw the water on the boy. Poor fellow. I feel sorry for him if he was injured in any way. The only peculiar thing about it was that you were not mixed up in it yourself and that you were able to get out. It seems that you surely ought to have been into it. I guess it was Blanche who always got you into trouble.

By the way if you see Blanche soon ask her for Ramises address for me will you please? I promised to write to him. He said I could get his address from Woodburn by way of you. He might have meant that I would write to you. I don't know. He said ask you anyway. I want to find out how he likes his work. I might [...] into the same as he if it is good.

It hardly seems possible that school can begin so soon. Time sure is moving. I feared time would go slow while in camp, but it doesn't. I am so busy I guess is the reason. You know when a fellow has all he can do time moves more rapidly. I sure wish I could go back to school with you this year. I hope you do not miss calling nights too much. I don't mean that I don't want you to miss me. I only hope you won't feel lonesome, and I hope you won't miss me like I will you. You see I will see none of the old school friends. I guess there will be a few back of the old students. I am sure glad to hear that the prospects for school are good. I was afraid school would be short this year. Say, I don't want you to work too hard in the office or in your school work either. Really it won't pay to work too hard. You must remember too that you have been working all summer. I thought when I came up here that I could send you some money if you would let me. I still would love to if I ever get any. I find however that it will take more to live in the navy than I expected. We have to buy cloathes [sic] and lots of things. I am in hopes that I may get something better if I have to stay very long. I will not draw any pay at all for some time yet. Then I owe some at home. So I will be somewhat disappointed in my expectations of helping you at the first of the year. I hope I can help you some in the second semester anyway if you need it and if you will accept it. Elma, I am not insisting upon helping you because I think you can't make your own way, but because it would be a pleasure to me to help you if I can in any way. I know what it means to work your way through school even for a boy. Really if I have any spare money it would be a pleasure to me if you would use it. I would be better off too, for I expect I would waste it if I just had it and had no use for it. I hope you don't take any offense at my offering to help you. I really think you understand the reason and spirit of my offer. If I have it to give I see no reason why you should not accept it either, if you need it. Of course you couldn't afford to let everybody know it but nobody need know it except you unless you want them too [sic]. Anytime you need anything and I can help you get it or do anything you want to do let me know. I sure would love to help you any time you will let me. If I haven't got any money at any time I can get it for you if you need it and want it. I don't want you to work too hard and I want you to have just as good time as anybody at college if I can help you in any way. Don't feel that you are asking a favor of me either to help you in any way that I can. I feel that I am asking a favor of you that you let me help you if I can. I won't expect you to feel that you are under any obligations to me either if I help your [sic] or by my offering to do as I am making the offer just because I would love to help you if I can. Always remember you are just as free as you ever were. Anything you want to do or say feel free to do it or say it. If we love each other as we think we do, we won't forget each other and we will be true to each other. If either of us find we have been mistaken it is best that we be as we are. I said once before if we really love each other I consider that we are engaged. If we are not really in love it is best that we be as we are. (You may have thought it strange that I did not ask you for a definite engagement before I left you. I feel that mutual love is all the engagement necessary and that is why I never asked you. I felt that you understood me too and that is why [...] have never said this before. I may have taken too much for granted. Have I? Believing that we really love each other and will be true to each other, I have offered to help you if you need it and will accept it, without fearing that I offer any offense by doing so.

You said you thought it nice that girls could do something while the boys are away fighting. The girls not only can do their share by work, but also by their influence. I know it is much easier for me to stay here in camp since I know your spirit and ideals. It helps us boys to fight when we know our sweethearts, sisters, and mothers appreciate the fight we are willing to make.

Well, I must stop before I get so much that I will have to send it by Parcel Post. With love, Elliott

AUGUST 5-6, 1918

Elma says she is missing Elliott "unusually much" because she has been looking at and listening to sailor boys all day long — at a band concert, at her teacher's wedding, and on the train, as she returned home to Franklin on Saturday night. She thanks him sincerely for his offer of financial help and agrees that no formal engagement is necessary because they can be just as true to each other without it.

At home
  Monday Night
  Dearest Elliott:

I have been wishing for you unusually much to-day. Why? Just cause I've been looking at and listening to sailor boys all day long. We have had a Marine Band here, some say it was part of Sousa's, don't expect that was true but they certainly furnished us some wonderful music. I believe the number I enjoyed most was "There's a Long, Long Trail." They sang one piece but I've forgotten what that was. A French Lieutenant spoke this afternoon to a perfect throng of people. He was great and the crowd went wild over his speech. I came home with a terrible headache like I almost always do when out in a crowd. Then, too, it has been so hot to-day and it still is. I'm expecting to melt and run away at most any minute.

Well I don't believe I have written to you since Friday afternoon so it is up to me to give an account of myself. I assure you the first thing that I was good Friday night. Sick! Oh gee I thought my time had come. I think I told you I had the headache when writing. It continued to increase until it developed into a genuine case of sick headache. However I was all O.K. by Sat. morning and breezed off to school as gayly as ever.

The train was reported thirty minutes late so I had time to attend my teacher's wedding before coming home. She married a naval recruiting officer who is stationed in B.G. at present. It took place in the

Baptist church. He wore his white navy uniform and she had on white too. They looked powerful sweet and happy. And I know they must have been just as happy as they looked. They left B.G. on the train I came down on and of course there was lots of excitement. There were several sailors and soldiers on the train, and they got together and gave a big yell for the "newlyweds." One frisky little sailor decided he would get fresh and stir up a conversation with a bunch of us girls. We answered his questions as short as possible and finally it dawned on him that we had no inclination to be bothered with him so he walked off. Of course I had to disgrace myself by making one of my horrible faces. An awful nice looking elderly gentleman who was sitting opposite me saw it and it almost tickled him to death. He laughed all the way from Bowling Green to Franklin. I suppose he was in the habit of seeing girls lose their heads over a uniform and I shocked him dreadfully by handing the dear little fellow a lemon. I think you should teach your cousins in the navy better manners than to try to flirt with a "little girl" that hasn't time for such foolishness and wants to be thinking about the one she really loves.

Blanche got on at Woodburn and came down with me. The train was so late we didn't get to go to the big tent show[12] that was in Franklin all week. We just came home, ate supper and went to bed like good little "chillun." Sunday was passed off in the usual way 'cept we came home after Sunday School just to see how it would feel to cut church and not get any points. We slept all yesterday afternoon and oh yes we went to the band concert real late and Blanche went to her grandmother's last night. That's about all that has happened since I "writ" to U. Hope you don't think I've been a very bad "little girl." I believe Delma has been kind enough to tell Thomas that he is wasting time when he's foolin' with me 'cause he doesn't bother me anymore. I am so glad for I don't believe I would be doing right to go with him. I think he does like me a wee little bit and I couldn't return it at all, at all.

I wonder if you love me just as good as you did the last night I was with you. I know I do and truly I believe I love you even more. If you should some day find that you had been mistaken, please be true to your promise and let me know at once. You talked in your last letter like you rather expected things to change — whether on your part or mine I do not know — but I feel that if any change should come it would have to be on your side.

~

Tuesday Afternoon
Bowling Green

I've just rec'd your nice long letter and I assure you that the green ink doesn't bother me at all. Why I would be glad to get a letter from you even if it was written with charcoal, so don't worry any more about that. You are a dear to offer to help me next year and far be it from me to take offense, but I know that should you help me you would be denying yourself of pleasures that you need and well deserve. If I know my heart I would not have you deny yourself of any pleasure for anything in the world, unless it would be giving you an added am't of happiness. I think now that I will be able to make both ends meet (as the old saying is) but if I should get in a close place, I promise to let you know and if you can help me out I would gratefully accept, but if it should be at a time when you couldn't, I would understand the situation and everything would be all right.

In regard to an engagement I understood how you felt about it and as we are I can be just as true to you as if there was a definite engagement. Now don't think I agree with everything you say just for the sake of being nice — I don't much think you'll do that but if you should be inclined to, know that I am sincere in whatever I say. If at anytime I should see things differently from what you do, I'd be telling you about it. I believe you would want me to, wouldn't you?

I am so glad you get out of detention to-day. Guess you'll be running around wherever you please by the time you get this letter. You said you might go to Sea or go East. I rather hope it will be East. I don't like to think about you getting out on the big wide ocean. I will try to get "Rameses'" address for you some time this week. I know Blanche has it for she spoke about hearing from him. She hadn't heard from Ira[13] in over a week. I'm afraid I'll have to be sympathizing with her before long if you go to Sea or even East. You have been so good to write to me so far but I can't expect you to always have time for such nice long letters. Yet if you should get too busy to write more than a card I would appreciate it just the same. Must stop and try to cool off a little bit. It was 105 yesterday and seems much hotter to-day. If you never hear from me again, you can know that I perished from heat.

With Love,
Elma

～

AUGUST 6, 1918

Elliott's sense of humor comes through in this letter when he talks about the "Jackies"[14] falling out of their new hammocks, although most of this letter is rather "blue." He observes that "the biggest fools in the company are getting the honours" and says the hardest thing to do is to obey some little "upstart fool" and "one-horse officer" who has a little authority and wants to use it.

Dearest Elma,

I will try to write you a short letter as I perhaps may have a few minutes. Gee! But it is hot up here to-day. It has been about the hottest day I ever experienced. This is the first real hot day since I've been here.

Well, we are still drilling, drilling, and then drilling some more. We got up at four o'clock and have been at it until a few minutes ago. Some of the company are drilling yet. The regiment goes on review to-morrow. They are getting ready for it. They want to make as good show as possible, even if they work us poor "Jackies" to death.

We got our hammocks yesterday. We have been sleeping upon [strike-through in original] the floor until last night. It was some fun to see the fellows get into their hammocks. About half of them fell out. About every half hour I was awakened by someone hitting the floor. I guess it was not very funny to the ones who fell. The hammocks are about six feet from the floor. I was lucky enough not to fall. One fellow had to go to the hospital. So you see it is rather serious, but it is funny just the same to see a fellow trying to hang ~~up~~on [sic] his bed. The regimental commander sent over for the names of all college men. I gave my name. I don't know what it is for but I am in hopes that I may have a chance to get into something better than I am in now. They want second class seamen, and so I may have to stay in it. It nearly always requires knowledge of mathematics or science to get a good job in the navy. You know I am rotten in math and I was bone headed enough not to study science. I may have to stay in something that I don't like just because of my failure to study the right subjects. They always told me that a fellow had a good chance to go to the top in the navy if he had anything in him. It doesn't look that way to me. The biggest fools in the company are getting the honours of the company. If a fellow has got plenty of brass that will get him farther in the navy than anything I have noticed yet. I guess you also know that I haven't much of that either. Perhaps I can learn to put on a bold face in time. I never wanted so much brass until about three weeks ago. If I just had H. H. Duvall's face, or bearing, I believe I could get somewhere. I may be mistaken in these ideas but they are my first impressions. I believe I am capable of an average rating if I stay long enough. I hope I won't have to stay long, but I am going to do my best even here. I would love to make good for you. If it was just for myself I would as soon do one thing as another while I am here, just anything Uncle Sam wants me. If I knew what I could do I would know what to study for and what to try to get in to. I guess a fellow ought to do all he can wherever he is. That is what I am going to try to do. My detention is up to-day. Perhaps I will know soon whether I have a chance for something or not. There were very few college men in our company. That gives me some hopes no one in the company has had more than two years in college. I guess you will think I am discouraged. I perhaps am a little bit, but not the first time in my life. My but it takes grit to go in to a thing with good spirit when that is really not a thing you want to do. My! It is hard for a fellow to give his best in war when he hates war as I do. I know it is my duty to fight and I love my country as much as anybody, but I think you know what I mean. The trouble is, it looks like I can't just feel that I am doing my best. I would love to do something bigger, and I guess I am not taking the interest in my present duties that I should. You said once you would love to know my problems. The greatest problem I have is, I just can't get into the work somehow with all I have got. Most of our problems are solved or have been so far. All we have to do is just obey. The hardest thing about the navy is you have to obey some little upstart fool who has a little authority and wants to show all he's got and then some. Gee! But freedom is a great thing. That's one thing a fellow doesn't get in military affairs. Of course military affairs are of a necessity strict. I guess I had better stop. I perhaps may have already made a wrong impression. I haven't really been mistreated myself. It is the way some of the little "one horse" officers talk to us all. I really don't think they have ever meant me in particular, but it always did make me sore to see others bawled out unnecessarily when I wouldn't care for it if said to myself. I guess I am just a little peeved, so I will stop.

I may get an eight hour leave to-morrow. If I do I am going to go somewhere if it is just outside the camp and lay under a tree. I just want to get out and be free again for a few hours. I was awful sorry that you were sick when you wrote me the last time, but I appreciated the letter all the more. That is alright for you to wait about writing for you have been so good about writing to me. I sure love to hear from you, but I know you will write me as often as you can. I hope you don't think I am too much discouraged. I admit I am somewhat but I will feel better to-morrow.

It is bed time and I will have to stop. Don't be surprised if you hear that I have fallen out of bed (hammock) and broken my neck. If I don't have such luck I will write again soon and try to be in better spirit.

Be good

With truest love

Elliott

LOVE LETTERS

AUGUST 9, 1918

Elma was in good spirits when she wrote this letter, despite the continuing heat and Elliott's blue letter. She has found a new pal who is "a good old sport" and she received a 97 on her first shorthand test. She suggests that Elliott's blues were caused by the color stationery she was using.

Friday afternoon,
   Dearest Elliott:
   I rec'd your little blue letter this morning. I have been expecting it ever since you have been there and so the only thing that surprised me was how you could be brave so long. I knew it was hard for you all along though you hadn't said a word before. I'll have to say — just for fun — that you're now enjoying about such freedom as we Rucker Hall girls had. Maybe your little case of the blues was due to the complexion of this stationary I have been using. If that be the case you might as well begin to cheer up for this is the last of it.
   I was feeling a little blue too when you wrote that letter but I'm lots better now. I've at last found me a pal here. One of the new girls who came last Monday is a good old sport. The other new girl is somewhat old maidish and Sophia [Lunsford] and I delight in doing things to shock some people's dignity. Why the first thing she did was to shoot terror through their souls by sliding down the bannisters. Last night we decided we would take a walk and you know me when it comes to walking — well, "Sophy" is right along with me. Two of our fellow sistern [sic] thought they would get gay and keep up with us but they succumbed at the 1st hill we met. But of course we couldn't attain much speed on account of the hot weather. Last night Sousa's Band played here and we took that in. It was about the same that we had in Franklin Monday but I enjoyed the repetition.
   Then I'm not only happy because "Sophy" has come to town but also because I passed my first test in shorthand Wednesday, making 97. I was rather pieved [sic] because it wasn't a 100 but was glad I didn't

flunk. Took up another shorthand class this morning — one for speed. You've been telling me all along that I was fast but believe me! I didn't feel fast in that class this morning when she dictated so fast that I couldn't get more than half the words. It comes at 7:30 and that seems dreadful early but it isn't quite so bad as four o'clock. And oh yes! Another thing that made me feel good was the fact that my typewriting teacher came around to me yesterday and told me that I did the most beautiful work of anyone in the class — so neatly arranged etc. etc. Wanted me to do office work, but I told her I hadn't had enough shorthand. Now you'll be thinking I have the big head but I think not. Oh yes — it makes a fellow feel better to have a few words of encouragement spoken occasionally. I think I'd like to encourage you a wee little bit but you'd say I was suffering from bats in the belfry or something like that if I should try. Honest your time is coming and I know you will shine brightly when it does come. Of course it takes a considerable am't of patience and sometimes even the doing of things one does enjoy doing. However we can just think that each time we overcome a difficulty we are strengthened that much. That's the way I like to look at it. "C"

Falling out of hammocks must be as great fun as doping[15] in Old Sem. Now please, dearie, don't you try that stunt of falling out for I fear it would not be half so jolly as watching other people. I can hardly wait to hear from you after you get out of detention. I believe you are going to be enjoying life the next time you write. You mustn't think Great Lakes is the onliest hot place there is cause every day this week I've just sweated great drops of perspiration big enough to drown a fly while pounding on old Remington. But to be sure that's nothing to compare with drilling in the "shunshine." Poor little boy. I just wish I had you close by so I could pet you ess a little bit when you come in all tired out and pieved [sic] at some old officer. But although I can't do that you can know that I'm sympathizing with you all the time. You said for me to be good but it's awful hard to be good for a long long time. Guess I can try. Have to ask you to go fifty fifty with me tho' on that.

Lovingly,
Elma

AUGUST 11, 1918

This letter was written on thin lined sheets of letterhead from The Navy Club of The Chicago Woman's Club. Elliott finally got a furlough, which he spent in Waukegan, Illinois. He is in much better spirits than when he last wrote and reports that he has a chance to go to the Municipal Pier School for Ensigns for six weeks.

Dear Elma:

I am on a furlow this afternoon. I am at the "Y" at Waukegan, Ill. It is a small town up here of about 30,000 inhabitants. This is my first shore leave, as they call it. I was out of detention Tuesday. This day I got off at 12 o'clock and have until twelve to-night all my own. This town is out about twenty minutes ride from camp. It cost me all the amount of 16 cents round trip out. I have been all over the city and have seen but few people here except sailors. The sailors are all so white that I can hardly distinguish them from the girls (at a distance). I mean their suits are so white. Their faces are not white by any means. They served supper to the men in uniform at the "Y." They said these 800 ate. They just served sandwitches [sic], cake and coffee, but it sure was good. I got in among the last ones and all the home baked cake was out. So I just got bakery cookies. As I came out there was an old motherly looking lady (but somewhat dignified) collecting (they charged a nickel or dime as the sailor felt able to pay). She smiled when I came up and says "you must come early next time. I had a special cake for you." Then she took a second look and says, "no I am mistaken it is not the sailor I thought you were." Then I began a conversation and we talked quite a bit. She was awfully nice and pleasant. She is the first girl I have talked with since here. She was about 60 I guess so don't get jealous. Out at camp there is a little fellow in my old company from Milwakee [sic] named Kunkel. I think about half the fellows out there thought we were brothers. We were together some and I don't know at the number who asked if we weren't brothers.

This town is on Lake Michigan. I went down to the shore and

watched the lake steamers come and go. The rowing, swimming, launching, flirting, and spooning. It seems to be a summer resort here. I really enjoyed it. I bought me a magazine and there was the finest shade I ever saw most. I lay in the shade and read or looked on as I felt like. There was a long pier running out into the lake for about a mile to the light house. There was a nice walkway all the way out fixed up so you couldn't fall in. So I walked out and took a fine view of the lake. It was awfully pretty and smooth to-day. That was my first time to see a body of water that I couldn't see across. There was an ice cream stand near the shore. I visited that once in a while. So you see I have had a real pleasant evening, but will you believe it. Everything I saw or did I wondered if you would enjoy it too, and oh how I wished I could have had these twelve hours with you, and that we could have been together. Elma, you get a wrong impression I am afraid when I talk about if either of us should find that we are mistaken in our feelings for each other. I am afraid you think I am forgetting you already. Elma, I am just so afraid sometimes that you might find out you have been mistaken. That is the reason I ever mention such a thing. Such thoughts as those would never enter my mind if I did not love you as I do. I believe you every word you tell me. I know you mean what you say, but Elma when we are away from each other I just sometimes think that it is too good to be true that you really do love me. I know I will never never c[h]ange. I love you and I know it. I know you have the same feelings of doubt about me loving you at times. I can tell from the way you write. I feel that I know I am not mistaken and I know I have not changed anyway yet except that I realize that I love you more and more each day.

It will soon be time for me to start back to camp. I am in better spirits now than last time I wrote. I think I am about to get a chance at a good thing. I am to be sent to the Municipal Pier School for Ensigns for six weeks. If I can pass the examination at the end of six weeks I get to go to school six more months in the officers' material school. I have a try out for a commission or chief Petty officer at least. I will have to be examined in Trigonometry, Geography, and current history. If I get into the school I will not be in the real fighting part of the navy but it is the merchant marine that I will be in. You know I am poor in math and I am not up very well in Geography. I am going to work every minute I have to spare for six weeks anyway. It is this way. I am just at the very bottom now of the navy. I am a deck scrubber. If I make good at the Ensign school I have a chance for the rank of a Gold braid in less than a year. It is a chance all odds in my favor. I can't loose [sic] anything and a big chance to make good. "Little Girl" if I do make good or whatever success I have I attribute it to the answer of prayer I have asked God to lead me every day and already I have an opportunity that is a chance of a lifetime. I believe too that your prayers for me have helped me and I want you to help me make good by your prayers whether I get into the school or not. I haven't asked to make good for my own honor but that I may be worthy of your confidence and love. So really if you want to help me as you have said before you do continue to pray for me. I am going to try hard and I now feel that I will have a chance to make good. If I loose [sic] it will be my own inefficiency. I was told to pack ready to be sent to Chicago to-morrow morning. I have heard since that we do not go for a few days, until several more men get out of detention. It might work out that I won't even get to try for it. I have signed up already, but nothing is certain in the navy. They might transfer me one day and put me back next. The company I am in now is a picked company of college and High school men. I think we will have a chance for something else if we should not get this. I thought it was all settled till to-day and that I would move in the morning but I am not sure now just what has happened or whether anything has happened. If I had had spherical Trig I could have gotten in the Ensign school for regular navy. I believe I would rather have the merchant marine though. If it was in time of peace I know I would. Perhaps I may get as good place as your friend Amerson anyway if I get into the school. The officers' material school is about the best opportunity for study there is in the navy. So you see why I am tickled to get a chance to study.

    They say the pier is a nice place to live and study. They tell me that they take us way out on the lake away from everything so we can study. If they do I may be dreaming all the time so that I can't study. If I am know that I am dreaming of you. If nothing happens to prevent me from going to the Pier I will be terribly busy studying for the next six weeks. I may not get to write to you so often even as I have been but don't think I shall have forgotten you. I will always be thinking of you and how I would love to win out in this big game of war and navy that I may be a little bit more worthy of the love you have promised me. Say don't let all those grass widows disgust you with married life. I guess that is a fine example of marriages when loved [sic] did not really rule their ideals of marriage. I have been in several homes. I mean I have lived in several. Some of them have been just as happy as folks can be on Earth. Some of them have been just as unhappy as could be. You were speaking of the little child who was so mean. That meanness nearly always goes with beating. A kid that is always being knocked on is nearly always meanest.

Well, it is about time for me to go back to camp. So I will stop for this time. I will send you my address as soon as I move if I do move. My address now is the same as before except it is Co., H. You can send it to the old address and I will get it, or you can send it to the new. Perhaps I will be more settled in a short time.

Don't ever think I am forgetting you or that I don't love you anymore.

With love,
Elliott

P.S. I am awfully glad if you decide to go home for a short rest before going to G.C. I know you need it. I would advise you to go home if you feel like you possibly can.

Your true lover,
E.C.

LOVE LETTERS

AUGUST 12, 1918

Elma is again in high spirits. Her classes are going well, and she and her new friend Sophia are having a grand time. She tells about going downtown to meet a troop train and describes the upbeat mood of the crowd. The rest of the letter covers many topics and is somewhat disjointed, no doubt because Sophia was "leading [her] a merry chase, turning [her] chair over and little things like that."

Monday Afternoon
2 o'clock
Extremely Hot
Dear Elliot:

I am in receipt of your card of Aug 9 and am tickled to death to know that you have at last gotten transferred. Hope you will like the bunch of college guys and I know you will stand a good chance for promotion now. I am just hoping that you will be able to get into something that you will really enjoy and feel like you are doing satisfactory work. I do hope it isn't as hot up there as it is here for, goodness gracious, if it is I can't see how you would be able to drill or do anything else. I can tell you right now that going to school in the summer time is some job! But don't you know, I think I am getting along beautifully. I got all the letters which the teacher gave, the very first day that I was in the dictation class and one of the girls who stays here said she was in the same class three weeks before she could get a whole letter. Now I believe I have a right to be a little bit encouraged. I'm most sure I will be able to go home in three more weeks. Oh joy! And after I have been to home a week I'll be bound for G.C. again.

Well, sir, my roommate has went. She left on the early train yesterday morning. We were up until 12 o'clock the night before and got up at 4:30. I claim I am almost up with you when it comes to losing sleep. I spent almost all of yesterday morning cleaning up but did manage to get to church by a fraction after 11 o'clock. Dr. Powell of Louisville preached an awful good sermon. Then after church I went on to dinner and of course we always have extra special on Sunday. We even had a half teaspoon full of ice cream apiece. Gee! I most foundered.

Sophia[16] [aka Sopha] and I had an awful good time sleeping yesterday afternoon and real late we all went to town and got ourselves some supper. Think of it some supper consisting of a whole pemiento [sic] sandwich and a saucer of cream. Then we were just in the act of going to church when we heard that a troop train was coming through so we immediately decided it was our duty to go to see the soldiers. We rushed madly down to the park and waited and waited and waited but no soldiers came. Finally it dawned upon us that we would have to go to the station if we expected to see any soldiers. Sure enough when we got there we found a great long train full of real live soldiers. The Red Cross girls served them with lemonade, cigarettes, flowers etc and they seemed to enjoy it so much. They were from Louisiana and my but they looked tired and hot. There was only one Kentucky boy in the bunch and he was a jolly little old kid. Said he had been telling those guys about Kentucky and they wouldn't believe him. But now he guessed they could see for themselves. One great big healthy looking fellow walked up in civilian clothes and the soldier boys almost snatched him on board the train. The little Kentuckian said "Say, we have a suit that would just fit you" and everybody just clapped for him. One of the lieutenants said some of the men had been in training only five weeks and were now on their way to France, where they would receive five more weeks training and then be rushed to the front trenches. That seems to me like it is putting them through in a powerful hurry. I hope you get to go to school somewhere. You may not like it but I believe it would mean a great deal to you.

I had a card from John Browning Saturday and as usual he called me Clarissa[17] and asked about Theophilus. He wanted to know if I was going back to G.C. Then went on to say, "It won't seem like G.C. to you with Theophilus so far away but you can find another Theophilus." Now what do you think of that? His address is Co. B, Signal Corps, College Station, Texas. And will you please write to him sometime soon and assure him that you are in normal health.

Well, well, well, we have just had a peck of excitement. Sophia and I got into a fight and when we got through fighting we joined in singing "So when I die don't you bury me a tall" and lo and behold the first thing we knew we had an audience below our window consisting of two boys on a load of logs. One of the girls hollered and said you didn't know you had an audience and one of the boys said but you have though. Now wasn't that excitement? But law, that's me all the time — to get into excitement when there is any body around to help me. "C."

The woman who stays here began playing [piano] at the picture show to-day and she said she was going to give us all complimentary tickets. We are just hoping we will get to go to-morrow night and see "To Hell with the Kaiser."[18] Don't guess a little child like me should see such pictures but nevertheless if I get a chance to go I'll run the risk.

You know how fond I am of bugs. Yes. Well we have plenty of bugs — the flying kind and crawling kind too. We study out on a back porch at night and although it is screened the dear little animules [sic] find some entrance. You remember you promised to protect me from bugs but you are failing to do so. Oh I guess I'll forgive you since you couldn't very well help me out being as you are so far away.

I sure am having the dickens of a time trying to write this afternoon. Sopha is leading me a merry chase. Turning my chair over and little things like that. I have to settle her about every fifteen minutes.

I guess I've written about enough for this time cause I realize that you are a busy little "Jackie" and don't have much time to read long drawn out letters like it is natural for me to write. Hope your eyes don't hurt too much when you reach the end of this. "Au Revoir, but not Good-bye." Heaps of Love,

Elma

~

AUGUST 14, 1918

Elliott says Elma's last letter was so jolly and full of her "giddiness" that it almost made him feel that he was with her again. He reports that things are much better since he got out of detention. He is using his free time to study trigonometry and to memorize the Navy manual, The Blue Jacket, *while he waits to find out where the Navy might send him.*

Dear Elma,

I just got your letter at noon to-day. I must say you and "Sofa" [aka Sopha or Sophia] are two gay chickens. I don't think I would like to prophesy what is to become of you. You are getting so gay. I don't think you used to do so many things as you keep telling me of now. I would just love to see you again. I just think I would enjoy seeing some of your "cuteness" again. If you keep on as you have since I left I think you and Blanche together will take G.C. this year.

I got your letter a few days ago answering my blue letter. If it was your stationery that caused it I sure hope you never use any more like it. If I ever get blue again I don't think I will tell you about it. You just write back and make fun of me. I think I know how you were at Rucker Hall now. I never had a letter to cheer me up more in my life than that one. I was somewhat blue when I received it. It was so full of life and you that it sure made me feel good to read it. I haven't felt blue one minute since I got it. Your letter that I got to-day was so much like you it made me almost feel that I was with you. It seems that your letters have all been so serious since I came up here. Don't think I don't like that kind of letters, but it just made me feel good to get one that was jolly and full of your "giddiness" as you love to call it. I thought perhaps you were feeling sad. I must admit I felt depressed from some cause or other and I always felt serious and so I wrote that way too. You know I am always serious so I have just been writing in my natural mood.

I have just got back from a review at the main camp. I have been on the march for two hours and a half. It is not so hot here to-day and I am getting used to it too so I am not tired at all. Our company has been having it easy now for about a week. We have done about 8 hours drilling in the week. We are a reserve company and are waiting for our time at the Pier. I don't know when we go. They say there are 2300 on the waiting list and that they take 100 each day. So it may be a month before I leave this camp and I may be moved at any time. There is nothing been said to us about going. They may have decided to do something else with us by this time. We don't have much choice. I still feel that something good is before me. They do not seem to be rushing this co. at all now in drill. We have about three or four hours each day off now in which I study. Some of the fellows do nothing. I have an idea that the fellow who puts in his time will get the best place. I do love to have a chance to study. Believe me I will take advantage of it. I will use all the time they give me for study. They say we get from 3 p.m. till 8 a.m. each day all our own if we go to the Pier and all time from Saturday noon till 8 a.m. Monday morning. So you see I will have it soft right if I really get to go there. I think I will get to go, but when?

It is much better since detention is up but we are not free yet.

They say this camp is the hardest in the station. I guess the camp we are in is always hardest.

I was expecting to go to Chicago Saturday but I guess I may not. I am broke and my dad hasn't yet sent me any cash. If he does send it soon I may get to go. If he doesn't and Uncle Sam doesn't come across soon I may be in close straits. They took my name yesterday for a pay number. So I may soon get a little change. I have been buying books as if I was in college again. I have begun to hone on Trig again. I have decided I will learn math as it is all important in the navy. Say, if you know any Geography or current history write it to me. I beg your pardon. I do not mean to imply that you could put what you know in a letter. I was just considering how little I know and before I thought I had said that. My! I sure have found out how little Geography I know.

I have one small volume of about 900 pages "The Blue Jackets Manual" that tells all about the navy. They tell me that we are expected to almost memorize it from beginning to end. I have started. I have memorized six rules for a guard — about half page. Don't you think I am progressing fine?

Well, it is almost chow time. I will have to stop and go to get some beans. They give us beans and bread for breakfast, light bread and white beans for dinner, [and] bread and "navy" beans for supper. Everybody eats beans in the navy and everybody likes them too. This is visitors' day, Wednesday afternoon. Thousands of mothers and friends are here. Most all of them have boxes of eats. Gee, but I get hungry when I see all of it and then I wish I had some friends living near here. Sundays and Wednesdays are the visiting days. I hardly ever go outside the barracks just because it makes me so hungry.

Guess I will write again soon. Don't you and Sopha get into too much meanness. The bugle blows; 5:30, and I must go eat.

With love as always,
Elliott

AUGUST 14, 1918

This is one of Elma's more serious letters. She is glad Elliott might get to go to school and encourages him to study hard. She shares his belief that God helps those who help themselves and says she is willing to make any sacrifices that will assist him in making good. She declares her love for him and wishes she could have been with him on furlough.

Wednesday
Dear Elliott:

I rec'd your letter written from Waukegan yesterday afternoon and the Views of the Navy this morning. I judge that you got to go to Chicago Mon. as this was mailed from there. I can't begin to tell you how glad I am that this opportunity has come to you. I felt sure that it would bye and bye. I do so want you to make good and I believe you will but don't rely too much on your own strength. God alone is able to help you win out and He is ever ready to help if we ask. I have never done anything very much worth while but I know I should never have been able to accomplish what little I have, had it not been for the guidance of My Heavenly Father. Of course I shall continue to pray for you every day. Study as hard as ever you can and don't try to write to me often. I shall not feel bad at all for I am willing to make any sacrifice that will assist you in making good. I want you to reach the top in whatever you undertake and this can only be done through hard work. Now I know you are going to do your very very best and angels could do no more.

And you have been doubting my love again. Please don't. Tell me. What can I do to prove to you that my love is true in every sense of the word. I have declared it with my lips and have tried my best to prove it by my actions but still you have clouds of doubt. I know it is natural but I wish you wouldn't. Perhaps I have not been writing quite as often as I did at first. The reason for that is — I have taken up more work at the B.U. and am trying to double up a bit in order to get in that week at home. You see it isn't because I've been entertaining some old slacker or flirting with soldier men or any other wild impracticle [sic] thing.

I know you must have enjoyed your furlough thoroughly but oh! What would I have given to have been with you. I could not have helped enjoying it. I always have wished and wished I might visit the Great Lakes and maybe I will yet when I gets [sic] rich. It isn't my policy to give up on anything, you know. Oh yes when I get the "blues" I feel somewhat down and out but I don't have those very often and when I do they don't usually last long.

Sopha and I got into some more meanness last night. We slipped out in the back yard and swiped a peck of pears. Mrs. Hughes almost caught us in the act but we religiously pretended to be getting a drink of water.

We don't think she suspected us at all. We took a strole [sic] of about two miles and consequently were somewhat hungry.

I haven't been one bit homesick since Sopha came. She almost takes the place of Blanche but not quite for she doesn't get down in the dumps like Blanche does.

I'm so hot. Just got to cool off some way or other so will have to stop. Again let me urge you to put forth your very best effort knowing that you will come out gloriously victorious.

With oceans of Love
From your "Little Girl,"
Elma

~

AUGUST 16, 1918

Elma is again in one of her "giddy" moods — stealing pears and playing pranks on the man who came calling on the youngest "grass widow" and threatening to write "crazy letters" to soldiers. She encloses a note from Sopha written in a countrified dialect in different handwriting.

Friday Night
Just in from supper
Dear Elliott:

I haven't improved one bit since you last heard from me, in fact I'm growing worse all the while. I mean Sopha and I together are. Wednesday night we went to prayer meeting and came right straight home and swiped some more pears. We have about gotten 'em all and oh! They were so juicy and sweet. I'm sure you will understand why they were so good... Last night the youngest grass "widder" had a fine beau and when we got back from the picture show we made things hot for him. Just as the clock struck 10, we lowered a big poster that read something like this:

10 o'clock
"No Man's Land"

He started up stairs and we vanished quickly. Not only did we vanish but we locked the door behind us. We let down some more gentle hints for him to leave like "Uncle Sam has a suit to fit U" and "Be it ever so humble, there's no place like Home." None of these made much impression for he lingered around till about 12 o'clock. In the meantime, we got his hat and lined it with pins. Also placed a cracker wrapped securely in a paper which said "Eat this when hungry," inside the band (of his hat). The girl says he isn't coming back anymore and we can't imagine what the trouble is. Have you any idea about it??? Somehow or other I didn't know my shorthand lesson to-day but I've already studied to-morrow's lesson real good so all I have to do is write to you but Sophia is anxious for me to finish as she has already got her epistle written. You see, she is goin' to town "mit mir" to mail this. Don't get excited and think she has read your letter because she's just trying to make you think so. I just told her what you said about us being gay chickens. She is very conscientious about reading other people's mail. Why the night the soldier man gave us a card to mail she wouldn't even read that because she didn't think it would be right. Listen — let me put you on to something — she is almost a man hater and vows she is going to be an old maid so I think it would be right funny if you would get some crazy old guy up there to write to her. The address is Miss Sopha Lunsford, 537 B.G. Ky.

There is another girl here who writes to a boy at Hattiesburg, Miss, and when some of us proposed writing him a crazy letter, she threw up her hands in horror and said, "No, no, he would never write to me again." I says I wouldn't write to such a foolish fellow. We are going to write to him anyway. You don't mind, do you? Now dearie, don't think I'm altogether wild for I'm still sane enough to love you in the same old way. I'm glad you like my foolish little epistles that is if you do. The reason I had been writing such serious ones was that I was almost becoming civilized when Sophia came along. Then I got "giddy" again.

She is pleading with me to "hurry" so will wait till I get down home and write to you all I please. Am going home to-morrow night.
With oodlings of Love,
From the "Little Girl"

~

AUGUST 16, 1918

Somewhar Nere a Pare Tree died wishing I war in it.
 Meester Cranfeld
 Chicagie, Illinoe,
 Dear Sir:

I would jist love the best kine in the world to writ you a note tellin' you of the progriss o' me chickins (and they railly air doin' fine and I got about too hins an' five frien size uns an' they air jist agroin to beat the mischief) now I'd jist tell you a lot more if Elimira would 'low me to but she 'lows as how you air her man and I kaint writ to you even if I air ole and gray.

You no them thar chickens they air jist some sites. They clumbs plumb up in my pare tree and eats up all the pares. Do you know what I can do to kep thim frum etin' all my pares?

Now don' ye tel Elmirie on me caze this ain' no note. This air jist a line to tell ye how me an the chickens air and to ask yore advise on thet pare question. Plese give Elmirie the receat in yore next letter an in that way I'll git it sooner and can stop thet raidin on my pare tree. We all send our bes' regardes.
 Your respichfuly,
 Grandma Sofirie

P.S. Plese don tell nobuddy bout my havin this here fine stashunerie caze they mite git me for usin it in war times but I done had this fer a long time why aktually my great granpaps dauter's, sister's, cussin's chile left it to me in her las will an testimonie.

P.S. Hars hopin this fines you well in min and body speshially yore mine caze frum yo last letter I rather thowt ye war unsound in min. Don't think Elimirie know I slipt that thar letter out an read hit.

Censored by,
M

~

AUGUST 17, 1918

Elliott still has no idea when or where he will be sent next. He has learned that if he gets accepted to the school on the Pier and then is offered a commission, he will be obligated for four years. He asks Elma for advice. He enjoys studying the different kinds of men he has met there, everyone "from the thief to the religious man," but doesn't know if he wants to make the Navy his life work.

Dear Elma:

I am still at my old post, Co H and have no idea when or where I will go. Nothing definite yet. I went to Waukegan again yesterday. I sure had a fine time. I have found me a pal too. He is from Michigan. His name is Lyons. We went together yesterday and stayed together all the time. He and I seem to have about the same ideals. He sure is a gentleman. I never saw a fellow more disgusted with the habits of tobacco and swearing in my life than he (unless it is myself). If there is anything I am certain of, it is two things, I will never swear or use tobacco. I don't hear so much swearing in the company I am in now, but ordinarily, you can hear someone swearing all the time. Rough, dirty language and swearing is the worst thing I see about the navy. I went to the Catholic church services this morning and the sermon was preached on profanity. It sure was good too. This morning was the first Catholic service I ever attended. It was rather strange customs, but I enjoyed the service. I have been going to the Protestant services before but there are so many go that one can't hear anything. There are not so many Catholics and one can hear so much better I think I shall go to Catholic services some more. All services are held by Navy chaplins [sic] anyway and there is not so very much difference after all. We have to go to at least one service each Sunday. I enjoy it alright, however. It is an impressive sight to see two or three thousand sailors all dressed in clean white suits bowing their heads in prayer, or to hear them sing. Every one seems devoted during the service but as soon as they return to the barracks the swearing and rough language starts. That was the real theme of the sermon to be just as consecrated during the week and in barracks as at church.

I went to the picture show last night and saw "Over the Top." I believe it was the best show I ever saw. I also went down to the lake again yesterday. The waves were running pretty high. The lake looked wild and lonesome too. I got some idea of the sea during a storm. I don't believe I would like a rough sea. If I get another leave while here I am going to Racine Wisconsin I think. My friend is going up there and wants me to go with him. He wanted to go to Waukegan yesterday and that's why I went back up there.

Well, I have been studying and reading every day and every minute of the day that I have time. It is almost a college atmosphere in this Co. It is like coming back to civilization to be in H Co. compared with Co B.

I went over to the main camp Library this morning. It sure is nice over there. I read for about two hours after church. We are not supposed to go over there but if we can avoid the guard we are O.K. I was about to pass the guard when he saw me and ordered "Halt." He asked me "where from?" I told him 6th Reg. He says "nothing doing. You can't pass." Then I took a second look at him and recognized an old G.C. fellow, Mr. Amos. I guess you may know him. He recognized me about the same time. So we had a little talk until a Gold braid came in view. Then I had to be moving for it is against military law to talk to a sentry. He told me to go on to the library if I wanted to. So you see I was in luck that time. I am going to try it some more. I like to read over there. If a fellow watches his chances he can get by the guards sometimes.

There is an ordained minister in my Co. [Keena] He is a graduate of Princeton University. He sure is smart too and is one of the most popular fellows here. He sure is a good scout. Then we have also a law student from Harvard. I was out practicing signals with him the other day. We were sending messages by semaphore and we talked quite a little about school, (by the signals). He is crazy about Boston. The navy sure is a good place to study men and especially here in camp. Every type of man from the thief to the religious fellow. It is a good experience to be here. I see now that my experiences here will be good no matter what I do after I get out.

Elma, there is one thing I have learned since I wrote you last. If I should go to the pier and if I should get a commission I would have to serve the full four years. Of course the chances are that I would have to serve it out anyway. What do you think about it. It is not compulsory. I do not have to go, but it is a chance to study and it will be equal to college almost not equal to G.C. though. If you would rather I would not tie up for four years I will stay in what I am in. Most anything worth while in here one has to sign up for at least four years. I don't want to stay in the navy for my life's work but I guess it is worth while to try for something good while here. Then I do not know whether or not I would get out anyway. What do you want me to do about it? Is it worth four years to be an Ensign or not? If I do not get a commission, of course I will not be tied up any more than I am already. That is a problem I am up against now. You asked to help me solve my troubles. Can you give me some good advice? Really, what I do now I want to do it all for you. It is you that I want to make good for. It is you that I want to live for so far as human folks are concerned. That is why I am always asking you. Elma, if anything I do does not suit you and you would rather I do something else I would be glad to please you if I possibly can. My whole life and hopes for earthly happiness now are with you. If I can do anything to make you happier I would love to do it. It would make me happy to do it. I do not expect you to always agree with me but that need make no difference between us on any subject. I love for folks to give me their own views. If we know other's views it helps us to see our own mistakes and especially when we get the views of those who are dear to us and whom we love. You said something about not agreeing with me always. I know you would not just agree with me because you wish to please me. If I am wrong it would please me more for you to disagree with me and show me than for you to agree and let me go on in the wrong. I want to do right and I always appreciate to be shown where I am wrong. I know you can help me many, many times for you have in the past. So know I am glad, if you honestly disagree with me, when you tell me so.

Elma you think I do not trust you as I should. Really I do trust you. I do not doubt you in the least. I never have since I came to see you just before I left. I never shall doubt your sincerity. I shall never forget you either. I think of you more every week and every day. You said not write you so often when I go to Pier. I am going to write you just the same. That is my best recreation and pleasure and I just love to write to you. So I am going to write every time I get a chance. There might be a time once in a while that I couldn't write but not often. I know if my letters mean the same to you that yours do to me, I will not give up writing to you for anything, but I also know one can really find time for anything he wants to do and not miss it either. One can't study all the time, or work either.

Be assured I love you as much as ever and I do not lack confidence in you in the least.

Say, don't you and Sopha do too much you may get in jail ("nicht"). I am awfully glad you have found a friend at Bowling Green. Blanche was talking of coming to B.U. when I was there. I was in hopes that she would go so that you would have your chum. I am very glad to know that you are making good as you are at the B.U. I knew you would. Please tell me of any success you may have, for nothing gives me more pleasure than to hear of your achievements. I know you will always make good at every thing you undertake, but I just love for you to tell me.

I know you will make good in the G.C. office this year. I hope you don't have to work too hard. It won't be long now until you will be going back to old G.C. I sure wish I could be there, too. I am getting some good experience here and get to see a great deal both of country and human actions and human beings. I am becoming better satisfied all the time not because I like the navy more but I realize the opportunity to make good by experience and associations with men. I really am not loosing [sic] by being here no matter what I expect to do. Elma, I believe I may be called to the ministry and have been sent here to study and learn men. I mean sent by God. I feel that way at times. It is a big opportunity for service preparation if I have. I know I expect to make the best of it that I can while here and remain true to my God and to you. Those are my two main ideals of life connected with service to both you and my God, if I am permitted to do so.

Well, I must stop for this time. I have written in a hurry as usual. Everything must be done in a rush here even on Sunday.

With most of love I am as ever yours Elliott.

AUGUST 18, 1918

This wide-ranging letter gives a good picture of Elma's daily life and concerns.

At home
    Sunday night
    9 o'clock
    Dearest Elliott:

Delma and Oral have just gone and I can't keep from writing to you. You can't imagine how much I want to see you after seeing them together. I went up to Delma's instead of going to B.Y.P.U. Wasn't I naughty? There was a woman up there who played the mandolin and we had some dreadful pretty music. I got me three more new pieces before I left B.G. yesterday afternoon. They were "Keep the Home Fires Burning," "Love, Here is My Heart" and "You Picked Me, When I Picked You, In Berry Pickin' Time." How do you like my taste in selecting music?

Well as usual the train was late last night. I went to supper then all the girls at our house fetched me to the train. Gee! They sure were glad to see me off. Sophia pretended she was extremely glad to get rid of me but I believe deep down in her heart she hated to see me go, just like I used to hate to see you leave G.C. when you went home for the week end. You didn't know I missed you all so much did you? Well nevertheless I did. Went to S.S. and Church this morning like a good little girl. Dr. McGlothlin preached and as usual it seemed like the best I ever heard.

You said something about me writing you some current history. I think I have kept you very well posted on the current history I know — for instance those things that take place around me every day. Of course now I have no objections to you using all this information freely. I am sure it will be of great help to you when exam time comes around. I broke the Sabbath to-day — washed my hair. Reckon I'll ever get forgiveness? Well this was one of these cases you've heard about called "ox in the ditch." Mama is dreadful worried about me 'cause I'm getting' gray headed. She plucked about a dozen gray hairs this afternoon. Ain't it awful? You will not want me if I have too many "Silver Threads Among the Gold" when you come back. It's bothered I am entirely. It seems that I want to see you worse to-night than I have since you've been gone. Perhaps it is because Delma and Oral were together. But if I would give worlds to see you I would not bring you back if I could. I know it is best for you to be just where you are. I almost dread to go back to G.C. for I know I will miss you even more keenly there than here at home. Although I will be very very busy, it will be hard for me to keep from thinking of calling nights, coasting parties and nights in the library. Of course you will be in such new surroundings that you will not be constantly reminded of the things of the past. The memories will be sweet, if I do feel a wee bit sad at times.

I wonder if there is any possible chance of you ever getting a furlough. If I just had something definite to look forward to it wouldn't be quite so bad, but I'll try to be good and not miss you any more than I can help. I suspect you'll be saying I have the blues but I was never farther from them in my life. I just want to see you that's all. It's growing late and I must take a little snooze. With love and a goodnight.

I am,
As ever yours,
Elma

~

AUGUST 21, 1918

Elliott comments on Elma's antics with Sopha and says he wouldn't blame anybody for swiping fruit, especially pears. He also mentions a new "point" system, which reminds him of the rules at Rucker Hall, the women's dormitory at Georgetown College. He says he doesn't know how soon he might get a point, but he already cut a baseball game that he had orders to attend.

Dear Elma:

I believe you have written me twice since I wrote to you or at least I have gotten two letters since I wrote.

Well, I don't believe you have improved any but I am not saying so because of the pears. I wouldn't blame anybody for swiping fruit 'especially pears. In fact I am about to get the opinion that it is O.K. to swipe anything that is good to eat. I am thinking that you are about the same as usual by the way you entertained the young man. I believe I have an idea about what you girls are capable of doing in fact most any bunch of girls. I expect I also have an idea how the fellow felt. I guess no sport objects to be joked by a nice little girl or two. (And I guess he is a "sport" by the company he keeps.) In fact I guess he enjoyed it. I don't mind folks having fun at my expense — and girls especially. And your shorthand lesson, that was alright. Be sure you don't let your studies interfere with your pleasure. You said Sophia was a man-hater. If you ain't careful you may be man hated by the widow's beaux anyway and I fear that might be worse for you while you expect to stay where you are. Don't think I will mind you writing to the poor soldier in... I don't believe you said. I used to wonder why so many correspondences sprang up in army when the parties were unknown to each other. A soldier is glad to do anything for a change. Things sure do get monotonous round here. A boy in the army is too glad to write to anybody who will write back. You know I don't care what you do so long as you can do it in accordance with your conscience. I trust you now absolutely and I expect to find you just as true to me when I come back as when I left.

It was awful sweet of you to write to me after your company left Sunday night. Yes, I liked the titles of your music find. I do not know any of it, except "Keep Home Fires Burning."

Really I didn't know that you hated to see me go home on weekends when in college. I knew that I would always most as soon stay at G.C. as to go home just because I could see you and if there was any chance for me to be with you I never went home when I could help it. I wrote home several times to tell them that I couldn't come home when they were expecting me when I found out that I could be with you. I am sure Sophia hated to see you go too.

Say, you write just the kind of current history that I want. I can read that much more interested than what I get in a magazine, although I did go to the Library Sunday evening and got so interested in a war article that I missed chow just half an hour. Now, I know that doesn't sound reasonable for me to do such a thing, but it is true really.

You asked me if you would ever get forgiveness for washing your hair on Sabbath. If you don't it is good night with me. I see little difference between Sundays now and other days. I have to wash clothes every Sunday and drill sometimes just anything they say. It is hard to tell when Sun. comes lots of times.

Say, you must not get too old while I am away. That is a bad bit of news that you are becoming gray. You must not allow your mother to pluck out too many or you might become bald and that would be much worse. Don't loose [sic] any sleep, however, worrying that I may not love you so well if grey. If I don't have to stay away much longer than I am expecting I don't think your grey hairs will make any difference. You were asking if I ever will get a furlough. I have been asking myself that question every minute I have time to think, and my thoughts are of how glad I would be to get back to see you. And believe me I will come back to Ky if I get a furlough and I won't be long in finding you (if it is O.K.

with you). I think it will be O.K. Nothing is known definitely here. I might get a furlough sometime and I may not. I don't expect I will ever know till I get it and get at least 100 miles out of camp. There are many things I would like to know. For instance what they expect to do with me. They told us yesterday that we would be in this camp for a long time. They do not seem to be moving the men round much now. The speculation among the fellows is that we will be here three months. I know that they know nothing about it however.

Say, Mrs. Macferan surely has been in the navy. We get "points" from now on. Three marks takes away our liberty for one week. That means we do not get to go out of camp on Sat., or Sunday. We get points for many things too. Even more, if possible than at R.H. That rule just went into effect to-day. I don't know how soon I will get a point. I cut a baseball game to-day when we had orders to go. I did it so I could get my clothes washed in time to write you. I don't think it will be reported as the regular commander was gone. I guess I would not have cut if he had been there.

Say, your friend Amerson went to sea two days ago. He is a third-class quartermaster now. I have learned that [h]is commander's job was just temporary. It sounds big to hear that one is a Co Comm, but really he is just about 50% worse off than if he is where I am. He has more work and very little more pay.

Well, I must stop this time.

Your sweetheart,

Elliott

AUGUST 21, 1918

Here Elma responds to Elliott's questions about whether to pursue officer training. She believes the decision of one's life's work is one of the biggest questions a young person faces, but only God can direct their course. She thinks if Elliott can get a commission, he should do so. She expresses willingness to make whatever sacrifices are required and believes it will give her a chance to do more for her parents in the meantime.

Wednesday Afternoon

Dear Elliott:

Since I have rec'd your letter this morning, asking me about the four year proposition, I have been thinking seriously about it. Considering all the pros and cons I have decided that if you can get the commission you should by all means do so. You may think that it doesn't hurt me to say that, knowing what it means, but I do believe it is the right thing to do. As you say, so many opportunities are offered to you and on my side, it will give me a chance to do a little something for mother and father. They are expecting so much of me that I would not disappoint them for the world. I am afraid both they and you put too high an estimate on me. I do try to live up to my ideals even though I seem frivolous at times. You said something in one of your letters about me being so serious since you went up there. You must remember this is a real serious time and when one feels responsibility resting on his shoulders it makes one more sober in his thinking. Since I have entered school here I have begun to realize what it means to stand face to face with the cold cold world. You know for yourself (though you did argue for woman suffrage) that it is hard for a girl to stand up under the strain of a business career. Don't think I'm complaining for I'm not. I just feel my weakness, especially was it so night before last when I cried myself to sleep. It was the first time I had done a thing like that for years but I was just back from home and I could not help but compare the love and kindness that I left there with the coldness of a place like Bowling Green. I haven't yet, for all my ambition, been able to convince myself that woman has any other place than in the home. But I know the experience I have already had and that which I will get during the four years you are in the navy will prepare me for any work that we might undertake together. You know, without my telling you that my greatest joy has been in doing church work, and nothing could make me happier than to know you had been called to the ministry. But dear, let me urge you to be dead sure about it. The descision [sic] of a life work is one of the biggest questions a young person has to face and if I could only help you in this, I would be very very glad but God alone is able to direct your course. You may think I am trying to preach a sermon but you asked me for my opinion and I have tried to give it to you. When it comes to advising I feel very incapable because I have never played the part of advisor — in fact I have always been the one to receive advise [sic] and you know you are older than I and I think it is your place to advise me...

I'm mighty glad you have found you a pal, too. I believe one of the greatest privileges in life is to cultivate friends. Mama has always told me to try to make friends wherever I go but I sometimes feel like I have failed sadly. Sopha and I are still loving each other. It won't be long before I will leave her. You see I'm thinking seriously about going home at the end of this week. I believe I could learn about as much in the next two weeks at home as I could up here, then I would be able to make a little more preparation for going back to G.C., to say nothing of just being at home. You must have felt queer when you had an old Georgetown guy to "Halt" you. Of course I remember Mr. Amos. He used to sit near me in English I. I have lots of memories connected with English class. Mr. Bell for instance and oh yes, you used to make dates on Monday morning. I wonder if you can remember anything like that.

Dear old days that can never be forgotten. I would have been so disappointed if I had not gotten your letter this morning for I walked all the way home between classes after it. I was fully repaid for my walk through the hot sun — I wouldn't ask for a sweeter letter and I had a perfect lesson in short hand too. I'm sure your letter helped me to [sic].

Must stop as we are going to prayer meeting and it is almost time to

start. Do your very best and trust God for guidance is the only advice I have to give you. With truest love,
  Elma

AUGUST 25, 1918

> *Elma decided to leave summer school early and take some time off before starting back to college in the fall, believing she could learn more "at home where peace and quietude reigns than up there where things were so disagreeable." Although she hated to leave Sopha, she was happy to be home.*

At Home
  Sunday Afternoon
  Dear Elliott:

What do you think of me? Guess I'm a quitter, slacker or something else, but I just couldn't stick it out another week in that hole in which I was staying. I came to the conclusion that I could learn more here at home where peace and quietude reigns than up there were [sic] things were so disagreeable. I am telling the truth when I say I don't believe there was ever a kind word spoken among the members of the family. I think you know what it means to stay in a place of that kind. I felt like if I ever got out of it I should never speak an unkind word so long as I lived. I didn't tell you quite how miserable I was for I thought it might worry you but now that I'm out of it I feel free to tell you. Poor Sopha, I sure did hate to leave her but they are going to move to another place in another week. I went around and bade everybody a fond farewell and to save my life I couldn't look like I was sorry to leave. Six of the girls came to the train with me and they tried awful hard to weep but nothin' doin'. They were too tickled to get rid of me to shed so much as one little tear.

I'll bet you won't believe me when I tell you I got fourteen letters and a card yesterday. Well now that's all right if you don't want to believe it but it's so nevertheless. Not a single one of them was from a boy. Ain't that marvelous? To satisfy your curiosity ('cause I know you've got some) I'll explain. It was the chain letter that the Y.W. Cabinet is writing. It has started around for the second time and the 12 letters that were in it were so long and interesting that it took me most a day to read them but it was heaps of fun. Everybody was talking about going back and it made me get all excited. And oh yes I was about to forget to finish telling you how I happened to have so very many letters. When I got home I had two letters and a card here. One was a big fat letter from June. And of course I loves to hear from my 1st husband. My 2nd "hubby" has barely sent me a post card — nothin' more so I'm about in the notion to get another divorce and try again. Startling news! Prick up your ears. Dr. Mitchell is to be hear [sic] next Sunday and preach. Dear Dr. Mitchell. I'm just wondering if he will bring his chewing gum along with him. But he's from G.C. alright and I shall grin to see him.

Frances Reagan and Miss Porter have been going to some University there in Chicago this summer and Prof. Fogle went way up there to see her, then when he got back to Louisville he called her up over long distance. Mary Anna [Beard] was in Louisville last week end and said she met them on the street and they were the happiest looking couple she most ever saw. Some folks think it is funny to be in love but I think it's grand!

Frances Reagan is going to teach school this year. Can't picture her teaching, can you? Gee whillikins! I sho' do feel sorry for you with all those points coming at you. Yes siree I can sympathize with you. But you're a good 'ittle boy and it won't be so hard for you to keep from gettin' any like it was for me. I'm bad 'es awful bad. Mama used to tell me I was when I was a little girl but I didn't believe her. Now I know I's bad.

I'm sitting here in the parlor just a wishing I had somebody to talk to but I wouldn't have nobody but U (even if I could). Oh, dear, I went to church this morning but I didn't hear what the preacher had to say for I was too busy thinking about you and wondering what you were doing this morning. If you want me to I can send you a calendar so you can find out when Sunday rolls around.

Delma begged me all morning to come up there this afternoon but I don't believe Oral loves me as good as you do and I fear if I should go I would be in the right church but the wrong pew. In other words, I fear that my presence might be superfluous. I 'member how it used to be in R.H. Oh we used to have various and sundry callers, didn't we? You were powerful brave to face all you had to — I mean to get to see me for 2 little short hours. I don't believe I ever did tell you about getting a letter from Mr. Tomlinson last week. In fact I forgot about getting it until this morning I came across it. He was writing to me about the Student Mission Band.

Well, I have to get up a talk for B.Y.P.U. and [therefore][19] must needs study a tiny little bit. I am almost to [sic] gay this afternoon to be at all serious. You don't blame me for feeling gay, do you? To think I am going to be at home for two whole weeks — it's most too good to be true. I'm still loving you with all my heart and hoping and praying that you will soon get a furlough.

As ever,
Elma

~

AUGUST 28, 1918

There may be a letter missing in the sequence, because some of Elma's comments do not seem directly related to Elliott's previous letter of August 21. She says she is sorry he thinks she doesn't want him to try for a commission. Although she would of course miss him if he were to stay in the Navy another four years, she thinks they should look at things in the light of the future and not of the present. She mentions that her parents are concerned that they will lose their claim on her after she marries.

Wednesday A.M.

Dear Elliott:

I was feeling awful bad until a few minutes ago. Your letter, at last, got to Franklin and made me forget how sore my arm was. I took my first "shot" for the fever last night and I guess you know just about how I feel.

I sewed all day yesterday and studied shorthand till 10 o'clock last night. I have an awful lot of work before me and Blanche wants to go back a week from next Friday — that is if the Hall is going to be open.

I'm sorry you took it that I really didn't want you to try for a commission for I do. I believe you wanted to and whatever it pleases you to do, it pleases me. Of course, I wish for you lots and lots of times, but because I am lonesome for you doesn't mean that I would have you give up an opportunity for advancement just to be with me a little sooner.

For example, I had much rather get a position here in Franklin and be with mother and father this winter but I couldn't think of doing it because of what it would mean to me in after years. We both know that we must look at these things in the light of the future and not of the present. Try to figure out just what this opportunity would be worth to you later in life and if you really believe it worth while don't turn it down because of the separation [sic] it would mean. Neither of us are very old yet and if we love each other in the right way we will be doubly happy when we can be to-gether. When I spoke of the matter to mother and father I did mean repaying them — you see it's like this, they seem to think (altho it isn't true) that when I marry, they in a measure lose their claim on me. For that reason, I feel like I want to do something definitely for them before I should marry. I don't know whether you understand me or not.

I know that you haven't a chance for the school yet but I have said this in view of the fact that you get it. The poem sounded just like you and of course, I loved it. Hope you will find time to write them often.

I'm sorry you were so near broke for I know after staying there all week you are anxious to get away on Sunday. Wouldn't it be nice if I lived up there close? I'd let you come out every time you could get off. You said something about coming to see me when you got a furlough if I would let you. That almost hurts my feelings. I never did refuse to let you come when I had any sayso about it — did I? Then why should you say if I would let you? When you talk like that I nearly feel like you don't love me very much. Now don't go and get the "blues" because I said that, for I meant no harm. It wasn't in the letter I got this morning but some other one.

There isn't anything much doing here and all I have to do is make preparation to go back to G.C. Everything is so nice and quiet here compared with what I'm used to that I can just sit and work and dream of you. I have just finished making a rose-colored middy blouse and I've been wondering if you would like it. You used to say you liked any thing rose on me...

Wish I was going to the Library to-night to study with you, but since I'm not, I guess I'll have to study shorthand all by myself. Don't think I'm forgetting you because this letter is a little short. I'm just feeling so bad that I can't think very fluently. I have felt worse to-day than I have in three years before but I'm expecting to be recuperated by morning.

Wif heaps of love,
Elma

AUGUST 30, 1918

Again there seems to be a missing letter or two. Elliott has apparently asked her advice about returning to college rather than staying in the Navy and working for a commission. She urges him not to make any decisions without asking God's guidance. At the same time, she is almost giddy thinking how wonderful it would be if they could be together again for their junior year.

Friday Night
Dear Elliott:
I don't think you would be considered the least bit unpatriotic if

you should come back to get your college course. You have again asked for my advise [sic] and I shall try so hard to answer you without considering self at all. Candidly, I do not see how you can get as much out of a course in the navy that would help you in after life (unless you expected to make it your life work) as you can in College. Of course, I know practically nothing about the opportunities offered. Neither do I know your Commander, but I can say that he would have to be a wonderfully brilliant man before I would put his advise [sic] over against Dr. Adams. I respect Dr. Adams more than any man I have ever met when it comes to real deep thinking and good sound advise [sic].

I believe the world will need capable leaders after the war far worse than the navy needs men now. (I am judging by the fact that the navy has refused volunteers.) Therefore I consider it a patriotic thing to do to come back to College if such a thing is possible. If it is not possible, do your dead level best to make good in the navy.

Now, please don't do anything just because I say so — again I say — take no step without asking Our Father's guidance. I know He will lead you in the right way.

Of course, I was thrilled thru and thru when I got your letter this afternoon and saw that there was a possibility of our going thru our Junior year in College together, but I have tried to forget for a time what it would mean to me and think only of what was best for you. I know it wouldn't be hard for me to work and keep up my studies too if you were where I could see you every day. I had a letter from Faith [Snuggs] this morning and she said everybody had been wondering what I would do without you. Oh! Wouldn't it be to [sic] good for anything if we could be together another whole year? I dare not think of it too much for fear I shall fly away on the wings of joy. Blanche came down yesterday afternoon and she and Lavinia [Payne?] and I held an indignation meeting about Zeta. They have held the names of the new girls back until the last minute, while they were sent to the Alphas several weeks ago. We have planned to rush the new girls madly and if the old Alphas get ahead of us they will have to hustle. Blanche and I are going next Fri and get everything good and ready. School begins on Tuesday, Sept 10. Faith says there is a fine prospect both for boys and girls. We have the names of about 40 girls who have reserved rooms in Rucker Hall.

Blanche spent the night with me and we had a most delightful time planning everything. She says Ira has been moved to New York but she has no idea what it is for. She said he was certainly one who keeps everything to himself. It seems to me that that is a pretty good sign they don't love each other. I just love for you to tell me things. I feel like you really care for me when you do. Come on and ask me anything you want to and if I don't answer it to suit you just disregard it.

I have had such a nice time this week sewing. You know that is such a delightful task to me especially, but mama is trying to rush everything thru so I can have a few days next week for real rest. I take my 2nd "shot" for the fever Monday and have an engagement with the dentist Tuesday so I don't imagine I'll find any of that very restful.

Oh! What wouldn't I give to know that you would be back, but do whatever you think is right regardless of what it may cost us in the way of sacrifice. As I have said before, I am willing to make any sacrifice for your advancement.

Lovingly,
Elma

~

AUGUST 31, 1918

Elliott wrote this letter while on shore leave at a beautiful park about 20 miles from camp. He jokes that after supper, he will be dancing and attending vaudeville shows and will forget all about his little Simpson County girl. He is still waiting to hear about the Officers' Material School. He heard that some fellows got 30 days' leave for the farm, and he thought about applying for that but was almost sure it would be useless.

Saturday
Dear Elma,
I take great pleasure in writing to you while spending my shore

leave. I am at a park about twenty miles out from camp. It is about ten miles from Ft. Sheridian [sic] I think. It is one of the most beautiful parks I ever saw. More pretty flowers and shade. I could spend a life time in it. If I could only be with you while here it would be an ideal place. I haven't seen so very much of the park yet. I have been reading a bit and resting from my morning's drill. The ladies here furnished all the entertainment and food too they say. I haven't gotten any of that yet, but I saw them fixing it. We are going to have pickles, sandwitches [sic], cake and ice cream. I thought perhaps I had better write before I eat or else I might not be able to write. They take up the time after supper dancing and at vaudeville shows. All free for sailors and soldiers. Isn't it great to be a sailor? I guess I will be dancing within a few hours and will have forgotten all about my Little Simpson Co. girl. Are you afraid that I will? I trust not. Don't fear. I do not forget you one minute.

Well, I had a chance to have transferred to the Aviators' Officers' training school yesterday. I decided not to try that. It is a big opportunity for those who like it. How would you like for me to be an aviator? I might fly away then some day to Ky, and make you a short visit. I could have transferred to a fireman too. I didn't want that, however. I am still waiting for the officers' material school if I stay here long enough. They are shipping the fellows out in a hurry. Three Cos. went out of our Reg. yesterday. Everybody is anxious to get out to sea as soon as possible. I am not so anxious, for I am afraid it will not be much better there than here. I am very well satisfied in camp. They called for firemen volunteers yesterday in our co. No one stepped out. Then the officer said you can go to sea to-day as firemen and twelve men out of 70 stepped out. So you can see from that example that most of the fellows are anxious to go out to sea.

Well, we get a holiday next Monday. I do not know yet whether or not we get liberty, but I rather think we will. If I do, I don't know where I will go. There are plenty of places, however. The people up here treat sailors like princes. They sure are nice. The South is noted for its hospitality but if it can beat the north in being nice to Sailors and soldiers they will have to go some. Everything does seem different though. I don't know in what way, but it just seems different. There's no place like Ky for me.

You were speaking of a furlough. Some of the fellows — just one once in a while — are getting thirty days off for the farm. I have been thinking about trying for it but I am almost sure it would be useless. Most all get ten days when they go to sea. Not all do. Every fellow is treated differently in the navy. So it is hard to tell anything about it.

The war news is certainly looking encouraging of late. I have been reading the articles of Mr. Simonds (I think that is his name) in the R.R. His article this month is the first to seem entirely optimistic. There are very few rookies coming in to the Station now. That looks better to me too. I got a letter from my brother [Isaac] who is in Md the other day. He says he is expecting to go to France most any time. He left home on the next day after I did. He seems anxious to go. If a fellow stays in camp a month or so he is soon ready to go somewhere, and he isn't very particular where. Then the real war spirit is different in camp.

Everything is rather noisy here. I can't write very well. There are too many things to disturb me. About twenty sailors already have asked me if this is Aug 31. I have said yes to all of them. I hope I am right for I try to be truthful. If it isn't 31st I sure have told a lot of "stories" to-day. More than usual. I try to be absolutely truthful when writing to you.

Gee but I wish I could be at Franklin to-day or else that you could be up here. You sure knew what appeals to me when you spoke of being in your parlor alone, and as if waiting for me. How I wish it could only be true that I could be coming! I know the happiest hours of my life have been spent there with you.

I am going out and see some more of the park and think of you and wish you were with me. I will write you again real soon, on Monday I expect. I haven't gotten any mail to-day. There wasn't any given out. Will not get any tomorrow either and I should have gotten your letter to-day. Won't get any Monday either as it is a holiday, but your letter will be appreciated all the more when I do get it. I will stop now and tell you more of what I do and see in my next letter.

As ever with love,
Elliott C

CHAPTER 6
September, 1918

Keep the Home Fires Burning[1]

> Verse 1:
> We were summoned from the hillside,
> We were called in from the glen,
> And the country found us ready
> At the stirring call for men.
> Let no tears add to their hardships
> As the soldiers pass along
> And although your heart is breaking
> Make it sing this cheery song.

Verse 2:
Overseas there came a pleading,
"Help a nation in distress,"
And we gave our glorious laddies.
Honour bade us do no less.
For no gallant son of freedom
To a tyrant's yoke should bend,
And a noble heart must answer
To the sacred call of "Friend."

Chorus:
Keep the home fires burning
While your hearts are yearning
Though your lads are far away
They dream of home.
There's a silver lining
Through the dark clouds shining,
Turn the dark clouds inside out
'Til the boys come home.

SEPTEMBER 3, 1918

Elma has just two more days at home before she heads back to Georgetown. She got her second shot for fever and had three teeth filled. She assures Elliott that this short letter doesn't mean she doesn't still love him, and she promises to write more when she gets to Georgetown and has more news.

Tuesday Night
Dear Elliott:
I'm a wee bit tired and sleepy to-night but I'm going to write a little bit any way, else you might be thinking I didn't love my sailor boy any

more. I've been writing so many letters within the last week that I'm afraid I haven't been as faithful to write to you as I might or rather should have been. But although I have written about 40 letters and cards to new students, I've been thinking of you and wishing I could be writing to you instead.

It was mighty sweet of you to wish for me when you were in that lovely park where the ladies were so nice to you. Don't you dare to fall in love with one of those fair damsels!!!!! 'Cause you see I'm just as good as I can be. Went to a sandwich supper last night and there were about 18 girls and 3 boys. Yes sir I was good —

Had three teeth filled this morning and oh! oh! but it sure did hurt. I've about decided that the best way to punish the Kaiser would be to grind all his teeth out. Took my second "shot" for fever to-night. Will have to take the last dose up to Georgetown with me. They sure are fixing their little daughter up this time. Just two more days to be at home. Guess my next letter will be written from G.C. When I get up there I'll have more news to write. Dr. Mitchell preached here Sunday and Dr. Adams was in Chicago Sat so I heard. That's about all I know. Now don't think I don't love you so good cause my letter is short. There just isn't anything happening here to write about and I've told you the same old story (not lie) so many times that I fear you are tired of reading it. But nevertheless, I love you. "The little girl."

∼

SEPTEMBER 4, 1918

This letter was sent to Elma's home in Franklin and then forwarded to her at Georgetown. Even in the face of great disappointment, Elliott remains confident and optimistic about his chance to come back to college. If things don't work out, he intends to get everything he can out of the Navy while he is there.

Dear Elma;

I guess I am "out of luck" on coming home to go to G.C. to college. I have not given up the idea entirely but I took the matter up with my battalion [sic] commander. He said it was useless to try for it, but I think I will see my regimental commander. There is so much red tape about anything that one does here it takes a month to find out about anything. I don't believe there is anything doing. I was in such hopes for a day or so after I got Dr. Adam's letter that I could hardly do anything. I wanted to come back to G.C. so badly. I could not see that it was unpatriotic to come back. That was the way my Co. Commander seemed to look at it. I am like you too in believing that Dr. Adams is a good person to go to for advice. I did not think he would do or advise an unpatriotic thing. Then I just wanted to know what you would say about it. That's why I wrote you asking what you thought of it. I know I will have little or no opportunity to prepare for after life's work here. My training here is all for the navy. I would much rather have the training at G.C. than anything I can get here, but to tell the truth I am about convinced now that I will have to stay here. If a fellow gets a thing that suits him in the navy he can usually put it down to luck. I don't want you to feel bad about it if I don't get back to G.C. I might have written before so as to disappoint you if I don't get back. Don't feel that way about anything I write you for as I have said before I never know what I am going to do or where I will go so long as I am in the navy. I will never be able to tell you for certain what I will do. I can only tell of the past as a certainty in the navy. I am going to do my best to come back and if I can't I am going to get all out of it I can while here. I think my little knowledge of Trig is going to get me into a school of some kind. All of our Co who said they do not know trig. were sent out to "somewhere" yesterday. I and all the rest who pretend to know Trig were kept here. It is the report that the fellows who left yesterday are bound for Siberia. How would you like for me to be sent there? For my part I wouldn't have cared if I could have gone too. If I get into a school here I am apt to stay here all winter. I am studying all my spare time on trig now. I find that I haven't forgotten it much. The Y is giving a class in Trig. I find I am about up with most of them in it.

We were supposed to get liberty Monday. I stayed here in camp and studied trig, and geography. I had been on liberty Sat and so did not care to go on Monday. I have decided to get a good place if possible and it can be gotten by hard work. So I am going after it. I have decided "the sooner I begin the sooner I win."

Well, I don't believe you and Blanche will let the Alpha's get ahead of you. If they should by trickery get more in members I know you will make up for it in your ideals and work. I realize now more than ever what T.θ.K. and Zeta[2] mean to real men and women of G.C.

You were saying that Ira doesn't tell Blanche what he is doing. I don't know his idea for not telling her. I know nothing gives me more real joy than to have you someone to tell about my failures or success. I feel that you are really interested and I love to tell you because I love you. Sometimes I may cause you to be disappointed in me. I hope you don't expect too much of me, for I know I am not capable of doing very much. I love for you to tell me things that you do, and that is why I judged that you would love to know what I do. That is one of my ideals for true lovers, that they really share each other's lives in full, by knowing and sharing with each other everything possible. When I stop telling you things and begin to keep secrets from you, you can know that I do not love you as I do now. If I did not [have] confidence enough in you to want to tell you all that concerns my failure or success I would not have confidence enough in you to love you as I do now. If we really love each other I think it is each other's due to know what we are doing or trying to do. I feel like, if we love each other, what concerns me concerns you. That's why I love to tell you all that I can.

I guess you won't rest much while at the dentist's or while taking your second "shot." Do you have three shots? I had three. They were for fever. My first and second did not effect [sic] me much but the third did. Most all were effected [sic] more by the first than the third. I hope your first is worse than the others so that you are already through it.

"Little girl" I sure wish I could come back to G.C. and I am hoping it is possible. I fear it is not however. I will know within a day or two now. If I can't I am going to do my best here and always hope that we may be together again soon. We must all endure hardships and make sacrifices now. So that is always a consolation to me when I think of our separation. So long as our true service demands sacrifice I am willing to make it and I know you are when it is necessary that we do.

It is raining and we are supposed to go to review this evening, but guess we won't. This is the first time I have ever had time to write a letter during drill period.

I must stop.

As ever with love,

Elliott

Tau Theta Kappa hall

LOVE LETTERS

SEPTEMBER 4, 1918

Elma wrote this long, newsy letter after she arrived back on campus, where she got busy recruiting new girls for the Zeta literary society and working in the college office. She talks about working registration at the office and names many of the returning students that Elliott would know. She mentions the sounding of taps and says it is thrilling to realize she is living in a military unit.[3]

Wednesday Night
8:30 o'clock

Well, dear, I just positively refused to do anything other than write to you to-night. The Alphas are giving a fine party down in Euepian to-night and all the new girls, Zetas and teachers were invited but it wasn't a bit hard for me to refuse the invitation. Monday Blanche and I, with others, met the trains all day long. The Alphas got perfectly furious because We Zetas would walk off with the girls before they had time to think. We sure did put one over on them when eight of us slipped off and went to the L + N depot[4] to meet the 5 o'clock train that comes from Frankfort. There were a bunch of boys around there and Robin D. Martin suggested that we take the new girls off at that station instead of letting them come on to the Southern.[5] Our plans were to get on and ride to the other sta. where other Zeta girls were to join us and of course, the Alphas had gone there too. But — we took to the Right Rev. Robin D's suggestion and what did we do but tell the 15 or 20 new girls that happened to be on that train to get off and off they got. The boys were so nice to help us and we marched gallantly up Chambers Ave suitcases + all. Blanche was almost afraid afterwards that it was a dirty trick but the boys said it was head work.

Mon night the Zetas had all the new girls up to Kate Shewmaker's, Lavinia Payne's, + Mary Eliza Bryant's room (which happens to be a great big room on 4th floor) and we had an old fashioned molasses candy pulling. They seemed to have a very nice time.

Yesterday morning I went to the office at 8 o'clock + worked madly until about 11 o'clock when the opening exercises were over and registration began. Then I worked more madly from then until 6 o'clock except for a few minutes for dinner. The boys went thru yesterday afternoon + I got to see all the new fellows. te! he!

I think there are two from Lawrenceburg, maybe more. One of them was Nolen Carter and he graduated at Kavanaugh High School. I took particular pains to remember his name, thinking perhaps you would know him. Some good brother fotched [sic] them over and I thought perhaps he was Rev Carter as he looked dreadfully like a preacher. This Carter boy breezed up to me to-day and asked me if I was Faith Snuggs and I says "not murch."

Last night all the Zetas took the new girls to the show. My! There was some thrilling picture on. "The Whip!"[6] We didn't know it was a 35¢ show when we planned it but nevertheless we forked out the cash and went right on. We can't help but believe the Zetas stand a pretty fair chance of getting their share this year. To-night is the 1st time the Alpha's have pulled off anything + they've been saying the Zetas were the only ones who had any life.

I have been busy with registration again all day to-day. Worked 8 hrs yesterday and practically the same to-day. Mr. Browning has almost agreed to pay me 25¢ an hour + let me work by the day. My job during the Registration has been assisting in receiving the money. I've been thinking of applying for the job of pay master in the navy. How would that suit you? I have my schedule made out for 33 hrs office work + 15 hours class work per week. Miss Iva Beard said I was a fool, Miss Porter said I was foolish + some of the girls say I haven't any sense, but they haven't told me anything new yet. Really, I think I will have no trouble in carrying it for I have it arranged so I get one hour of recreation every day and that will make my expenses beautifully and probably leave me enough to go to Blue Ridge[7] on in the spring. I must make good for your sake as well as for the folks at home. Dear old Dad has worked so hard + he and mother have sacrificed so much that it is up to me to make good. Dad opened up his heart to me just before I left home and said he would like for me to go on and finish college, then work two yrs before marrying and that was just what I had planned. Oh! Doesn't

4 yrs seem a long long time?? But maybe we will be rewarded for waiting.

Ira came this morning and he + Blanche have gone to the show to-night. It is raining but I guess they don't mind much. Maybe you think I didn't feel blue when she went down but — I did. Don't you know he came this morning + told me he was leaving to-night altho Blanche didn't know he was to leave so soon. I think he has been home most a week but hasn't been with Blanche but one day. I wonder if you would do me like that. I can't believe that you would. When Ira leaves this time he is to be put on a submarine chaser and can't come to port for 18 months. I do hope you won't get into anything like that.

The Prof Puncher, Mr. Duvall is back, got transferred from the navy. I think it a shame that such pills as he and Bush could get off + you couldn't. Most all the preacher men are back such as Mr. Eddings, Bro Hinds + Bro Sebastian. I hope you have no difficulty in recalling these classmates of yours. Eddy Tomlinson came in to-day. Things are beginning to look a little more naturel. And oh yes. "Stumpie" is here + is just as cute as ever but he sprained his other ankle this morning. Wasn't that too bad.

Poor Ruth Carson had an attack of appendicitus [sic] yesterday morning and had to be operated on to-day. Her mother got here just before the operation. Her mother has heard Ruth talk about you so much that the 1st thing she did when she met me was to ask about you. Lots of the folks have told me to tell you "Hello" for them but I can't remember who all. Lutie is back and I told her about the boy you spoke of in your last letter and she said she thought he was engaged. She seemed terribly surprised that he liked her so well.

Listen, tell me something about your ownself next time you write. For instance do you still wear your glasses? Blanche has some now but she hardly ever wears them. I wear mine most all the time.

Taps are just sounding and my! But it is some thrilling — I can't realize that I am living in a Military Unit. They started work on the barracks this morning…The training or rather drilling proper begins the 1st of Oct. However they are to make a start in the morning.

The President's reception takes place to-morrow night. I haven't as yet made up my mind whether I shall go thru that agony or not. It's awful hard to be nice to folks when you are all the time wishing for the one you really love. Do you ever find it that way? Maybe you don't think of me so much after all. I just can not keep from being lonesome for you no matter how hard I work or what a gay time I appear to be having. I haven't the least doubt in the world that I love you enough to be true to you forever.

As ever, Elma

P.S. I appreciate you not yielding to those fast girls. Always be strong...

SEPTEMBER 8, 1918

Elliott has given up on his dream of returning to college this fall but is determined to do his best in the Navy. He asks Elma to tell him all she can about school when she has time to write. He had planned to go to Chicago on leave and see either a war exhibition at the art institute or a Cubs game, but he drew guard duty so decided to stay closer to camp and spend his liberty back in Waukegan.

Dear Elma,

I guess you are back at dear old G.C. to-day. I never really knew how much I did think of Georgetown until during the last few days. I guess it is all over with my dream of coming back. The Commander says there is nothing doing. So I guess it is up to me to do my best here. Is G.C. looking as usual? I know you will have lots to tell me when you get settled. I got your little letter the other day. It was not appreciated any less than your other letters altho it was less in itself. I know you were busy and will be until you get all fixed up at school. It is alright when you are so busy or are tired not to write. I know you will write me when you can. I know what it means to be busy (and tired too) and I don't want you to do too much this year. Gee but I never wanted to go to school so bad in my life! I always thought I knew what an Education meant to folks but I never knew as I do now. I want you to tell me all you can about school. Don't think it is tiresome to me for I will be glad to hear anything of G.C. I don't want you to think I will ever get tired of you saying you love me either, as you intimated in your letter. The greatest pleasure I have ever gotten from words are those words "I love you" when spoken or written by you. And I love to read them over and over in the same letters. So don't be afraid I don't want to hear them any more.

Well, I am back in Waukegan to-day. It is such a beautiful day. I came up to-day to go to church, a real church. I haven't gone to a service outside the navy since here. I think it will be a real pleasure to go again, when I do not have to, as I do in the navy. I had planned to go to Chicago and see the War Exhibition[8] there, or the World's Series[9] baseball game, but it fell my lot to guard four hours last night and so I decided I wouldn't go so far, so that I might get more sleep to-night. There is quite a contrast between my two plans as you see. I think my later is an improvement over the first.

I have nothing new to tell you about my work. It is the same old monotonous routine of drill and details. I am hoping that I may get a change soon. After the fifteenth of this month I will have been here two months and will be eligible for any of the schools. We have to be here two months at least before we can get into the school which I have been waiting for.

I don't think I told you about the nice lady I met last Saturday night on the car. I was coming back from the Park. She came in and sat down by me. She said she was from Ala. Said I favored a Mr. Ingersoll that she knew there. (I wasn't wearing his watch either, or talking infidelity.) She said she came almost speaking to me before she saw that I wasn't he. We didn't talk long for she got off the car soon. (She was an old lady.) I came near getting a girl at the Park too. I was awful hungry and had just started over to where the ladies were serving supper to the sailors. I was passing through a nice shady corner of the park and seated on the grass were two nice-little-painted-faced-girls. They seemed very lonesome and as if they were looking for a beau. I was hurrying past as though business was calling me, when a wee sweet voice said: "Hello Jack! Don't you want a sandwitch?" [sic] I thought, "I sure do" but I quickly replied,

"No, thank you. I have just eaten at the canteen lunch counter and am looking for my friend." I didn't see any sandwitches or I might have said yes. They had a small box, but I thought perhaps they had no more than they should eat alone, and so I told the little story. That's the only thing I didn't like about the Ravinia Part [sic] — the girls who were out there. That is an unusual thing I assure you for a sailor to refuse to eat, and I guess the little things were surprised that I did. And it wasn't the eats I was refusing but the company. Sailors are constantly tempted by such girls everywhere up here. That is about all the kind of girls I have had an opportunity to meet since here. The society belles and the community flirts. That kind of girls are the kind sailors seek as a rule but they don't appeal to me in the navy uniform any more than in my civilian togs. It sure is disgusting to see the flirts round camp and in the town here in the vicinity of the Station.

I was on guard the other night, last Saturday night, for the other section of our barracks from which I stay in. When I went in there, there was one fellow in there who had not gone on liberty. We got to talking and he told me his name was Chapman. He is a cousin of the Mr. Chapman of G.C. I guess you know him. He knew John Browning, Sister Stone, and Luttie Williams. He seemed like an awful nice fellow and by the way he reminds me of Ira Porter, only he is almost red headed. He and I have almost been as chums ever since we met. He went to school at Berea last year. He seemed to be very much interested in Luttie (Is that the way to spell it?). In fact I believe he is crazy about her. He said he used to go with her some and was in school with her? Is Luttie back this year? If she is ask her if she knows him. He told me some news about Miss Williams. He said she is very wealthy. Has eight automobiles. From seeing her at school I never thought about her being so wealthy.

Well, I have wished all this week that I was a Jew. All Jews got five days furlough this week beginning Sept. 2. Jewish New Year or something I don't know what. I haven't wished for the Jewish blood for the race's sake but for the furlough, see? Another fellow (from Ky, too) got three days to come home to take his third degree in the masonic order. When I get back in Ky I am going to join the Masons so I can have an excuse to come home for a few days. I can't think of one thing to claim a furlough for so I see no chance that I ever get to come back to Ky. Perhaps I may get back some sweet day. I got a whole extra hour liberty to-day. We had chow at eleven instead of twelve. I am at the "Y." There are about three or four hundred jackies writing in here. I guess there are many fellows here who have a "little girl" back home to write to the same as I have. If a speaker to a bunch of Jackies wants to get their attention just let him mention "the girl back home" or the fellows [sic] "sweetheart" and everything is silence in a moment. Most all of them know how to appeal to the sailor to by referring to it. This morning a fellow was teaching a Bible class at our barracks. Everyone seemed to be getting tired as the talk was dry and rather long, when the old gentleman began to tell us about his son in the navy who has crossed the ocean fourteen times with 35,000 soldiers since he joined one year ago. Then he said his boy was expected to land in U.S. any day now from his last voyage (and if safely) is to marry a girl from Cal. this next week. When he mentioned the girl all the Jackies clapped their hands and listened attentively to the rest of his talk. It is wonderful how many fellows will tell you about their sweethearts back home, and wives, as many are married. All the real men that I have met and know in our barracks have said something to me about their "little girl" back home. And I know how they feel to know that they have one back home to be true to, and who will be true to them. Such a fact makes life really worth living, and our country worth fighting for, and it makes the navy life much easier. I must stop this time. Tell me all the news when you have time to write.

As ever with love,
Elliott

SEPTEMBER 8, 1918

This letter from Elma is filled with details about students returning to Georgetown, including names of students and faculty. Elma is rather jealous of all the couples on campus and disappointed that so many of the men besides Elliott were able to get furloughs but says she enjoys sitting in her room all by herself writing to him. She is tickled, though, that the boys now must live under rules as strict as the girls in Rucker Hall.

Rucker Hall
Sunday Night
9 o'clock
Dearest Elliott:

I'm sitting here in my room all by myself (Thank the Lord) with everything perfectly straight and "cozy" — and can write to my hearts [sic] content for once more. Have been here since Friday night and everything has been in such a stir that I have only had time to drop one card home. Your last letter followed me up and I got it Saturday morning and oh! how glad I was to get it. Dear, I know if I could see you I would love you to death. I don't believe I love anybody very much but you 'cause I'm not a bit thrilled to see the girls. Mary Anna [Beard] came in just a minute ago and Blanche [Hall] almost went into fits over her and I wasn't a bit tickled. She hadn't been here but a little while when someone called for her downstairs — she just flew. I know it was Gene [Martin]. That made me so homesick for you. Another thing that is going to make it hard on me is that Ira [Porter] is coming to-morrow. He's home on a furlough and comes over to-morrow to stay until Friday. Blanche doesn't seem to care at all. Her whole time is given over to working for Zeta. There are only three new girls here now and they are just as good as Zetas already. I think we stand a real good show. We are going to meet all the trains to-morrow so it will keep us stirring. I'm awful scared the Ciceros are gaining ground for they have a good bunch of workers who have been here several days and the T.θ.K.s didn't show up until to-day. I don't imagine the boys [sic] societies will do much this year anyway because everything is so changed. I'm almost afraid I've come to some other school besides G.C. Absolutely nothing is the same. They have changed the schedule completely. Classes begin at 10 o'clock A.M. and run till 5 o'clock P.M. That is in order that the boys can get their military training early in the morning. They are going to build barracks on the back campus for the boys who can't get rooms in either of the dormitories. They are talking of knocking the insides out of Old Sem and fixing it up like the government wants it. What tickles me so is that the boys are under more rules than the girls now!! Every girl in Rucker Hall is rejoicing over that fact but we get on a "turrible" long face when they tell us that we can't have but one day (probably 3) Christmas. That means "little Elma" doesn't go home anymore for a long long time. This may be gossip what ain't so. All the town boys have to go into barracks and get out about like you all do. And, oh yes, they're expecting 250 boys and 125 girls. Every room in R.H. is already taken and the Logan House is full. Blanche has gone down there to see some girls to-night and that's how I happened to be having such a nice time...

No boy is allowed to work in any way to pay their tuition. Consequently two girls are to have charge of the Book Store and they're to do heaps of things that the boys have been doing — for instance — Mr. Browning wants me to take Mullins place — think of it! Have to help keep the books straight and I never kept a book in my life. He said Mullins didn't know anything when he started and he thought I could do as well as he did — so I guess as how I'll be trying it. They want me to help some way about Registration. Can you picture me sailing around with a very important air offering my assistance to the poor little green Freshies? Mary Anna dashed in just then and sure enough it was Gene that wanted her. She said give you her best regards.

I have so many things to tell you that I can't think very clearly and I'm afraid this will be like scrambled news.

As we came back we met Mr. Bell and his wife in Louisville. They too were on their way back. Mr. Sisk and his wife were with them and he asked about you. Most all the old students are seeking information concerning you and it sure does keep me busy but I don't mind.

I hear Prof Fogle and Miss Porter down below in her studio, but I'm not thinking they'll be talking so loud very long. In fact I don't hear them any more scarcely now. He has been over here ever since I came and they have been to-gether constantly. He isn't going to teach at all this year but some other man from Camp Taylor[10] is going to teach French. There are lots of new Profs. I'm in love with the woman who took Miss Howards [sic] place. She's a perfect angel! You see she's in love — engaged to a man who has gone to France — She showed me his picture this afternoon. She, Blanche, Lelia [Harris] and I took a little hike to the country this afternoon. She is real young and "turrible" sweet. The first thing we saw Fri. afternoon when we got off the train was William Bower and Viola [Beagle] — then I got a glimpse of P.J. Arnold and Sally Ford Moore to-day. I'm having such a delightful time standing back watching all the old cases. They sure are taking advantage of their liberties. I was about to forget to tell you who was to have charge of the training but perhaps you had already heard. Tis no more nor no less than Brothers Arthur Freeman, Ogden, Siler, and Redding. Maybe there is another boy but I've forgotten who that is. Prof Martin is one of them too.

John Conn is coming back and Coker is already here so they say but I haven't cast my optics upon him as yet although my heart is yearning for the joys of that moment...

Lavinia and I joined the church[11] here to-day but you wouldn't think it from the stories I tell, would you? We went to B.Y.P.U. to-night but there weren't very many there. I think they have most played out. I found myself looking across for you ever once and awhile. I guess you'll think I'm just raving but sweetheart, I am in dead earnest when I tell you that I love you more to-night than I ever did before in my life. I feel like I would be willing to do anything if I could always have the hope of being with you again sometime. Of course I was disappointed that you didn't get to come, but yet I hadn't dared hope very much for I felt like it was hopeless. Do your very best there and I will do my best here. They have offered me $200 for 4 hrs office work a day but that won't cover my expenses and I am going to try to get in 5 hrs a day. I think I can manage it alright that way. I am going to write to you just as often as I possibly can but of course time will be scarce until we get everything straightened out, anyway. I hope my letters haven't been far enough apart to cause you any disappointment. Am thinking of you and praying for you every day. From your own "Little Girl" Elma

SEPTEMBER 11, 1918

Elliott is feeling homesick for Georgetown College, especially after receiving Elma's report about the returning students and activities on campus. It has been raining all day and he has been studying military rules and customs in the Navy manual, The Blue Jacket.

Wed night

Dear Elma:

I got your letter to-day. It seemed like a terrible long time since I had heard from you but I knew the reason and that is O.K. Let your work come first and write when you have time as I know you will. Your letter made me homesick more than I have been since here. I wanted to come back to G.C. so bad when I read all the news. But I can't say when I will ever see G.C. again. I hope it won't be long. I imagine it would be great to see all the "old lovers" strolling the campus again and I know it ~~will~~ would [sic] be great to be back with you. I hope I won't have to stay away so long as Ira has before I get to come back to see you for a little while.

You give good tidings for Zeta but I hate to hear that T.θ.K. isn't doing so well. I know many of our best workers are gone and Cicero's best men are still there. I mean best man. That is Bill Bauer, but I believe T.θ.K. will come out O.K. for what it stands for. I can't conceive hardly of G.C. students being in school under such rules as we are here. If they are you girls sure will have it over the boys, for I know you couldn't be under more rules than I am. I never do anything except what I am told to do, and be assured that I won't be punished for it.

I have been studing [sic] all day to-day. It has been raining. But I have to study what they tell me. I have to study a book they call "The Bluejacket's Manuel." It is about 900 pages of military rules and orders and customs. Believe me it is hard too.

I think you will be running the whole school next. I am sure G.C. couldn't run this year without you, but there is one thing strange that anybody would ask you to take Miss Mullin's place. I am not uneasy that you will fail in anything you undertake and I know you can do anything Mullins could.

You don't mean to say Miss Howard is really gone! I don't see how Rucker Hall can exist without her. I guess she must have left just because I did not come back for she knew how much I loved her. There is one more thing I can't imagine. That is that an angel could take her (Miss Howard's) place. I am sure glad you like the new lady. Perhaps you will have a friend at Rucker Hall this year. But then I won't be there to get you into trouble. You could get along perhaps with Miss Howard this year.

I hope they don't torment you too much by asking you about me. Perhaps it won't last long when they all find out about me.

I know the military affairs will be well managed by Ogden and Siler and Prof Martin. I thought Freeman was thoroughly disgusted with G.C. last year from the way he talked. Those fellows took their training about 11 miles out from this station at Ft. Sheridian [sic]. How does it happen that Conn is back? I thought he had a prominent job. And yes I sure would love to see the meeting between you and Coker, (provided neither of you saw me).

I am glad that you have so many chances for work but I fear you are undertaking too much work if it is over 4 hours each day. Don't work too hard. How many studies are you going to take? It seems to me that they could afford to pay you more than they are, but I do not know what girls usually receive for office work. I am going to help you a little if I can. I have never drawn a cent yet. I guess I may draw a little about the twentieth. Then I won't get much. A second class seaman can't draw but within one month of his pay. I owe some too. I can't be able to help you before mid-year I don't expect. Then if you will let me I perhaps can help you a little.

Well, I went to church last Sunday and I never enjoyed myself more in my life. I went to B.Y.P.U. and I believe it was one of the best meetings I ever attended. Then church was fine too. They had a social hour after church and the folks treated us Sailors as if they had always known us. There were not many present however. And again I have been mistaken as another fellow. When church was over a nice looking girl came dashing up to me and says, "What is your name please?" I told her and she said when I came in the door she almost had heart failure for she thought I was her friend who was on the station. I told her I was sorry I had proven such a disappointment to her. Then she said she had a special invitation to a wedding and so rushed away. Of course I took her reason as said, and went on about other folks' business. The minister's wife came round and introduced herself to me and she was the pleasantest little lady I've seen since here for honestly she reminded me of you. The preacher was fine too and one of the best looking men I ever saw. Well it is about bedtime and I won't have time to write any more before to-morrow so I will stop.

Two fellows are sitting by me, one on each side arguing about the time when the war will be over. One of them has just said he would not take an Admiral's place if he knew he would have to stay four years. The other fellow asked him why and he said, "Hell, I want to get married." That was the most public acknowledgement of that fact I have heard since here. It is hard to write when everybody is talking. I must stop this time.

With love,
Elliott

SEPTEMBER 14, 1918

In response to Elma's request, Elliott describes his physical appearance, then says he has taken the hint and will send her a picture as soon as he can get some money to have it made. He still hasn't given up hope of returning to Georgetown. He talked to the commander of Perry Camp about a possible transfer and received some encouragement.

Saturday night
Dear Elma:
I am surprised at you again. You ask me to write you something about myself! Honest I thought that was all I had written since here. I thought everything I had written you had been boasting of what I had done, or expected to do. I don't know just what to tell you except the question you asked me. I wear my glasses most all the time only I broke them the other day. I sent them out by a fellow and had them fixed and am wearing them again now. I weigh 163 pounds, am sunburned almost as black as a negro,[12] have had my hair cut rather short (although I kept all they would let me). Otherwise, I guess I look as I did last time I saw you. Is that what you want to know about me? Say, I think that was a nice little hint sure enough. Want to know how I look eh? Well, I will send you that picture just as soon as I can get some money and a chance to have it made. I haven't forgotten that I promised you a picture and I will send you one some of these days when you are not expecting it. Gee, but I am some sight in a sailor's uniform. While you are waiting for my picture and are giving me a little hint once in a while I would be glad if

you would send me a little picture of yourself. I wrote home for them to send me the one I have of you there but it seems they couldn't find it among my vast possessions. I didn't think I could keep anything, and I couldn't in detention but I can keep a picture now if I can get one. That is all stuff they put up to "Rookies" about sending everything home. A fellow can keep anything in camp he wants bad enough to move it. If a fellow is willing to carry it in moving he can keep anything.[13] What a fellow has to have makes about all he wants to carry however.

Well, well, I am glad to hear that Anderson County has a representative or two at G.C. I sure do know Mr. Carter. It was his father who gave me the pull in the debate decision at Danville last year. Nolan's father is a good friend of mine. You were mistaken once in your judgement of Carter's father, for he is not only not a preacher but is an infidel so they say. He is a lawyer and is considered the best in Lawrenceburg, and one of the best in Ky. He was once Lieutenant Governor of Ky. (I thought perhaps you would like to know of my store of historic knowledge). He was acting governor for one day and therefore he is called Governor[14] in his home town. I guess Nolan is a very smart fellow. He has that "rep" at least. I never went to school with him but very little. I think he is an orator. Put T.θ.K. wise on that subject for he is a good man. Tell me the other Lawrenceburg fellow if you know him or her. I want to see if I know him. I sure think it nice of you to take the new girls to the show and I imagine it will have the desired result. I hope so. If Alphas can get ahead of Zetas in anyway [sic] I would love to hear about it especially so long as you and Blanche are there together.

Well, I really don't see why you had not just as well join the navy as a paymaster as undertake what you have. Really I am afraid you are undertaking too much. Remember "Little Girl," those you are trying to reward by your hard work, and expect success by such, do not want to see you work too hard. Your health means more than all you can gain by work. For my part I know I don't want to see you work so hard if you can help it. I don't think you are crazy by any means, but I fear you are over ambitious to succeed. Be your own judge however. I do not really know one thing about office work. I would advise you to try it and if it is too hard give up a part of it.

Well, you say you had planned four years before you would consider marriage. Well, that seems like an awful long time to wait, but I see little chance now for me to get out of the army [sic] in a shorter time than four years, and I propose to leave it all to you. If you feel that you should not marry sooner than four years, I will be glad to wait that long if there is any hope that I can get you then. I had hoped that the war might end and circumstances permit an earlier engagement than four years. Of course I never dreamed of asking you to consider such a thing as marriage while the war lasts and I am in the navy. I really think it is foolishness for folks to marry under such conditions. Well, marriage with you is my greatest earthly hope of happiness, but it is useless to write about it now until conditions have changed.

I think if I should come back to Ky, I would see you in less than a week's time if at all possible. I know I wouldn't stay in Anderson Co and you in G.C. for a week without seeing you.

I hope you get to go home during Xmas and that the report you have heard is a false one. I can't imagine old G.C. with military barracks on the campus. Well I haven't entirely given up hopes of coming back to G.C. I stayed in from liberty to-day to see the ensign who is commander of the Perry Camp. I went to see him. He said (after asking me a few questions) in a very pleasant and in a seemingly interested manner that he would fix out an application for me Monday if I would come back. The other officers I have seen wouldn't even talk to me about a transfer. He said he had nothing to do with deciding it, but that he could fix up the letter for me. I got more encouragement this morning than ever before. I guess you will think I am just trying to keep you disappointed all the time, but I'm not. I would love to come back if I could. I am afraid I am too old to have a good chance. I have heard of one or two fellows from the station who has [sic] been transferred. That's why I keep trying. I think I will take it to the recruiting officer if I don't hear from this satisfactorily. Don't expect me to come back until you see me, but there is a chance yet that I get back on the strength of Dr. Adam's letter.

Ira is to be put on a submarine chaser? I don't think I would like that station any too well, but it seems that most all the fellows here want that or the aviation. In fact I do not care much where they send me. One thing sure I do want a man's job if I do anything. You know I came up here with the idea of a radio operator or getting in as a yeoman, but I wouldn't have either if I could help it. Yeomen and radio operators as a class are "sissies." When a yeoman passes everybody sings out, "Hello Mabel" or "Hello Sister Roadio." They call the radio operators Roadio Men because they do not drill but do road building and general detail work. There are a bunch of yeomen in our barracks now. They are all either Jews[15] or full brothers to Sister Stone Mullins[16] etc.

I think I could get in as a radio operator anytime I want it. If I can't get anything better I think I will just [be] a seaman. Really I won't have much say about what I do. They put us where they want us. If they knew I could make a radio man I expect I would be put into it. I am going to keep it a secret as long as I can. Duty on a submarine wouldn't be so bad except for the exposure. They tell me there is as much exposure on a chaser as there is in the trenches. I don't know about it or anything else in the navy except just what I've seen. That is very little. I have been here [for] two months and haven't even seen a ship or a naval boat. I have done nothing except construction work and infantry drill. I can't see that I am doing but very little here to help win the war. I am now thinking of getting into the gunners' mate school if I don't get in the officers' material at camp Dewey. They told us the other day that we get a chance next month for the Officers' Material. I saw Mr. Amos to-day. He says J.J. Ford got into that school the other day. Ford tells Amos that he sure has to study over there, that G.C. is a kindergarten compared with it. So you see what I am trying to get into. Seven men from this Co take the exam next Friday. I don't think there is any chance now to get to go to the Pier.

Say is it cold down there? I have been about to freeze for the last week. They won't let us wear our sweaters or our blues. And the wind blows about sixty miles an hour and seems as cold as if it came off an iceberg. Civilians coming into the camp for the last two weeks have been wearing overcoats. It seems as cold to me up here now as it does in Ky at Christmas.

I was supposed to go on liberty to-day or else work. I went out the gate this morning and bought me a big piece of chocolate cake. Then came back in and slipped off to the library and studied. I guess if they had found out that I was in camp and not working I would have about 4 hours guard duty to-night. Everybody gets by with just as little as possible here and I am a follower of the camp policy when it comes to getting out of work.

I must stop as taps are blowing. What time do they blow at G.C.

As ever,

With love, Elliott

P.S. Is Joe Bailey back this year?

∼

SEPTEMBER 15, 1918

> *This is another of Elma's chatty, newsy letters, where she reports on the goings-on at school. It is easy to picture the students welcoming each other back, asking about old friends and former classmates, competing for new members of their literary societies, attending the President's reception, and getting settled into classes.*

Sunday afternoon

Dear Elliott:

This is a rainy Sunday afternoon but I have been having such an exciting time, in fact I'm about to get campused already so soon. You see I don't care how often I get campused this year so I'm reckless. Now you'll be thinking I've done something terrible so I spect as how I had better begin to explain. Harold Snuggs came in last night. He is on his way to Mussel Shoals, Ala and stopped off for a few days. He and Roland [Snuggs] took dinner in Rucker Hall to-day and all the crowd that generally runs together ate at the table with them. After dinner we went down to the Logan (Senior) House and were playing and singing and having a jolly time when Mrs. McFerran called Faith and told her no such was allowed and she must entertain her brothers in the Hall alone. "Stumpie" Porter had stopped in, too, and this interference [sic] of Lady Mac was very disturbing. Not to me particularly but to the others. I vanished upstairs and took a nice little nap so the madam would forget about us having been down there before I came back. See? Now was that so very terrible? I had had the "blues" all day but that little bit of excitement 'most chased them away. I was awful sorry my letter made you so homesick. I try to make them as cheerful and interesting as I can but deep down in my heart I'm so blue and lonesome for you. I feel like I can hardly stand it sometimes. It's cowardly in me to tell you but I haven't anyone else to tell. It may be awful in me but I feel more free to tell you about my affairs than I do the folks at home. I guess it is natural though. When you love anybody you want to tell them everything.

Sunday night [at] 10:30 o'clock

The supper bell interrupted me and this is the first chance I have had to get back to my letter. I went to B.Y.P.U. and we had the biggest crowd. Everybody met to-gether in the room down stairs. Another girl and I sang a duet. You can imagine how beautiful it was.

The president's reception was pulled off Thursday night and although I had to make myself go down, I went into the affair with all my might and did my best at entertaining about half dozen freshmen. Among them was Mr. Routt. I spose [sic] you know him as he seemed to know so much about you. He told me some powerful nice things, for instance, he said you were the only man in school the year you graduated and took off all honors. Well, I almost knew that before he told me but I enjoyed hearing it like I always do anything that concerns you. I'll bet you think I'm silly for all time writing something like that but I'm sincere. I feel like if you think enough of me to offer to help me, that you won't mind me pouring out my heart to you.

I'm falling more in love with Miss Howard's successor every day. She is going to teach one of the girls' Sunday School classes and she made a lovely talk to us this morning. She seems to be so consecrated and is just 24 yrs old. If our plans work out right that is how old I will be when we can be together. I love to think and dream of that time.

I have sure nuff sad tidings from T.θ.K. They got only 17 new members and Cicero got 53. Alan Jennings came in Thurs night and between then and Saturday night he won 10 of the 17 who were gotten. Isn't that pitiful? None of the T.θ.K.s were inclined to work much, consequently the results. The girls are to sign up to-morrow night and I will tell you about them in my next letter.

John Conn came in to-day. I just saw him pass, therefore I can't tell you how he happened to come back. It is rather mysterious for when he started up here he said he was only coming two years.

Before I forget it — don't you need your fountain pen? Please let me send it to you for I'm sure you would like to have it. When you go out on a furlough you might find it handy. Don't fail to tell me in next letter. You ask me about what I was taking. I have five subjects, each three hours a week. French 3-4 with that red-headed Miss Mabley for a teacher — my but that will be trying! Education 1-2 and what do you think — Prof Rhoton hit me with a question the 1st one, the 1st day. It was "What is the mind." I wanted to tell him it was something I did not have but instead, I delivered a very psychological answer. Then the 2nd day he asked me if the mind was in the body. I told him I didn't think it was confined to the body altogether for one's mind might be a 1000 mi. away. Then of course everybody larfed [sic] and asked me where mine was. I see I'm doomed to have a dreadful time in that class. I am taking English 5-6, a Shakespearian course, Bible 1-2 and went to sleep in class the 1st day it met. And last but not least Political Science. I believe it is going to prove my most interesting subject for you know how Prof Hill makes things. He is going to teach it with relation to present War Situations. I like my office work more each day. Mr. Browning is the most agreeable person to work with I ever saw. He never gets in a hurry or disturbed about anything and of course that suits me. The only trouble I have is enduring Dr. Mitchell who raves around continually like some wild animal. He never knows whether he is walking on his head or his feet. I tried to write some names for him Saturday and he had me to make about 50 changes in them before I finished. That's just a tiny little sample.

Wilbur Fields is back and he was asking about you. Said he had written to you but never got any answer. Mr. May has been here for a few days before going to the Seminary and he asked me to remember him to you when I wrote. You notice I am more particular about delivering the boys' messages than I am the girls'. There's a reason for all things. Ha! Ha! Joe Bailey isn't back. He's in the army. Oh! I most forgot to tell you about my encounter with Coker in Education Class. I marched in and sat myself down by him and bless pat if he didn't get up + move. They all teased me terribly about it. Must stop or I might exceed the postage limit and how could you ever get it out when you are broke. Lovingly, Elma

P.S. This was written by candlelight and it is now 11:30 P.M. So excuse mistakes, please.

∼

SEPTEMBER 17, 1918

Elma says prospects are looking favorable for Georgetown, with 306 students already registered, and she is delighted with her office work. Her main complaint is that Dr. Mitchell walks around and chews gum from early morning until late at night. She says another student from Anderson County has enrolled, so she thinks this might be her chance to gather some valuable information on Elliott's history.

Tuesday Night
9 o'clock
Dear "Tot:"

I have so much more time to write to-night than I will to-morrow night that I'm getting a day ahead of myself. I got your letter which was written Sat night, to-day at noon and the minute I read it my hopes went flying sky high. Faith tells me that Amos is coming back. If that be true why didn't he say anything to you about it? Old G.C. sure is getting full. 306 have registered already and more are trying to get in every day. I say trying because some don't have enough high school credits to get into the Military Unit. Prospects certainly look favorable. I'm still delighted with my Office work. I put in 5 hrs to-day and had four classes. Please, dear, don't be afraid of my working too hard 'cause goodness knows I never was accused of anything like that. The only thing I stand in danger of now is suffering a nervous breakdown as a result of working in the room where Dr. Mitchell is. He walks and chews his gum from early at morning until late at night. Mr. Browning has been searching diligently trying to find some trip to send him out on but as yet hasn't succeeded. There certainly is a wide contrast between the two people for Mr. Browning never gets fussed or in a hurry about anything.

I didn't get to go to chapel this morning but they had their first rally. Elected Gene Martin president of the student body. I'm awful glad. That shows that T.θ.K. is still shining a little bit for they ran Sis Mullins for every office and he never did get in. The boys began football practice this afternoon. Now there I go again. Saying something to make you homesick. Maybe you'll get to be one of them yet. Oh! Listen, Anderson County has another representative. Somebody from Sinai. I believe his name is Atkins or something similar. I was making out an order for some Biological apparatus when Mr. Browning was registering him and didn't realize what was happening until I heard the word Sinai, then it was too late to get the name. Mr. B said "I believe Cranfill was from there" and the boy said oh yes I know him well and about then Mr B gave me the wink and when he was gone he told me that might be my chance to gather some valuable information. My! But I have a wonderful opportunity to get a bit of your history. Doesn't that thrill you? You know the funny thing to me is that all these Anderson County boys waited until you left, then came flying to Georgetown like mad. Can you xplain? And you thought I was hinting for a picture. Well maybe I was but I never dreamed that you would catch on so readily...I imagine it is wonderful to be wise...I'm powerful glad you told me a little bit about how you look for if you should have dropped in kinder sudden like, I might never have recognized you. I thought Ira was the blackest fellow I ever saw and if you are like him I don't know what I'm going to say.

Is it cold? Well I should ta to [say so]. We've all been shivering and shaking around for a week but I know it isn't anything to compare with up there. Just got to close as I'm exceedingly sleepy. Then too Blanche is keeping up so much noise snoring I can't do much good thinking. Understand? Be real good and don't get the "Blues" whatever you do.

With lots of Love,
Elma

MARCIE MCGUIRE

SEPTEMBER 18, 1918

Elliott turned 22 years old on the day he wrote this letter, although he doesn't say anything about that. This is his first mention of La Grippe or Spanish Influenza, but the earliest cases at Great Lakes were reported on September 8.[17] He says that half of his company has gone to sick bay, and the whole of Camp Perry will be quarantined.

Dear Elma:

I will write to you to-night for fear that [I] may get sick. The camp is like a hospital. Everybody has La Grippe or Spanish Influenza as they call it. I have escaped it so far, but I guess half of our company has gone to the sick bay. I guess it is nothing dangerous but it makes everybody feel terribly bad. There were not enough in our co. to go on review so we haven't had drill to-day, but have been pretending to study "The Bluejacket's Manual." I have been to headquarters twice to-day visiting the Gold Braids' Abode to see more about coming to G.C. I have to go back in the morning at 7:30. I sent in my application for transfer Monday and fixed up a new one to-day with Dr. Adam's recommendation. Really things are working in my favor now for a transfer. Would you be surprised to see me coming down Jackson Street someday with my old sea bag on my back? It has taken a long time but I really feel that luck is coming my way, or else they would never have asked for a recommendation. Still it may all be a dream or a vain hope but I feel that I may be back in Georgetown soon. Don't look for me too much for I am only telling you my best hope and not a sure thing. I guess I just keep telling you that I may come back enough to keep you expecting me and then as I don't come you are disappointed. Perhaps that is why you have felt so blue at times. If it is, I am sorry, but I just love to tell you all and that is why I keep telling you. You said you would rather tell me your affairs than your folks at home. It certainly is that way with me. I don't want you to feel that I expect you to tell me everything unless you just want to. I do love to read anything that concerns you or anything that you are interested in or interests you. Of course I have no right to ask after your affairs and I do not expect you to tell me unless you just want to.

One thing about my coming back to G.C. is that I will not be able to help you any I am afraid. I am counting on helping you with all I can spare so long as I am here but if I get back it may take all I get to be able to get back (if I do at all.) To-morrow is pay day and my but it is exciting to guess all the time how much I am going to draw. No one knows until he gets his pay envelope.

You asked me if I wanted my pen. No. I would rather you keep it. I do not know how long it would be mine if I had it here. You see one thing doesn't always remain in the same person's possession here. Then I really don't need it. They won't let us carry anything when we go out on furloughs. I can keep a pen in my grip. So you see if you can use it you need it more than I and I would rather you keep it. If I ever want it I will let you know. See?

You were speaking of Mr. Routt. I guess it is Paul Routt. He went to Transylvania last year. It was quite a surprise to me to hear that he was in G.C. He was a frat man at "Transy." So I guess he will be some swell at G.C. I guess you will know already my opinion of him. He is one of Lawrenceburg's dudes if it is Paul. I imagine he would make a typical Ciceronian. I guess you will think that it is hard for me to talk about him as you said he was saying nice things about me. He was just telling you stuff when he told you that I was the only man the year I graduated. There were ten men in my class and eight girls.

Some of the men in my co. have been taking the exam for the Officers' Material School. They say the exam is terribly hard. So you see my chance for that is slif [sic] if I stay here. They are examined in U.S. History, Geography, English Grammar, Current History, Algebra, Trig, Arithmetic, Geometry and Logarithms. You see they have to know a few things that I don't. I. Q. Ford is in that school so I hear.

I am so sorry that you feel blue at times but I think I know how you feel. I could stay here perfectly satisfied and never think of being homesick or blue if it wasn't for being away from you. When I told you your letters made me homesick, I just meant that it made wish so much to be back at G.C. with you or where I could just see you once in a while. If we can't be together I guess we will just have to wait and bear with the circumstances. Perhaps it will be so that we can see each other again sometime before long. I don't want you to stay away from receptions and entertainments if you can enjoy them. Perhaps it will help you to pass the time.

Well I am sorry about T.θ.K. I knew most of our good workers of last year were gone but I was in hopes that some of the others would wake up. John Browning and Stevenson and Ramises were about the ones who got the men last year (and yes Harold Snuggs). He was best of all. Perhaps T.θ.K. can make up by efficient work? I still have faith in them. I say Jennings ought to have a medal.

Well, I like your course but if I come back I will have to take all science I expect and Math. I just keep saying "if I come back." I can't help but feel that I am.

I am sorry you have to endure the remarks of the Education class. I think you were right however for I know my mind is far away most all the time.

I guess I know why you never tell me what the girls say about me. They don't say anything, but I don't care so long as you think of me and love me.

I will have to stop this time. Hope I may see you soon.

As ever your lover, Elliott

P.S. My pal is sick to-day in the hospital. He and I were expecting to go to Chicago Sun. They say the whole of Camp Perry will be quarantined Sun. So I won't get to go anywhere I guess. E.C.

SEPTEMBER 21, 1918

The whole station in under quarantine for La Grippe, but Elliott is still lucky enough to be well. They don't have enough men to form a drill company, so all who are well have to do "detail work" in order to keep them in the fresh air as much as possible. All liberties have been cancelled, there are no church services, and the Y.M.C.A.s are closed. A new order just came out from the war department to let people return to college, but the quarantine might affect Elliott's chance of returning.

Dear Elma,

Well, I am staying in camp this week end. I do not get liberty because everybody most is sick. The whole station is under quarantine for La Grippe. I am still lucky enough to be well. I guess colds don't affect me as I do not catch this one. I have been rolling a wheel-barrow all afternoon and don't you know I enjoy it? I worked in a bank two days this week. Wasn't that good — but by the way it was a sand bank, and I was using a shovel. Since so many got sick we do not have enough to form a drill company and so all who are well have to do detail work. They won't let us stay in the barracks hardly any. They want to keep us in the fresh air as much as possible.

I sure am glad to hear that there are so many in school this year. And actually you tell me that my old friend "Slip" Elmer Adkins is there! Say, he lives within a couple of hundred yards of me. He and I are therefore pretty well acquainted as we also went through high school together. I don't want you to get too well acquainted with him for he knows too much about me. He is truthful fellow too and therefore you must not ask him about me. It is a funny thing to me why all the fellows wait until I am gone to come to G.C. Perhaps the folks of Anderson Co thought they could not afford to let me be the only representative lest the county's rep[18] be spoiled. Mr. Adkins was teaching school[19] when I left home and said there was no chance for him to go to college. Really I am delighted to hear that Anderson is waking up to her educational advantages.

I am glad again to hear that Gene and a T.θ.K. is President. Poor Mullins, I guess she was very much disappointed.

I am very glad you find Mr. Browning so nice to work for. I am sure he is. But I can imagine about how Dr. Mitchell would perform while chewing his gum.

You mentioned football practice. How do they seem to think football will be this year? Don't think the mentioning of football will make me homesick. Between me and you, I am not so crazy about football as many might suppose. I like basketball much better.

Well, I am still living in hopes of coming back. I filled out my final application yesterday and of course haven't had time to hear from it yet. I have talked with several who tell me that I will get to come back O.K. (If I do I guess you will see all the Anderson fellows leaving.) I do not know what effect the quarantine would have on my being transferred. I hope it would not keep me here. The great trouble that I fear is that I may be transferred to something else before I hear from my application. I was sure I was to be sent to sea yesterday. A bunch of us fellows were told to report at headquarters yesterday at one o'clock (that is the regular time for shipping out). We went up, about fifteen of us. We lined up and the Ensign stepped out and asked how many of us wanted to be machinist's mates. Eight fellows stepped out and he drafted two more from the other end of the line from which I was in. The rest of us were dismissed and I went back rejoicing.

If I had known that I will have to stay here I would have been glad to get it but as it was I wanted to wait for a little while. You said Amos was coming back. I guess I am the fellow who first told him he had a chance to go back, for he told me about a week or so ago that he did not know anyone could do it. One fellow from this company said he had an officer friend who told him that a new order had just come in from war departments to let men go back to colleges. That fellow said he was going back if he does not get into the Officers' Material school. He took the exam this week. He says he knows I will get to come back but I don't know it until I am back in Georgetown again. Then I don't know how long I would get to stay.

Since everybody got sick we have put on our blue suits and sweaters. To-day the sun has been shining warm. Yesterday it snowed a little bit. If the weather would stay as it is to-day I think the Grippe would soon cease. It is pretty tough to stay in camp two weeks without being out at all. I would most as soon go through detention. I was planning to go to Chicago to-morrow with a Mr. Lyon. He is in the hospital and I do not get liberty. I can't imagine what we can do to-morrow. They say there is to be no church services and all the Y.M.C.A.'s are closed. I wouldn't be surprised if we have to work. It would be just like them to make us work on Sunday.

My company commander is sick too now. We have a new fellow in charge. I don't like him much but he is better than our regular one. I haven't seen my regular commander smile since I have been here. I think he would die if he should just smile once.

It is terrible to be in suspense. One day I keep hoping that I may get to see you real soon. Then perhaps the next day I just about decide I won't get to see you for a long time. I wouldn't get homesick any at all if I didn't want to see you. I know that I never would get so I would be satisfied when I can't see you once in a while no matter what I was doing. (That sentence sure is well constructed. I never heard such a racket in my life as the fellows are keeping up round here. One minute I am living in the present, next in the past. That's why I mix my tenses up so.) You mentioned or I did, that your letters make me homesick. Only when they remind me of the many pleasant times I have spent there at G.C. with you. When you mention them I think of the good times I could have if I could just be with you once in a while.

Well, I just now got back from chow. We had potatoes and maccarona [sic] and two small slices of tomato, bread, and tea. That is about our usual line of feed. We usually have all of it that we want, but we soon get tired of it, because we get it over and over each week.

Here goes the bugle again. It is muster this time.

Muster is over and this is now the regular time for noise and then more noise. I am sure it is even more disturbing than Blanche snoring.

I am in hopes that I may be in Georgetown sometime next week. If I am not I guess I won't have much chance to get back. I will stop this time.

With love as ever,
Elliott

~

SEPTEMBER 22, 1918

This is another of Elma's upbeat letters in which she provides plenty of descriptive details and an entertaining narrative, making it easy to picture life on campus in 1918. She still enjoys her office work and has been assigned to do typewriting for the commanding officer of the Student Army Training Corps on campus. Almost in passing, she mentions that she has heard awful things about the Spanish flu and hopes Elliott has not been sick. The flu had apparently not yet reached campus, but on September 24, Louisville papers will report 100 soldiers at Camp Zachary Taylor ill with influenza. By the end of the month, the camp hospital will be caring for more than 2,100 cases of influenza.[20]

The Zetas put on a show

Dear Elliott:

Just back from BYPU and church and Dr. Eberhardt preached especially to the young ladies. When he described the kind of girl a young man should seek for a wife — my heart sank plum down to the floor — He said she must be devoted to her ideals — courageous strong in character and willing to sacrifice for the sake of others. That's not me 'tall. The prospects for BYPU are good this year. We're going to have a meeting of all the old officers to-morrow night and divide things up again. I never was mixed up in quite so many affairs — as a naturel [sic] consequence I'm afraid I'm not doing anything well.

Am still delighted with my office work. Keeping books is heaps of fun. The Commanding Officer of the S.A.T.C. who happens to be 2nd Lt Aldis I Harrington from Kansas City, Mo arrived last week and the second day he was here Dr. Adams snatched me up and handed me over to him to do any typewriting that he might desire. They moved a typewriter back in Dr. Adams office and fastened the Lieutenant and me up in there by ourselves. To tell the truth I was a wee bit nervous for a while but I soon discovered that he was a perfect gentleman and became quite composed. Of course all the work was new to me but he was so nice and patient with me and never seemed the least bit worried with my stupidity. He is a little bit gray headed but has a very young face — is a graduate of the University of Illinois. Now please don't get excited and take it upon yourself to think I'm in love with him – no – no – no – never. I say again I do not love anybody but you and I know that love becomes deeper every day.

The Alphas and Zetas gave a joint program last night and both societies gave a living moving picture show. Neither one knew what the other had planned. I played the part of a dude and Beulah Porter who stays at Old Sem this year borrowed Gene Martin's suit for me. Blanche [Hall] was an Old Farmer and Lutie Williams was a country boy. We are all disgraced for life (according to Mrs. McFerran) for Dr. Adams slipped in and saw a part if not all of the performance. Those who saw him said he wasn't a bit shocked at our attire but Mrs. McFerran thought it horrible. The Alphas had seven girls dressed as boys — I guess you'll be as badly shocked as Lady Mac when you hear all these wild things but that was really my first experience at playing the part of a boy and I made almost as big a hit as I did in the part of Clarissa. Oh! The awful part about it is that Gene knows I wore his suit. He breezed up to me to-night at BYPU and said hello! My suit! — Embarrassed — oh mercy. I turned all colors. Beulah promised not to let him know who wore it and now I'll never hear the last of it.

Excitement — whew! I was most gobbled up by a real live bat just then. Had to roll under the trunk for protection. All the girls in this end of the hall are in confusion. I have now fled to the study room and have the door shut and barred against all wild animals.

Hope you haven't been sick. I've been hearing some awful things about that Spanish Influenza to-day. I scarcely knew whether to write or not. I'm expecting you so soon but I decided it would be best to go on and write. Oh! I most forgot to tell you that the Alphas and Zetas each got 24 when they signed up last night. Be good and come back to me real soon.

With heaps of Love, Elma

SEPTEMBER 25, 1918

Elliott is still feeling healthy although the whole camp remains under quarantine. Reports say there are 6,500 patients in the station hospital, plus many more who are not sick enough to be in the hospital. He heard that 83 men died, and the company officer was seeking men who had experience as undertakers and embalmers.

Wednesday night
Dear Elma:

The "old lady" has just finished his washing and so now I will try to write you a little. It is 7:30 now and I have to help sweep the deck at eight and be in bed at ten minutes of nine. So I may not get this finished but I will write what I can.

I am still feeling good although most everybody else is sick. They claim now that the epidemic is checked. They had published in the station paper this morning that there are now 6,500 patients in the hospital (there are 45,000 men on the station). Then there are many who are sick but not bad enough to be in the hospital. Also many are now out of the hospital. So you can have some idea of how the epidemic has been raging. I guess it is O.K. for me to write this to you as it was published in the Bulletin the station paper. They claim that 83 died yesterday. That is just news. It may not be so. I don't believe it. But there has been a great many who have died, because an officer came into our company the other day seeking men who had had experience as undertakers and embalmers. They say they went all over the station seeking them. They got one from our co. It really has been terrible I guess at the main hospitals. I am judging from reports. Of course I have seen very little of it and it is not advisable to believe anything that you hear around here. Well, well, here I go telling you such disagreeable things. We are now under quarantine. The whole station. The report is that it will last 21 days. I am sure however that that report is half imagination.

I am still in hopes of returning to G.C. I was called to the main station yesterday about it. They asked me a few questions and dismissed me. Said I would hear from it sometime one way or the other. There is so much red tape about everything in the navy that we never know anything. It may be a week or two before I hear and I might hear tomorrow. I am in hopes I will hear soon or I might be shipped out and then I guess I would be all out of luck. If they wait very much longer I will be out of luck for school anyway for I won't be able to catch up with the classes. I think our company will be sent out real soon. They sent out ten yesterday and ten more are to go real soon. Then there are not very many left. I shouldn't be surprised if we should go at anytime and yet we might be here some time yet. I guess I am too anxious to find out for sure whether or not I will get back. And to tell the truth I find that the greatest thing I look forward to is seeing you. The longer I stay here the more I see that my chances of going to the top are few. One hundred and eight men took the exam for the Officers' Material school this month and two passed. So you see how much chance I would have to get into that school. Those two who got in were from our co. I know that neither of them know but little in books. Both of them had a pull and their physical build with the pull got them in. I can't find anything in the navy that I care about doing especially. There is nothing in the navy that will help me out in after life that I have been able to find out about, unless it be some trade and I never expect to follow a trade. Then you can't get much chance at a trade for they are all filled up. So if I am not lucky enough to get in to some school somewhere I am apt to have to go to sea as a seaman. I guess that is about as good as any of it except an officer. The chances for an officer are few.

Gee, but it gets monotonous staying here in this same camp doing the same old things over and over. If I do have to stay here (I mean if I can't get back to G.C.) I hope I will be sent out of this camp real soon.

Well, I know now that they couldn't get along at G.C. without you. You must be simply great to be the secretary for everybody in college, especially the new ones. I am sorry you think you are so selfish and bad. It is terrible that you are so bad. I think Dr. Eberhardt had just such girls as you in mind when he was describing the girls who would make good wives. If he didn't I would if I should describe my ideas of them.

I am not at all shocked at your behavior in Zeta and I really would love to have seen you.

Are the same rules on for callers this year at G.C. as last year? I just want to know if I will get to see you any if I am lucky enough to get back.

I will try to write you again and not in quite such a hurry Sunday if I am still here. Perhaps I will know for sure by that time whether or not I will get to come back, if I don't know by then I will have about given it up.

As ever with the most of love, Elliott

SEPTEMBER 28, 1918

The station administration claims that the flu epidemic is under control, but 57 deaths were reported in one day. Apparently, the government was trying to keep the pandemic under wraps in order not to affect fund drives. Elliott guesses that Elma finds his letters very dull now, with nothing going on but the daily routine of work. He says he shovels coal one day and sand the next, then alternates on sand and coal.

Dear Elma:

I am all dressed up and no place to go this day. They do not even have church to-day. I have just been to a Bible class. A fellow from Williamette[21] [sic], a small town about four miles out from camp talked. He made a nice talk too. His subject was the prodigal son. The YMCA get the men outside to teach the classes. We get to hear some good talks too. They do not have church because of the influenza epidemic. The station is still under quarantine. They claim that the epidemic is under control now. There are very few new cases, but there were fifty seven deaths yesterday on the station. So you see it is not over yet. Gee, but it is a pitiful sight to see some of the fellows as they come back from the hospital.

I was just a little disappointed yesterday that I did not get a letter from you. But I know it is alright. I will hear perhaps to-day if they give out any mail. They did on last Sunday. In your last letter you seemed to be expecting to see me real soon. I was in hopes when I wrote last that I would get to see you by this time, but I have never heard from my application any more. I still have hopes that I will hear soon but I may not. If I do not hear from it this time I am not going to try to put in another for it would be useless I think. I may be too old to be granted a transfer.

I sure would love to come back to school but I joined the navy to do what Uncle Sam wants me to do. If he would rather I shovel sand and coal I can do it, but I will never like it. One thing however I won't be in much danger as long as they keep me here. Gee, but I would rather be in the trenches than here. I keep hearing of fellows who are going back to school. They claim it is easy to get such a transfer but I have never talked to anyone on the station yet who is sure that he is going back. Most all the schools begin about the first of October, however. I am in hopes that I may hear from my application about the first. Then this epidemic of influenza would prevent anyone from leaving now I guess. I am going to take it as being the best for me if I have to stay here or if I get to come back. It is really a great experience to be here and it would be much greater if I could ever get out of this camp.

Since I have been under quarantine I guess you find my letters very dull. There is nothing going on but the daily routine of work. We shovel coal one day and sand the next then alternate on sand and coal. It is very easy work. We just have to stay on the job from 8 to 11 and from 1 to 4 o'clock. Then we don't have to do anymore than we want to. The boss usually puts us on a job. Then leaves. We work or loaf as we choose and you can guess which we do (which I do at least). Once in a while we get a boss who makes us work. The thing that makes it seem hard to me is that I feel that I am capable of doing something more worth while than shoveling sand. I guess the naval authorities know better and it is only up to me to do as they say whatever it is.

Everything mostly is quiet to-day except a baseball game out in front of the barracks, and a card game just to my back a little ways. Our company is going to play a match game of ball this afternoon. I may go if there is nothing more exciting. They have just started the card game of late. The fellows can't get out to spend their money so they began to gamble and give it away. We have some very fine fellows here in this company and then we have some who are tough.

Have you ever met my friend Adkins any more? I am sure he may have something to tell you when he gets a chance for the asking or perhaps without the asking. I hope you get acquainted with the Anderson folks that you see all the folks over there are not really to be judged by me. It really is an intelligent and respectable people that live there.

Well it is doubtful whether or not I see you for a long time yet but I will always be looking forward and praying for the time when I can be with you again. Oh but the happy happy memory of those last few days I was with you! Every day when I am not busy and many times when I should be busy I suddenly awake from a pleasant speculation of the future or from the pleasant memories of the past with you. It is hard that we are really separated just when we came to the realization of our love for each other but I know the separation already has made my love for you stronger. I never dreamed that love could be so sweet or that one human life could mean so much to another as you mean to me. I realize each day that your love means more and more to me. Everything I have done since I left you I have thought of you and many times when I am tempted to do wrong I think that it would be displeasing to you (and the Lord only knows I have temptations enough). It is my love for you that always helps me to do right and it is not because I only want to please you but it is because I want to be worthy of your love as nearly as possible. It sure makes life more worthwhile when I think that you do really love me and that I can expect to come back to you (when the war is over at least) and prove to you that I really love you. If I don't get to come back I will still love you just the same and I will have the same hopes for the future only I may have to study and work longer before (may I say our dreams come true?) and we can be together for all the time. If that time was possible I believe my happiness would be complete. I hope you don't really get tired of me telling you that I love you. Then I know you love for me to tell you for you say you do and I know how much I love to read those words from you. If I write to you at all I have to tell you that I love you because that is all I want to tell you and I just love to write it although I would much rather have a chance to say it to you again.

    I will stop this time still hoping that I see you soon but with less faith that I do.

    With the most of love,
    Elliott

CHAPTER 7
October, 1918

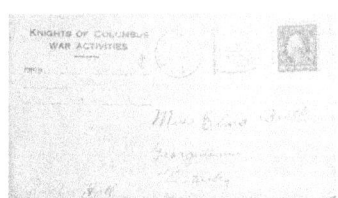

I Don't Know Where I'm Going But I'm On My Way[1]

Verse 1:
Goodbye ev'rybody, I'm off to fight the foe.
Uncle Sammy is calling me, so I must go.
Gee, I'm feeling fine,
Don't you wish that you were me?
For I'm sailing tomorrow
Over the deep blue sea.

Verse 2:
Take a look at me,
I'm a Yankee thro' and thro'.
I was born on July the Fourth in ninety-two,
And I'll march away with a feather in my hat,
For I'm joining the army.
What do you think of that?

> Chorus:
> *And I don't know where I'm going*
> *But I'm on my way,*
> *For I belong to the Regulars*
> *I'm proud to say*
> *And I'll do my duty night or day.*
> *I don't know where I'm going,*
> *But I'm on my way.*

~

OCTOBER 2, 1918

Elma says it breaks her heart to give up the idea of seeing Elliott soon, but like him, she believes God knows what is best and they must "trust in Him and submit to His Great Will." She is considering giving up all outside work except office work and classes, although she loves all the social activities. She asks Elliott's advice and signs off, "Let's cheer up and be brave to-gether! Always hoping and praying for better things."

Wednesday Night
Dear Elliott:

I feel meaner than a dog because I have waited so long before writing to you, but, dear, it is not because I love you any the less. You see I just had such hopes of seeing you at any time that I kept putting off writing. Then I failed to get your Wed letter on Sat like I usually do and I felt so sure you were coming then. But Mon the letter came and you said in it, that you could perhaps tell me something definite in your next letter which I generally get on Tues so I waited a little longer + it came to-day. Now that is the reason I have been such a long long time writing to the one I love better than anyone else on earth — even than mother and father. It almost breaks my heart to give up the idea of seeing you soon but God knows what is best for us and it only remains for us to put our trust in Him and submit to His Great Will.

There was a Rucker Hall reception last night but I was so lonesome for you that I just couldn't get up nerve enough to go down and make myself agreeable to strangers. I stayed in my room and thought of you and the dear dear hours we have spent together. I would not take the world for those few happy moments we have spent together and oh! How I long for the time when we can start on "the long long Trail" together. Don't feel too bad about it if you don't get to come back because you would have to be sent over to State[2] anyway. All the Navy boys, so they say, are to be transferred over there where they have a Navy Reserve. Of course, I would be glad for you to come even to State for we could see each other occasionally at least.

I had such a good opportunity to stir up a conversation with Mr. Adkins this afternoon if I had only had the courage. He came in the Office and I was in there all by myself. He asked me about returning a key and I told him as how he'd have to give it to Mr. Browning. I was all the time trying to screw up my courage to have a conflab[3] but I didn't get it keyed to the right pitch. Last night one of the new girls said she had always led her class in math but she had met one fellow by the name of Adkins that was going to make her work her head off. There's where Anderson Co brains are beginning to shine again. Really, this boy reminds me of you some. He is so gentlemanly and reserved.

The boys were inducted into Military Service yesterday and we had a holiday. The program which lasted from 10 to 12 took place on the Hinton Field. A big flag was raised on the chapel tower and Dr. E.Y. Mullins of Louisville gave the address. The Young Woman's Christian Association presented a large flag of orange and black, called the battalion flag, and Beulah Rusk gave the address for that, Lieut Harrington accepted it.

The Zetas initiated their new girls Mon night and we had a young banquet after the initiation. I helped serve and had so much fun. Ate ice cream all the time they were giving toasts. The boys had a gay time that night too. They had one of their fine parades in which they made music with tin pans, buckets, etc. It lasted almost all night and the interesting part about it was that they circled around Rucker Hall + made their artistic music. It is now 10 o'clock and the boys are serenading but I guess taps will sound in a minute and they will have to roll in. The uniforms haven't arrived yet but things are beginning to move off in military fashion.

I had to lead the Y.W. to-night and made a talk on Morning Watch. That begins in the morning + I expect to remember you each morning. I am a leader in BYPU this year + Blanche who is President of our section informed me a few minutes ago that I was to get up a program for next Sun night. I know I am attempting too much for I notice that I am feeling tired these days like I did in the Spring. I put in 7 1/2 hrs in the Office to-day and had one class.

I have been thinking about giving up all my outside work and devoting all my time to the Office work + classes, but it will be so hard to do it. The Mission Band had its first meeting Mon night and although there were only a few there Prof Ragland seemed to think a good year was before us. I would hate so bad to give up my place in that — as well as in Society, Y.W., BYPU + Sunday School. Tell me, dear, what you think I should do about it. I don't think I would feel a bit tired if I only had someone to love me up once in awhile and encourage me to press on. Your letters are as sweet as can be but they can't quite take the place of you.

Let's cheer up and be brave to-gether! Always hoping and praying for better things.

Your own "Little Girl,"
Elma

OCTOBER 2, 1918

Elliott hasn't received a letter from Elma in a week and he worries that she might be sick. He is no closer to coming back to school than when he wrote before and hasn't heard anything from his application yet. Camp is still under quarantine although the flu seems to be under control. The executive officer granted liberty but the citizens in the neighborhood objected, so liberty was restricted again.

Dear Elma:

I have been disappointed now for a week as I haven't gotten a letter from you. I do not know what the trouble can be. I am afraid you are sick. I hope you are not. They are terribly careless here about handling the mail. I sometimes have failed to get mail for a week after it is in the post office. Of course a week is not long but it is so much longer than usual that I can't help but fear that something is wrong. Last week end as I did not hear from you, I just thought you were expecting me back in G.C. and did not write but as this is Wednesday and I haven't heard, I begin to fear you are sick or something.

Well, I don't see that I am any nearer to coming back to school than when I wrote before. I haven't heard anything from my application yet.

Gee, but things have been exciting round here to-night. One real sure enough fight and two or three boxing matches for fun. When two fellows here have trouble they make them put on boxing gloves and fight it out. These two fellows had a quarrel to-day and so to-night they had to fight. It was exciting to watch. I see now where I don't fuss while here. They fought until both were exhausted and finally one knocked the other out.

I went on review again to-day. A Danish prince was present at the station and so they put on a special review for his benefit and entertainment. Our company has begun to drill again now and we have the distinction of being first company in the battalion. That means we are the best drill company on the regiment, but I guess we have been here longer than most any other company. This makes three days that we have drilled now in succession and it seems so good to be off detail again and to see most all the fellows back. The influenza is about under control now. We are still under quarantine however. The executive officer granted liberty but the citizens objected in the neighboring towns and so liberty was restricted again. I don't have any idea when we will get out again, but hope we may by this week end.

They came round this afternoon searching for men to play football. They are aiming to get a team for the regiment. I expect I could get on the team if I tried but I hardly think I will try. I fear that I would miss a good chance for a transfer or something. If a fellow gets on an athletic team of any kind he has to stay on the station until that season is over. So I would have to stay here until after Thanksgiving if I should get on the team. I hope I get out of here before that time.

I saw Roy Martin Sunday afternoon. He has had influenza but he doesn't seem to have been very sick. He tells me that Jack Morris has graduated from the Officers' Material School and that he now is an Ensign. He was telling me of Dutch Volmer and others of G.C. who are making good in the army. Dutch is Captain now. Cecil Anderson is a Major. I guess all the G.C. fellows will make good but me. George Mitchell is at Princeton University in the Paymaster's corps. J.L. Ford is in the officer's material school here now.

"Little girl" I have watched the fight to-night until it is most taps. I will have to stop for this time. It is just like being in detention again. I have been under quarantine now for three weeks.

I hope I get a letter to-morrow from you and that there is nothing wrong. If I get impatient when you can't write me don't think I am out of humor. I feel sure you will write just as often as you can. I can't help but feel lost, lonesome, uneasy about you, or — or — something. I just love to hear from you so much and I am disappointed when the time passes and I do not hear from you. Your letters mean so much to me.

If you are sick let me know. I will try to write more next time. I haven't much to tell you as I see so little these days.

As ever with love,
Elliott

P.S. I am out of stationery and can't get any more till I get liberty. So I have to use "Y." E.C.

OCTOBER 5, 1918

Elliott is in much better spirits since receiving a letter from Elma and finding out that she does not have the flu. He heard that 150,000 Navy men are to be allowed to go back to school and he feels certain he would already be back at Georgetown if not for La Grippe. He is also in good spirits thinking he will finally have enough money to help Elma out a little, so she doesn't have to work so hard and doesn't have to give up the activities she enjoys.

Dear Elma:

I never felt in better spirits since here. I feared you were sick with influenza or something as I did not get a letter from you for so long. I got your letter this afternoon and when I learned that you were well I am now perfectly happy (so far as I can be here). Of course, it hasn't been very long since I got your last letter but so many being sick round here made me feel uneasy about you. I am so sorry you were so disappointed that I did not get back to G.C. I was disappointed too, but I have prayed over the matter and I am perfectly contented to accept whatever comes to me now. I believe God is able to keep me where he wants me and I believe, in fact, I know He is leading me where he wants me. Perhaps he will not always lead me where I want to be (most of all with you) but I have faith to believe it is best for both of us although separation is hard. Little girl your letter to-night told me plainer that you love me than any letter I ever got from you. It was almost like being with you to read it. You have little idea how I missed your letters. I just didn't have heart to do anything. But now I will never get so impatient again. I wouldn't this time only I felt so sure you or your folks were sick. I just imagined every thing bad that might have happened for you. Don't misunderstand me. I did not think for once that you were forgetting me. I never feel any doubt any more as to your love for me. I haven't had one moment's doubt since I left you in Bowling Green. I have already read your letter three times. If you don't have time to write to me as often as you have been and feel that you have to write as often as I do don't feel that way. I will be contented to hear from you just as you feel like writing. I am not so very busy these days and I just love to spend my time writing to you. There is so little that I see these days I don't have much to tell you. I will love you just the same and know that you are just as true to me, whether I hear from you so often or not. I could read your letters all the time and never get tired. I have read all of your old letters over two or three times on Sundays when I have nothing else to do, but if you are too busy I can be patient and content with what you can write. I know you are too busy. I hate to know that you have to work so hard. I hate to see you look tired as I did last spring and with the work you have I know you will be tired. Well, I just as well tell you. I think I still have better news now than ever. I began this letter with the firm resolve not to tell you but every time I write I want to tell you. So here goes. I want you to be prepared if this is mere hopes too, not to be disappointed. That is my only reason for intending to keep it from you — that is to save you any more disappointment. Here it is at last. I was called to the Main Station again yesterday about my transfer. I feel sure that I will get it now.

Sunday morning 8:30

    I was interrupted for chow and had to wash my clothes after chow. I will now finish writing to you. They told me at the main station that I would be notified sometime this next week when my transportation papers were fixed up. So that sounds like I am to get back sometime yet. I really think I would have been back already if it had not been for the Grippe. They devoted all time and energy to check that and so other things were delayed. They tell me that 150,000 navy men are to be allowed to go back to school. It might be a week or two even yet but I think now I am sure of the transfer. (I am not telling you to keep you from writing again but I hope I will really be back this next week.) They have so many applications that it takes some time to get it all fixed up. Of course it may fall through yet but they just the same as told me Friday that the transfer is granted. But you know I thought I was going to the Pier once. I was told on Saturday night to get bag and baggage to go out on Sunday morning at 8 A.M. Then I did not get to go. It might be the same way again but something tells me that I will get back. If I get back I get my transportation, tuition, board, and thirty dollars per month. So if I get it I think it is a great opportunity to get my education and my greatest hope of all is that I will also have something to help you too. Of the thirty dollars per month I ought to be able to help you too if you will let me. I guess six dollars will be taken out of it for insurance each month. I know you couldn't have any excuse for not taking it if I am going to school too at the same time. I guess you get tired of me offering help and never doing anything, but I haven't gotten anything yet. I have been here three months almost and have only drawn thirty dollars. But I am supposed to draw each month from now on. I just got my pay number last month. Nothing would give me more pleasure than to help you some so that you wouldn't have to work so hard. You asked me if you should give up your outside work. I would hate for you to have to give it up for I know how much you like it but if you have too much I believe it would be best to give up something for you can't afford to do too much and risk your health. That is worth more to you than all else in the world. Really I don't know how to advise you. I think you know best and do as you think best. I hope to be back in the near future. If I get back perhaps I can help you in some way. I know you can help me just by getting to see you once in a while.

Well, I have told you enough again to disappoint you more than ever if I do not get back. It is not sure yet but I feel most sure now that I will be back in a week or so. I hope if I do get back that I don't have to go to State. I don't see the idea anyway of sending them over there. They are giving army drill now in the navy. The same rules apply to both army and navy in the matter of camp training. Seamanship can only be learned on board ship. So I do not see that a naval unit is necessary. The authorities here did not ask me if Georgetown has a naval unit but asked if there was a military unit. If they send us back knowing that there is no naval unit I can't see the idea of sending us to State. They are even sending some back to High School. I am beginning to believe the war may be over soon. The news in the paper this morning was so good. Then they are sending so many back to school both from the army and navy. All the fellows here seem to be afraid the war will end before they see any service. I hope it does. I would love to see service too. I would love to go to France as well as anybody but I would much rather not go if the war will end. When the papers came in this morning and the fellows saw the headlines, "Germany Asks Peace," it was almost a mob scene in the barracks. Everybody was yelling and talking. Of course they all knew that the war was not over but they talked as if it were. All of them began talking of what they would do as soon as they get home. Some were offering to sell their suits (uniforms). We all had a regular jubalee [sic]. My but this would be a happy world if peace could reign again. All the Jackies pretend to outsiders that they like the navy. But most all of them like about like I do. You know about how that is from the way I write. I am just like the others. I tell everybody that I like it fine (everybody but you). So if I come back don't be shocked if you hear me say the navy is the finest place on Earth. We are really forced to give that impression to outsiders. And really there are good features about it but it doesn't suit me when the war is over.

Yesterday we didn't do a thing all day. I read until late yesterday afternoon. The day before was a big day. Secretary of the navy Daniels was here. They called a special review for his honour. He made a big speech. All the men on the station were assembled. Believe me there was some crowd. I was so far back that I couldn't hear a word he said, but I got to see him as he and Capt Moffett drove past in a big machine. I was lucky I had a pass to go to Main Station. So I got to ride over in a bus. The others had to march over. It was about an eight mile walk there and back. I also got out of cleaning up the barracks. I got back at six o'clock. The others got back at 7:30.

Well we are still under quarantine, and there is little telling when we will get out although there are few new cases of influenza now. I think we will be given liberty next week.

Hello, I have just gotten back from church. This is the first time we have had church for three Sundays. We had to fall in for Bible class about 9:30, then church. It is after 11:30 now and chow at 12. We have to take a hike this afternoon of about eight or ten miles I guess. They had a hike yesterday. They gave us the privilege of going or staying here. Nobody hardly went. So to-day it is compulsory. I do not know what time we will start. It is getting cold again to-day. It looks and feels like snow.

Well, I am amused somewhat at you saying "Slip" Adkins is reserved. I thought he was everything else but not reserved. Say, you are right in thinking him a gentleman but when you become better acquainted with him you will find he is not reserved, by any means. And I can tell your girl friend that she will have trouble keeping ahead in math class that Elmer is in, or any other class as to that matter. He is one of the best students I know. Mr. Adkins had a brother in G.C. several years ago. He is a preacher. He was pastor of Helen Saunder's home church once. I saw him once last year and he was complimenting Helen very much and asked if I knew her. If I know Slip, I don't think he will ever make a preacher. I am anxious to know if he is a T.θ.K. If he joined Cicero I will lick him. I don't think I ever talked to him very much about Society, but I know I have told him everything else about G.C. — even you as I expect you will find out if he gets acquainted with you. Well, well, here goes the bugle again. It is medical inspection this time.

5 p.m. I will try to finish now. I have just got back from a ten mile hike. Gee but we had some fun. I had the best time I have had since here. About 400 of us went out to a big farm. The owner of it is president or manager of Armour + Co. So you have an idea about what kind

of place it is. They told us to come in and make ourselves at home. The lady said the house, garden, orchard, and farm was free to us. We went in and made ourselves at home. I made myself comfortable or rather uncomfortable in the orchard and garden. I never ate so many apples hickory nuts and strawberries in my life. Those were the first strawberries I ever ate in October. They sure were good. And we ate grapes too. I never saw so many apples. Believe me 400 sailors ate some of them too. They had swings and seats, tennis court and a big Victrola. I did not go in the house. It looked to [sic] nice for me. It did not look like home. So I went to the barn. It was most like a mansion. The fellows sure went all over the place from the cellar to the top of the windmill. I never knew what the large sailor's blouse was good for until this afternoon. They make a fine sack to carry apples in. This is visitors day and as we came back the folks all along the way after we got in camp kept smiling and saying, "They surely get plenty of chow. They have such large stomachs." The lady told us to take all the apples we could carry. So we took them to accommodate the lady. When we left she told us we were welcome anytime we would come out. We started at 12:30 and got back at 5 P.M. I guess we stayed over an hour at the farm. We did not have to go on this hike to-day but I volunteered and am not sorry that I did. We took our time going out and back. We did not have to keep step. So I was not tired at all when I got back. Before I came here I couldn't hardly have walked eight or ten miles. Now it doesn't make me tired at all. I guess we average much more walking than that every day. I know I am always much tireder when I drill, we did not take guns to-day, only belts and canteens. Well, I guess I have about exceeded the postage limit this time sure enough. I hope I will get to see you soon. Of course even yet I may not get to come back but I feel almost sure now that I will. I might not get my papers fixed up even now for a week or two. Everything is so slow in the navy. There are so many to be taken care of. We have to stand in line for half an hour even to get a drink in the navy. I guess I get in too big a hurry when I want to see you as bad as I do now. Gee wouldn't it be great if we can be together again this year or just for a time at school or even if I have to go to state, I could see you most ever week anyway. That would be oftener than I could call I guess.

    I could rave on all day but I guess you will be tired before you get through this now. If you have time to write don't put it off expecting me for I may not come. If you don't have time and are tired don't write till you feel like it. If I don't see you be good and don't be too disappointed.

With the most of love, Elliott

OCTOBER 6, 1918

Elma is in high spirits as she writes one of her "giddy" letters. This is the first letter where she mentions the flu, but she seems more interested in telling about other incidents. At dinner, Mrs. McFerran announced that the girls were not to leave campus for the rest of the day because several of the boys and two girls had developed symptoms of the flu.

Rucker Hall

Sunday–1 P.M.

Dear Elliott:

I will start your letter now but I guess I'll be interrupted before very long for dinner — in fact, I almost hope I will 'cause we had eggs for breakfast and you know about how much I love 'em — it might be compared to my love to Miss Mabley.

I have just heaps to tell you and sceercely know where to begin at. 1st

— June is here — she came last night and brought her sister to school. She is going to spend a few days of her vacation here before going back to her work in the Bank. She is crazy about her job and I'm thinking about going up there in the mountains and work this summer. What do you think about it?

Well, the Tigers put up their first fight yesterday afternoon, when they met the Camp Buell team of Lexington. My! I say they brushed them away — 32 to 0 in favor of G.C. But the funniest thing happened when I breezed out there about 3:30 o'clock and seats being greatly in demand, I happened to drop down by a very distinguished personage — none other than Gov Carter of Lawrenceburg. We managed to stir up quite an enthusiastic conversation but I will relate only the most interesting part of it. Coach Thomasson sent out Gene Martin in the 2nd or 3rd quarter and as he was going on the field, the Gov asked me his name. When I told him Martin he inquired if it was the one who debated at Danville. I explained to him that this didn't happen to be the one, then he proceeded to tell me that he was one of the judges and that Cranfill + Martin represented Georgetown. He added very earnestly that he considered Cranfill a splendid debater. My little heart just went flippity flop and although I longed to say a lot of nice things about you, I merely told him that Georgetown was very proud of you.

Say, didn't your ears burn during all that discussion?

Oh! Let me tell you a little Rucker Hall gossip. Excitement was abroad in G.C. last night between eleven and twelve o'clock. Some girl who chanced to be gazing out of her window spyed two boys sitting on the ground beneath our window. She immediately hastened to tell us about it. There were a bunch of girls already in our room, so we turned out the light and crowded around the windows for to see all that might happen. Soon they began to move slowly around and just then a little note went floating down from some higher region. Of course it was impossible to know from whence it came. The next thing I knew — a little rock swatted me on the elbow and one sang by Blanche's ear — landing safely in the middle of our room. Well, it was easy enough to understand the purpose of these little weapons of war — our presence was interfering with the proceedings so we withdrew for a few minutes then upon our second observation we saw a rope being gently lowered from a window above. Just at this point, Mrs. McFerran was informed and all our excitement ended in a very prosaic fashion. Talk about sceered freshmen — we had a bunch of them. They felt sure it must be some desperadoes who had no other motive than to steal them away before ever the day should dawn again. At least we succeeded in calming these young inexperienced children and peace was beginning to reign once more — when! Lo some drunk men came along, cussing + swearin' something awful. Confusion sprang up again + it was early in the morning before our weary eyelids closed in slumber. That explains why I went to sleep in church this morning.

3 o'clock I have had my dinner now and am all settled down here in my room, for goodness knows how long. Mrs. Mac announced at the table that Dr. Adams had requested that we do not leave the campus any more to-day as several of the boys are sick and have symptoms of Spanish Influ. Two girls are also threatened with it. We are wondering if we will have classes to-morrow. I wish I knew so I would know whether to study or not.

I'm awful sorry you had to wait so long before hearing from me — hope you got my letter yesterday all O.K. I started this week's Georgetonian to you but it may lose out before it gets there. It will come nearer telling you the college gossip than I could. A bunch of girls have been in here, just scared to death about the Spanish Influenza. Several of the Freshman are just sure they are going to take it and die. All of them have discovered some pain or other since the announcement at dinner. Blanche predicts about twelve cases in the Hall before night.

I know you are tired of this raving for really raving is all I have done in this little epistle. This would be the mostest ideal day to take a nice long strole [sic] with you but instead of doing anything so delightful, I guess I shall have to take it out in dreaming. Wouldn't it be a terrible old world if people couldn't dream? Perhaps some day our dreams will come true, but in the meantime, we must be contented to perform the monotonous tasks of every day altho' many times they may seem entirely worthless. We can never achieve great things except thru faithfulness to little duties. With lots of love,

From The Little Girl

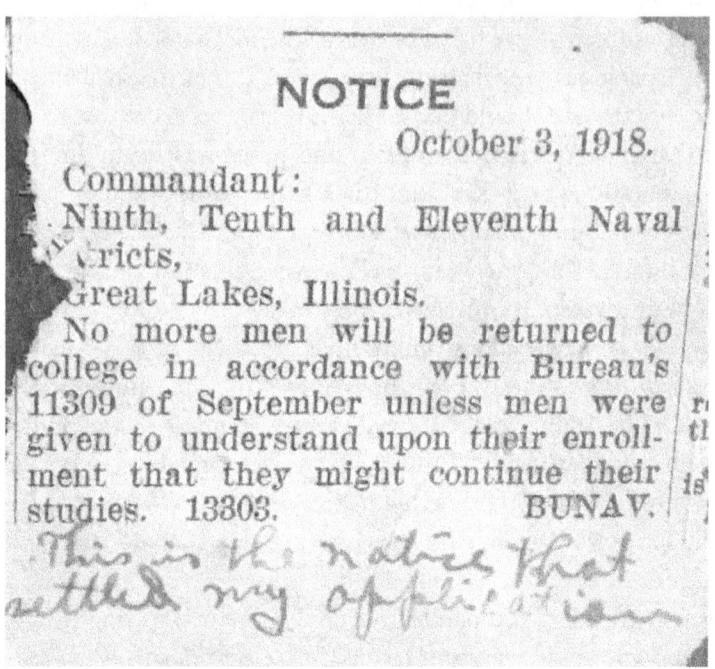

OCTOBER 9, 1918

Elliott finally has definite news about his transfer. No more men will be returned to college, so he is out of luck. He is sorry he told Elma his prospects looked good because he knows she will be disappointed again. He feels he has only himself to blame for asking "that fool company commander" first instead of going straight to headquarters when he got Dr. Adams' letter of recommendation. The quarantine has been removed.

Wednesday night
 My dear "Little Girl:"
 I at last have definite news about my transfer. I am out of luck. I wrote to you on Sunday night and Monday morning an official notice

came out in the Bulletin, the Station paper, that no more men would be returned to college. So there is no more hope that I get back to school unless the war is over. It looks now like the war might be over soon. I was disappointed again but I am used to it now. I wished I had not written that my prospect of returning was good. I know you will be disappointed again when there was really no occasion for it if I had just not written as I did and waited till I knew for sure. It is that way in the navy. One order may be given and at any time an order just contrary will be given. I don't want you to feel too badly about it. It really was my fault. If I had gone on to headquarters when I got Dr. Adam's letter and not asked that fool company commander I would have been in school now. I must confess I was too ignorant to know what to do. He was the cause of about a week's delay in my application, and I lost out by about a week. I learned a lesson by it however that will stay with me. I will never again put off doing a thing that I want done so long as I stay in the navy. The greatest disappointment is that I was so sure of seeing you again real soon. Now it is hard to tell when I will get to see you. But it is alright. The war will be over some day. Then I will be back to see you. And perhaps I may get a furlough sometime. And I have great hopes that it may be soon. In a way it will be great to stay in the service till the war is over and come back with all the other fellows who are away from their sweethearts. I really believe you will feel prouder of me if I stay, and come back when the war is over than if I should come back to school and that is a consolation to me. If I stay here there will never be any reason for anyone to call me a slacker. Some poor ignoramus might say we were trying to get out of the war by a pretense of being of greater usefulness after completing our education. You know I don't feel that way about it. I really think it requires more patriotism for a fellow to stay in school now than for him to join the army and fight. I also believe he is doing a greater service for his country if he will stay in school. It is for that reason that I put in my application. That is the only reason I would come back to school. But every body don't [sic] think that way. I have heard several in this regiment say that it was only a slacker who would go back to school. It was such a good chance too, to get my education. A fellow couldn't ask better, but the opportunity is gone and I have no one to blame but myself and no one to disappoint by it but you and myself.

Well our quarantine was removed to-day. There is great rejoicing in camp to-night. It is just a month now since we have heard the shore call on the bugle until to-night. It did sound good to hear it once more. Second class seamen can't get out except on Saturday or Sunday. So I will not get out till then. I get liberty on Sunday. I think I will go to church again at Waukegan, if nothing happens.

A good Baptist friend of mine just now interrupted me to give me a big piece of chocolate cake which he got from home. My but it was fine. His name is Kay from Missouri. He and I are going on liberty together Sun. I also got a Ky friend of mine, Mr. Cook, to take some kodak[4] pictures for me this afternoon. If they are any good, do you have any idea who they are for? They are very military or were intended to be. You may not like them. Mr. Cook is from western Ky. Says he knows where Franklin is, has been there. He is a graduate of Vanderbilt. He has a friend at G.C. he tells me, a Mr. Flannery, Flannigan, or something like that. You may have met him by this time. Say it is very nice of you to send me the Georgetonian. I haven't gotten it yet but guess I will. It will be great to read one again. I have been intending to subscribe for it but I guess I am apt to move at any time and then I wouldn't get it.

"Little girl" I have gotten things fixed up now so that I can send you what money I have to spare and so I am going to send you some right away (perhaps about 20th this month) as soon as I get it fixed up. So if you get an insured or special delivery some of these days you will know what it is. I am telling you this because I thought perhaps you wouldn't want anybody to know that I send it. There is no need for anyone to know it except you and me unless you want them to know it. I don't want you to write back that you don't want to accept it for it will only be a pleasure to me to let you have it and I know you need it — what little I can send — if you are working 7 1/2 hours or five hours as you said you were going to. Of course I can't send you very much as I don't get very much, but I would rather you use what little I get than anybody on earth. My dad doesn't need it. And if I ever get a chance to go to school I can get what I want from him. There is nothing I can do with it here except waste it as will be the case if I carry it about with me. Or I am apt to get it stolen. Somebody loses money every day. If they ever catch me off guard or if the rogues suspect me having money I am apt to lose it. I owed some money as I told you. I bought a bond the other day and signed it over to them. The payments came out of my wages each month for ten months. I was expecting to pay it all off right away is why I told you that I couldn't help you any before Xmas. I don't know how much I will be able to send you but I hope it will be enough each month so you won't have to give up any of your outside work. If I can help you enough I hope you will give up some of your office work. Little girl I hope you don't think I am offering what little help I can give because I think you couldn't get it O.K. I am asking it because I love you and want to see you through college without working so hard as you did last spring in so much as I am able to help you. I hope I will be able to get a higher rating soon. Then I will be able to help you more. I have written as though I was about to bestow a fortune, but not by any means.

Well, I really think you would enjoy working in the mountains for a summer. I know I would. I didn't know whether to take it seriously or not, whether or not you really are thinking of working next summer up there. Does June look as she used to? I would love to see her.

I am afraid you told Mr. Carter your feeling about me rather than the general opinion of G.C. He really is a good friend of mine or else I am deceived in him. He pretends to be at least. So if he was saying nice things of me I am afraid he expects too much of me.

I went on review again to-day. Our company was about the best in the regiment again to-day. Our drill exercise was almost perfect but not because I was in it by any means.

We got news here Sunday night that the war was over. I had just finished my letter to you and started to mail it when the news came in.

In ten minutes the whole camp was in an uproar. Everybody was yelling. The band was playing and everybody was in a terrible jubilee. The report was that Germany and Austria both had submitted to President Wilson's peace terms. Assembly was blown and the regimental commander made us a speech saying that it might all be a rumor and for us all to go in and go to bed and wait for definite news before further celebrations. We all went in and to bed. About the time we all got into our hammocks assembly blew again. We all dressed and rushed to headquarters. The commander told us that definite news had come in from Chicago that the report was true. That an armistice was signed, a crushing defeat had been dealt upon the Germans on the Western front, and that peace negotiations would be entered upon immediately. So you can imagine what followed until about 11:30. Then there was a blue looking bunch next morning when the paper came out, although there was really good news. I sure will be glad when we can celebrate peace again.

It is time all little sailors were in bed so I must stop.

With love, Elliott

~

OCTOBER 11, 1918

Elma says she is proud of Elliott for being so brave in the face of such disappointment, and she thanks him for his offer to send money to help with expenses. The school has been closed for a week, with about sixty cases of flu among the boys and twenty among the girls. Elliott's friend from Sinai was carried to the hospital, threatened with pneumonia. The president, vice president, and dean of the college and their wives are working in the dorms to care for the students who are sick. Students who are well are devoting their time to "Red Cross work" and getting very little sleep.

Friday Afternoon

Dearest Elliott:

I just know you have the sweetest spirit of anyone in the world. I could read between the lines of your letter I got to-day and everything spelled disappointment but not bitter disappointment — it was brave disappointment. I just wished I could put my arms around your neck and tell you how proud I am of my brave sailor boy. I can't refuse to accept your offer of help any longer if it will really give you pleasure. It is a hard struggle for me and every little bit will help out so much, but please don't deprive yourself of every bit of spending money. You are human like other boys in some respects and I know you like to have a good time once in a while and it is impossible without a little extra money.

I guess I had as well tell you about the conditions here. School has been closed since Monday and there are about 60 cases of "Flu" among the boys and 20 among the girls. Several of the boys are very sick — threatened with pneumonia. Elmer Adkins is one of them. He was one of the first to take it and was carried to the city hospital. They called his people Wednesday morning and I haven't been able to hear from him since. It is impossible to get any help of any kind either nurses or cooks so we who are well are devoting all our time to regular Red Cross work.[5] Dr. Adams and Mrs. Adams have charge of the boys in Pawling Hall, Prof. and Mrs. Hill at Old Sem and Dr. Mitchell at the Jameson House. It is where the Taylors lived last year and has been turned into a dormitory this year. Lieut. Harrington has detailed certain boys to assist at these various places. Walter Jackson nursed the boys at the Jameson House for 4 days with only 8 hrs sleep. Yesterday he keeled over and it is reported to-day that he has a very serious case of it. We girls have been taking care of the 20 girls here and also helped prepare the meals for those who are sick at each of the dormitories. Blanche and I got 3 hrs sleep last night, after a hard day yesterday. So many of the girls have gone home that we who are left have quite a responsibility. I helped prepare the suppers here in Rucker Hall last night then went over to Pawling and washed dishes for about an hour, came back to my patients and got in bed at 12. At 3 Blanche and I were called out to take Dr. Moore and Beulah Rusks' places so they could go to see about a boy who was thought to be worse. Besides all this I worked 2 1/2 hrs in the Office this A.M. I got in a little nap this afternoon and am feeling quite spry again. Poor Blanche never stops a minute, and she has all the symptoms of the "Flu." I'm afraid she will do like Jackson and be sick sure enough. I haven't thought about feeling tired for I thought you might come at any time and that helped me along so much, but when I got your letter to-day I at once realized I had nothing to look forward to — I mean definitely — That's alright for God knows what is best for us. I'm praying and hoping that the war will soon be over. I'll try to let you hear from me often for fear you might be a little worried about me taking the "Flu." With the most of love,

Elma

P.S. I will send you the Georgetonian each week.

OCTOBER 13, 1918

Elma is in one of her blue moods, and her roommate Blanche is having "one of those awful despondent spells when she wishes she was dead and all that stuff." Mrs. McFerron has asked them to give up their room for two girls who are getting over the flu and whose rooms are being fumigated. Elma is also tired from working all day in the office and tells about an incident with Arthur Freeman that made her "sure nuff mad."

LOVE LETTERS

Pawling Hall

Dearest "Sailor Boy:"

The calendar says this is Sunday night, but otherwise I would never know it. We have had no church service of any kind to-day and have worked like mad all the day except for a little while this afternoon when Blanche and I slipped off and went down to Old Sem to see Beulah Porter. She is living down there this year with Mrs. Lowe. We were seeking excitement and we did find a big bunch of folks down in the parlor playing and singing. There were several boys but they were all Freshmen except Stumpy and Chocolate Snyder.

Oh! Let me tell you something awful, terrible, dreadful, unbelievable — but nevertheless true — Blanche and I have turned out to be thieves. Really I hadn't stolen anything since Sophy and I made raids on Grandma Doty's pear tree — until to-day. After we had finished serving the sick girls — we dived into the ice-cream freezer, got us two big saucers of pineapple ice cream and sneaked away off on the back campus and et it, we did. Then, when it was all gone we still had a longing for some more so we creeped back to the place where the freezer once stood but lo! It had vanished. While we were seeking it, we found a basket of apples and they looked so nice and juicy that we tuck [sic] us one apiece.[6] Was that very awful to do on the Sabbath? I hope you don't think so for I have something worse than that to tell about. Oh it's a whole heaps worse for real live men are concerned in this next wild adventure. The time was just after supper, the place was the back porch of Rucker Hall, the characters were three young freshmen, Blanche, and I. One of the young gentlemen is alarmingly distinguished. He is none other than the son of the Gov of Porto Rico [sic] — in other words Mr. Holmes Yager. This fine personage appeared down in the kitchen while we were preparing the suppers and behold! When he entered, the servants fell upon their knees before him (so to speak). After all the sick folks had been fed — Blanche swiped a big saucer of gelatine and we were standing on the back porch eating when Mr. Yager and a Mr. Bromley came up with a long hungry look on 'em and we proceeded to feed them. I might say by way of explanation that these young gentlemen had come to get some ice for Pawling Hall — but it took them about half an hour to get it. When the saucer of gelatine had been devoured Mr. Yager went in the kitchen and got a great big saucer full and we all ate out of that same saucer. If I catch the "Flu," I'll be bound to say that's where I got it — won't I? I was strolling thru the hall a few minutes ago and Miss Armstrong snatched me into her room and axed me if I would take some grapes to the "Fluenza" girls for her and I told her how much delighted I would be to do it. After the task was completed she asked me to sit down and chat for awhile but I told her I had to come home and write a letter and what do you think she said? Well, it was this: "Give him by best regards." So these they are.

I'm so much afraid you are going to think I am wild and wooley tonight, but you see hospital duty naturally has this kind of effect on me.

Really, I started to write to you this afternoon and I just wanted to see you so bad that I was afraid to write for fear it would be a blue letter so I thought over the only Sunday we ever spent together and dreamed of the time when all our Sundays would be spent to-gether. It looks now like that time might not have to be so far off after all. I get so impatient to see you sometimes that our separation seems like an eternity. If you had gotten to come back to school you would not have had to go to State for I was talking to Duvall yesterday and he said he had just received orders to stay here. Don't feel too bad about missing your transfer for I know it will all work out alright in the end.

I got a letter from home yesterday pleading with me to come home, but as I have stayed with the "Flu" this long and not taken it I think I shall stay on. State has been given two more weeks and I have heard rumors of us getting some more but I can't help feeling rather doubtful about it. It was announced that school would begin Tues, but I'm sure half the folks will not be well by that time and the rest of us are too tired to get down to studying. I haven't been able to hear from Adkins only in a general way and that is they said they were all getting along O.K. If he had been worse I am sure I would have heard. The only real dangerous case is a boy out in town named Oldham. He is not expected to live. I guess you knew that the State Board of Health of Kentucky had ordered all schools, churches, and picture shows closed until the epidemic could be checked. That explains why we had no church to-day.

I hope you and your friend got to go to Waukegan to-day. If it was as pretty there as it was here, it was some grand day — — My! Don't I wish I could spend one such day with you in such a spot as you have described Waukegan to be. It seems strange that some people are permitted to be to-gether all the time and others have to be separated all the time. There are Viola Beagle and Bill Bauer, who are scarcely ever separated. He had the "Flu" and she went down to Old Sem and spent the day with him last Sunday so they say. But that isn't so strange when Mrs. Beagle already calls him "son."

Oh! A girl came in just then and told us some startling news. Said President Wilson had ordered all schools closed for an indefinite time. We're hoping that this may be true.

Blanche and I have a terrible silly spell and I giggle awhile between each word. I'll try to get to be a little more sensible before I try to write again. I'm afraid you don't love silly letters like you do sensible ones. But you know me and you know it takes all kinds of moods for me so if you expect to love me at all you'll have to love me when I'm foolish.

With heaps of love,
From your giggling "little girl."

OCTOBER 13, 1918

Elliott has had trouble sleeping since receiving word that his brother Isaac is sick with pneumonia at Camp Meade, Maryland. But he is proud to report that his company was chosen to march in the Liberty Loan parade in Chicago and their picture was on the front page of the paper.

Dear Elma:

I have just been reading since twelve o'clock. I almost fell asleep. I couldn't read any more and so I will try writing to you. So long as I am writing to you I am sure I will not become sleepy. I was on guard last night after an afternoon of hard though pleasant work. I stood guard from eleven to one. Then I have been somewhat anxious about my brother [Isaac] who is seriously ill at Camp Meade Md, with pneumonia. I couldn't sleep very well for the last two or three nights on that account. I just got the news from home on tenth that he is ill. I haven't heard anymore since. Perhaps I have been unduly alarmed. I hope I have.

I said I had hard work altho it was pleasant. Our company was choosen [sic] to go to Chicago yesterday for [a] parade in behalf of the Liberty Loan drive. About 5,000 Jackies marched down there in the parade. I never saw so many people in my life. It was a nice little trip and quite an honour for the company that it was selected as one for the parade. Only the best companies on the station were selected. We marched all over Chicago it seemed. Secretary McAdoo was there and Teddy Roosevelt. It made me feel fine to be in the company marching down the street in company front [sic] and all the crowd cheering. We were leading the parade. It started at one o'clock and lasted until five. So you have an idea as to the size of it. There was a band of 500 pieces. The newspapers had photographers taking pictures of the parade. This morning when I bought a Sunday paper what do you think! There was our company in a big picture on the front page. The commander told us when we got back that our company was best in the parade. So the paper proved it by putting the picture in. I cut the picture out and stuck it in my ditty box. If I think of it I will stick it in my next letter, so you can see how we looked. You can't recognize me among so many but you will just have to take my word for it that I am in it. We could only recognize one or two in the company. Then we knew that it was "us" because of the position and we were able to recognize the commander.

I am out on liberty again. It seems like I had just escaped prison. Just think four weeks since I have been out of camp. I came up here to go to church to-night. I am somewhat afraid there won't be any for the "Y" and all public places are ordered to be closed by the state board of health due to the influenza epidemic. I do not know whether church will be open or not. I rather think it will however. Everything seems rather dull round here this afternoon. Not many folks out.

Oh yes, I have some "great" news for you. I just weighed a little while ago. I weighed 173 pounds. I guess you wouldn't know me now, I am so big. I just weighed 146 when I enlisted.

I went over to Main Station the other day to register so as to be able to vote in the coming [midterm] election (by mail) and I saw a fellow from Ky. He said he was from Shelby County and knows all the Shelby bunch at G.C. He knows Mary Anna Beard. He said he went with her this summer. Can you imagine that? (By the way he knows Gene Martin). Are you surprised that he should? I talked with him quite a bit but I have already forgotten his name. He knew Paul and Mary Thompson, Ralph Henderson, Roy Martin, and all those folks. I saw a good many from Ky that afternoon, but nobody that I knew. There are five Kentuckians in my company.

Well, little girl the news this morning looks like the war might be over soon. If the Germans agree to accept our own terms I can't see anything to prevent the coming of peace soon. This winter anyway. I can't figure out any way for the Germans to work a trick if they really do what we ask by evacuating conquered territory. The German note seems to mean to me that they are ready to evacuate. Everytime I begin to write to you I can't help but think all the time of the time when I can come back and be near enough that I can see you when I want to. Elma I never really knew how to appreciate you and your love for me until I left you and have been up here and see the type of women that the sailors associate with and that are continually round the camp. It is the most disgusting sight to me that I have ever seen to see the men and women carry on as they do round the station. It makes one almost feel that there are no decent folks in existence. Then when I think of you and know that you really love me I am the happiest fellow on the station I believe. It seems funny to see the way the sailors act and then to hear them talk. It seems to be their pride to talk of the time they can go back home when the war is over to the girl they love. The majority of fellows will tell you about and seem to delight in talking about their sweethearts. Then they go to Chicago and these towns here and carry on in a way that seems to me they couldn't go back and claim the love of any respectable girl. Of course that is not true of all by any means, but I really believe it is true of a majority. I can't help but ask every day what will be the real effect upon the morals of future generations due to war conditions. It may be that I am becoming pessimistic but I am afraid ideals will be lowered due to war conditions and environments of training camps. It will certainly be up to those of high ideals to do some active service when this war is over. When I am in better moods I love to think of the opportunity I will have to try to do good when the war is over.

Well my friend seems to be anxious to go out someplace so I will stop this time. Little girl don't feel disappointed because I did not get to come back to school. It is a great experience to be here. I am getting experience that will benefit me all my life.

With most of love,
Elliott

P.S. I have been wondering if school has been dismissed yet. You were saying that you thought it might be. E.C.

~

OCTOBER 14, 1918

Elma is in one of her blue moods, and her roommate Blanche is having "one of those awful despondent spells when she wishes she was dead and all that stuff." Mrs. McFerron has asked them to give up their room for two girls who are getting over the flu and whose rooms are being fumigated. She is also tired from working all day in the office and tells about an incident with Arthur Freeman that made her "sure nuff mad."

Monday Night
Dearest Elliott:

I guess you'll think I'm writing rather often, but I'm so lonesome to-night that I feel like I must have a little chat with you. Blanche is just the opposite to what she was last night. She has one of those awful despondent spells when she wishes that she was dead and all that stuff — Gee! But she makes me feel miserable when she begins to weep and wail around. To add to the misery of the situation, we have been driven from our room to one that has neither sheets or pillow cases and only a little cover. Mrs. McFerran wanted ours for two girls who are just getting over the "Flu" and whose rooms are being fumagated [sic]. I know I shouldn't complain for I have an idea that you are sleeping in far less comfortable surroundings all the time. I guess I'm a wee bit tired 'cause I've worked eight hours to-day in the office. School doesn't begin until day after to-morrow. I'm hoping something will happen to put it off a little longer. I don't believe I want to go back to school at all.

B'lieve I'll quit school and run off and do something wild. What would you say if I should? Oh! I know you wouldn't care — very much — especially after I tell you what I have done to-day. I walked all the way from the Chapel Building to the Post Office with Robin D. Martin. You see Jessie Beagle was sick in bed with the "Flu" and you were way off at Great Lakes so we thought as how we'd just walk along side by each. Then I had an awful lot of Office mail which he kindly offered to take for me — and what an awful time he did have. When an officer came breezing along he spilled all the mail in a desperate effort to salute. It was terrible funny but I dared not laugh — much.

Mad! My! I was sure nuff mad this afternoon. Long distance called for "Dutch" Lehnard. I went out to get someone to call him to the phone and spied Arthur Freeman standing on the porch of Pawling Hall talking to Holly Stevenson so I axed him if he would like to make himself useful as well as ornamental. He says yes and comes marching in and up to me. Since no one was around he proceeds to pat me gently on the cheek. Fire and brimstone! It made me so mad!! I had almost as soon had a scorpion touch me. I would have probably boxed his young jaws, if I had not been afraid of alarmin' Dr. Adams. Believe me, he didn't try it anymore.....You know he always was the biggest fool anybody could find, but since he has gotten a faded uniform he thinks he can do very much as he pleases but I have an idea he will learn a lesson or two if he fools around me.

I don't wonder in the least at you boys having no confidence in girls. I'll agree with you that the majority of them are fickle as the day is long.

How I long for the time when I shall not have to fight the world alone. It is such a hard hard battle with so many temptations. It takes a powerful strong will to go through. I know you are strong for you have told me enough to show that you are, and I believe I am fairly strong so to-gether we would be doubly strong, wouldn't we?

Several times you have asked me if you might say "our dreams." If you love me — as I love you — it is perfectly proper to say our. For my part, I can't think in any other terms. It seems so natural now for me to take you into consideration in everything I do, and I believe you feel the same way about it. I sometimes fear that you have doubts and if you do, I hope you will tell me. We want to be always perfectly frank about our feelings and I want you to feel free to tell me everything that you would like to. That is the way I feel toward you and if you do not feel that way, please tell me.

With lots of love, Elma

OCTOBER 15, 1918

Elma says she has been blessed that neither she nor her folks have been sick yet, and she prays that Elliott's brother will recover. Blanche is still despondent and Elma is out of patience with her. She says it reminds her of when her mother used to have such periods of despondency.

Tuesday Night
Dearest Elliott:
Just a note to tell you how sorry I was to hear about your brother being so sick. I do hope that you have had news that he is better before this. It certainly is a distressing time now. So many of the girls have been worried because of sickness at home. I feel like I have been greatly blessed in that neither I or any of my folks have been sick as yet. Blanche still has her spell and it is even worse to-night than it was last night. I do wish I had some patience with such conduct but I have absolutely none. She would be decidedly the finest girl in school, were it not for these periods of despondency. Mother used to have them when I was growing up and now I am forced to put up with them during my college career. You won't have them, will you, when time comes for me to be with you? I know I ought to do something for Blanche, but she provokes me so that I dare not speak to her for fear I say something I shouldn't.

I went out to Prof Raglands [sic] this afternoon with Miss Iva Beard and Lelia Harris. They do have a real sweet home. Mrs. Ragland served lemonade and cake and we had a lovely time. Stayed about two hours. If you get this last week's Georgetonian which I sent you, you'll see that

Prof Rhoton has left us. The man who is to take his place hasn't arrived on the scene. At least I haven't seen him. Dr. Leigh has had the "Flu" and six of the boys in the Chemistry Department ordered $5 worth of perfectly beautiful American Beauty Roses for him. I saw them this morning before Roland [Snuggs] took them up to him.

Don't forget to send me the picture of your company. I'm so glad it is the best on the Station. Am worried to death because you're getting so fat but I guess I can stand it if you can. I believe I'm falling off. Will try to be your little girl when you come back.

I am praying that your brother will recover and that you will be kept strong and brave.

Lovingly yours, Elma

~

OCTOBER 16, 1918

> *Elliott has received good news from home that his brother is doing better. He encourages Elma to take care of herself and not work too hard or expose herself to the flu if she can help it. He tells her that her experience with Arthur Freeman is typical of a soldier's or sailor's lack of respect for women, but he had hoped she would never become acquainted with the soldier's "spirit of indecency."*

Wednesday night
Dearest Elma:

I have gotten three letters and the Georgetonian from you this week. I got one letter and the Georgetonian to-day. I am so glad when I hear from you. I just love anything you write me. The last two letters were your extremes. One very gay, the other is you disgusted and out of spirits. I know just how you feel in the latter one but it has been a long time since I have felt gay once. There is a great tendency here for me to get soured on the world and lose absolutely all confidence in humanity. Everything I see here is serious. If there ever was a true saying it is that

"War is Hell." Many times since I have been here I have been so discouraged that I just feel that life isn't worth living anyway, and I don't care what becomes of me. Then I think of the happy hours I have spent with you and so long as we love each other I can see great prospect for happiness in the future. All is pleasant then and I love to think of the time when we shall be together again. I never love to write to you when I feel so discouraged for I know it makes you discouraged too. I can tell you this experience here is teaching me the seriousness of life and I see that life is to be a battle all the way through. I always thought I had been up against the world but since I came here I find I never had met the coldness of it at all. I have always been under a Christian mother's and father's influence. I have always had their advice and council [sic]. Now I am face to face with the world all by myself. I know just how you feel. You are in the same condition (almost I must say) as I. This is the most trying time I feel for both of us. Our greatest period of temptations. If we can both conquer alone we shall be strong when we can be together. Little girl I may not really know how you feel but I think I do. But when we are really sane, and look at things properly, life for service is really worth while, and I have had plenty of evidence that there is a great God to give comfort and courage when we are out with the world since I have been here. And the greatest comfort I have is that I have a brave little girl back home whom I can love and who loves me. Of course we both feel our disappointments and discouragements, but the time has past [sic] with me when I any longer doubt you in any way or your love for me. You can rest assured of my absolute and lasting love for you but I must admit that I am very very weak myself and temptations are a thousand times more than I had at G.C. when I had you to help me. Your experience with Arthur Freeman is typical of a soldier's or sailor's conduct or sense of respect for women. It seems to be a spirit among men who are wearing the uniform to think it is their privalege [sic] to do just as their natures desire with women. (And it seems to me they do it round here.) I do not know who are to blame for it, the men or women. I always knew Freeman was more brute than human but I really thought he would show more decency than he has to you. I was really in hopes you would never become acquainted with this soldier's spirit of indecency. I know it is not your fault in any way that he acted as he did. Men of Freeman's character who have been in a military camp for a while are apt to do anything. I have become acquainted fully with such men since here. I think I can conquer the temptation myself by having you to love and to love me. Take Freeman's conduct as a matter of course. That kind of conduct is to be expected of men without honour or respect for themselves or others. If I were there I think I could teach Mr. Freeman a lesson of respect for you at least, if it became necessary. You may think that sounds different from my usual tone. I really am convinced that physical strength is about the best thing to teach some folks decency with, and now I would love to try it once as an experiment. I will tell you now that you may be surprised to find other just such men if you ever meet those who have been in a real training camp. So you can always be on your guard. There are gentlemen however in the service. Don't take it that I mean all men in the service are not gentlemen. Any real gentleman will stay or can stay a gentleman in the service but I mean if a man is inclined to be indecent he is apt to show it up when he puts on a uniform.

So all I can say is cheer up little girlie. Let's be brave as we can and do all we can to serve our God and country. Some day we can help each other. Remember there is a promise that we will not be tempted more than we are able to overcome. Let's be true to each other and live for service and we shall be rewarded. Do not ever think that I doubt you in the least. I doubt myself but not you.

You were telling me about your pleasant little walk with Rev. Martin. That is alright with me if you are not afraid of Jessie when she gets well. I would hate to hear that you have suddenly become bald headed. That would be terrible.

I must say that you and Blanche are becoming regular burglars, but I don't blame you. I think I told you once before that I have about decided there is nothing wrong about taking anything to eat, and especially ice cream.

Well, I went on liberty Sunday to go to church. All the churches are closed here. There is nothing doing at all.

Well, I have been working some of late. Have been getting up at four o'clock all this week. We have been drilling for a big parade to-day. We were on parade this afternoon from one till 5:30. We had all the drills songs and everything that we have learned besides a sham battle. It was all in behalf of the Liberty loan. The battle lasted for about 20 minutes. Believe me I got some idea of what a real battle sounds like anyway. They used cannon, rifles, machine guns, a tank and aroplanes [sic]. The uproar was enough to deafen one. It may not be long till I will be in real battles and not sham ones. I can tell you it won't be a pleasure to me to be in one either not that I am afraid but I just hate to think of taking part in such things. After the battle was over we all went to a boxing match, rather four of them. The station champions were fighting for their honour (if it can be called such).

I got those pictures the other day I am sending them. I guess they look a little bit like I do. You can tell me if they look anything like I used too [sic].

I got good news from home to-night. My brother is better. I was so uneasy about him.

You were talking about your bed being bad. Then comparing it with what I have. I hope you never have to sleep as I do. I haven't slept in a bed now for three months. It has been on the floor or in a hammock. I would much rather it was the floor all the time. But then when I compare my comforts to those of the fellows in France, I know I am lucky. I don't mind the physical hardships of military life. In fact they are easy for me. I have done harder work all my life. It is the consciousness of war and what my energies are being exerted for the mental effects that are hard.[7]

You must take care of yourself during the flu epidemic. Don't work too hard if you can help it. I love to hear that you are well and able to help those who are sick, but don't expose yourself if you can help it.

Don't get too discouraged. These are hard times and we must all be content with things as they are, and make the best of them. It looks now that the war might end soon. If it does or don't [sic] end we must try to do our best and try to be as brave and contented as possible.

It is time for taps. I will have to close this time.

With most of love, Elliott

P.S. It is rumored that we may be sent to-day up in Minn to fight forest fires. I hope we are but I think the chance is small that we go. E.C.
P.P.S. I am sticking in that cut of our company on parade. I thought perhaps you could get an idea of what the Jackies look like on parade.

∼

OCTOBER 17, 1918

> *Elma is in a lighter mood, and Blanche has recovered from her despondency. Classes are back in session and students are back to behaving like students — making fun of their professors, cutting classes, annoying Mrs. McFerran, and going on excursions into town and along the creek. Elma says she has been "unusually smart" today and has read several fine articles on the war, which she would like to talk to Elliott about. She also mentions reading a wonderful biography about an educator, Alice Freeman Palmer, who was an advocate for college education for women.*

Thursday night

Dearest Elliott:

Have been bad all day to-day. Isn't that unusual? I couldn't help it 'cause Mr. Browning ran out of work for me and I had to loaf a little bit. That inspired me to loaf some more, so Faith and I cut Bible and sat in the Library and read all the time we should have been listening to Dr. Thompson shoot theological treatise a mile over our heads. Mercy! Mercy! I 'most go mad over that subject and it worries me so 'cause I was expecting to enjoy my Bible course.

Since Prof Rhoton has gone, some fine man that favors Prof Ragland has come to take his place. We already had an assistant math teacher in the form of the prissiest little man I ever saw. He has an electric iron and presses his suit every day. He has a most awful squeaky little voice and they say the 1st time he met his class he sat for 15 minutes without uttering a sound, then said, "I believe this is the 1st time I have met the class." Well I started out to tell you about our Education Class that met this afternoon. Prof Richardson was supposed to teach us and we stayed 10 minutes and decided to leave. We knew very well that he was standing out in front of Giddings Hall talking to this prissy little Prof Kirton but we marched sedately out by his side and off across the campus. The poor man never suspicioned that it was his class filing out.

(Intermission) Blanche has just been telling me about one of Mrs. McFerran's fits that she witnessed to-night. Somebody threw a pillow in the parlor and oh! Stars and Stripes! How she riz up on her dignity. From the demonstration Blanche gave I think it must have been similar to the time she got insulted at us sitting on the porch after we got back from Church. Can you remember? Also the night when she rushed back to straighten the rug. I had such a good time this afternoon. Took a book, "Alice Freeman Palmer's Biography," which I am reading and went down back of Rucker Hall and had the best time all by myself. The book is just wonderful and I hope you will read it if you ever get a chance. Her husband[8] wrote the book and he evidently must have thought her an ideal woman. But I guess all men look on their wives that way if they love them in the right way. Much fun is made about love but wouldn't this old world be empty and void without it?

I've been unusually smart to-day, in that I read some fine articles on the war. One was by Simonds[9] in the September Review of Reviews. Another one was in the Nation. Everything seems to prophecy peace at an early date. Won't it be great!!!! I'd like to talk about that time but you said in one of your letters that you didn't like to talk about it so I will refrain from it.

Blanche and I went to town yesterday afternoon, got some eats and went out the Paris Pike till we came to the Elk Horn, then we turned to the left and followed the stream down by a slaughter house. There we watched a negro skin a beef. Then we proceeded on our way, following a spooky little path until we came to a dear little spring trickling out of the wall and some nice flat rocks on which to sit. There we settled ourselves and ate and dreamed for about two hours. During that time a canoe with two men in it passed by. They were fishing but I don't think they were much successful.

Well, dearie, the lights are out and I'm out in the hall where it's terribly chilly and Blanche's trunk isn't a very comfortable seat so I'll have to hush for this time. I do hope I get a letter from you to-morrow — With a great big good-night — and a whole lot of love.

 Elma

∼

OCTOBER 17, 1918

> *Rumors are that the sailors may be sent to Minnesota any day to fight forest fires. Smoke can already be seen at camp. Although Elliott says he would like to go, he is not sure how much use he would be fighting fires because he has a sprained ankle. Three days earlier he was standing in a marching column at the main camp, waiting for his work assignment, when a coal truck knocked him and two other fellows down.*

Thursday night
 Dearest Elma,
 I just got your note written Tuesday night. I just know you are the sweetest little girl in the world. You show your love for me in every way possible. It is so sweet of you to sympathize with me when I am worried or in trouble. I have had good news from my brother. He is better but of course he isn't out of danger yet. He is apt to get a furlough as soon as he is able to go home or at least they have been giving those sick in the navy furlough.
 I guess I did not get one of the Georgetonians as it seems you have sent me two from your letter. I sure was surprised that Prof Rhoton has resigned. He is the last "prof" I would have expected to see leave. What will you "young people" do without him? I certainly did enjoy reading the *Georgetonian*. I almost read all the ads I think. I went to a football game this afternoon. It reminded me a little bit of school life. The first thing that has resembled school since I have been here.
 Well, you say you don't like it because I am getting so fat. Don't

worry. I really don't look any larger much than when you saw me. It is my hardened physical condition that makes me weigh heavier although I do not seem larger. I asked a fellow to-day how much he thought I would weigh? He guessed me at 150 pounds. My usual weight really is about 160 or 165 pound. I had fallen off a lot when you saw me last.

There is quite a rumor to-night that we may go to Minnisota [sic] to fight fire.[10] We were told to be ready to go on ten minutes notice. I would really like to go. It would mean some unusually hard work but if we could help stop it, it would be a great service to those living in the region near the fire. It must be terrible up there. The wind has suddenly changed this afternoon. It is from the direction of the fire. I don't know how far it is from here to the fire but the smoke is so thick here on the station it seems like a heavy fog. I am afraid I wouldn't be much use fighting fire I don't expect. I got my ankle sprained the other day, about three days ago. I guess I was very lucky that I escaped getting my foot mashed off. I was standing in marching column with the Co at main station. We had been sent over on detail work. We were waiting to be assigned work. I was talking and paying no attention. All at once something struck my arm. I jumped just in time. It was a big truck load of coal. It just missed me enough to catch my heel under the fore wheel. It knocked me down and tore the heel entirely off my shoe. So you see I was quite lucky to escape with only a sprained ankle. It has been real sore but I have only missed one half days drill with it. I have been limping considerably but it is getting better now. If the truck had hit my foot an inch higher up I guess my foot would have been mashed off. I guess I was partly to blame. A fellow is supposed to watch out for himself in the navy and I will from now on, but all trafic [sic] is supposed to stop or wait for a marching column to get out of the way. Then the driver didn't even blow his horn. The truck struck two other fellows too. The others were not hurt at all. I thought the company would mob him. I think everybody in sight cursed him but me. I guess if I had really been hurt they would have thrashed him anyway. I don't think I cursed him out loud but I felt like it too. He must have been a green driver or something. But one thing sure I will watch out for my self after this.

My friend from Princeton came back yesterday from a 15 day

furlough. He had the flu. His name is Keena. He is a Presbyterian theological student. He and I go to the "Y" each morning for morning watch. We go together. There was another fellow named Wahn. He has been transferred to another camp.

Well, I am sending you a little money in this letter. It is not much but perhaps it will help you a little. I was supposed to have drawn pay this week but they say it is to be next week. I may have some more for you then. I never know how much I will get until I get it. Of course I will have to keep enough each month to have some money all the time, but I don't want any more than I need. So I will be very glad to send you what little I have to spare. It is really the greatest pleasure to me that you will accept the little bit that I can send you.

With lots of love,
Elliott

~

OCTOBER 20, 1918

Elma sincerely thanks Elliott for the money and the photos he sent. She says Elliott is the only one she can come to "with all [her] little joys and worries." She mentions the idea of service and her belief that God has work for them to do. Almost all the students have recovered from the flu and classes will soon start for real. She reports that a fellow student, Jessie Beagle, died, but it's not clear whether she died of the flu.

Sunday Afternoon
3:30 o'clock
Dearest Elliott:

I can't begin to express how much I appreciate your kindness to me. The Special Delivery came yesterday just about noon and I was so thrilled. The money will help me out so much, especially since the board has been raised to $25 a month. But dearest, please don't deny yourself too much for my sake. If I knew you would go without things that you really want and need, I would refuse at once to accept any more.

The pictures came Friday and they are just grand. Well I should say you don't look fat — not in the least. Several of the girls say you look better in uniform than in civilian clothes. It doesn't matter so much to me what you have on so long as it is you. Of course though at a time like this, the uniform looks especially good to me. Yet, I'm not half satisfied with just seeing you in a picture — I want to see you in reality. Poor little boy — you're all the time gettin' your ankle sprained. I hope it is most well now and that you are just as happy and contented as can be. I love to hear about your intimate friends, for friends are so essential to happiness. Neither this year nor last year have I had a real close girl friend. I didn't miss it so much last year when you were here with me, but I am so lonesome for one this year. It hurts me because I can't feel free with Blanche to talk over little things that naturally come into one's mind but I can't to save my life. That is the reason I write you so many little things that are of no importance whatever. You are the only person in the world now that I feel free to come to with all my little joys and worries. I never felt free to tell mother everything for she didn't always seem to sympathize with me and now since I have been away from home, I have always been careful about what I write for fear it will cause mother and father unnecessary worry. They are both old and I feel like they have had enough trouble to bear without my telling them every little thing. I just love for you to tell me everything and because of this I feel free to tell you everything that happens. You certainly have proved your love for me and I am happy in that love.

I was so glad to hear your brother was better, 'most as glad as if he had been my brother. If he should get a furlough, I wish you could come home too but — I 'spose there's nothing doin'. However, your time will come I'm sure. Let me beg you not to allow yourself to get "blue" and despondant [sic]. I know it is terribly hard to keep from it sometimes — in fact — this very day I have felt like I would love to give up school and go home. But it is only when we lose the bigger vision of Life that we fall into such moods. When our thoughts become self-centered and the idea of service is forgotten. God has a work for us to do or else we would not be here. And dear, I feel more and more like that work is to be done in China. I have often laughed when people mentioned my being a missionary but deep down in my heart I have had hidden feelings about the matter. One thing has always been uppermost in my thoughts no matter what my task has been — that was the preparation for some definite service. I believe we have always been alike in that respect.

I have been truly enjoying a day of rest. Didn't get up until 10:30. Dr. Eberhardt held services for the girls in Eupian at 11 and I went to that. And now I am spending the afternoon with you (in thought at least). It is a very pleasant way to pass off time, I find.

Jessie Beagle died yesterday afternoon. It was a shock to everyone, although she had been in very poor health since last February. I feel so sorry for Robin D. Martin. They say it is almost killing him and I know it must be for he was so devoted to her. A death is always sad but the death of a young person like Jessie, for whom so many hopes have been built seems unusually sad. Almost all of the students have recovered from the "flu" and I guess classes will turn from camouflage to the real thing once more. It seems impossible to get straightened out to work this year. I'm wondering what will be the next thing to turn things topsy turvy. Perhaps all these disturbances are naturally to be expected in a training camp although this is a very very small one. The number in this unit has been limited to 160.

I'm wondering if you were sent out to fight fire. That must be something on the order of fighting Germans. I hope you didn't go for I shouldn't think it would be very good on your sprained ankle. You've been giving me advise [sic] — now — I think it is my turn. Be real careful with that ankle — if I'm not mistaken you told me once that you had had your ankle sprained several times.

I started you a little box yesterday. If you fail to get it let me know so I can send you another one. It isn't much, but I thought perhaps you would enjoy it a wee little bit. Must close and go to see a patient of mine that got sick this afternoon. If you ever need a nurse just send for me. I'll come flyin', you bet.

Wif [sic] lots of love,
Elma

~

OCTOBER 20, 1918

Elliott describes his trip to Chicago, where there were bands playing, singers and speakers all over the city, airplanes dropping advertisements, and crowds and crowds of people. But the thing he enjoyed the most, much to his surprise, was the art museum. He encourages Elma to be as patient as possible with Blanche. Apparently, both Elma's and Elliott's mothers were "troubled" in the same way, with what Elliott refers to as "nervousness."

Sunday morning

Dear Elma:

How are you feeling this gloomy morning? Or is it gloomy in Ky? It is raining here and is real dark for day time. I am not feeling very good this morning. I have the headache. I guess I took one drink too much last night. I went to Chicago yesterday and did not get back until one thirty last night. I guess it is the loss of sleep that gives me the headache. I was up later last night than I have been since in the navy. I did not come back till my full 12 hours were up. I usually come in about eleven. We got out about three hours sooner yesterday than usual. We usually get out about one o'clock P.M. Yesterday they let us off at ten.

I had a real nice time yesterday seeing new things. There certainly was plenty of excitement. Chicago was trying to go over the top yesterday for Liberty Loan as it was the last day. Bands were playing on every street corner. There were singers and speakers all over the city. Aroplanes [sic] were dropping S.O.S. advertisements all over the city, and crowds and crowds of people. (It was most like county court day in Lawrenceburg or band concert at Franklin.) The most interesting thing I saw however was the art museum. I have always read of art and listened to speeches (and saw picture shows of art at G.C.) on art but I must confess it never interested me much. Yesterday I saw the real stuff and believe me I did enjoy it. I stayed in the art building about five hours. I believe I could stay in there all time and never become tired of seeing the different things. No use for me to try to describe any of it to you. It is something that can't be described. It is just wonderful. I would have given anything to have had you with me yesterday. I know you would have enjoyed it as much as I. If you should ever be in Chicago don't miss seeing the art museum. There were all kinds of jewelry, needlework, Oriental and Egyptian arts, Greek and Roman sculpture, paintings of all ages, bronze and silver work. I asked the guard (one guard for there were perhaps a hundred or more) the estimated value of the museum. He said it was impossible to set a value on the collection. He said there was one painting of Ennes that they had been offered $200,000. I guess I did not see one tenth the contents of the building during the time I was there, and of course what I saw was just a rapid survey. The building was immense. I did not go through near near [sic] all the rooms. I walked till

I was most tired out. Well, I guess this raving will have about the same effect on you that the same kind of talk has had on me in the past. I know now that art is something that can't be appreciated until seen. Don't get it into your head as I did that you can't appreciate art until you have seen it. Of course I don't mean to say that you don't already appreciate art, but I didn't. See?

Hello! I have been "falling in" and "falling out" for church and Bible class for the last hour or so. A new chaplain preached this morning. He was good too. The sun has come out. Now it is the most beautiful day. My head doesn't ache any more either. Do you reckon all the change has come 'cause I began to write to you? I know everything seems much pleasanter for me and everything always seems bright when I am thinking most of you or when I am writing to you.

The Y.M.C.A.'s [sic] and libraries opened again to-day. They have been closed now for six weeks. I think I shall go to the library this afternoon. There goes the bugle again. Chow! Chow! Yes I must stop to eat although I'd rather write. You don't believe it, do you? It's so anyway.

Hello again! When I went out for chow they made me come in and put on my leggins. Said I couldn't eat without them. It is so funny here. One meal they won't let us go if we have on leggins. Next time they won't let us go if we haven't them on. It all depends on how they feel. We have some time round here keeping on the uniform of the day. Well, what do you think we had apple pie for chow. They said it was pie but it must have only been samples from the size of the pieces.

I tell you I am unfortunate to-day. I can't keep my hands clean as you can tell from this paper. I have been interrupted so often that I can't keep my hands clean. I guess you wonder why I never get some stationery. I will tell you. I don't have room to keep anything hardly in the ditty box that they let us keep.[11] So in order to have room for things that I absolutely have to use in the navy I use the paper that is furnished at the different organizations. It is always handy. I know you really don't mind or at least I hope you don't. If I had any place to keep it I would get some stationery. Here I go again, have to fall in for a shot in the nose. They give us a shot every day now to prevent colds or gripp etc. It sure ought to prevent disease from the way it tastes and smells. It sure would be a crazy germ that would try to live with such environments.

In one of your last letters you said you were at Prof Ragland's and liked his home. I did too. I ate dinner there once and have been there several times. I can't admire the professor so much but what I have seen of his home it seems almost ideal to me. There seems to be such freedom or frankness and devotion among the whole family.

You were speaking of Blanche's spells of despondency. I was in hopes you would not be bothered with that this year. I mean I hoped that Blanche would not be troubled by them. It is really bad on one's spirits. I am sure Blanche can't help it. I imagine it is nervousness that causes it. My mother used to be troubled in the same way. I wouldn't know what to say to you but I think you should be as patient as possible. She might get offended if you show impatience with her and you might really loose [sic] a very good friend when you were not thinking about it or really do not mean to offend her. The least little things used to offend mother with her neighbors and sometimes it caused hard feelings on her part when I am sure no offense was intended. She was sick and perhaps it is the same with Blanche. I think Blanche is a friend that you should appreciate. She certainly doesn't seem to be of the ordinary type and she seems to be truly in love with you. So I would try to cultivate patience lest possibly there might be a chance that something come between you to injure your friendship for each other. Of course I don't think there is any danger of you offending her, but if it is really nervousness that troubles her you might offend her before you think about it when she is attacked by her spell. You asked if I would have such spells when we were together for all the time. I certainly hope not. I don't feel as if I would ever be despondent or unhappy if I had you with me. I don't think I am of a very moody disposition. It is very seldom that I change spirits. I am more or less gloomy all time, however. I often wish I could be sunny and jolly like other people but I am — well, you know me, that I stay just about the same way all time. Of course, I must say I feel gay once in a while especially in past when I was with you. Really haven't you nearly always found me in about the same spirits at all times? Truly I think I am. I may be mistaken.

Two fellows cut church to-day. The commander caught them. He made them wash all the sneeze curtains this afternoon. (I guess I better tell you what they are. They are curtains made of white cotton that hang down between each hammock to keep us from breathing each other's breaths when we sleep.) There are about 100 of them. So you see they will have quite a washing. Each one is about six feet square. I won't miss church any more. I'm telling you I won't.

Well I will stop. It is such a pretty afternoon I think I will go out for a little walk and a dream.

With most of love,
Elliott

P.S. I am sending an answer to Blanche's note if I get back in time from my walk. I have to go on guard at 5 o'clock. It is two now. E.C.

OCTOBER 22, 1918

Elliott thanks Elma for the big box of candy she sent and says he has been eating candy all day. He talks about a special review for some rear admiral and mentions that some new fellows have come into the company and changed things so they are not so good as they were; he says he feels like a rookie again and was "never so tired of doing nothing." He talks about the "funny system" for how they pay sailors and says when he gets paid again he will send what he has to spare.

Tuesday night

My dear little girl:

I got the nice big box of candy that you sent me. I got it yesterday. It certainly is good. I have been eating candy all day almost, except while drilling and on review. I was a little surprised to get the box simply because I got a letter from you yesterday morning and not a word about the box. It sure is sweet of you to send it. I gave some of it to a friend or so who have been giving me of their boxes. One of them said tell "you" that it was the best candy he ever ate. Of course he didn't know who "you" were but I told him my girl sent it. I agree with him too that [it] is the best I ever ate. The box was in such good condition too. A good many boxes that the fellows get here are all mashed up. That one was just as if it had been handed to me. I certainly thank you many many times for it.

We had a special review to-day for some rear-admiral. Every time some big guy comes here we poor "gobs" have to suffer by staging a review. I'll get back at them some day — when I get to be Admiral. They came round to-day and asked all high school graduates to step out. I don't have any idea what it was for but it may mean that we move sometime. I don't care. I never was so tired of doing nothing. I have been here now for 13 weeks about and haven't done anything since the first three weeks to learn anything new.

We have to go on review again to-morrow. In fact we have to go every Wednesday. Some new fellows have come into our company now and it is not so good as it was. They have changed us all around and I feel like a rookie again in my new place.

You were saying that you do not enjoy your Bible Class. I don't wonder at it. I like Dr. Thompson fine as a man but I don't think he is a very good teacher. It is too tiresome to listen to him. I never listened to him ten minutes in my life without being ready to fall asleep. That is the reason I did not take Bible last year. I was trying to wait for a new teacher or I was in hopes they would get a new one. I don't know why but I never could listen to him. I think I have heard you say it is the same with you even before your last letter.

You were saying the new teacher favors Prof Ragland. We have a "Y" secretary here in the fifth Reg who looks almost exactly like Rag. The first time I saw him I almost spoke to him thinking it was Rag. Prof must have almost as many likenesses as I have. When I was in Chicago the other day in the art museum a very distinguished-looking lady came up to me, stuck out her mit, and I "shaked" her hand, and she calls me "George" and wants to know how I am liking the work of my Uncle Sam. I says I beg your pardon but I think you're mistaken. When she took a second look she realized the fact. But we had quite a little talk after that. She said she had three sons and two nephews in the service. I sure do feel sorry for all the poor fellows who have been accused of favoring me since I came here.

Really, I was in hopes Mrs. "Mac" would be a little more reasonable this year (as I was gone) but I guess she will always be the same old sister so long as she stays at Rucker Hall. That's one thing I guess she is glad of this year that I am not there to mess up her rugs. It may be best that I am not there this year. If I were there I expect I would get you into trouble about "goodnight" time or when Mrs. Mac came in to fix her rugs. You know I don't 'spect I could be civilized at all if I should get to be with you again. You know how hard it always was with me after you were so good to tell me the first real good-night. Even on Monday nights now about 9:30 I often think of those dear moments when you really first showed me that you loved me. Especially the first time I asked you to kiss me you said "no" but your eyes told me that you would. That was the happiest moment of my life. Always, before that night you tried to seem as if you were unconcerned about me coming etc, but I thought even before that night that perhaps you loved me. And when I really knew you did I was so happy. I think perhaps I will try for a furlough about Christmas if I can't find an excuse before. I have a little business to see to about then that I think I can get off for. I think I will make it seem a little more necessary for me to go home than it really is. Do you think it would be wrong when I want really to see you? I think perhaps I can get a furlough about that time anyway. That's what they tell me at least. It seems like an awful long time to wait but even I might not get to come then. They do not grant furloughs much.

You said something in your letter about me not liking to talk about the time when peace will come. I must have been asleep when I wrote that for I made a mistake. That is the only happy prospect I can see. Therefore I just love to think, pray, and hope for the time when peace comes and I can be with you again. So it was a mistake when I said that. I love for you to think of that time too and for you to talk of it. So don't think that I don't like anything you may say or hope for at that time. Somehow or other I feel that perhaps peace will be signed this winter. Everything looks favorable. I sure hope it is.

You were speaking of the book you have been reading. I sure would love to read it. I may be able to get it at the library. I will try for it. You are certainly right. If a man really loves his wife or a woman he thinks she is perfect.

I have been reading of the history of the allied navy and its actions during the war. I find that the real head and commander of the allied operations is Admiral Beatty of the British navy. So it has been very interesting for me to read it. I also saw a book in the library here on the revolution in Russia written by Miss Bessie Beatty. Are they relatives of yours? You should get acquainted with them as I am. See?

I was called to headquarters to-day and given back my application to be returned to school. They refused to grant me the transfer because of the order that I was telling you about before.

I expected to get a letter from you this afternoon but did not. I guess I will get one to-morrow.

Well, I was expecting to have some more money for you this week but I was told that I would not get any pay this month. Next month they claim they will pay all that is due us. If they do I ought to draw a right respectable little bit. The way they pay us off is a funny system. Some fellows here in this Co haven't drawn a cent yet. One fellow drew $40 last month and $30 this. He enlisted just as I and at the same time. I don't understand it, but of course it is safe and I will get all that is coming to me sometime. When I draw again I will send you what I have to spare.

It's time for sailors to be in bed. So I must stop. I thank you again and again — many many times for the candy. It is so sweet of you to send it and the candy is so good. I also return your goodnight and wish I could receive a real one from you real often.

With most of love,
Elliott

OCTOBER 24, 1918

This is another of Elma's "giddy" letters, filled with free-flowing thoughts and images, composed of short paragraphs and anecdotes, with plenty of dashes and exclamation points, a sprinkling of slang and foreign phrases, lots of nicknames, and exaggerated emotions. Classes are back in session, and some students, including Blanche, have been teaching labs for professors who had the flu.

Thursday P.M.
5 o'clock
Dear Elliott:

Have just finished up a day of four classes in which the climax was reached. Got called on in Polly Science but thanks be! Happened to know it. When it comes to enduring three classes in the afternoon I almost have nerves. But poor old Blanche was a nervous wreck at noon and she has to teach Physics Lab for 4 hrs this afternoon. She just hates it too. Prof John Conn formerly known as "Chinc" Conn has been teaching one of the advanced Chemistry classes since Dr. Leigh has been ill mit der Flu. He chanced to get your address from me a few days ago.

I've been having a most delightful vacation from Office Work this week. You see it happened like this. Wee Willie has been on the firing line in the basement of the chapel building. Dan is sick and nobody else knew how to manipulate the furnace. That's how it all happened. 'Spect as how I'll be sorry when the pay day comes around but nevertheless it wasn't my fault for goodness knows I was perfectly willing to work if I had had someone to give it to me. However he has someone over to fire now and I feel myself getting down to work again in the "mawning."

I saw Mr. Adkins walking around this morning and he really spoke to me. I was so thrilled!!! But the think [sic] that worries me is that he looks like he is afraid of me. Unless something can be done, I doubt if I ever get close enough to him to gather any information which I presume he might be able to give me.

7:00 P.M. am so horribly miserable now. I am afraid I shall never be able to finish this tender epistle. I saw a girl eat 9 rolls for supper and I thought I would try to keep up with her so I most killed myself but didn't succeed in hiding but six. They say this same girl ate 14 biscuit [sic] for supper last night. Yes, she's a Freshman. Blanche says she's glad I put that last in or else you might have thought it was my roommate or Sufferin' Susie. My! We had some fine dinner to-day an extra special in the form of camouflage beans. I was in the act of partaking freely of them when lo! My eyes beheld an almost unspeakable sight — ooh! It wuz awful — a nice fat, juicy worm, a whole inch long — right in the middle of the bowl. They's what I call camouflage beans. Gee! Don't it make you hungry to hear about it? 'Spose we change the subject.

The T.θ.K.'s intended to have an open session next Saturday night but Dr. Adams has ordered all literary societies suspended pro tem. I was so sorry 'cause I had received a special invitation from Mr. Roland Snuggs. Perhaps the invitation won't get very stale before the suspencion [sic] is lifted. The boys aren't doin' a thing in the line of study this year — attend classes when the spirit moves them — but bless your life they step around when the commanding officer speaks. They have to line up in front of Rucker Hall every morning — raise the flag — call the roll, then march down to mess. This morning I heard the old officer bawl one fellow out 'cause he answered in a low voice, soon afterwards he called Coker's name — and oh! My — I believe you could have heard him at Great Lakes if you had been listening. John Conn was figuring on giving his class in Chem a test to-morrow but he offered to let them off if Coker would consent to give an hours [sic] lecture on alcohol. Coker hadn't decided to-day whether he would take him up on the proposition or not.

Well, I'm about to run out of foolishness. Did you ever hear of anything so unbelievable?

Am glad you got the box and sincerely hope it will fill your sweet tooth for a bit. I'm glad your friends enjoyed it too but if it was the best you all ever ate I'm afraid you haven't seen much candy — — Maybe I can send you some more some time if you really enjoyed it.

Oh! It will be grand if you can get a furlough Christmas! Of course it would be nice to get it sooner but lessons would be hanging over my head and we are all still clinging to the hope of a slim vacation Xmas.

There is some danger of not getting it because of the time the Flu has swiped. Dear, dear, I can scarcely wait to see you. But I guess I'll just have to. And you say you think of me about 9:30 on Mon nights. Well, I'll have to confess that I thinks about you too at that time when that old bell rings. It used to take the joy out of life in those days, didn't it? It still does — but now it is at 6:30 A.M. instead of 9:30 P.M. It is also aided by the shrill bugle notes — some duet that would make Julius Caesar turn over in his grave.

I must needs stop now and lose myself in "La Mare an Diable" or "The Devil's Pool"[12] taught by one —— of the reddest headed women in G.C. [Miss Mabley]. Please don't think I'm absolutely insane. The fact is I had some fermented grape juice a few nights ago and haven't exactly recovered as yet.

Asever, [sic]
— Your Little Girl

OCTOBER 24, 1918

Rumors are that Elliott's company is to stay at Great Lakes all winter, but he says they hear everything around there except the truth. If he could study he wouldn't care so much, but it is too noisy and "a fellow has so little time to call his own." He was happy to hear Elma talk about their future work together and says that if God wants to send them to China he says will gladly go, although the missionary field never had a special appeal to him. His ankle is getting better and he was not sent to fight the fires.

Thursday night, 7 P.M.
Dearest "Little girl:"
This has been a rainy day to be sure. It has rained without ceasing since about four o'clock yesterday afternoon. It is still pouring down as if it might rain forever. I haven't had a thing to do to-day except two

hours guard duty. I have to guard from one to three in the morning too. It seems that I always get those hours at night. I have tried to study a little and washed some and read some more. Gee, but the days seem long when there is no drill. I got some new dope to-day. They tell me that this company is to stay here all winter. We hear most everything round here (except the truth) but I shouldn't be any surprised if we do stay here all winter. I sure hope I don't have to, but I may. If I could study any I wouldn't care so much, but I can't study any round here for the noise and a fellow has so little time to call his own that he can't study much.

I went to a picture show at the "Y" last night. It was a pretty good western story acted by Hart. Then they showed some war pictures. It was good for a change. I never was very crazy about movies however.

Well, if I look better in uniform I guess I had better stay in the navy all the time. For goodness sake I hope I don't look any worse than I did in civilian life. Really I didn't like the navy uniform much before I enlisted but since I have seen the sailors and soldiers together I now think the navy uniform looks better. That is the blues do when they are worn with leggins. It is much easier to keep the sailor's suits clean too (except the whites).

Well, well, don't worry about my ankle. I have had enough sprains to know how to take care of one by now. I had almost forgotten about it till I got your letter. No really I have had a pretty sore foot. It was hurt worse than I thought. It is about well now however. It is a little bit sore yet but I can walk O.K. now. This time makes three times that one ankle has been sprained. The other one twice. It does seem that I am unfortunate.

You were speaking of close friends. We don't as a usual thing have time here on camp to form intimate friends, but it seems that one fellow here and I have almost the same ideals of life. We went on liberty one Sunday. His name is Kay. He is from Mo. We got to talking of our past experiences. He told me all about his girl back home. He seemed so free with me I just had to tell him a little about you. We have been the best of friends since. I was really a little surprised to know that you and Blanche are not the closest of friends. I knew you were not last year for you told me so but I thought you told me that you had changed toward her. As you have been so plain as to say what you have I will tell you a little secret too about her. Somehow or other I never looked upon Blanche as an ideal girl by any means. I never had any reason whatever to distrust her and as you always seemed to like her so well I tried my best to like her but I must confess I never was very crazy about her. For the life of me I couldn't say why. I always suspected that you knew I distrusted her and I always felt like a hypocrite because I told you I liked her when I didn't. I have really tried to like her and she has always been perfectly nice to me and why I never did like her I couldn't possibly explain. I am sure she knows I don't like her for I never could pretend I like a person if I don't. If she doesn't know it please don't ever tell her that I don't for really I would love to like her, because I really think she is crazy about you. You may be surprised to know this as I was to know that you do not share even your secrets with her. And I never in my knowledge of her saw one single thing to dislike about her. You say you love to tell me little things that you do not feel like telling anyone else. Be sure that I love to hear anything that affects you, your pleasures, worries, or happiness. If I can ever be of any help whatever to you in any trouble be sure that it will be a pleasure to me to do all I can. I would be glad to do anything I can to make you happier. It certainly is a joy to me to know that you love to share with me your secrets and feel free to tell me every little thing that affects you. I feel the same way by you as you can judge from my letters. If you ever get in trouble of any kind or are worried about anything tell me about it if you will. Of course I know I can't help you so much when I am so far away but always know that I love you and would love to do anything to help you be happy. I know you get discouraged at times and so do I. It always does me good for you to encourage me when I am blue.

You were speaking of our future work. You have little idea how much happiness it gives me to hear you say those words and to plan for us to work together. I can't say that the missionary field ever had a special appeal to me, but I have always wanted to do whatever God wants me to do. I want to serve Him and if he wants me to work in China I would be happy to go there and the happiest thought of all is that I will have you to help and encourage me. If we could do most good by our work in China I would love to work there. I really feel that God has a work for us to do together and if you are called to work in China I believe I could willingly go there with you to work. I have felt since I came into the navy that God is giving me this chance to learn men and different parts of the world and its needs. I know God was leading me to enlist in the navy. I couldn't be contented at home at all or at school or anywhere except here. And really I have been satisfied in conscience since I came. I think we will know our work when it comes time to begin whatever it is or wherever it is. Everything I consider doing after the war is over I think of you and love to think that we can work out our life's work together and I am so glad to know you feel the same way about it.

I was awful sorry to hear about Jessie Beagle's death. I did not know that she had been sick at all. She seemed like such a nice girl. I really never knew her personally. I know Robin D loved her and I know it must be a terrible blow to him. It always seemed hard that young people of such true characters and promising lives should be taken away but God knows best and must work his own plans and it is for us to only submit to them and know that it is best in the end.

I was not sent to fight fire. I guess the people got the fire under control without any "Jacky" aid. I don't think any sailors were sent at all. I never heard of it if they were.

Taps have blown and I must stop. I haven't read this over. I guess it is full of mistakes. I have been interrupted every five minutes. I hope you continue to feel free to tell me all that you want to and know that I love you.

Yours,
Elliott

OCTOBER 27, 1918

Elliott writes about going to Lake Forest, Illinois, a city of millionaire's residences, and comments on what a pleasure it was to get out alone, where he could think or dream, away from the noise of crowds. Then he tells about an adventure that seems totally out of character for him, saying he has gotten to be "a real ship jumper deserter or something."

Dear Elma:

This is a rainy afternoon and because of that fact and also the flu epidemic there isn't much doing. I have been riding round most all afternoon. When I first got out it was not raining. I went down to Lake Forest Ill for a while. There didn't seem to be much going on down there except funerals (there were three). It was too sad for me so I didn't stay long. That was the first time I have ever been there. It is one of the nicest looking towns I have seen since in this country. It is a city of millionaires' residences so they tell me. I saw some of the prettiest homes down there I have ever seen anywhere in my life. It looks more like a big beautiful park than a town. The houses are far apart and large oaks and elms everywhere between. It must be an awful beautiful place in summer. I am so sorry I did not go there during summer while everything was green. You know the only two thoughts I had while walking round there all by myself was to think of you wishing you were with me and wondering if you would love to be there with me in these strange but beautiful places. The other was to wonder how many of the folks who lived in those mansions were (or are) really happy. I walked all the way out to the lake shore. I had little idea where I was going. I didn't care. I just felt that I wanted to get out of sight of a crowd for once where I couldn't see folks. Do you ever feel that way? It seems that everybody else up here loves the crowd but me. I went down from the park which bordered on the lake to the very shore. It was a rough climb through thick brush and down a bluff of bout 100 yards. My! But the lake was rough. I stood there for an hour most I expect watching the big waves roll in on the shore. It seemed so different to what I am used to. The noise of drums and bugles and command on the drill field. Then I go in to hear the uproar and noise round the barracks. It is just a pleasure to me to get out alone and think or dream. When I think of it it seems to be so strange a disposition, but I never did like the noise of a crowd. I saw that it was about to rain so I started back toward the young men's club. I looked all over town for a church on my way back but I was unable to find one anywhere. So I decided I would come to Waukegan if by chance the churches here might be open. Sure enough the Baptist church is. So I am going to church after awhile. The "Y" also is open here now. It seems that the flu is getting better now. I sure hope the country will be rid of it soon.

Well, I've gone to two picture shows at the "Y" in camp this week. So you see I am getting to be a movie fan. A show is going on now here but I am well contented writing to you.

Talk about excitement. I had an adventure yesterday. I have gotten to be a real ship jumper deserter or something. They sent about 30 of us fellows way over to a new camp that is being constructed, to work. When we got there and worked a while, some of us decided there wasn't much use working. So we slipped over and lay down behind a lumber pile. Then we had our blue suits on under our whites (accidentally C?) as we have to wear whites on detail work. As we were not working we decided we had just as well go on a little liberty. There happened to be a hole in the fence so out we crawled and round a factory off to north Chicago after we had slipped off our whites and rolled them in some paper we had in our rufer [sic] pocket (by accident). We stayed out until muster time last night about eight o'clock. We got a big oyster stew for supper in north Chi and had a very good time. We walked boldly in the gate by the guards as if we had legally gone out on liberty. No one ever suspected us, but I hardly think I shall try it again. That is most equal to some of your experiences, isn't it? For fear of getting in the brig I don't think I will ever do it again. If a fellow gets the brig it means bread and water to eat, no pay, and pretty disagreeable work for from 10 to 30 days. So I guess you see it would be best to avoid that. When a fellow stays in the same old hole for a week he gets so he doesn't care much what happens so he gets out for a while. It pays however to obey and I shall try to most all the time from now on. I think I know how you girls feel who have to stay at Rucker Hall under such strict rules.

A bunch of us fellows were walking through camp the other day and found someone's love letter on the street. It was not even in an envelope. So we read it. It was one that Prof Daniel would call slushy. All the fellows saw a great lot of fun out reading it but it really had a different meaning to me to what one of its kind used to have. Some folks have a funny idea about love. Last night after I went to bed, a fellow and I got to talking. By the way he is a Kentuckian from western Ky. His name is Cook. He pretends to be wealthy. I guess he is. He was telling me about a trip to Blue Ridge that he had and of meeting a girl down there. He said he had been engaged to a girl for two years. Then she lost her health and that on that account he never expected to marry her. He said it would be foolish for he would just be marrying a Dr's bill. That made me think he didn't care much about her if he thought more of his pocketbook than he did of her. I like the fellow pretty well but I can't give him much on that. He said he never expected to marry anybody else but still he wouldn't marry her. And he gave the above statement as his reason. I never even told him that I had a girl after he gave me his idea, and I didn't give him my idea about it either, but I think it would have been different to his. If I didn't think enough of you to spend every nickel I ever expected to own for you if sick I could never ask you to love me I don't think, and especially I think if the girl I was engaged to was sick I could put a cure for her or an attempt at least above my pocketbook or else I wouldn't ask her to marry me. It's church time I must close.

A big "good night" with lots of love,
Elliott

P.S. This letter is rather abrupt in places, at the end especially. You may think I'm going crazy but I'm no worse than usual. I haven't had one good place time or chance to write to you since here. It's always written in a rush. I think you know don't you? E.S.

OCTOBER 29, 1918

Elma hasn't written for almost a week and says the last two or three letters were only "silly little notes," so she is going to try to be "a sensible little lady" and write again. She tells about two students who are seriously ill and may not recover, which has made her very aware of the uncertainty of life. She feels it is unfair to be separated so long at a time like this and is jealous of the couples who fill up the parlor almost every night.

Tuesday Night
9:15 o'clock
Dearest Elliott:

    I haven't written you a real sure enough letter in a long time. The last two or three have only been silly little notes, so I'm going to be or at least try to be a sensible little "lady" again. I was most awful disappointed 'cause I didn't get any letter to-day but I didn't much blame you for not writing when I've been so bad. Blanche got two letters to-day and one of them was five folders. Wasn't that disgraceful?

    I wanted to write to you so bad last night but four hard lessons were hanging over my head. I had worked seven hours in the office and was so tired that I felt like I would like to have been way out in the country somewhere with nobody close to me but you. For the last week I've had a terrible longing to live in a far distant country where everything is quiet and peaceful like with never a responsibility or care — nothin' in the world to do but love and make you happy. Wasn't that a selfish desire? I can't help it, for life seems so short and uncertain that it seems unfair to have to be separated so long.

    Judd Summers has been at the point of death for the last week, but it is thought now that he has some slight chance of recovery. Viola Watson had the flu the same week everyone else did and got up in time to start back to school as soon as it opened. She was in classes all day Saturday and was taken with spinal meningitis Saturday night and everyone says there is no possible chance for her. Such incidents as these are what makes one realize that life is indeed uncertain.

The 9:30 bell has just run and oh! How it takes me back to certain Tuesday nights when life was brightest. You ought to see Gene [Martin] and Mary Anna [Beard]. They are us all over again only worse if possible. He even calls her up two or three times on Sunday. There are more cases this year than you ever heard of. The parlor is full most every night. We wouldn't like that much, would we? I don't believe it would do at all for us to be in a crowd. If you get a furlough Christmas, you'll come down home or go as I do want you! Mercy! It thrills me so to think about it that I haven't any sense. I just love you so good. I think, however, you know it well enough without me telling you.

We have had very exciting times in G.C. this afternoon. The new professor who took Prof Rhoton's place got so mad that he dismissed Education class this afternoon. All because a bunch of folks were just outside the window making too much noise. He called them down twice and they paid no attention but continued their disturbance by throwing some gravel into the room. This was the climax and he blew up, dismissed the class and flew out of the room, but alas! Jimmy Moreland had sailed to the window and warned the guilty parties who disappeared immediately. A little later in the afternoon Prof Hill had to go out on the campus and bawl a bunch of boys out. Things are quite wild and wooley this year. Bill Bauer says the boys aren't a Georgetown bunch at all. Haven't the Georgetown spirit. They are just people that haven't any purpose in life and have drifted in because of the S.A.T.C. They say one of the fine lieutenants is a champion crap shooter (is that the way you spell it?)

Well, dear, it is impossible for me to think of anything else as a crazy old girl is in here rattling as hard as she can, telling all her affairs, never seeming to realize that it is extremely annoying. Blanche is enduring it like a martyr. About 3/4 of the girls in the hall loaf in our room and I have to seek some other place to study. I think I'll apply for single room next yr. Must say goodnight before the lights go out — course I never could write it in the dark —

With the most of love,
Elma

OCTOBER 29, 1918

Elliott's long chatty letter reads as though he and Elma were having a face-to-face conversation about shared experiences. He seems much more confident in himself and in her love for him, as he openly shares his thoughts and teases her some. He tells her about his dad's plans to remarry a "grass widow" and shares "a bit of gossip" about the woman's history. He ends with the latest rumors about the companies that are moving out. He adds a P.S. urging her not to get her hopes up about his getting a furlough.

Tuesday evening

Dear Elm:

Professor Conn! I am surprised and yet glad to hear that "Chinc" is so fortunate. I feel quite distinguished to have once been a roommate of a G.C. Prof. Has Chinc ever fallen in love anymore? I wrote to Conn but I never heard from him. I guess he did not think enough of his old roomie to write to me. No I don't guess he ever got it. I have been expecting to write to him again but never have.

I am glad to hear that you have had a little vacation altho [sic] you do not seem to have desired it. I wish something could happen so that you wouldn't have to work at all. I mean outside your study.

And you think Mr. Adkins is afraid of you! Well! Well! That is the first time I ever heard of Slip being afraid of a girl. You must have a peculiar appearance to him. When you know him I don't think you will think he is afraid of you or any other young lady. He's quite a ladies [sic] man or (at least he thought so) in his home town. By the way I got a letter from Mr. Fields last night. He says Adkins is a Ciceronian and is trying to be a frat man. So you know by that that he isn't afraid of you.

You made me terribly hungry by telling me about all those rolles [sic] you ate, but the beans didn't seem to make me hungry at all. I have those every morning for breakfast. Yes worms and all. Camouflage beans is a special dish in the navy for all occasions. I was surprised to know that you can't eat as much as the new girl. It must be terrible to be beaten in an eating contest by that much. And the grape juice had its effect evidently judging from your letter but you know my drinks all seem to have a depressing effect upon me. (I haven't had one now for a few days. C?)

I guess I have an idea how the fellows step around at G.C. When the officer gives a command we all step. Everything we do round here is "On the double." "Shake it up." "Hurry hurry." "Wake up." Get the hap out of your head." "Get a little life, you!" "Where do you think you are, at a picnic?" "etc etc" We do everything on the run except when we draw pay or go to chow. My, but we get orders round here. We march everywhere we go (except to bed). But I imagine it seems funny to be under military authority at college. You said the boys don't do much study. It is absolutely impossible to study here although we just fool round doing nothing three fourths of the time. I guess it is the same way in the college unit. Fellows here who know about it say that one can't study. I don't think however that it will be long now until the war is over. It seems that Austria and Turky [sic] are out now and I think Germany is ready to quit too.

Well, I guess that Greek (to me) stuff you are reading, about the Devil and the war, is a suitable subject for war times when you have that red-headed sister for an instructor but I don't like it when it is the cause of you having to stop writing to me. My but you think I am selfish to say that, especially when you had written 12 pages.

Well, I got a long letter from my brother [Isaac] yesterday. He has been in the hospital for 30 days. He is able to be out again now he says. He says he weighs 125 pounds. He weighed 175 when he enlisted. He surely has been sick to fall off that much. He says he has just gotten two letters during that time. They were special delivery from his girl. His girl is the one that I used to go to see [Grace Crossfield]. He beat my time "C." He says that his girl says my dad is about to get married again. I can't hardly believe it but I guess she ought to know for it is her aunt that he is talking to. My dad's girl is a grass widow, weighs about 230 pounds and uses snuff. I can't imagine it is true but it is I guess. I must say my dad and I would differ greatly in a choice but it is his business and if he thinks he could be better satisfied if married again I hope he does get married. I know he has been the most unhappy man I ever saw since mother died. I am afraid he will even be worse dissatisfied if he gets married again. I don't mean because of the woman he is about to marry but because of the comparison between her and mother. The lady he is talking to doesn't look very well but she is really a very fine Christian woman. She is about 45 I guess. Dad is about 63 years old. She has been very unhappy because of her marriage. A fellow came in there from the west. He began to talk to her. He went to see her for about two years and married her. They were about 40 years old each of them. He lived with her during their honey-moon. They went up in Ohio for about a week. He sent her back home. He pretended to be going to the west on business and told her that he would be back in a few days. When he did not come back, she was terribly grieved, and later she heard from him that he had gone back to his living wife out west. She never saw him afterwards. That was the meanest man I ever heard of. It was even worse when you knew the woman and knew how much she loved him. Perhaps this is a bit of gossip and a story that doesn't interest you in the least but it is very interesting to me for it is a story in which my dad is very much concerned if the gossip is true. I think it very apt to be true for my dad was talking to me even before I left for the navy. Ever since I have been grown dad seems to have delighted in telling me everything and especially since mother died. He told me that he doesn't love the woman but that he thinks he can perhaps be better satisfied if married. I fear very much that he won't be even as well satisfied as he is for I know how much he loved his first wife. I beg your pardon for taking your time by all this family affair but it is of great interest to me and that's why I am telling you.

Well, I may be moved out soon. Every company in this regiment goes out to-morrow except two. My Co is one that stays here. Eight of us go out too. There won't be more than 20 of us left here in this company. And for that reason I expect to be going out soon. I may not be however. The eight men who go to-morrow go to New York City to a drafting school. I stepped out for it but they wanted college graduates and just eight. So they got the number they wanted who had had more college than I. I expect to get something soon for I am going to try for the next good thing offered. Everybody is in great spirits to-night especially those who are moving to-morrow. There are fifteen companies in the regiment. There will only be two to-morrow night and our company will be terribly small.

They are sending out a lot of fellows as firemen. That is the only thing in the navy that I absolutely don't want. Most everybody is the same way about it. Therefore they draft men for that. I might be drafted for it but I don't think there is much danger. One Ky fellow in our company was sent out as a fireman to-day however. They wanted him to be a yeoman, and he refused to take it and so they sent him out as a fireman to spite him I guess. It sure was a dirty trick too. Our company commander was sent to sea too the other day. They are getting ready for a large number of rookies I think. They say they are expecting 3,000 new men this week. Gee but I would love to have gone to New York to school for about six months or a year. The draftsmen study mechanical drawing mostly I think.

I guess I had better stop or else you will never get it all read. Be a good little girl and stay as happy as you were when you wrote the last letter.

With love,
Elliott

P.S. You said you hoped I got a furlough Xmas. Do not look forward to it as a certainty. It is very doubtful whether I am able to get it. Really now I am expecting to be in a school for something by that time. If I am I don't expect I will get off until I have finished. So don't let me make you think I am coming back when I haven't much chance to come. Be sure I will be back the first chance I get. And the only thing I really want to come back for is to see you. Say I just ate the last of the candy about two day [sic] ago. I certainly did enjoy it. It was so good. And I think it even tasted better to me because it was you who sent it.

E.C.

OCTOBER 31, 1918

Elliott has finally gotten word that he is going to sea on a draft bound for Pontiac, France. He says he will tell her all he knows as soon as he can and signs off, "So long."

Wednesday night
Dear Elma:

I am moved to Company seven 16th Reg. It is an outgoing camp. I am liable to be leaving any minute I guess. I am going to sea as a seaman I think. That is the dope at least. I have it pretty straight that I am on a draft bound for Pontiac France. What I am to do or where that is I have little idea. I will write you as soon as I get a chance and find out where I am going. This card is a picture of my Co on the march. The arrow indicates me. Will tell you all I know as soon as I can. It has all happened since 6 o'clock, moving and all. It is 8:30 now.

So long,
Elliott

OCTOBER 31, 1918

Elliott has been "standing by" all day awaiting orders, expecting to leave at any time. His excitement about the impending journey is evident here, with "everything ... in a stir and hurry" and everybody "laughing and having a big time." He says Elma can still write to him, because the mail will follow him. He mentions several things in this letter that Elma has told him but that are not in any of her letters from this month, so perhaps one or more of her letters went missing.

Thursday night
Dear "Little Girl:"

I was expecting to leave for the East to-day but didn't. I wrote you a card last night expecting to go out this morning. I have been "standing by" all day awaiting orders. It is the general rumor that we go to Philidelphia [sic] from here, from there on to New York City and then to France. It is all rumor. We do not know where or when we go but one thing is pretty sure we will be going soon. As a usual thing men stay in this regiment from one to three days. Sometimes however they stay for a month or so. So I do not know how long I will be here. Everybody is tickled most to death to know that we are about to get a chance to do something ~~good~~ worth while. Three big 16 to 20 coach pullmans went out from this regiment this afternoon. So you see some men are being sent out. I would like to have a rating before I go to sea but I will have even a better chance after I get out I guess. Our company was not supposed to be sent out but they got a call for so many men from our regiment. They had to send all the men out of the regiment even some of the company commanders and platoon leaders. I don't guess there were more than 30 men left in the whole regiment. There were about 1300 when the draft came. Everything was running along quietly and in the same old way for our company till yesterday about 5 P.M. We had just gotten back from review and were lazing round when a yeoman suddenly appeared and said be ready bag and baggage by 6:30 to go to camp Luce. We had to go to chow and get our belongings together. At 6:30 we started on our four mile march to camp Luce. We got here about 8 and got all fixed up for our stay here. If you want to you can write to me. I will get it even if I am in the East, for my mail will follow me. If I move in a day or so I will send you my address. If I should go directly on to some foreign service it may be some time before I get a permanent address. It may be some time before I get another letter from you unless I should stay here for several days, as mail will follow me slowly. I got a letter from you yesterday morning. It came just in time. You asked me what I did with my extra hour. Believe me I but [sic] it to good use sleeping. I wouldn't care if they would give us an extra real afternoon. Gee but I wish I had been at G.C. to use that hour calling. I never would have slept if there was a chance to call provided it was you on whom I was calling. I think you have quite a funny organization for the old maids. I guess it is something like Hog Heaven Court? (Nicht) But I don't think our court even had refreshments except night air. I am not surprised that Truth game got you into trouble. Truth is a hard game to play in this old world.

I guess I can forgive you this one time for the terrible crime you have committed by being unable to give Mr. Eddings the information he desired. I don't blame you for walking with Mr. Eddings or giving information either. (Excuse these blots two fellows are wrestling on the table while I write). Don't worry. I have nothing to forgive. If you can get the forgiveness of the O.M.C. don't ask for mine.

That library rule is the limit! Don't you know it is best that I am not there? I know I would get you in trouble sure if I ever caught you at the library and of course you couldn't afford to give up studying there some and I would stay there all the time looking for you. Take my advice and don't get into trouble by breaking that rule. "C"?. My but ain't I getting selfish?

I am sorry that you are so out of luck about going to town. That must be terrible sure enough that you and Blanche both have to stay in.

Just now got the news that I am on draft 923. I go to New York City. I am apt to go to-morrow but do not know for sure.

Well, I thought I would get to see you Xmas but it seems now that I may be out of luck unless the war is over by that time. Personally I believe it will.

Everything is in a stir and hurry to-night. Everybody is laughing and having a big time. So my thoughts are scattered as usual.

I must stop as it is time sailors are in bed so the bugle says.

I will write you a letter as soon as I get a chance and as soon as I find out where and when I am going.

With the most of love,
Elliott

P.S. It is snowing up here to-night and is cold as mischief. E.C.

CHAPTER 8
November, 1918

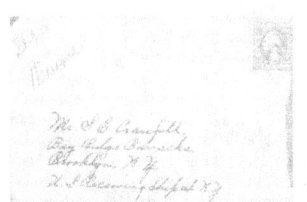

I'll Come Back to You When It's All Over[1]

Verse 1:
See that lonesome lassie kiss her soldier boy goodbye.
Her poor heart is beating fast,
This one kiss may be their last.
Don't you worry, dearie, let me try and dry your tears,
I may be gone for many days, perhaps for many years,
But...

Chorus:
I'll come back to you when it's all over, all over,
Back to you and fields of clover.
We'll start our sweetheart days all over
If your heart still beats as true.
There is a duty that ev'ry man should do.
My life defends it, but my heart belongs to you.
So pray for the day when it's all over 'cause I'm coming
    back to you.

Verse 2:
See that lonesome lassie watch those soldier boys return.
She is looking ev'rywhere,
Something tells her he is there.
Soon her sweetheart threw her a kiss
and proudly marched ahead
With joy and pride she marched beside
Her soldier boy who said...

Chorus:
I'll come back to you when it's all over, all over,
Back to you and fields of clover.
We'll start our sweetheart days all over
If your heart still beats as true.
There is a duty that ev'ry man should do.
My life defends it, but my heart belongs to you.
So pray for the day when it's all over 'cause I'm coming
    back to you.

~

NOVEMBER 3, 1918

By this time the Navy is sending about 1,000 men each day from camp, so Elliott expects his turn will come soon. In the meantime, he is enjoying the relative quiet, with only 12 men left. Although he misses Elma, he does not regret his decision to enlist and trusts that God will bring them back together at the proper time. After the war, he can rest easy in conscience, knowing that he did his duty and did not shirk responsibility.

Sunday morning
  Dearest Elma:
    It is pouring rain and everyone seems to be quiet. So I will write to

you. About half of our section left yesterday for the East and so there are only twelve left. We are staying in new barracks now. They are double decks, and are divided into four sections or rooms, two below and two above. I am on the upper deck. Since about half our bunch left we are having a pretty nice quiet time of it. I like it much better this way when there are not so many together. I expect I will go to-morrow. Our commander told us he thought we would go either Monday or Tuesday. We had to wash up all our dirty clothes yesterday. They are sending out about 1,000 each day from this camp. So I guess from that my turn will come soon. I haven't been doing much since I came to this camp. I was put on mess gang. Three of us have to feed twelve men. That's all we do. It takes about an hour after each meal. We do not even have to do guard duty so long as we are on mess. All the other fellows have to go on detail work too from this camp. We get no drill whatever. I think by the time we leave this camp I will be an expert at washing dishes and serving chow. When the war is over I think I can get a job perhaps as a cook. I have been lucky before. I never had been on mess before. Until we came to this camp five men had to feed 200. Believe me they had a job too. I was lucky enough to escape it.

I got your letter written on Tuesday night. It was sent over from Camp Perry yesterday. It was such a sweet letter. I am sorry however that you thought I failed to write because of the kind of letters I had been getting from you. I don't appreciate your gay letters any less than your others for I know both are from you and it is you that I love. I don't want you to change one bit either. I love you when you are gay and when you are serious. When you feel like writing your gay letters know I appreciate them for they are you in your gayer hours. Don't think I have forgotten you when you were "giddy" as you called it. (I should say when we were gay for I think it belonged to us both don't you?) I think I wrote just the same however. I guess it was a delay in the mail service that you did not get it. You may think I am changing from my letters but I am just about as gay as ever. Everything I see here is mostly serious but not altogether. Then I see things brighter than it may seem in my letters. I love your "silly" letters as you call them just as well as your others for I know both are typical of you. I am sorry you have to work so hard that you can't write to me when you feel like it. I have enough coming to me too that you wouldn't have to work quite so hard for a few days if I could get it, but there is so little certainty when I will get it. I may not get it till the war is over. They pay a fellow when they feel like it in the navy.

You were saying you wished you could be way out in the world alone with me. You don't know how often I wish that might be true. And if it could only be for a little time now I think I would be much happier. I never knew that folks could want to see anyone so badly as I do you. And you said without responsibility! Wouldn't it be great to just feel free once, that no responsibility of any kind was resting upon you. But then when we think aright the old world wouldn't be worth living in if every one of us did not have a responsibility to meet and did not owe a debt to others. I find that since I know that I love you and can expect you to help me some day to meet my responsibilities it is much easier for me. I wonder if you feel the same way? How I wish for that time when we can help each other to meet our responsibilities in this world. Don't you feel that it will be easier then? But I don't think it is a selfish feeling that prompts us at times to wish we were free from our responsibilities but it is more a realization of our weakness that makes us wish to be free from it. And life certainly is uncertain in these times and it is short at best. When we love each other and see no definite time when we can be with each other again it is hard to be separated. The only consolation I have when I feel that I just can't wait to see you again is that there is one who can protect us in all life's uncertainties and dangers and bring us back together at the proper time. If we trust Him will he not bring us together at the proper time and will we not be happier for the separation. I remember you said in one of your letters a long time ago that it was strange how some folks got to stay together all the time and how others were separated. I don't know how often I have thought of that statement since. You know I often feel that it is all my fault that we are separated. I could have stayed at home and gone to school perhaps this year in the S.A.T.C. Then I think would I ever feel as much at ease when the war is over? Or would you think as much of me? You know I have no excuse whatever for staying. No home folks to care for. Nobody but you that I want to stay out of the war for. Would it not have been very selfish to stay out and at school with you when so many have to leave their wives. It must be much easier for us to be separated now than if we were married. When I think of the many who have left their sweethearts and wives, I don't think I could ever be easy in conscience after the war is over if I should have stayed out. You cited Bauer and Viola for example. I often wonder if such as he wouldn't feel better when peace comes if he had been in the real service. It is a nice excuse to say you were in college preparing for a bigger service while the war was on. That is O.K. too if a fellow's conscience will let him honestly say it, but I must confess that my conscience told me that I wasn't doing my duty while in school. That's why I enlisted when I did. Anybody that knows me knows that I hate war and would never enlist if I could help it, but the fellow who has stayed out or hunted an easy job in this war will be counted a slacker when it is over. The only thing that makes me want to be out of the service now is I want to be with you but will it not be worth the sacrifice for both of us if I feel that I have done my duty? If I had honestly felt that I ought to serve in the navy, and then stayed out even because of my love for you and because I could be with you do you think you could love me as well? I thought all these things over before I enlisted. I tried to solve it in a way that we both would be happy when the war is over and I could feel that I had done my duty. By the way I think the war is about over. They are gambling 10 to one in N.Y. so they say that war will be over in twenty days. I haven't seen a paper for two days but it looked good then. I may not get to come home Xmas I as [sic] hoped but now I am in hopes of coming home for good by spring. Then too I am just as apt to get home Xmas if I go East or to France as if I stay here. For I am just as apt to be back in this country then as not. I will never have any idea where I will be. If I can get across once or twice I will be much more apt to get a furlough than if I stay here. You asked if I would come to your home. You bet I would. I would go anywhere to you. When I do get a furlough I am coming to see you wherever you are. So don't worry I will come to Franklin if you want me to. I think I told you I thought I was bound for Pontiac France. I misunderstood the name. It is Paullic.[2] I think it is spelled that way. Many are being sent to Brest France too. Of course I may not be sent either place and I may not even go to France. I don't know where I am going. I doubt too whether they will let me tell you where I am if I do go to overseas duty. I guess there will be a very close censor if I do go. But I can still tell you I love you. Paulliac is on the a [sic] river just north of Bordeaux I think. It is a big U.S. Naval base. I think it is just off the coast of Bay of Biscay a short bit. The report is that we go there but rumor after rumor is all we hear in this camp.

You were talking of Gene and Mary Anna. I hope they do love each other. I think they are a nice couple. I just love to see folks that really love each other. I used to laugh at them but I know how to appreciate their feelings too. If there are so many cases in G.C. this year I mean so many in the parlor we couldn't be together there could we? Would we ever be satisfied to just sit up and talk as we used to? No I couldn't but I could sit up and talk O.K. (or look at you at least) if there were too many round. I could do anything that is necessary if I could just be with you but I would much rather be with you alone as we were the last time I was with you.

You will have to quit being so popular if you expect to have quiet in your room. And you were talking of the roughnecks at G.C. this year. Fields wrote me the other day. He said the reason T.θ.K. was behind in numbers this year is that the C.S. type is more abundant in G.C. this year than usual.[3] He seems to think T.θ.K. is holding her own alright. I am so glad too. By the way have they had that entertainment yet? And did you go?

I have had a very good time to write to-day. Everything is quieter than usual. Elma, I may not have so much time to write when I get East or to France. I hope I do. If so I will write just as often as I can. If I don't you won't think I think any less of you will you? You see I never know now what I am going into, or where I will be. I will think of you all the time and write as often as I can. I may see a lot of the world now if I really get to go to foreign service. Always remember me in your prayers and love me as you do now and I will be happy and contented till war is over. Then I am coming back to you for good as soon as possible.

With most of love,
Elliott

P.S. This is a little poem I wrote this afternoon. Do you think there is any truth in it? I know it is true. That's all that makes men fight and win is love for their women and home.

～

THE MAKING OF A SOLDIER

> *I*
> *One has asked "What makes the soldier great?*
> *What makes the soldier brave?"*
> *"Tis race-blood, the spirit of his kin," some say*
> *"An ancestrial [sic] gift of power*
> *to a chosen man whom God gave*
> *The spirit and power to win in the battles of his day."*
>
> *II*
> *But 's not this makes a soldier win, not this makes him*
>   *brave*
> *Nor machine-like drill, or knowledge in arts of war;*
> *Or general's skill, nor national banners that wave,*
> *Insignias of truth in peace, honor, and victories in war.*
>
> *III*
> *But 's the little cottage on the hill,*
> *The garden, fields, flowers—home not race—*
> *Childish chubby arms that clasp*
> *a father's and a mother's neck*
> *Childish curls that loose [sic] a tanned hard set*
> *and a brave white face*
> *As lips meet in love ere he's gone*
> *for battle field or gun-swept deck*

IV
It's the little woman's hand he's pressed
(the girl he loves you know)
'Tis the woman's lips he's pressed,
the tear he saw in his sweetheart's eye,
'Tis the eyes and lips that promised him love ere he'd go.
These make the soldier brave and great;
these make him fight to win or to die.

V
One sweet kiss of love
from trembling lips the soldier loves, one sigh, one tear,
One last hour alone, one fond good-bye,
And the soldier will meet the fiercest foe without a fear
Of the barrage of steel, of the Hell of gas and fire,
to live or to die

∼

NOVEMBER 5, 1918

Elliott is still at Camp Luce waiting to move to Brooklyn Navy Yard. He says the commander has lectured them about the kind of women they can expect when they get to New York, but he says his love for Elma and his desire to be a real man will keep him clear of their temptations. He references another letter from Elma that appears to be missing from the sequence.

Tuesday Evening 1:30 P.M.
    Dearest "Little girl,"
    I have just moved from the 16th to 17th regiment. I am still in camp Luce, but my next move will be for Brooklyn Navy yards so I am told. I still don't know exactly when I go, but it is apt to be to-night or in the morning. I was all packed up just ready to leave the 16th when the

mailman gave me the special delivery letter. It is the sweetest letter I have ever gotten from you I believe. It might have just seemed so, because I was not expecting to hear from you for a while, as I was expecting to be moved before this time. It is awful sweet of you to send me another box but I expect it will be an accident if I should get it. I appreciate it just the same. If I should stay here for a day or so I would get it. Little girl you don't know how many temptations I do have in this camp life, but I can meet them all for your sake and by God's help. And your letter will help me so much. I don't know but I don't believe I ever could have met all the temptations if it had not been for my love for you and my knowledge of you and confidence in you. I think it is very doubtful now whether or not I go over sea as the war news looks so good (not only looks good but is good). I may not get farther than New York. I hope I do get to take a trip across the sea. The commander just now told me that we will be off the station by seven o'clock in the morning. I will write to you just as soon as I get my new address. It might be some time before I get fixed up permanently again. The commander gave us a little lecture just a little bit ago. He advised us all to write to our mothers as soon as we get on board ship as it takes a long time for a letter from a ship to reach its destination. So you see that sounds as if I might be on a ship shortly. So don't worry if it is longer before you hear from me than I expect it to be now. Nobody here knows what we are to do or where we will be sent from N.Y. The commander also gave us some advice as to our money when we get shore leave off ship. He said there were women always looking for the man in uniform around port and it is their money they want. They are here too as I guess most sailors know. It is just such women that makes life hard for the sailor who tries to be decent. But my love for you and my desire to be a real man can keep me clear of their temptations. I am sure it was your knowledge of such conditions that made you write the sweet letter that I just received. I can assure you conditions will never be worse anywhere than round Great Lakes. From my experience here I can assure you that I can be absolutely true to you. So don't be afraid. And don't worry about your work with Dr. Leigh. I may be mistaken but I took you to mean that you do not much like to work for him in a private office. You know that is the one big objection I have to girls working in offices. Some men try to take advantage of such occasions and lead girls astray. However I would have the greatest confidence in Dr. Leigh in fact most any professor that I know in G.C. But as we both understand each other and as I have absolute confidence in you I would like to give you just this little bit of advice. Don't trust men too far. I mean all men for you don't always know them. Now don't think I distrust you one bit for I never had the slightest distrust of you in my life. I think you know that if I had not trusted you absolutely I never would have acted toward you as I have. You know I have never had any other motive in my asking privileges [sic] of you than love and the deepest trustful love for you. If I did not love you as I do I would never dare say these things to you. I would not say these things except I feel perhaps I know men and their motives at times better than you. I appreciate every word of advice you have ever given me and I hope you don't think I am going too far now. I really think you can trust Dr. Leigh absolutely. And I think that is just the reason you were selected for the office work just so there wouldn't be any suspicion as to the motives and intentions of the profs at G.C. You know it is not every girl that could work with a man in his private office. I think all who know you trust you absolutely and that is why you were given the job and you can know that I trust you absolutely and for that reason I assure you that you can trust me also wherever I go. It is much easier to be pure when one has confidence in a girl whom he loves and who loves him. I hope you don't think I say these things because I distrust you for I never trusted you more in my life.

I will have to stop this time. I will write you again as soon as I get a chance.

They say we get up at 3:30 to-morrow morning if we do not go out to-night.

Don't fear that I forget you or my God wherever I go or whatever I may be doing. I have written this with about ten fellows up on the table and yelling and talking. It may be rather scattered and rambling. Be good and know that I love you more every day.

As ever with love,
Elliott

NOVEMBER 8, 1918

The inside address on this letter is Bay Ridge Barracks, Brooklyn NY, U.S. Receiving Ship. Elliott arrived in New York just in time to witness "a wild celebration," after a false report that Germany had signed the armistice. He reports that "One couldn't hear anything but horns and whistles. Streets were jammed. Guns were firing, bells ringing, bits of paper were flying in the air, so that one couldn't see anything." No more transport ships are being sent over, so he doesn't know whether he will actually be sent to France or not.

Friday

Dearest Elma:

If you will excuse the pencil I will write you a brief letter. My baggage hasn't arrived yet, so I have no ink or pen. I got to New York City about four o'clock yesterday. Then it took until about six thirty to come on over to the barracks. My! But New York was wild yesterday. They almost mobbed us poor sailors as we came through. It was for joy however for they were celebrating victory, rather peace. There was a false report that Germany had signed the armistice. There are so many reports one doesn't know what to believe. I really believe the war is over and it is the truth now I guess that the armistice has been signed. I can tell you N.Y. was a happy city yesterday as we came through. One couldn't hear anything but horns and whistles. Streets were jammed. Guns were firing, bells ringing, bits of paper were flying in the air, so that one couldn't see anything. These scraps of paper were dropped from the upper windows of the buildings until I believe the streets were covered at least six inches everywhere. There was a holiday from two o'clock on the rest of the day. We little sailor boys felt grand as we marched through, all the people cheering and yelling bravo and brave.

Well, I certainly had a big trip from the Lakes to N.Y. I came over the N.Y. Central route by way of Chicago, South Bend, Toledo, Cleveland, Buffalo, Albany and then down the Hudson River to New York City. It sure is beautiful scenery along the Hudson. We didn't stop anywhere much except at Utica N.Y. We stopped there about two hours. I passed West Point, Bannerman's Island Arsenal and Sing Sing prison, Rockefeller's and Vanderbilt's homes. It was quite an interesting trip for me. I am now stationed right on the shore of East river. I got up this morning and looked out on the harbor. I could see a hundred or so big ships, gun boats, battleships destroyers etc. It looks like the navy here. I don't feel like a dry-land sailor "no more." All the four months I stayed at the Lakes I don't feel that I learned one thing about the navy. It was so different there. At the Lakes we were afraid to speak to an officer. Here we don't even salute when we meet them. We are treated like men and human beings here. Everybody seems to be on an equal officers and all. We don't have anything to do here. We are sent here to be assigned duty on board a ship. I don't know when I will leave here. They say as a usual thing the men don't stay here long until they are put on a ship. This is a new place just opened up a week or so ago. We get fifteen hours liberty every other night only twelve hours a week at Lakes. We get good chow here too. I had eggs (C?), baked apples, cocoa, butter, oatmeal, and coffee cake and fried potatoes for breakfast. I got beans at Great Lakes. So you see there is quite a contrast. Then the food is well prepared here. One fellow said when we got here last night that this is paradise compared to Great Lakes. He certainly was correct too. About half of the men here have foreign service stripes. It is interesting to talk to them about their experiences over seas. Most all the big ships here in the harbor are camouflaged. I guess all of them have seen foreign waters. Of all funny designs of paintings and colors they have them. I guess it is about a mile across from the barracks to the New Jersey side and when I first got up I couldn't see one ship in the harbor due to the painting. There was some fog but not much.

 I was talking to a C.P.O. this morning who has been to France. He says the war is over. He says a great many of the transport ships leave this dock and that none have been going now for a week. He said two transports were called back about a week ago even after they were two days out. That sounds good to me, when they say no more soldiers are being sent over. I don't know whether I will see much service or not. I would like to go over at least, but believe me I am ready to come home as soon as Uncle says he can do without me. I don't think I ever knew what an education can mean as well as I know now. I would sure love to be back in school as soon as the war is over. I can be satisfied here O.K. till the war is all settled. Then I want to come back. If I had known the war was so near over I don't think I would ever have enlisted, but I guess it is worth the experience.

There goes muster so I will stop this time.
I will write again soon.
With most of love,
Elliott

ARMISTICE DAY

NOVEMBER 11, 1918

Elliott jokes that he has just been over in New York viewing their future place of business on Wall Street and their future home on Riverside Drive. He says New York is the wildest place he ever saw, with "noise noise noise and people crowded till one can hardly go anyplace" but if all the world is as happy tonight as New York, there ought to be a grand time. He says it is a great experience for him to be there and he is enjoying it very well, but everywhere he goes in the vast crowd he is lonesome for her.

Dearest "Little Girl:"

I am leading a gay life in the big city of the world. I have just been over in New York viewing "our" future place of business — Wall Street and "our" future home on Riverside Drive. Of course I don't mean I have already selected the spot and dwellings without your consent and judgment but I have just been over to see the communities see? New York is the wildest place I ever saw. Noise noise noise and people crowded till one can hardly go anyplace. If all the world is as happy to-night as N.Y. there sure ought to be a grand time. I thought there was some excitement here the other day when I came in but nothing to compare with to-night. I stayed here in the "Y" last night and am staying again to-night. The whistles woke me up about two o'clock this morning and they haven't ceased one bit all day. It is now seven P.M. The noise seems to be worse now than any time to-day. All business is closed to-day (except saloons). I never saw quite so many drunk folks. I think I am as proud that it is no temptation for me to celebrate by getting drunk as any one thing I know. You know there is a holiday for we even got half day off in the navy. All ships in the harbour are giving a holiday to their crews. Sailors and soldiers! There must be a million in N.Y. to-day of all nations. I guess I will get off most every night for a while. They haven't finished the barracks yet where I am living. We have no heat as yet and no jackstays to swing our hammocks to, and so they are allowing us to come out and get a bed. We get liberty every other night anyway. It is a great experience for me to be here and I am enjoying it very well but you know everywhere I went in the vast crowd I was lonesome. I wanted to see you. I never wanted to see you so much in my life as since the news came that the war has ended. It is such a time to be happy and to rejoice but it isn't easy for me to feel real happy any more when I can't see you. I wanted to write to you last night but I came down here with a sissy sort of fellow who was bound that I go with him to a show. I went. The show was good but it lasted until 11:30 (and we went in at eight). So it was so late when I got back that I did not have time to write. I hope you will forgive me for putting of [sic] writing to you for a show for it was not my own desire but another's persistence. The fellow's name is Tabor. He is a musical artist or thinks he is at least. He planned to take me over to the Grand Opera to-night but I accidentally missed him on purpose for I know you would be jealous if you should see me keeping company with "her." Sister Stone isn't a beginning. Then I wanted to write to you. I never loved you so much in my life. When I left you and didn't know how long it would be before I saw you again, I wondered if I would still love you as well after a long time as I did on the night I left you. The longer I stay away from you the more I love you and the more I want to see you. I guess you felt the same way when I left you about yourself. But there will never be a doubt now as to how long I will love you. I know I will be the happiest fellow in the world when I can come back and see you again and just enjoy your company for a while and can love you as I did when we were together last. Perhaps it may not be so long now until I get out. The general opinion is that the Reserves will get out within three or six months after the war is over. I guess that will mean after peace is signed however. I am going to put in another application to come back to school at mid-year. I fear it will be useless but I might get back, and now I could certainly come back with an easy conscience although I haven't done one thing yet that is of any benefit to the government. I have done all they gave me a chance to do however. I don't know one [thing] more about seamanship now than when I enlisted. One can't learn seamanship except by practice, and I hadn't even seen a ship till I got here. I haven't been on one yet. I am not doing one thing here, except have a big time. I shoveled sand for about thirty minutes to-day. I have read and run round all the rest of my time or sat on the sea wall and looked out on the harbor at the ships. I expect I will be sent to duty of some kind soon. I hope I am. A fellow gets tired doing nothing. Then it makes me want to come back to school and to see you much more when I realize that I am doing nothing. The rumor now is that we go to Bordeaux France as guards to guard government property there. I hope we do but it is all speculation. We have no idea where we will go. I think we will be sent out soon because of the lack of accommodations that we have in our barracks. I was billeted yesterday. They say we do not stay long after we get our pay numbers etc. After the twentieth I am supposed to draw my pay every two weeks. I have been wishing for that day now for about a week. I was expecting to draw again on the fifth but I got here on sixth so I had to wait until 20th. Now don't get it into your head I am broke as yet. I ain't.

Well, as luck will have it a Ky boy just now breezed in and wants me to go with him to the subway station that I happen to know from last night's experience. So I will stop this time and write again real soon. It seems a long time since I have heard from you but I know how long it takes. I have been expecting the box you sent to be forwarded but it hasn't come yet. I may never get it. I don't know whether it will be sent or not. Letters will be sent sometime if they are not lost on the way.

With a loving "goodnight," Elliott

NOVEMBER 12, 1918

Elma says that Georgetown also had "a fine parade," and the SATC boys got to be in it, but the "poor girls had to stand in a line on the sidewalk with [their] hands folded and never utter a sound." The college president has been thinking of taking away the girls' self-governance "because about half a dozen fast girls have been doing things they should not....Some girls have been slipping off and going to Lexington in cars." She also mentions a wounded French soldier who has arrived on campus and will finish his education at Georgetown.

Tuesday Morning
  8 o'clock
  Dearest Elliott:

Although I have four classes to-day and have not so much as looked at any of them, I'm going to write a little letter. It has been over a week since I last wrote, but really seems more like a month. Your letter written from Brooklyn came yesterday and I enjoyed the description of your trip so much.

Have been getting along beautifully with my work — even with Dr.

Leigh. Took off my first trial ballance [sic] Saturday and found that the books were out of ballance [sic] $123.65 so I have before me the most delightful task of finding the said amount.

You were telling about the excitement in New York on Thurs. Well Georgetown wasn't very far behind I'm telling you. It was about 1 o'clock when the bell began to ring and everybody struck out for town where we found excitement running high. I got out of all my classes except Prof Hill's. But believe me he went on as calmly and serenely as if nothing had ever happened. Still more excitement went on last night. Had a fine parade. S.A.T.C. boys got to be in it but we poor girls had to stand in a line on the sidewalk with our hands folded and never utter a sound. You can imagine how painful such an ordeal would be with everybody rejoicing around you. Dr. Adams is disgusted with Rucker Hall girls he says and is talking of taking Self Government[4] away from us. All because about half a dozen fast girls have been doing things they should not. A bunch of us went walking Sunday afternoon and met two girls with boys walking out on the Frankfort Pike, some distance the other side of where you turn off to go to the Old Mill. Dr. Adams happened to see them and had them campused for two weeks. All kinds of wild things have been going on around here this year. Some girls have been slipping off and going to Lexington in cars. It sure is awful to have to suffer for the transgressions of others.

A wounded French Soldier arrived here Saturday night and is going to complete his education in G.C. He can speak English fairly well — well enough to say that the American girls were more familiar with men than any he had ever seen. He got that impression at a party which was given by the Society bunch on the night of his arrival. Georgetown played the Wild Cats over here Saturday afternoon and got beaten by a score of 21 to 3, Jennings made a drop kick and that was the only score Georgetown made but it was a good close game. "Dutch" Lehnhard starred and Bauer got through the line and had only one man between him and a touch down two times but that one man brought him down both times.

State brought a band along with them — it was some band too for it had one piece of the Franklin band in it. Do you have any recollection of hearing that Band?

I'm all upset 'cause Blanche is talking seriously of going home to stay until Christmas. She had the "flu" and is so nervous now that she can't stand any excitement or worry at all. I sure will be lonesome if she does go, but I imagine I can get more studying done for there is always a big crowd in here to see her and I know if she leaves there'll never be anyone in here.

Another Library Rule has been made. No girls are allowed in the Lib in the daytime because it is to be used as a study hall for the S.A.T.C. boys when they are not in classes. The girls are at liberty to use it from 7 to 9:30 at night and no boys are allowed in during those hours. This is getting to be one fierce place...

"Bill" Bauer, Clyde Mullins (in other words Sis) and some other boy were expecting to go to Camp Hancock Georgia this week but an order came out in last night's paper saying that draft calls were cancelled and they may not go. I was so thrilled until I saw where the Navy would take no steps toward demobilization but that it was thought they would be sent to France to guard until peace terms could be drawn up, which would probably take two years.

I heard last night that Delma and Oral went to Nashville, Tenn Saturday and got married. I sure am glad for they were in love alright and had been going to-gether ever since they were kidds [sic].

Oral is expecting to have to go in the next call and he decided he couldn't go without marrying first. The whole business was planned the day before and I guess they are supremely happy since he doesn't have to go at all. She may be proud of him but I don't believe I could be.

I hope you do get to go to France, for I feel like it will be such an education for you. I really believe with what you already have, it would mean more than four years in College. Don't worry about leaving me – 'cause I can manage to do something until you get back. The way looks dark and lonely many many times but I am willing to face it, in order that you may be great. I am expecting you to come out of the Service, a man in every sense of the word.

It is about Office time and I must go. Let me beg of you to enjoy the opportunity that you now have and be assured that I am thinking of you and praying for you every day.

Yours with love, Elma

LOVE LETTERS

NOVEMBER 14, 1918

Elliott is very lonesome and says it "feels so queer walking round in a crowd all the time and never seeing a soul that he knows." He has moved five times since coming to New York and has become separated from his old company; he is now in a barracks with "a bunch of strangers." He says he doesn't like the East much and has decided that a southerner is "always a southerner at heart no matter where he goes." When he picked up the evening paper, he was excited to see the headline, "Navy releases college men."

Thursday night

Dearest "little girl:"

How are you to-night? If you feel as lonesome as I do you do not feel extra. I wrote you a letter this afternoon and was going to mail it when I came out on liberty. I forgot it and so I am writing an absolutely new one with the same contents. I am writing again because I thought perhaps you would get it sooner. Then it helps me to pass off the time. You may think it sounds queer for me to say I am lonesome in New York City, but I never felt so lonesome in my life. One feels so queer walking round in a crowd all the time and never seeing a soul that he knows. I am in a barracks now with a bunch of strangers. I don't know a soul. I was with a part of my old company but I have been moved so much that we are all separated now. I have been moved five times since I got to this station and yet it is a very small place. I was with a good friend of mine, Mr. Keena from Ohio. I think I have written to you about him before. He was put on board a freighter to-day bound for France. He is a graduate of Princeton. I expect I am apt to be put on a ship in a short time now and yet I might be here for some time yet (unless I get mustered out C). Don't think I'm coming home 'cause I fear it will be some time yet before we get mustered out.) I think I will begin going to headquarters every day and ask for a furlough until they give me one. Do you think they would ever get tired enough of me to grant me one? I believe I have been in long enough to rate one and really I am going to try about the twentieth I think. I guess there's not much chance but if I never ask I will never get anything. I wish they would let me come home in time to begin the second semester of school. You know I have some hopes that I might since conditions are changing so rapidly. I am at the Brooklyn Y.M.C.A. Have just been singing and had a pretence [sic] of a movie. I would call it a fake however.

I have been watching the mail list very closely of late (two lists each day of incoming mail are posted on a bulletin at the P.O.). You have no idea how much I miss hearing from my "little girl." It seems like an age almost. Of course I know you haven't had time yet to send me a letter since I sent my address but I was hoping I might get a letter that you might have sent to Camp Luce and which had been forwarded to me. I never wanted to see you so much in my life as since I came to N.Y. I don't like the East much. I know now why a southerner is always a southerner at heart no matter where he goes. Ideals and conduct are much better in the South.

Say, Elma, I just now picked up an evening paper. The first thing I see in big headlines on the first page is "Navy releases college men." The article says that college men who now wish to return to school may do so and says for candidates to see their commander if so desiring. So I will march up to my captain to-morrow at eleven A.M. and see what he says. Really I may get back to school by mid-year as I have mentioned before I would feel free to come back now too if I get a chance. I would love to take a trip across but I believe college would mean more to me. Living conditions in the navy here are not bad but military life when not necessary doesn't appeal to me. I realize that I have done nothing and my stay in the navy so far is an absolute failure, but I do feel I could have done more if I had been given a chance. Of course it would take some time for me to get everything fixed up even if they accept my resignation and they may not. I would have a better chance I know if I was on a ship and had seen some sea service. I may have to stay in for so much active ship service. Perhaps I will know soon. I may have to get another recommendation from Dr. Adams (if he will recommend me). I gave in his other letter in my first application and never got it back.

It is now about 11:30. I have to get up at five in order to get back to camp in time. So I will stop.

With much love,
Elliott

NOVEMBER 14, 1918

Elma was in high spirits when she wrote this letter. She tells Elliott to "be sure and take in all the sights" in New York for both of them, so he can show them to her later. She says it would "beat office work all to smash."

Rucker Hall
> Thursday Night
> 8 o'clock
> Dearest "Sailor Boy:"

I think you must be having a gay time rambling around in the big city. Be sure and take in all the sights for both of us then maybe a few years hence I'll let you show them to me. Wouldn't that be de lightful? 'Twould beat office work all to smash I imagine. Say, I'm getting so interested in Political Science that I'm sceered I'm going to turn out to be a suffer igit.[5] Honest to goodness, I enjoy it more than any subject I have this year. That's saying an awful lot!!! For I'm in love with all my books.

I had to stop just then for Blanche to read me a proposal which she got to-day. It was from a young scape goat that went to school to her two years and of all killin' epistles, it surpasses everything a mile. She is endeavoring now to frame a consolatory answer. Here's hoping that she will crush him gently. I believe she has smashed more tender young hearts than any one person I know.

The Frenchman has been furnishing a great deal of amusement around the campus of late. He went up to one of the Freshman boys and asked him if he should have a bath before he left the campus. The poor Freshie finally discovered that he wanted to know if he should have a pass. He must be having great difficulty with his language.

Now for the big confession which I have to make. It is relative to something that is far worse than anything I have ever done before — oh yes! It is even worse than your going to the show with Mr. 'Sis.' Of course I'm just as sorry and penitant [sic] as a little girl could be and solemnly swear, never to do it again — until I do it again next time. Really I just couldn't help it cause it all happened 'fore I knew what was going on. Lest you get unduly wrought up about the matter I will hasten to tell the whole story: The shades of evening had begun to fall, the moon was rising over the skeleton tree tops, silence reigned supreme, I was stealing gently from the Hall of Pawling when lo! The image of a man appeared by my side and there it remained until I had reached the Hall of Rucker. It was none other than your friend and admirer, Mr.

Vaughn, who did not cease to sing your praises during the entire journey.

Well, dearie, I believe I'm tired of raving. I want to tell you one thing in real seriousness, that is — I love you — better every minute. I know just how you felt when you wrote to me on the 11th. I'd almost be afraid for you to walk in on me here in Rucker Hall for I know there would be danger of me shocking somebody to death. I hope when you do come back, we can have a little while all by ourselves. I'm just selfish enough to wish a thing like that.

Faith had a letter from John Browning last night. He is in France and has been there since Oct 1. He said he walked into a "Y" but one day and whom should he find but Coach Hinton. Can you picture the meeting?

There is to be another game here Saturday with St. Mary's. Hope we have better success than we did with State. The boys were all packed up ready to start for the Officer's training camp this morning and received orders about 20 min before train time to stay here. They sure were a disappointed bunch. I must stop and write mother and dad a few lines to let them know I am still thriving nicely. Be a good little boy and don't get into too much mischief while you are running around loose in N.Y.

Wif heaps and heaps of love

From your "Little Girlie"

NOVEMBER 16, 1918

> *This starts out as one of Elma's "blue" letters, which often follow her "giddy" ones. She has not received a letter from Elliott for a while and knows that he "must be out on the deep blue sea somewhere." However, the letter is written in installments over a period of several days, and she seems to perk up somewhat as she reports on various campus activities. By the time she signs off, she has read in the school paper that the Navy boys are expected to be back in school by mid-year and says, "Ee!! Don't I hope so."*

Saturday Night

Dearest Elliott:

I am the mostest disappointed and lonesome little girl to-night that you ever saw. Have been expecting a letter from you for the last three days and here it is Saturday night with not a word since Wednesday. I know you must be out on the deep blue sea somewhere. No matter where you are, I hope you are happy.

The "Tigers" played St. Mary's this afternoon and licked 'em up but as I didn't go, I can't tell you the details. However the score was 20 to 0 in favor of G.C. And there came very near being a fight between Prof Hill's brother, who was umpiring, and one of the Saints.

The Student Friendship Drive has been on this week and we're trying to raise enough to pay "Bobby" Hinton's salary while in France which amount is $1800. We lack a heap sight of reaching it yet but Prof Hill is on the job as chairman and you know he always puts things through.

The Zetas gave a fine program to-night or rather Prof Ichie gave it for them. He gave an illustrated lecture on France and it was extremely interesting. Of course he had visited all the places and knew so much to tell.

I'm writing to-night 'cause I think I'm going out to dinner to-morrow. Think of it! The first time I ever had a chance to take dinner out of Rucker Hall. Blanche, Lelia Harris and I are invited down to

Mrs. Harts [sic]. I sure am thrilled over the prospect. And don't you know. Blanche and I had two invitations to feasts tonight. One down to the Senior House and another here in the Hall. Since it is raining we preferred to accept the one inside. Then too the one we accepted is going to have wild duck. She got a big box from home and she lives in Arkansas.

We elected officers in Zeta to-night. I was the only one who was a candidate for treasurer consequently was duly elected by acclamation. Quite a desirable office, you'll have to admit since, if I'm not mistaken, you had the pleasure of holding it in T.θ.K.

I have something very distressing to tell you. I'm gaining every day. Weighed this afternoon and it was 135 lbs. Have gained almost 20 lbs since last summer. The harder I work the more I gain and of course it doesn't matter how tired I get. I don't get one bit of sympathy. I felt so elated yesterday afternoon when Mr. Browning said I had worked hard all day and turned off so many jobs that he thought I deserved a vacation of ten minutes. That was after I had worked from 1 o'clock to 5:30. Wasn't he sweet?

I don't believe I have ever told you about coming so near getting proposed to, have I? It happened this way. I was in the act of taking my departure from the Office a few evenings ago, when Wee Willie remarked that he was so tired. I said, "So am I." He said, "Tired of what? Study?" I said "No. Tired of living." He said "Tired of living alone?" I said "Yes." _____ Silence _____ ensued.

The feast is spread so I must go. Will finish in the morning.

It happened to be Sunday night before I got back but I'm here and will proceed. I did take dinner down at Mrs Harts [sic] and had the goodest time. Such a good time that we stayed for supper. Had rabbit and all kinds of rare eats. Had lots of fun playing with the children too.

Next week is test week and oh! How I dread it!!!!!!!! These are the first tests that have come along.

Monday Morning. This certainly is a chopped up letter. So many folks came in our room last night and raved around until the lights were out that I didn't get to finish.

I saw in the *Georgetonian* where the navy boys were expecting to get back in school by mid-year. Ee!! Don't I hope so. Just think if I can pass in everything this year I'll be a Senior next year and you know what that means, if you come back. I can't realize that I have only two more sets of final exams between me and seniority. Haven't any more paper, so will have to stop.

With all my love,
Elma

NOVEMBER 16, 1918

Since Elliott arrived in New York, he has had more time to write long, philosophical letters, although he has to use a box for a desk and a tin pail for a seat. In this letter he talks about what it's like to live under military rules, raves about the kind of fast women he has encountered in New York, expresses his appreciation for Elma's love and what it has done for him, and reflects on the mistake he made in volunteering for service rather than waiting to be drafted.

Friday night

Dearest "little girl:"

I got your nice long letter yesterday which was written on the 12th. My how glad I was to get it. I have been perfectly happy ever since. I enjoyed reading about all the excitement too. Things almost as wild as you and I used to pull off have been happening I believe. Perhaps they are worse. I don't think we ever broke many rules did we? At least we were not caught and that seems to be the main idea these days is to keep from being found out. That is a special idea of the navy that one rates whatever he is able to get away with. Believe me we take some wild chances too. I say you must be living under military rules from what you tell me. These are sure bad times in my estimation altho I hope and believe the worst is now over. Gee but I know what it means to be under strict rules. And you mentioned the fact that you have to suffer for the sins of others. I know how to sympathize with you there. There isn't a day passes that I do not suffer or stand some punishment for the fault of someone else. I can't get used to it either. I say it is a wrong system wherever it is practiced or under whatever circumstances. I can stand any punishment for a fault of my own but it gets next to me when I have to be punished for something someone else has done.

    You were speaking of the French man's idea of the American girls. He must have landed in New York City. Talk about your fast women. I never saw fast women till I came here. I have been out on the street most every night since I came here. It is a common sight to see soldiers and sailors walking even in the most public streets with their arm round a girl and I have seen them in the day time. I have gone to the movies several times. That is the style here at the movie for the boy to have his arm round the girl. On the day of the celebration here the soldiers and sailors were going through the crowd, and most any good looking girl they saw they would go up put their arms round them and kiss them. That may sound unreasonable to you. I wouldn't have believed it if I had not seen it happen. I did not see it in a single instance but I venture to say in more than twenty different instances. Then I hear the sailors talk round here about the women in New York. It is unbelievable if I had not see [sic] what I have seen them do publicly. I hear boys talk who have lived here all their lives. They confirm most any report that I might have heard. I never dreamed that society could be so corrupt. It is the so called better class too. You know them, the society folks, but I know you don't know them as I have seen them in New York City. I do not think all women here are that type but most all that one sees on the streets round where the men in uniform go most. That is what makes the soldier's life hard for a man who wants to be decent. To be plain a soldier can't be decent and stay on the streets in this city, unless he just looks straight ahead and keeps moving at a rapid pace. I have quit going anyplace except to the Y.M.C.A. since I found out the real conditions round on the streets where the sailors usually go. I guess you get tired of my eternal ravings about women. The reason I say so much about them is because I know now how to really appreciate you for I know I can trust you. I don't believe anybody appreciates or honours true womanhood, I mean the purity of true womanhood more than I do. Another reason I am always raving about women is that I can appreciate what your love and my love for you has done for me. If it had not been for my determination and desire to be true to you I could never have come back from the navy a true man or a gentleman. If my confidence in you and my love for you could never mean more to me than that I have room to be grateful to you. And oh how happy I am when I think of your purity and know that you love me. Really that fact makes it comparatively easy for me to be clean and to live a straight life.

I am sorry Blanche has been sick and I hope she doesn't leave you for I know you will miss her very much, but I fear you won't miss as much of your present company as you think you will.

I was so glad to hear that Delma is married for it was evident that she loved Oral. And I am very glad that he doesn't have to go to war. You know I look at being drafted in a different light to what I did. I think it really was the right thing to do. I don't think anybody will look at it that way but I think I made a mistake when I volunteered. I am glad I volunteered however for I got an easy conscience by doing so, but I lost out just what time I stay here. I am not learning anything. Of course I am getting some experience in the world (mostly of temptations). The reason I think I made a mistake is that after I got into the navy I just had to wait for a draft in the end. I have no choice whatever in what I do. So you see I just stood by doing nothing until the draft needed me and by the way it hasn't needed me yet. I find the military service is a draft system all the way thru and that's why I say the man who waited was the real far-sighted man. I do not know how long I may have to stay in the navy and for me it will be a waste of time. Now that the war is over I can't take any interest in the work at all. In fact I am not having any work to do. I hope I leave this place soon. A big bunch went out of this barracks to-day for Key West Fla. They were taken alphabetically and ran just down to my name. I wanted to go on that bunch just because it was going South. I may be among the next ones who go.

You said you hope I get to go to France. I would love to have the trip, but I can't agree with you that it would equal four years in college, for you know if I should go just on a ship the chances are I wouldn't see much, not apt to be more than one port. You said you expect me to be great. If my greatness all depends upon my success in the navy I'll never be more than a two by four. Absolutely I can't succeed in the navy. I realize it absolutely and I have given up hope of making good in it. You have no idea how many resolutions I have made and how much I have tried to succeed because I love you but there is no chance here for me. It must be in another field if I ever gain success. Therefore the sooner I get out now the better satisfied I'll be. The reason I can't succeed is it takes two or three enlistments to win a commission in peace times and [I] could never stand that. I can be a true man so long as I love you. I can be that in the navy or anywhere else but it is not always easy.

I never have got to see about coming back to school yet. I went to request mast to-day and stood in line for two hours to put in my request. Mast was closed just before I got to the window. Nearly everybody was asking for 48 hours leave. We just get one chance each day to put in a request of any kind. I guess I will have to wait till Monday now as they do not have mast on Sunday. I guess I will be shipped out before then. That is about my luck. Perhaps I will get out by mid-year. I have hopes that I will.

I happened upon an old friend of mine from near home to-day. He just got home from a 13 day furlough. He has been in the service for 9 months. His ship was rammed by an oil tanker about 700 miles out from N.Y. It sank within five minutes he said. It happened at 12:30 at night. He was in the water one hour. He lost all his clothes and possessions. I guess he had some narrow escape. He had made one trip across already. He told me the report was out in his neighborhood that I am dead. Said he heard that I died at Great Lakes of the flu. He said he was very much surprised to see me, and I was as much so to see him. I guess there isn't much sense in this letter. A fellow has been talking to me all the time since I began to write. I like him fine but best if he is silent when I write to you. It is now time for taps. I will stop.

With the most of love,
Elliott

P.S. I have the best of accommodations for writing. I have a box for a desk and a tin pail for a seat. You don't wonder that there are so many blots do you. I have to reach out arms length to reach the paper at all. E.C.

MARCIE MCGUIRE

NOVEMBER 19, 1918

Once again, Elliott has gotten his hopes up that he can come back to school, only to have them dashed. He went to see about coming back to school but says there is "nothing doing" because the officer in charge is "the biggest nut in the navy." He is now "all packed up ready to be sent aboard" the U.S.S. Maumee, an oil ship.

Dear Elma:

I am all packed up ready to be sent aboard a ship. I may go tonight and I may not go till tomorrow. I am to be on the U.S.S. Maumee. It is an oil ship. That is all I know about it for sure. I do not know where it goes or when. One fellow who is going with us has been on it before. He is going again by special request. He says it has a nice bunch of officers and that it is a nice clean ship. He said it sailed from the Mexican coast before and landed at Scotland, Ireland, and France. So the chances are that I may see quite a bit before I get back. I went to see about coming back to school. There is nothing doing yet, especially with these officers. I will have a much better chance to get out after I have been on a cruise. Then I could not expect to enter school now until mid-year anyway. The officer in charge here is the biggest nut in the navy and I wouldn't be afraid to gamble on it. I am really glad I am going on one trip at least for I would hate to say I had been in the navy and never on board ship. They say we can have a great time on the Maumee. I did want to be on a battle ship but as the war is over I would much prefer the freighter because they have to stay three months on a cruiser once on board. At least that is the custom. Then on the freighter we are not under such strict regulations. Then the battle ship does not always land when it goes across. One fellow told me he went across six times and never did land at all (on the other side).

Say, I got the *Georgetonian* to-day. I enjoyed reading every word of it, especially the report about navy men although that report isn't official so the officers here claim.

By the way I have some great good, excellent, scrumptious news for you. I just know you will fall over when I tell you. He looks just as cute as ever and he's really a sailor going out to-day on the battle cruiser Huntington. He says he thinks he will be back to G.C. by mid-year. Yes sir-ee I really saw your good friend Fulton. Fulton Miller I mean. Now isn't that good news for you?

Seemingly you are the most penitent little soul I ever knew for your would be faults of walking with the men. I always told you I had no objections to you going with the men but I didn't really think it would come to this. Really I am surprised at you going with Mr. Vaughn. Isn't that sarcastic? And doesn't it really sound like me? Seriously I do not mean any of that. I think a whole lot of Mr. Vaughn. He is a dandy fellow and I really think he does like me and I honestly appreciate his good feeling for me, and he really likes you too. I think he is a real gentleman, and I have no thing to say against it.

Well, "little girl" it may be a long time before I hear from you again and you may not hear from me for some time. I will write just as often as I can. I hope you don't miss my letters too much. I know how I will miss your letters but I will get all of them some time. It may be that I won't hear from you till I get back if I go across, but I really hope I will get out when I get back. Address my mail:

S.E. Cranfill S2C
Receiving ship at NY
Bay Ridge Barracks, C23
Brooklyn, NY

This is my complete address. It will follow me O.K. If I get a new address I will send it as soon as I get it. If I really get the trip I expect to it is a valuable experience for me. I have seen many things valuable to me educationally already. I know it is hard for you to tell just how I feel about the navy. I like it one time when I write you and hate it seemingly in my next. As a fact, there is much good to be gotten if attentive and much that is unpleasant. I have really tried to tell you both sides as they are and as I see them. I try to get the good in practice and avoid and overlook the bad as much as possible.

Gee, but you made me feel good when you said we might see New York together. I don't care whether it is New York or not but I will be happy if we may be viewing "some place" some day together. And I sure hope it isn't many years (yes years did you say?) if it must be years. Well, you expressed my sentiments exactly when you said you wanted us to be alone for awhile when I get back. I don't think it selfish at all either. I think we have a perfect right to wish to be alone. You wouldn't shock me to death I don't care what you should do when I come back if it was because you love me. In fact I wouldn't care who knows I love you so far as I am concerned. And I am prouder of the fact that you love me than anything I know.

I just got a letter from my brother [Isaac] to-day. He just the same as told me that he is engaged to the little girl at home [Grace Crossfield] whose picture I was showing you. I used to go with her a little. He has loved her for a year or more, but he didn't seem to be sure about it. I guess the separation has made him sure. He says he will not have to go to France now and that he thinks he will be home by Xmas.

Be good and know I am not forgetting you if you do not hear from me as often as you have been. I hope I will be back home by midyear. I may not but I will be back as soon as possible.

I will stop this time.

With love as ever,

Elliott

NOVEMBER 20, 1918

Elma took time out from studying for tests to write this short note to try to cheer up her "sailor boy." She says she knows just how he feels upon seeing the "corruptness of Society," since she felt something like that while staying in Bowling Green. She encourages him to be "brave and strong" and to believe that everything will work out alright in the end, even though he may feel at times like he is entirely out of luck.

Wednesday Night
10 o'clock
Dearest Elliott:

If you'll excuse this paper, I'll write you a wee little note and tell you I'm still loving you harder than ever. Honest to goodness this is the onliest paper I possess and I just had to write to-night and try to cheer you up a bit. The letter I received to-day seemed to indicate that my sailor boy had the "blues." Please, don't let them get the best of you, 'cause it won't do. I know just exactly how you feel — at least I imagine it is something like I felt while I was staying in B.G. and seeing the corruptness of Society. I had my eyes more opened then than ever before and of course that was nothing to compare with N.Y. Be brave and strong. Everything will work out alright in the end, though you may feel at times like you are entirely out of luck.

I've been studying, studying, studying for tests. Had French this morning and have English and Education to-morrow. Bible and Political Science Saturday. It is the testing time sure enough for I haven't had much time for study.

I wrote 150 letters this afternoon — however, they were on the multigraph. You didn't know I had gone into the printing business, did you? Well, I had my first experience at setting up and taking down type this afternoon. Then operating the machine wasn't such a very easy job, but I'm still surviving.

It is too cold to go out in the hall and the lights are about to go out so I must say "good night." Don't get insulted at this little message and I'll do better when tests are over.

With worlds of love,
Your little girl

∼

NOVEMBER 23, 1918

Elliott finally got paid so he was able to send a little to Elma to help out with school expenses.

Dear Elma,

Yesterday was pay day and I am sending you a little gift. It has been some time since I had a pay day but I got $73 yesterday. I am keeping enough to have a "big" time on "C" till next pay day. I will write you a letter to-night. I thought I had better register this for safety.

        Elliott Cranfill
        U.S.S. Maumee
        ℅ Postmaster of New York, NY

∼

NOVEMBER 23, 1918

This letter was written on the U.S.S. Maumee. *Elliott says he is "a real sailor now" although his ship is broken down and won't move for at least 45 days. He was afraid the ship would be an old greasy dirty ship but was pleased to find it had a piano, Victrola, violins, a library, a cat, and real beds. He put in his application for a discharge but expects it will take a while before he hears anything.*

Dearest Elma,

It has now been several days since I wrote to you. I could have written while on board ship but letters mailed on the ship are censored. So I thought I would wait until I got liberty to write to you. I was set free to-day at one o'clock to do as I please until Monday morning at eight A.M. Forty-eight hours the longest time I have been free since I enlisted in the navy.

Well, I am a real sailor now although my ship doesn't move. It is broken down and they expect it to take 45 days to get it repaired. So I am apt to be here at the Brooklyn dock some time yet, perhaps all winter. I am on a regular naval ship. It is an oil supply vessle [sic] about 700 ft long and perhaps one hundred ft wide. It carries 200 men as the crew. It is all steel and only about three years old (what will be its size when it is grown?). It carries 3,000,000 gallons of oil as a cargo. So you see it is some ship. It is clean too. I was afraid it would be an old greasy dirty ship but the oil is all below and the crew lives on the second deck (that's from the top). It is a real home, except the woman. We have a piano, victrola, violens [sic], library, and a cat. And we really have beds too. Gee but I sure have slept the last two nights. We have good eats too. I have to get up now at six instead of five and I can go to bed at 7:30. I used to have to wait till 8:30. I begin work at 8:30 and work till 11:30, begin again at one and quit at 4:30. I am helping paint the ship now. It is some job too. Being on ship is far better than the training station. Really a ship is something decent to live in and there is something attractive about it. All the fellows are genial and pleasant. I find a ship is really what I thought the navy would be when I enlisted. If I could stay on a ship all the time I could be much better satisfied, but the navy isn't my calling as I find it on ship. I put in my application for a discharge this morning. The Captain read an order to us yesterday from the Bureau of Navigation which said men in the U.S. Naval reserve force would be allowed to resign as soon as possible to return to college and business. He told us to put in our applications immediately if we desired to go back to school or business or for any other good reason. It will be sometime before I hear from it I expect, for it has to be sent to Washington, D.C. to be passed upon by the bureau of navigation. I think I will be able to get out O.K. It may be some time yet. I really hope it is before we sail, for it might be a couple of months before I get back from the cruise once we get started. I would like to get the trip but I'd rather come back to school.

I had a terrible time at Bay Ridge for the last day or so that I was there. About 200 of us were called to the draft office for different ships. We all had to stay in the same little room all the time waiting for our ship to call us. I had to sleep on the floor two nights. The place was crowded, dirty, and full of cigarette smoke. I was there two days and two nights before called to the ship. I don't know why, but they wouldn't let us go to our barracks till wanted. I sure was glad when they called out for the Maumee draft. They put us on a boat, The General Putnam, with six other small drafts and started out across the harbour. We started at 12 o'clock. They took us way up the Hudson River and took about 100 men of the battleship Rhode Island, which was lying at anchor up there along the six other battle cruisers. Then they turned round and headed for Bay Ridge again. We had no idea where our ship was, we expected to see it every one we saw during the whole trip up the Hudson. When we got back in sight of Bay Ridge we all began to fear we were going back, but finally they took us in to the dock and put us on the Maumee. We landed at about 6:30. So you see we had quite a little trip anyway. We got a good view of New York, Brooklyn, and Jersey City along the water front. The Rhode Island is a dreadnaught. It is the first one I ever saw. Those boys sure were glad to get off of it too. Everything is regulation on a battleship. That is one has to be in uniform all the time and work under strict orders and rules. I am glad I did not get a battle ship. We can wear dungarees on our ship. (That is the navy term for overalls.)

Well, yesterday was pay day and I sent you a little gift this afternoon by registered mail. I don't know whether or not you will get it or this first. The 20th was pay day on the station. So that day I was put on a draft and couldn't draw. I came on to the ship and they gave a special pay day for our benefit. I get paid every two weeks now so they say. I thought perhaps I would be able to help you more than I have but it takes more for a sailor to live than I thought. Then while I have the opportunity I want to see some of the educational parts of New York. I will send you some more if I don't get out any ways soon. If they won't release me another way I am going to buy out or try it at least. They say they let us out if we pay $60 dollars for our uniform. If I can't get out any other way I am going to try that after a while. I think I will get out O.K. however. Say they made me put my name and address on the outside of the registered letter. I hope you get this first so there will be no occasion for embarrassment on your part if anyone should see the letter.

I would have sent it by special delivery but I feared it might get lost. Elma, I can't help you much because I am paying off some of my debts at home, but really it is the only pleasure I have while in the navy to send you what little I can spare and know that you think enough of me to accept it. I wish I could pay your way so that you wouldn't have to do outside work, for I know you must be tired to do school work and office work too. Perhaps we shall both see more prosperous and happy days in the future.

Well, you told me such an interesting story about your proposal. I mean you started to tell it. You stopped just at the exciting part. I was getting very much wrought up when silence ensued. I hope you are not really tired of living. Cheer up. Now that the war is over, you may not always have to live alone (unless it is of your own choice). My! I believe I would be the happiest creature in the world if I knew I would be free again in a short time as I really hope I may be.

When you write to me now address it U.S.S. Maumee ℅ Postmaster at New York NY and I will get it O.K.

I am at the "Y" to-night. I think I shall go over to New York to-morrow and to church to-morrow night. I wonder sometimes what church would be like in New York City. I may never find the way back to my ship Monday morning but I think I will. I went over to the Sailor's "Y" on the other side of Brooklyn to-night and there was such a crowd I could hardly get in. So I came back over here.

Well, I guess I had better stop this time for I doubt if you can ever read all this junk now. I have tried to tell you a little news to-night, something about what I am doing, something besides the one thing I want to tell you all the time.

With love,
Elliott

~

NOVEMBER 25, 1918

Elma was "happy beyond words" to receive Elliott's letter saying he wouldn't sail for some time and still had a chance of getting out. She especially misses him on Saturday nights when everyone is having a good time while she sits in her room and "wishes and wishes" for the time when he'll be back. There are still several cases of the flu in Georgetown, and the ban is only partially lifted. There is only one church service per week, and picture shows and public gatherings are still prohibited. Reports are that the flu is as bad in Lexington as it has ever been and State University is still closed.

Monday afternoon
Dearest Elliott:

I was a bit surprised to-day when I walked in to dinner late and Blanche told me I had a special delivery up stairs. I had had a feeling that I wouldn't hear from you any more for some time and of course I was happy beyond words, even so happy that I didn't take time to eat but two muffins 'fore I rushed up to my room and devoured every word of your little epistle. My! but I was glad to hear that you would not sail for some time and that you would have some chance of getting out before the time was up. Oh! Please hurry and come back to school, for it sure is lonesome without you. Most everybody has a gay time on Saturday nights this year 'cept me and I just sit up in my room and wish and wish for the time when you'll be back. But, of course, we couldn't enjoy the crowd so very much. Could we?

The registered letter hasn't come yet. It will perhaps get here some time this afternoon or to-night. It is lovely of you to always think of me when you are payed, but please, dear, don't fail to keep every cent you need. I am getting along fine and making a little above my expenses besides daddy sends me some occasionally. The work doesn't seem to be hurting me one bit. I even lived through test week and almost believe I passed in everything. In fact, I made 98 on my French test but there isn't any telling what the old sister will give me for the quarter. I did most disgracefully on Political Science but I'm hoping Prof. Hill, out of the goodness of his heart will donate a C to my records. You know I was a bit scared up over Bible but it was easy as dirt, and although I hadn't read but one lesson during the whole year, I crammed the night before and have a faint feeling that I may have punched Dr. Thompson out with an A. Education was somewhat wild and woolly and it's hard to tell what Prof. Richardson might give. English was comparatively easy and I guess I can count on a B in that as Prof Daniels acquired the habit of giving me B last year and I am sure it would be impossible for him to go above that.

'Suppose we change the subject. Mr. Browning (dear little Wee Willie) has symptoms of the "flu" and is absent from the Office to-day. As a consequence I am endeavoring to hold the fort and have nothing to do but write to you and answer questions, over the 'phone and otherwise. I can't see the necessity for me to hang around just for that, but Dr. Mitchell insists that it must be done.

Mr. Adkins went home this week end. The reason I happen to know is — in the absence of the Pres., V. Pres, and Dean on Saturday, Mr. Browning had to sign the boy's papers who were requesting a weekend furlough. When Mr. Adkins came in to get his signed, I smiled at him so sweetly like and he smiled back in the same manner. That was all that happened. Never a word spoken. I have a most awful curiosity to know what he would say, should I be afforded an opportunity to converse with him. There is to be a masquerade party in the gymnasium Thanksgiving night and everybody is figuring on having a lively time, even to Seniors. I am planning to represent "Little Bo Peep" that is if I don't take a fit and stay at home. You know they had a masquerade party year before last but I didn't go because I had a sick roommate.

We had preaching at church yesterday morning for the first time since the first Sunday in October. However the ban is only partially lifted and we are allowed only one service per week. Picture shows and public gatherings are still prohibited. They say the "flu" is as bad in Lexington as it has ever been and State is still closed. There are still several cases in Georgetown. For instance Prof Daniel had to miss his classes two days last week because Mrs. Daniel and the baby had the flu.

We had a little sample of military punishment this morning. A young fellow was made to pick up paper on the campus for a few hours while he was guarded by an armed soldier. That was right exciting in such a place as G.C.

Great preparations are being made for the Thanksgiving foot ball [sic] game. It is to be at Danville again. Dr. Adams and Lady Mac are laying their plans to keep the girls from going and you know it is worrying me most frantic. I would be sure(?) to go along if not prohibited.

Oh me! Oh my! That 'phone just keeps me bobbing up and running after somebody all the time. I really don't believe people would be so troublesome if they only knew how very busy I was and how much I dislike to be interrupted in the middle of a most important sentence. Guess who is coming to G.C. to-day. I had a letter from home Saturday, saying "Jake" was there and would come up here to-day and pay us a little visit. I rather imagine he will miss teasing us to-gether. Even if he should tease me all by myself, I believe I will be right glad to see him. And you tell me my most adorable Fulton has sailed. Were it not for one thing I doubt if I should ever be able to withstand the shock. That's that I have the privilege of writing to Fred Amerson. Yes siree! I have written two letters to him and he is now in the Officers Training School at Hampton Roads, Va. Ira Porter is there too. They got in the 15th of Nov. Oh yes I know all about him, 'cause you see I'm Dr. Leigh's Secretary these days. Why I even wreite to "Slim" Taylor sometimes and Hayden Roberts. Yes he is in France now. It certainly is nice to be able to keep up with your real intimate friends, especially in war times. Really, laying all jokes aside, I do miss the bunch of fellows that had been here both years that I have, for instance John Browning, Harold Snuggs, Joe Bailey etc. Although I miss these terribly, it is nothing to compare with the way I miss you, of course.

Dr. Mitchell has just blown in and of all the dashing around and smacking of gum, he do beat all. He is talking to me in a blue streak all the time and I just say yes or no and keep on writing. Sometimes I say the right thing and sometimes I don't. Little should I worry about him. Thank goodness! He has breezed out in the hall for a few minutes so I will proceed. He is the most nerve racking man I ever did see. Now he has returned again and all I can hear is the never ceasing popping of his gum. Oh it is music fit for the gods!!!!

Dear, I certainly am glad you are situated more comfortably now than you were in the Station. It must have been miserably uncomfortable during all those months. Hope you won't freeze this cold cold weather. I sent you a sweater just before you left Great Lakes but I suppose it was lost before it reached you so I'm trying to chase it down. If I ever find it I'll save it for you or send it on, just as you like.

Well I think I shall plead with Dr. Mitchell to let me off so I can go to town and mail this. Be good and don't do anything I wouldn't. And come back just as soon as you can.

Yours with love,
Elma

NOVEMBER 28, 1918

Elma received the money that Elliott sent and says she has more to be thankful for this Thanksgiving than any girl she knows — her health, a home with loving parents, and one who loves her sincerely. The only thing that would make her joy complete is to be with Elliott.

Wednesday Night
Dearest One:

It seems that you have done everything possible to prove your love to me. The little (?) gift came yesterday, and I was too much surprised for words. You are nothing less than an angel to me and I can't think of a single thing to do to pay you even in a small measure for all you have done for me. I just know I have more to be thankful for this Thanksgiving than any other girl I know. What more could one ask for than health, a home with loving parents and one who loves sincerely and whose love you can return. There is only one thing more which would make my joy complete, and that is to be with you. Blanche received a delightful surprise to-night when she got a letter from Ira saying he would be here to-morrow night or Friday morning. It hasn't been but about two months since he was here but I have never seen anyone quite so elated as she seemed to be. She read a little poem to me last night that went like this: "If He Came Now"[6]

If he came now!
My heart would be like a once quiet street,
Hung with gay lanterns on a fete night, wild
With singing! And my heart would be a child
sleepily waking to a kiss, then flinging
Sleep from it, spring[ing]
with all too ready feet,
Out of the night, into the world again,
and finding that its toys were all once more

> *there where it left them, waiting on the floor*
> *to be played with again. My heart would be*[7]
> *an opened book that had been left too long*
> *upon a dusty shelf. It would be a song*
> *in a young mouth. And it would be buds, too,*
> *opening under the moon, and shivering at the dew,*
> *but liking it.*
> *And it would be a flame,*
> *red in the night. I used to be glad when he came,*
> *but not so very glad — because I thought*
> *that I could always have him. Then war caught*
> *him up from me, and bore him out*
> *to be where danger is; and killed my doubt,*
> *my hesitation and half fears. Ah, how*
> *I would run to welcome him, if he came now.*

Blanche will soon have a chance to welcome him and how I wish that I might hope for my turn soon. Doesn't the part about doubts, hesitations and fears being killed, fit our case right well? I never felt so sure of my love for you as I have the past week. I believe real love is the kind that develops by gradual growth. I haven't much faith in the instantaneous kind that doesn't last after marriage. I have been watching married people particularly of late and I am about to come to the conclusion that happy marriages are very very scarce. Now I'm not saying they are impossible for I believe they are if the parties understand each other properly beforehand.

Do you find it hard to be contented with the routine of every day life? I remember when I was in High School. I had marvelous dreams of College life and I was dreadfully impatient to get through the little insignificant tasks that I was then performing and get out into something bigger. Now that I'm nearing the end of my College career I have the same restless feeling. I am eager for the time when I can launch out into the bigger fuller life. Oh! If you were only here that I might talk over my plans with you and feel the thrill of partnership. But perhaps I am giving to much thought to the future and not enough to the present. I guess the main thing now is to make the most of present opportunities and let the future take care of itself.

There was a big chapel rally to-night for the game to-morrow. I was so tired after having a general house-cleaning, then going to town this afternoon that I preferred to stay at home and write. However Blanche and Lelia made me read them a long long story before they would let me do what I wanted to. The lights have just winked, reminding me that I was invited to a feast but I didn't care about going 'cause it was in honor of a visitor in the Hall and I'm terribly skeered of strangers, you know.

Mr. Browning really has the "flu" as well as all his family and (Miss) George Newell has had it too. Now isn't that just too bad! I'm having a comparatively free time during Mr. B's illness. Dr. Mitchell has the grand idea that I should sit in the Office and waste my time doing nothin'. But I'm not particularly fond of drawing pay for nothing when I'm not supposed to so I runs off home and enjoys myself while time and opportunity is afforded.

Prof Hill made a splendid talk at Y.W. last night on the Thanksgiving spirit and I felt dreadful mean and ungrateful when he got thru. I wanted to write you a little letter right off and tell you how very much I appreciate what you are doing for me but I had such a painful headache and was so sick that I thought it would be best for me to wait until to-night, when I felt more like it. I hope you have a pleasant Thanksgiving and get just lots of good things to eat. I do wish I could have sent you some kind of a box but I have so little chance to fix up anything of the kind up here. Maybe some day I can prepare you all the good eats I want to, but I believe I promised to be good and not get off into the future any more to-night. The girls have come for me to go to the feast so I guess I can't resist any longer. With the very mostest of love, I am as ever,
Your "Little Girl"

NOVEMBER 29, 1918

This is another of Elma's "blue" letters, which was forwarded from the U.S.S. Maumee to Elliott's home in Sinai, Kentucky, on December 16. Elma was in her room, as lonesome as can be, looking out across campus at all the couples who had recently been reunited since the soldiers and sailors returned from the war. She asks Elliott's forgiveness for telling him "all these horrible feelings" but says if she doesn't get a letter tomorrow she is going to stay in bed all day Sunday and Monday.

Friday Night
 Just After Supper
 Dearest Elliott:
 I didn't know it was possible for anyone to be as lonesome as I have been to-day. Just now there is noise, noise everywhere but never a friendly sound. I sat down by the window this afternoon and as I looked out over the campus, I saw Blanche and Ira coming across, then Gene and Mary Anna. And in a few minutes along came Stumpy and Jessamine. It was almost more than I could stand. When the mail came around at dinner, a letter fell at our door. I just flew to get it and lo! It was to Blanche from Ira and there she was at that very minute sitting

down in the parlor talking to him. It almost made me feel like the saying: "Every dog has his day" is a false one but I guess it always proves true in the long run. So many of the boys have been in on a furlough in the last few days, for instance, "Jake," "Little Pat," "Doodle" Sullivan, Fred Amerson and Francis Glenn, and of course Ira. Now it isn't much wonder that I have been feeling exceedingly lonesome, is it? But I'm mean and selfish for telling you all these horrible feelings I've been having. Won't you forgive me since I haven't anyone else to tell them too [sic]. I used to burden you with all my little worries every two weeks, didn't I?

We had the fine masquerade party last night and I got gay and went. Dressed up like an Indian girl, with my face all painted and everything till I doubt if you would have recognized me. Can't say that I had a good time, but it was a new experience at any rate. They or rather we did the grand march and Virginia Reel, then the Glee Club sang. They served apples, pears and popcorn.

The game yesterday was distressing. I wrote a letter for Dr. Leigh today in which he said the score of the opponents was so large that he would conserve space by not telling it, however, I'm going to tell it. Centre[8] 83 and Georgetown 3. But the score wasn't the worst part. Nearly all the boys got knocked out. Coker got his ankle hurt right badly, Dutch Lehnhard had his collar bone broken and the covering from one of his ribs torn away. P.D. Powers got three ribs broken and pushed in on his lungs so they began bleeding and they feared last night that he was going to take pneumonia. I think there were some more slightly wounded but they were the most serious. They said the Centre team looked like giants beside our boys. Their lightest man weighed 50 lbs more than our heaviest, so they said.

It is now an hour later. There has been a crowd in here and the last one has just made her exit. Blanche has gone down and I am all alone much to my joy. I'm not half so lonesome when I'm by myself as I am when there is a bunch of gossiping folks around. Don't you think I'm awful to-night? Believe I'm soured on the world. No, that isn't it. I can't think of a single thing in this world that would make me feel good except — to see you for a while. I honestly believe I'm bad off and getting worse all the time. If I don't get a letter to-morrow I'm going to stay in bed all day Sunday and Monday. I may anyway as Mr. Browning is still sick with the "flu" and there isn't much to do in the Office. Sure 'nuff I haven't had a letter from you since the register which came on Tues I think. It seems like ages and ages. Please please please do all you can to get out as quick as possible. I fear I shall die if I don't get to see you some time soon. Ira expects to finish at the Officers Training School in April and get his commission. Then come back next year. Blanche and I are planning to try to get a room down at the Senior house. Seniors are allowed to have callers at their own discretion and to have them down there too. Won't that be scrumptious? Oh dear, dear, I had most forgotten that I have four classes to-morrow and haven't so much as peeped into a book yet and it [is] nearly 9 o'clock. I must get to work and try to forget how lonesome I am, until Blanche comes up at least. Again, I beg you to forgive me for telling you how blue I feel… I'll probably be over it by to-morrow and my next letter will most likely be some kind of a silly affair. Anyway I'm the same "little girl" regardless of the mood in which you find me.

With loads of Love,
Elma

CHAPTER 9
December, 1918

Smiles[1]

Verse 1:
*Dearie now I know
Just what makes me love you so
Just what holds me and enfolds me
In its golden glow.
Dearie now I see
Tis each smile so bright and free
For my sadness turns to gladness
When you smile at me.*

Verse 2:
Dearie when you smile
Everything in life's worthwhile
Love grows fonder as we wander
Down each magic mile.
Cheery melody
Seem to float upon the breeze.
Doves are cooing
While they're wooing
In the leafy trees.

Chorus:
There are smiles that make us happy,
There are smiles that make us blue,
There are smiles that steal away the teardrops
As the sunbeams steal away the dew.
There are smiles that have a tender meaning
That the eyes of love alone may see,
And the smiles that filled my life with sunshine
Are the smiles that you give to me.

∽

DECEMBER 1, 1918

Elliott begins this lengthy letter describing the entertainment he enjoyed at the Brooklyn Y, including "a great discussion of prohibition and temperance," quite a bit of singing of patriotic and popular songs, and a violin recital by a little girl and her brother. He mentions trying again for a furlough and says his ship is now expected to be in New York for at least two months. He devotes the rest of the letter to describing his views about love and marriage.

Sunday morning

Hello, "little girlie," How are you this fine morning? I am feeling fine except a slight headache. I guess it is caused from loss of sleep. I have lost about four hours sleep each night now for three nights in succession. I was on watch two of them and last night I was listening to a great discussion of prohibition and temperance. The subject was being debated in the literary society of the Brooklyn Y. Two ladies discussed it at first. Then the question was opened for common discussion. That's when the fun came. Everybody wanted to say something. It was the prominent business men of New York + Brooklyn who were debating the subject. I found that all the objectors to prohibition among the number last night were lawyers and revenue men. One of the ladies was a candidate for vice-governor of N.Y. this last election. She is a brilliant woman too and it seems that she understands the liquor question and the game of politics also. Those lawyers were asking her questions and she always got the best of them in the argument. The other lady was the president of the W.C.T.U.[2] of Brooklyn. I don't know when I have enjoyed an evening more than that last evening. They had quite a bit of singing of patriotic and popular songs. Then a little girl and her brother gave several pieces of music on the violin. A sailor or anyone else can always find entertainment of the highest type at the Y.M.C.A. You know I am becoming more in love with the Y every day. You know I can't see why our churches can't take up the social question in a similar way to the "Y." In the debate last evening one fine young lawyer popped off and asked what New York would do without saloons for a social gathering place and as a place of amusement and pastime of the poor and laboring class. (I never heard that argument for saloons before.) The lady said the Y.M.C.A. could do a great social work if it would use the same plan of huts in the labor section of New York just as among the soldiers in France. She said substitute Y huts for salloons [sic]. Don't you know I think that's a great idea. Why couldn't churches and Y.M.C.A.'s establish reading rooms and places of amusement for the poor? I believe it is a practical suggestion and I believe Christian people and business men would support the idea. She said the Y.M.C.A. has become a rich man's club. And no one could doubt that if we go to the Y.M.C.A. in any city. And our churches are more or less the same way. You know there are many people who never go to church because they feel they are out of their place when meeting with the more prosperous ones.

Well, I will stop preaching for a while and tell you how much I appreciated your letter which I received yesterday just before coming ashore. I think each letter I get from you is the sweetest one I have ever gotten. I sure wish I could take Ira's place and you Blanche's in seeing each other for just a few days. I don't mean I want to take their pleasure of being together. I mean simply that I wish we could be together too. I have asked for a furlough twice but there is nothing doing. I tried to get a furlough at Bay Ridge and on the Maumee. I am going to try again soon. I am really due a furlough and I might get one. The reason I haven't said anything about it is I don't want to have you expecting me and then not get to come. It is hard for a fellow to get a furlough in the navy. Then I have been hoping that I might get out next month. I heard a fellow say this morning that 400 had been already released from Bay Ridge since I left there. They haven't been sent home as yet but have gone back to Great Lakes for transportation. One can't always believe what he hears in the navy. So I do not know that it is true. I am just hoping that it may be. They say now that my ship will be here for two months. So if it is, I will have time enough to find out if I am to be released soon or not.

Say, that little poem was great. It certainly is true too about separation killing doubts. I felt sure of my love for you before I left you, but I must confess I was not always sure, but when I left you I ceased to doubt any more. I agree with you that real love is an increasing sentiment. And I think when a girl and boy begin to feel that they love each other they then should think of their ideals and life plans and see how nearly they agree. You know I really think there is a possibility sometimes for unhappiness when there is real love between the man and woman who are married. For instance the girl might have a certain work planned for her life and the man a conflicting plan for his life. In such a case I think there would be a chance of discontent even when the two love each other. You know I never talked to you very much about my life plan. In fact I have no definite work except I want to do a work of service of some kind to man and to God. I have taken special notice ever since I began to feel that I loved you to see if our ideals and ideas were in conflict. And I never have yet seen one instance where we would have conflicting ideals of life. I do not mean that we both would always agree in opinion, but differences of opinion need not cause discontent between lovers. I believe our ideals of life are the same and that is one reason why I believe we love each other and why I believe I could be happy with you as a partner and helper. That is what I see in true love a desire for partnership and sharing with each other coupled with the instinct of love between man and woman. I know that is what would make me happy in marriage is to have a woman that wanted to help me live and do my work and I wouldn't ask a girl to marry me unless I felt that I could give my whole life in harmony and devotion to common ideals and work between us. All said I think to truly be happy a man and woman should first have the feeling of love natural for man and woman. Then I think they should make sure that their ideals and plans for life work do not conflict. In that last I also mean to include that there should be an equality in ideals of manhood and womanhood, as purity of both man and woman. Then I think there also should be agreement as to faith and worship in religion. Then if true love of the man and woman exist, I see no reason why they should not be happy in marriage. I think the desire to share and help each other is the great and first essential to happiness in married life. I know it is as you say. The most I dare say of marriages are not as happy as they might be just because the man or the woman has something they feel is their own and they do not want to share with the other. It might be personal secrets or personal inheritance of money, or fruits of personal effort. I think in real love there is a sharing of all these and that such a sharing makes love sweeter. Often I think personal secrets that are sometimes kept back by the man or the woman until after marriage cause jealousy and discontent. Faults and missteps confessed in love before marriage are often easier forgiven than after marriage. That's why I feel free to tell you all of my shortcomings as well as my secrets. I love to talk free to you and have you talk free to me, because you know my one hope of happiness now is to make you my wife if you feel that you can always be happy with me as a partner. If you ever feel that there is a possible chance of unhappiness between us let's discuss it in time. If you can't be happy with me I don't want to make you unhappy and I am sure I will do the same by you. I have wanted to say all this before but I wanted to talk it and not write, but this morning I just felt like saying it in this letter so I have. You know we have really never been together a lot although we really have had a pretty good opportunity to learn each other. And up until the time I came to the navy I really had never seriously thought of marriage and love as I have since separated from you. For that reason I never had the opportunity of saying just what I thought about it. I feel I know you have considered my proposition of marriage ever since I left you and you know that has been my most occupying thought since I left you. Now by this don't think I am trying to hurry your absolute decision. Marriage should be the last step after we finally understand and know each other. I am just saying this so you will know me better. You know I will have nothing to offer you as a home for perhaps a long time yet, and we are young both of us and true love is worth waiting for. The greatest evidence of my love for you is that I never see, hear, or have anything that I first do not wish you could share with me. From your letters and gifts I know you feel the same for me. My only idea of marriage is happiness for both myself and the woman. In giving you what little I have been able, I have not done it because I feel so much that you need it or not at all that you couldn't get it elsewhere. I just give it because it is happiness to me to share what I get with you. Once you wrote as if you feared it might mean a hardship or sacrifice for me to do without pleasures here that I might have with the money that I send you. Not at all. The pleasure I get of sharing with you is far more than I get from anything in New York. So "little girl" when you consider marriage with me think of us both, our ideals and plans. Perhaps we will be together again before long. Let's not be hasty about decisions although I believe we are both old enough now to know what marriage means. It is either a lifelong happiness or regret. Let's make sure it's never the latter. We've never yet had any differences, and let's make sure we can be happy by really becoming acquainted in time. I think many people even marry before they get acquainted. We can know each other before marriage just as well as after if we are free with each other in our ideals and plans and if we always continue in our truthfulness to each other. You know I have told you that I have not always respected my ideals as a true man should. I have done many wrong things in the past. I have told you that I did keep company with the wrong kind of girls once. But honestly I told you all. I never was guilty of the worst. I am thankful that I met you in time. It has been easy for me to be a real man since I learned to appreciate real decency in women by knowing you and your ideals. In fact I never went with but one real girl before I met you. I have told you of her. I have even told you I think that I did not respect her ideals of decency at first. That is until she forced me to. She forgave me for my ungentlemanly conduct and I went to see her for sometime afterward.

I really think those days when I first started out have been my worst although you know I have many faults now. I am more thankful that you too have overlooked these worst faults that I have confessed to you, than for any other one thing I know, unless it is the fact that I met you as early in life as I did, and have really found my ideal woman to love and trust. Really I want you to know me as I am that we may never make the mistake that is often made in marriage. I hope you don't take me for what I have been, for that isn't worthy to offer you at all, but I hope you can take me for what I can be by your love and help.

You ask me if it is hard to do the routine of everyday life. I should say it is. I know how you felt in high school and now. But, Elma, I want to tell you that when we get in real life routine won't be ended. Life is a big job of little duties. It is a problem that will take all we've got to solve our part and that part may be small as to what we may have dreamed of. I really am getting a taste of the competition of life in the navy, and I am just beginning to enter the fight now. I have failed in the navy so far although I haven't had the opportunity yet that some have had and I had never had any practical experience to get me by.

Then the usual success in the navy is a gradual advancement from the lowest routine to the higher. We have to take our turn at the apprentice. Then after experience we become master of the job and it is routine and experience that calls for advancement. School is the apprenticeship of life in whatever we try for. I find that the fellows who have served their apprenticeship in the navy are the highest now. And apprenticeship is all routine. So also I believe the student who does best the routine of every day will get the good job in life. I don't want to discourage you, Elma, but when you get into what you think is that bigger life you will find the same routine of perhaps bigger duties. You'll be discouraged and disappointed when you step out of school. I thought I had met with all society and competition in school, for I have really been in life as I thought ever since I started to school. But society is different, life is different from school life. Don't let this discourage you. I haven't the blues to-day. I am happy as I can be so long as I am in the navy away from you. I don't think I have been idle since I came to the navy although I haven't studied books much. I have had a good opportunity to study men and life since here for life is what society makes it and society is what the individuals make it. I am associated with every type of man. I have a chance to get his ideas and ideals and his business views and experience. Life's going to be a big job even bigger than we think while in school, and the success we dream of in school won't be ours for the asking. It will require a whole life's work to really gain success and that life's success will be determined by the way the little duties have been done. You know I wrote you once before that I never was really impressed with the bigness of the world and the meaning of success till I came to New York City. It is that idea of continually being on the job that wins in a place like New York, and it's routine. It's competition in routine.

I hope you enjoyed the feast and I know you did. Say mentioning the feast made me think. Don't worry about sending me eats. I know you don't have time to fix them up with all the work you have to do and then I know you have no place or chance to fix them up in Rucker Hall. It's alright. I enjoy them very much because they are from you and I know you want to fix them up for me. I really have plenty to eat now anyway. Then the hard part about it is when you have worked hard and taken care to fix something for me it gets lost usually. It really is seldom that a fellow gets a box thru O.K. Letters usually come O.K. But they don't like to fool with boxes in the military mail. It's alright. I know you can't send me much while I am in the navy. I will be out by and by and some day we will be happy helping each other. Your nice long letters are enough to satisfy me and repay me so long as I can't be with you and if I could be with you, all I want is your love as you can honestly give it to me.

I guess I had better stop this time as this is exceeding long already. I hope you don't misunderstand me in this as to my purpose in this lengthy discussion of marriage and love. I just want you to really know me and my ideas about it and as we can't talk I write it. I know letters are not always plain and are sometimes misunderstood. My real idea is that we know each other in true love.

As ever your lover,
Elliott

P.S. I love for you to talk of the future. It is the happy prospect for me and not the present although I am trying to do well my duties of the present. E.C.

EVENING DECEMBER 20, 1918

By this time, Elliott has gotten out of the Navy and returned to Kentucky. It appears that he went straight to Georgetown to see Elma while school was still in session before heading home for Christmas break. There are no letters telling of his planned departure, so it may be that he wanted to surprise her by showing up on campus with no warning. We can only imagine their joyful reunion. When he arrived at home, he found two letters that had been forwarded to Sinai from the U.S.S. Maumee in New York, including Elma's "blue" letter from November 29.

Dearest "little girl:"

How are you feeling by now? I hope your head isn't aching so badly as it was this morning. Well, I most lied to you when I promised to write to-night. It is 9:30 and all of them are in bed. They all just talked and talked so much I couldn't get a chance to begin any sooner. I guess you will find out how home folks can talk to-night also. But I guess I have time enough yet. When I got home I found two letters here for me from you and two more from my brother. They were letters sent to U.S.S. Maumee at N.Y. They have come back to Sinai. Gee! But I am glad one of yours didn't come to me before I got out. I say it was some blue. I don't think I ever knew "my little girlie" to be so out of spirits. I am so glad I go [sic] back before I got that one. I know how you felt however and I know how to sympathize with you when you felt so badly. The other one was you again in better spirits. I know I was to blame for you having the blues. I should have written oftener than I did but it just seemed I couldn't get a chance any oftener, but it's all past now and we needn't miss each other so much now. Oh how glad I am that we can see each other and be together again as we can at school.

Well, I got home O.K. last evening about four o'clock. No, I wasn't all that time with Miss Corbin. My brother [Cal?] had some business in town and I had to wait for him. Then the ford [truck] was broken and we had to drive. So that is why it took so long. But it was as I expected it would be. No one was at Lawrenceburg to meet Miss Corbin and so it was up to me to see that she got to Alton. Consequently I had to drive out with her the four miles and hunt up her folks, but she was seemingly perfectly thrilled by the experience and everything passed lovely. I had no trouble finding her folks after I got to Alton although no one at Lawrenceburg seemed to know Ben Moffett. When I got to Alton I found his name in Anderson is not Ben at all but Lou Moffett. I must say she acted a perfect lady and I was just as good as good could be and so everything was O.K. I got her down there in time for dinner (I don't mean in time for mine but her's [sic] for I didn't stay. No. No. Not at all.) It did not seem to me that the young lady got any too hearty a welcome. The old lady her aunt didn't seem greatly thrilled at all to see Lot, and by the way she wasn't home anyway but we found her across the road at a neighbors. Her aunt said she didn't get the letter and was not expecting her. That's my yesterday's experience only my brother said that when he saw me with the young lady that he just imagined it was my girl (you C) who had come home with me for Xmas. As he had never seen you I could forgive him for mistaking Miss Corbin for you but if he had ever seen you I think I could [sic].

Say, the fire is out and I am sleepy. I believe I will finish in the morning for the mail doesn't leave till one o'clock to-morrow. A loving good night.

Morning 10 A.M. I am all set for work. I have on my old overalls and rubber boots. I went after a horse for my dad this morning out in the field. I put a shoe on it and hitched it up. Then I went after the cows and milked three and now I am going to strip tobacco as soon as I have mailed this letter. By the way my dad has gone to town to-day to get his marriage license. He is to be married to-morrow afternoon I think. I don't know whether he is going to take a honeymoon trip or not. He has been in such a fizz this morning I haven't gotten much out of him. And last night he didn't have a chance to tell me anything. In fact I guess there isn't anything to tell except he is going to get married. So you see I have come home to his wedding bells, and I only hope they will prove to be joyful.

"Little girlie" I hope you feel better this morning and I hope you have the loveliest time Xmas that there is to be had. I think I shall put in most of my Xmas working.

I heard this morning that one of my brothers is coming home to-night [Isaac?]. I don't know whether it is for good or not but I hope he is. I hope the other one may get home too before I come back to school [Tom?].

Well, have the biggest time you can for both of us in Franklin. I can't see you but I'm thinking of you. I will stop this time and write you a long letter Sunday or first of the week. Be good till I see you after Xmas holidays.

With all my love,
Elliott

P.S. Pardon my stationery. This is all I can find on the place and I left mine at G.C.

E.C.

MARCIE MCGUIRE

DECEMBER 21, 1918

Elma is back home on Christmas break and gives a full account of her trip to Franklin on the train, with much information about the train schedule and delays, and comments on various passengers. Despite the late trains and special trains and missed connections, her father was right there at the station to meet her when she arrived at 9:30 p.m.

Saturday Afternoon

Dearest Elliott:

I seat myself here in the parlor before the fire with not a single soul around to bother me and with the memory of night before last as my inspiration — to write you a little letter. It seems quite a time since the last time I wrote you a letter but it hasn't been so very long after all.

I've been having such a good time to-day helping mother with the Christmas baking. It would have been a little(?) more fun if I had been preparing it for you.

I guess I had better tell you about our exciting trip now. After I left you I finished breakfast and then completed my packing and got Jim to send my suitcase to the station. Then I went to town and got a box of aspirins, however I never did take one until last night. From town I went to the far depot and bought about a half dozen tickets. As luck would have it the train was about on time and when we got to Frankfort we had to wait awhile for the Louisville train. We tried to get on three trains before we struck the right one. It came at last! I was just seated comfortably when I spied an elderly Franklin man who was carrying on an extended flirtation with two fast girls. Blanche and I watched the performance closely all the way to Louisville and I must say our disgust was too much for words. Just before we reached Louisville the G.C. Crowd got together and sang merrily.

Upon our arrival in L. we rushed to the Information Bureau and learned that our train was 45 min. late. Blanche and I left the crowd and crossed the street to procure ourselves some dinner. When we had devoured our order, our appetites were still not satisfied. We then decided to go up town and try some other place. We waltzed up and down 4th Street until we found the Dairy Lunch Room. There we entered but after waiting some 15 min. we took our departure without a morsel to eat. Our next stop was at the Benedict[3] and such a dinner as we did order — country sausage, chicken croquette, fruit salad, green peas, orange pie etc etc. I claim we didn't leave that place hungry. It had begun to rain again and there we were eight blocks from the depot with no umbrella. We marched down the street just as if the sun had been shining brightly. When we reached the station we greatly favored drowned rats. Little did we worry for we had had something to eat and that was what we started out for. Upon looking around we noticed the crowd which was coming down our way was conspicuous for its absence. We asked some girls who were waiting for the Henderson train where they were. There [sic] reply was their train left at 3:10. We staggered to the Information Bureau to learn that a special train had been made up as No. 7 was 1 hr late. We were greatly relieved to know we had at least one more chance. It came in about 4 o'clock and stood in the station 1 hr. before leaving. The thing was a mile long, dirty, and filled with the most common crowd of people I ever saw. I got home about 9:30 and daddy was right there to meet me. I never did sleep quite so good as I did last night.

They're wanting to eat supper so I will have to stop. Am expecting to hear from you right soon. Delma ran in to see me a minute this morning and she is just as sweet as if she wasn't married.

With the mostest of love,
Elma

DECEMBER 22, 1918

Elliott is back home in Anderson County. He says things have really changed since he left home, but the neighborhood seems about the same except that most every young fellow is in uniform now. His brother is back from the Army and is "straight and strong looking." His dad has gotten married. The country church finally held service for the first time in four months on account of the flu. But he finds he can't be very well contented at home anymore and is always restless and discontented when he can't see Elma.

Sunday night

Dearest "little girl:"

Everything is quite [sic] and still. I am all alone in the big world to-night and have nothing to do but think of you and so I will write a little letter again. The folks are all gone. My dad got married this afternoon and he is staying away from home at the bride's home for the night. My brother [Cal?] and his wife have gone to my sister-in-law's father's. So you see I am all alone and quite lonesome. But no it's not so bad when I can think of you and write to you.

The wedding ceremony was performed to-day at two o'clock. I went and took my dad so as to keep him from having to get in the mud (then you know I wanted to learn how it should be done any way). I don't know how long it will last but they seem to love each other very much now. They act like a couple about eighteen or twenty. Really I believe my dad acts most as silly over his new wife as I do over you, and you know that is saying he seemingly likes her pretty well.

The wedding is about all the excitement I have had to-day except I went to church this morning. There were about a dozen present but we had a pretty good service at that. It was the first service held in the church for four months on account of the flu. They most missed having services to-day for the housekeeper had gone visiting and left the house locked up. They finally found some keys that would unlock the doors. They had a business meeting too, and called a pastor and elected clerk and treasurer. Of course the pastor had already been chosen before to-day, but they only went through the formality to-day. By the way I had to do some nice talking to keep them from electing me clerk. You see I am never at church here much and I thought it best to have some one who could be present more. In fact I have been thinking seriously of moving my membership to Georgetown. It seems they are so good to me here they want to give me a job every time I go to church. I feel mean to never do anything but I just can't do much at home in church when I go to school at Georgetown. In fact I don't do much anyplace.

Well, little girlie how are you enjoying home? But I know you are having a good time for it's been so long since you've been home. Things have really changed considerable since I left home last summer but I find the neighborhood about the same only most every young fellow I see is in uniform now. A good many are coming home now. My married brother [Tom] came in this morning. He looks fine. He is so straight and strong looking. He looks a third larger than I do so everybody says although I even weigh the most. The folks at the wedding said this afternoon that I really am beginning to look like a man now and not like a kid. Don't you know I feel grand to come back and be told that I have really grown up at last. But the worst of all was my new stepmother made fun of me with my flat hat on. She said I didn't look like anybody she ever saw.

I guess if the flu is as bad in Franklin as it is up here (or I mean if folks are scared as badly in Franklin as here) you won't get out very far from home. How is your mother? I believe you said she was sick. I hope she is well and I hope your instinctive feeling that you would have flu hasn't come true, and that it won't.

Well, Elma I find I can't be very well contented at home any more. When I have been home a day or so I begin to think of Georgetown or Franklin all the time. No really I don't think of either Georgetown or Franklin but of a little girl that sometimes lives in G.C. and sometimes in Franklin. No place looks good to me any more unless I can see you once in a while. Every thing and every place seems lonesome without you. I am always restless and discontented when I can't see you. You know I really felt like I would love to stay in the navy until I got one trip across the ocean but I just felt that I couldn't wait until I could see you.

And now I am so happy that I did really get out and came back to see you when I did since I got that letter from you. Really I didn't know you did want to see me so much till I got that letter and until I have been with you. I would far rather see you than any place in the world. Of course, I knew that all the time but I thought it was my best chance sometimes to see the world. I know now that I could never stay away from you without seeing you at all another five months and be even so well contented as I was this time. You know two or three have asked me since I came home what kind of a change has come over me. They say I am not a bit wild as I used to be. I wonder if folks see any change in you. And my I know I feel a much greater change in myself than I show. I fear I don't tell folks what I really know has caused my changed actions. I expect I had better stop as I haven't had any excitement as yet 'cept what I've told.

A jolly Xmas and lots of love,
Elliott

DECEMBER 22, 1918

Elma is happy that her parents are so interested in Elliott and willing for her to do anything she wants to do for him. They also seemed disappointed that he wasn't coming to visit.

Sunday Night
Dearest:
I'm terribly lonesome for you. Have been right here at home all day — resting and reading. Have read a book and a half of required English this afternoon.

Father and I went to town last night for a little while to see Santa... and Santa was so nice as to give me a very tiny little present to send to you and I'm starting it with this letter in the morning. It isn't very much and not half so nice as what you gave me but I'm sending it just because

I love you. I'm so happy because mother and father seem to be so interested in you and so willing for me to do anything I want to for you. I think Jake fixed things up for you. He told Papa that he was proud to claim you as his friend. That wasn't all he said about you either. Mother and father both seemed to be really disappointed because you were not coming down. What do you think of that? It makes me so happy to see them coming across so beautifully. It would hurt me to go against their wishes in anything.

Delma ran in to see me a minute yesterday morning. She and Oral have just moved to themselves and she is starting to [set up] housekeeping. Happy well I should say so. She asked about you the 1st thing. Won't we have a good time when we can go to see them?

Well dear I'm sleepy although it is only a little after seven and besides there is nothing to tell. I do hope I get a letter in the morning telling me all about yours and Lot's trip home. I'll be writing to you again ere long.

With bushels of Love,
The Little Girl.

P.S. You can tell how sleepy I was this crooked writing.

∼

DECEMBER 25, 1918

> *Elma is bubbling over with joy and says she feels like a "real sure enough little girl" on Christmas morning. She says this has been decidedly one of her happiest Christmases. The only thing that would have made it perfect is his presence.*

Christmas Morning

Dearest Elliott:

I feel like a real sure enough "little girl" again this morning. I'm having the goodest time. Daddy woke me up with a great big kiss and told me to get up and see what Santa had brought — just like he used to do. Course I didn't need much urging and when I discovered I went into thrills!!!! Mother had fixed up a lovely box with all kinds of dainty hand made things in it and some money too! On further investigation I found a pair of the best looking brown shoes (which you must be sure and notice when I come back) and a check for $25.

Now, can you imagine anybody being more spoiled than I. It is beyond my power of comprehension to understand how anybody as undeserving as I am can be so fortunate. This has been decidedly one of my happiest Christmas. Just one thing more would have made it perfect, and that is your presence. However I got a letter from you yesterday morning and four or five Xmas cards from the girls. Then another and even sweeter letter from you this morning and several more Christmas cards.

I hope you will like your stepmother even if she does make fun of your little pancake hat. Don't let what she says bother you 'cause I think it is real "koot" [cute].

2 o'clock P.M. I had to cease writing and help some with the dinner. Now it is all over and even the dishes are washed. I say we had lots of good eats, if I did help fix 'em. My! Wouldn't I be thrilled if you would come walking in this afternoon!!!!!! You asked about mother. Well, she is improving rapidly but she still looks thinner and paler than I ever saw

her. She has been real sick and father wanted to send for me but she would not let him. Dad is in better health and spirits than I have seen him for two or three years. He and mother are both as jolly as can be. Yesterday was their 36th wedding anniversary. I am invited to a little party to-night but I sure do hate to go. I had almost rather take a French test but goodness knows they would say I was stuck up if I dared refuse. I came home with the determination not to accept a single invitation and here I am fallin' down on the very first one. I've been staying right here at home and didn't go to S.S., church or B.Y.P.U Sunday. I went to town Mon. morning and everybody I met asked me why I wasn't at church. I was surprised at so many missing me. The B.Y.P.U. president informed me that I was to have a part on the program next Sun. night and I insisted that it was probable that I would not be here. I guess I will hear from Wee Willie in the morning. I don't much believe he will ask me to come back on Sat but if he should I don't imagine I could let you know in time to come on Sunday. Anyway it isn't fair for you to come back early when you don't have to. Nevertheless I'll drop you a card as soon as I hear.

It is snowing just a tiny little bit this afternoon. Wouldn't it be fun if we should get to go coasting again? Even more fun than it was last year! Be good and have a happy Xmas. From one who loves you dearly. The little girl.

∼

DECEMBER 26, 1918

Elliott's Christmas was quite the contrast to Elma's. The only gifts he mentions are the buttons from Elma and some stationery from his new stepmother. He worked all day Christmas stripping tobacco and then hauled hay all the next day. He is glad Elma's parents approve of him and hopes they will never be disappointed in him.

Thursday night

Dear "little girl,"

I just got your nice Christmas present this evening. I got your letter yesterday but the box did not come until to-day. The present sure is nice. The only funny thing to me is how you happened to know that I didn't have any buttons. You couldn't have given me a better gift, for I never had a real nice set of buttons before, and what I had got lost while I was gone.

I don't know whether you will get this or not before you go back to school. I was expecting to write to you last night, but I worked all day yesterday and your wish about my glasses came true. I broke them and so I had the headache. Then I got your letter saying that you had sent me a present. So I thought I would just wait another day. Yes, I even worked all day Xmas day. We finished up stripping tobacco. All of dad's stock was about to freeze to death before he got the tobacco out of the barn. I don't know but I got along as well yesterday at work as I ever did on Christmas day before and I don't think I ever worked on that day before. I have hauled hay all day to-day. You see I am a real farmer this week. My brother and I had an accident. We went to help a neighbor hang a big hog. We left our horses standing on the roadside. While we were helping an auto came along and scared our horses. So they ran away with a load of hay. However they didn't hurt anything for a fellow stopped them after they had gone about a half mile. You see this is all the excitement I am having and so I have to write that or nothing.

I have an invitation to a party to-night but I hardly think I shall go, for I hardly expect I would see you there and that is the only person whom I wish to see to-night.

I don't expect I would have written to you?? But my step-mother gave me a nice box of stationery for Xmas. I think she is real nice to me don't you?

Well, I certainly appreciate anything that Jake said about me. And I am certainly glad that your folks are willing for you to talk to me. I would hate for you to do anything against their will for I know that they expect good things of you. I am sure they have reasons to expect you to do well too, that's one reason I always feel unworthy of your love, because I really know how little I have done and also know how little one can count on me doing. If you can love me I hope I will be able to make you happy and that's about all I could ever expect to do. I hope your parents may never be too much disappointed in me. I know I could try to make them like me, but they might not. I hope that they may like me better if they ever know me, and I think they will when they know that you really love me. You know it is a big thing for a fellow like me who has nothing in the world, to ask a mother and father for the only child they have – and a fellow too whom they have never seen but little and about whom they know so little. We can't wonder that your mother and father should not be anxious to give you up without first wanting to know something about me. I have known that they couldn't be crazy about me as yet. You have no idea how glad I am if they really can give their consent for me to talk to you and love you. And I hope they can be content to trust your happiness with me when the time really comes for me to ask them. I have often thought it must be awful hard for parents to give up their child to a fellow in whom they have no confidence. Of course, it isn't giving their children up for good but they feel that it is in a way. You don't know how much I appreciate anything that Jake has said that will make your mother and father willing for me to love you and for you to love me.

I guess I had better stop. You may not get this till I see you, but I guess you will.

I thank you again and again for the nice present and for the love you show me by sending it. I guess I will see you again soon.

With most of love,
Elliott

P.S. I would love to see Delma + Oral. I am so glad they are happy. Perhaps we can visit them sometime. Would that suit you? It would me.

Before Texting

While reading these letters, I was struck time and again by how young my grandparents were and how their concerns were very much like those of young lovers today. If they had written Texts or Social Media posts instead of multipage letters while in college, they might have sounded like this:[1]

June 6, 1917 - Elliott @ ElliottCranfill
You ought to see me with my overalls on, and my big straw hat. You wouldn't think I had ever been inside of a college. #FarmHand #GC

June 12, 1917 - Elma @ ElmaBeatty
Since I got home Mother has turned everything over to me. Talk about college folks not knowing how to work -- I say it is all nonsense. #domesticScience #keepingHouse

June 6, 1917 - Elliott @ ElliottCranfill
I am trying to find out what lucky fellow was sitting in the swing with my girl after I left. Am rather lonesome but hope it will not last. #Luckyfellow

June 12, 1917 - Elma @ ElmaBeatty
When I think of that night I begin to quiver and quake. It was nothing short of a miracle that Miss Howard didn't tell. #porchswing #ravingmaniac

June 6, 1917 - Elliott @ ElliottCranfill
I didn't have time to say how much I did enjoy being with my girl, for it was so late. Indeed I had many things I would like to have said. #mygirl #banquet

June 12, 1917 - Elma @ ElmaBeatty
I went to the plays but they were not quite as good as expected. Instead of the "League of Youth," they gave the "School of Scandal" and no one liked it very much. #devilsplay

July 8, 1917 - Elliott @ ElliottCranfill
Got my grades to-day and felt like "shoutin" for I was at a sanctified meeting when I opened the letter. #collegedays

July 8, 1917 - Elma @ ElmaBeatty
Had a "large time" in the city. Everybody and his dog was on parade. On our way back we had a "blow out" and didn't get in until eleven o'clock. #July4 #TinLizzy

July 22, 1917 - Elliott @ ElliottCranfill
Have been to 3 lawn parties and a Sunday school picnic since I got home. Also heard the Honorable W.J. Bryan speak on Prohibition the other night. #lawnparty #prohibition

July 22, 1917 - Elliott @ ElliottCranfill
Got about 8 miles from home and about halfway to a party and didn't get any farther. A candidate was speaking right in the middle of the road. Of course it was blockaded. #Villagelife #politics

August 6, 1917 - Elma @ ElmaBeatty
@Jake is expecting to sail for China the 16th of the month but has not yet been released by Uncle Sam. #missionarywork #wartime

August 27, 1917 - Elliott @ ElliottCranfill
I guess I will get to come back to college O.K. Neither of my brothers at home have been called yet and my other brother has been exempted on account of weight. #war #draft

August 27, 1917 - Elliott @ ElliottCranfill
So much for women reforming politics. Some of the women here voted for the candidate who would haul them to the election in an automobile, a rather cheap sale I think. #womansuffrage

December 19, 1917 - Elma @ ElmaBeatty
You missed all the fun by not being with us from Frankfort to Louisville. A bunch of us Georgetonians sang, yelled, etc. until the passengers looked as if they would like to throw us out of the window. #Homefortheholidays #15rahs

December 24, 1917 - Elliott @ ElliottCranfill
It seems I have joined the Hospital Corps since I got home. Every one of the folks here were sick when I got home. #hospitalcorps

December 27, 1917 - Elliott @ ElliottCranfill
I hope you took a good look at the present you sent me or else you might think I had just returned it to you. #handkerchieves #Santa

December 29, 1917 - Elma @ ElmaBeatty
I met @Jake down town this morning and he at once began teasing me. He immediately said he should take it upon himself to enlighten people around here a bit. I just dared him to tell any tales out School. #hushhush

June 7, 1918 - Elma @ ElmaBeatty
I am home again and mama and papa have most talked my head off. I wasn't expecting anyone to meet me but them and when I walked off the train right into @Delma's arms, I was quite surprised because you know I had not written at all. The trunks and all landed safely with me. #homesweethome

June 7, 1918 - Elliott @ ElliottCranfill
Forgot to tell how I spent the time in Frankfort. I went to the pool room first and had several very interesting games then I went in and took a few drinks and a smoke and finally I went to the show and saw most all of a "wild west" or a "Buffalo Bill" or something. #justkidding

June 11, 1918 - Elma @ ElmaBeatty
Didn't do anything Saturday afternoon but read and watch the eclipse of the sun. #eclipse

June 13, 1918 - Elliott @ ElliottCranfill
I am going to-morrow to town to see if I can get any idea about when I may have to go to war. My brother goes 26. He is talking of joining the navy next week. There are only thirty more in Class I in this county besides the newly registered ones of June 5. #war #draft

June 15, 1918 - Elma @ ElmaBeatty
I haven't said much about the war, but we all want to do our part toward "Making the World Safe for Democracy." #democracy

LOVE LETTERS

June 16, 1918 - Elliott @ ElliottCranfill
The home folks think I am "playing off" on them. They say they're going to put me to work to-morrow. They say I am pretending to be sick. Can you believe that? They are going to put me to use a cradle. #cuttingwheat

June 17, 1918 - Elma @ ElmaCranfill
Am all fixed up and feeling very much at home. At present I am sitting in a porch swing, enjoying a nice cool breeze and doing something I really enjoy. The place has a big yard with a lawn swing and settee in it and the porch is all fixed up with chairs and a porch swing. #Boardinghouse #bowlinggreen

June 19, 1918 - Elliott @ ElliottCranfill
You ought to see me about Saturday night or the last of the week, with my beard a week old and my old dirty harvest clothes. You would think I was a tramp. I believe @Elma likes a mustache? I don't think I will shave it off anymore till I come to see her. #farmwork

June 21, 1918 - Elma @ ElmaBeatty
I am coming from a state of darkness to the light with regard to conditions in the world. Since I have been in this place I have seen enough to open my eyes and I am thoroughly disgusted every day with the way the boys and girls carry on. #SocietyBelles #WaysOfTheWorld

June 23, 1918 - Elliott @ ElliottCranfill
I am getting to be a "big bug" since I got home. They had the speaking advertised in the county paper and on bills all over the county. Just think my name among all the other preachers and politicians of the county. Believe me I made some speech. Just about ten minutes long, but I am sure that was long enough to those listening. #WarSavingsStamps

June 23, 1918 - Elma @ ElmaBeatty
I was exceedingly smart this morning. Got up at 10 o'clock. Oh, yes. I went to church alright even if I did miss Sunday School. We were a little late getting there and I went strolling in, took my seat, glanced around and whom should I see sitting on the same bench but @Thomas Meador. #JustFriends

June 26, 1918 - Elliott @ ElliottCranfill
I got my questionaire to-day. And when I get it filled out I will know whether or not I can join the navy, I guess. If I get another chance I am going to enlist. If I can join the navy, I am going to do so immediately. #Draft #Navy

June 26, 1918 - Elma @ ElmaBeatty
This morning the whole student body marched down town and joined in a "farewell party" held for the eighty boys who left for camp to-day. It was the first time I had witnessed anything of the kind and it certainly was heartrending. We didn't follow them to the train and of course I guess it was worse up there. #ArmyRecruits #TroopTrains

June 30, 1918 - Elliott @ ElliottCranfill
Well, I got through with my W.S.S. work O.K. I had to do some pretty hard work and I met some disappointments. I lacked five dollars making my quota of $2000. My district is composed of very poor folks. Most everybody pledged some but many only bought one and so you can see that doesn't count very fast. #WarSavingsStamps

June 30, 1918 - Elma @ ElmaBeatty
Got a card from @Harold Snuggs. He is in Elizabeth, N.J., in some kind of chemical school. Said he was enjoying his work fine altho the other night they got gassed with NO2 and his hands were all burned with nitric acid. But he said that just relieved the monotony. #ArmyTraining

Epilogue

After Elliott returned from the Navy in December 1918, he and Elma continued their junior year at Georgetown College, and they wrote to each other and visited during school breaks. By the summer of 1919, Elliott was back to work on the family farm, and Elma was working at the college office to earn money so they could return to school for their senior year. By then, they were beginning to talk more seriously about marriage and sometimes expressed impatience to be together, although they agreed they should finish their studies first. In a letter dated August 3, 1919, Elma writes, "Let's don't forget to use our heads some and look at things from a business point of view. We must always remember that it takes more than love to make the happiest home."

They wrote to each other two or three times a week whenever they were apart. Their letters were long and heartfelt as they shared their "ideas and ideals." When Elma's parents got sick, she struggled with whether to stay in school or quit to help them at home, but she ultimately decided she wanted to finish her education. Elliott fully supported her in this decision and said, "I would much rather you have the education you have than for you to know all about cooking and housekeeping or a whole lot of things you could make by staying at home. I want a girl who can be some company for me. I don't want a girl who can just keep house and cook." Elliott also worried about leaving his 65-year-old father to run the farm alone but felt that young people would do better to prepare to live up to their ideals and perhaps do some good in the world. In contrast, if they stayed home with their ailing parents, all they could hope for was to provide a little rest and comfort to them.

The entire collection includes letters written in the spring of 1920 as Elliott and Elma impatiently looked forward to their wedding. They graduated in May 1920 and were married at the preacher's house in Louisville, Kentucky, on June 15, 1920. Shortly after graduation, they obtained their teaching licenses, and in the fall, they began teaching school, first at country schools in Buckeye, Kentucky, and Taylorsville, Kentucky; then at Elliott's alma mater, the Kavanaugh Academy in Lawrenceburg, Kentucky; then at Bowling Green Business College; later at various colleges in Mississippi and Texas. They both earned master's degrees at the University of Michigan, and Elliott eventually earned a Ph.D. in Economics from Louisiana State University. In 1948, they returned to teach at their alma mater, Georgetown College, and remained there until they retired. They moved to Florida in 1965. They were active in church and community their whole lives. Elma died of a stroke in January 1984; Elliott died of congestive heart failure in July 1986. They were married 64 years and had two daughters, Juanita and Gwen; two grandchildren, Marcie Slone and Skip Slone; and three great-grandchildren, Melissa Slone, Matthew Sleadd, and Isaac Sleadd.

Lexicon

B.G. = Bowling Green
BU = Business University
BYPU = Baptist Young Peoples Union
C = See
C.P.O. = Chief Petty Officer
C.S. = Ciceronian Society
G.C. = Georgetown College
O.M.C.?
R.H. = Rucker Hall
S.A.T.C. = Student Army Training Corps
S.S. = Sunday School
T.ø.K = Tau Theta Kappa, men's literary club at Georgetown College
U = You
W.C.T.U. = Women's Christian Temperance Union
W.S.S. = War Savings Stamps
Y.M.C.A. = Young Men's Christian Association
Y.W.C.A. = Young Women's Christian Association

Dramatis Personae

- Acton, Herr — One of the 25 Georgetown College students riding home on the train with Elma during Christmas break 1917, who walked downtown to see a movie during their layover in Louisville.
- Adams, Augustus Franklin — The 1920 *Belle of the Blue* lists an Augustus Franklin Adams, who "has not been so successful with the fair ladies at Rucker Hall."
- Adams, Malden Browning — Dr. Adams (referred to as "Dr. M.B." in some letters) was president of Georgetown College from 1913–1931. The 1918 *Georgetonian* describes him as "first among this majestic body, one whom everyone learns to love and reverence." They say, "Who else but Dr. Adams could keep the college in so flourishing a condition in such hard times? Who else could instruct us in the right path as well as Dr. Adams?" During the flu outbreak, Dr. and Mrs. Adams had charge of the boys in Pawling Hall.
- Adams, Miss — Elma mentioned a Miss Adams when talking about woman's suffrage. Possibly Miss Adams was running for office in Simpson County.
- Adams, Mrs. M.B. — The students dedicated the 1919 Belle of the Blue to Mrs. M.B. Adams. During the flu outbreak, Dr. and Mrs. Adams had charge of the boys in Pawling Hall.
- Adkins, Elmer. — Elmer was one of the Anderson County men who entered Georgetown College in the fall of 1918. Elliott refers to him as his old friend "Slip" and says they lived within a couple hundred yards of each other growing up in Sinai. He taught country school before he started to college at Georgetown. Elma thinks he is reserved but Elliott says he is everything but reserved and is in fact quite the ladies' man. He says Elmer is one of the best students he knows. Elmer was one of the first students at Georgetown to come down with the flu in October 1918 and be taken to the city hospital.Alexander girls — Friends of Elma's from Franklin, who hosted a picnic at Drake's Creek.
- Allen, Mrs. — Apparently owned the boarding house in Bowling Green where Elma took her meals while attending Business School.

DRAMATIS PERSONAE

- Amerson, Fred — A fellow Georgetonian who, according to the 1918 *Georgetonian*, left school when he "felt the claim of war stronger than the call of books" and was in the Officers Training School at Hampton Roads, Virginia, along with another Georgetonian, Ira Porter. Elliott ran into Amerson while at Camp Perry in Great Lakes but later heard that he had left for sea as a third-class quartermaster, his commander's job being just temporary.
- Amos, Mr. — A fellow student from Georgetown College whom Elliott ran into at Great Lakes when Mr. Amos was doing guard duty and Elliott was trying to get to the library. He later ran into Mr. Amos again while he was waiting on his chance for the Officers Material School. Elma says she remembers him sitting near her in English I and mentions him in connection with Faith Snugg, perhaps as her boyfriend or fiancé?
- Anderson, Cecil — One of the Georgetown College men who made good in the Army and became a major.
- Anderson, Katherine — Katherine Anderson from Charleston, South Carolina, was in the class ahead of Elma. The 1919 yearbook describes her as a gentle, unassuming person who always lives up to her ideals and says "from early morning until late at night she can be found in one of the laboratories, either analyzing an unknown, examining bacteria, or perhaps testing the strength of an electric current."
- Armstrong, Miss — Elma mentions her in her letter about the flu in October 1918.
- Arnold, P. J. — Elma mentions him dating Sally Ford Moore.
- Atkins, Elmer — See Adkins, Elmer.
- Bailey, Joe — Joe Bailey was in school with Elma and Elliott during their first two years at Georgetown but served in the Army during the fall of 1918.
- Bauer, Bill — Joseph William Bauer wrote to Elliott while at training camp. He was in Elliott's rival literary society, the Ciceronians, but Elliott seems to have admired him, describing him as "Cicero's best man." According to the 1919 yearbook, Bauer, "claims to have attended classes and to have been presented with some very creditable marks."
- Beagle, Jessie — There is a woman named Beagle listed as a sophomore in 1917. First names are not given for underclassmen in the yearbook. Elma reports that a Jessie Beagle died of the flu in fall 1918. She was apparently close to Robin Martin.

DRAMATIS PERSONAE

- Beagle, Viola — Viola Pearl Beagle was in the class of '19 and a Zeta. She was described as "a regular ray of sunshine, the kind of person who makes you feel better when you meet her."
- Beard, Iva — Iva Beard from Shelbyville "honored the class" of '19 as a teacher of Latin, as well as fellow classmate. She was described as "full of vim and go and always ready to give the class a push when it begins to bend beneath its heavy responsibilities."
- Beard, Mary Anna — Mary Anna from Shelbyville, Kentucky, "a sterling girl," was described in the 1920 yearbook as one of the smallest members of the class but one whose quiet unassuming manner and loveable disposition had won a large place in the hearts of her classmates. She apparently dated Gene Martin.
- Bell, Mr. — Elma mentions having memories of him connected with English I class, but doesn't say what those were. She also mentions him having a wife.
- Bishop, Miss — Someone Elliott's cousin teased him about when she told him a Bishop wanted to see him.
- Bowen, Major Marmaduke — Elma describes him as a "big man from Louisville" who made a stirring patriotic speech.
- Bower, William — There is a Joseph William Bauer in the class of '19, president of the Ciceronian society, described as "Enthusiasm, that's Bill all over." He was said to belong to the cult that takes as its motto: Don't let your studies interfere with your college education. Elma mentions him going with Viola Beagle.
- Bromley, Mr. — Elma mentions him in connection with an adventure involving Holmes Yager, in which they all shared a saucer of gelatin.
- Brown, "Tubby" — Elma mentions "Tubby" Brown on the train ride home after their sophomore year in college.
- Browning, John Thomas — John Thomas Browning, from Dry Ridge, was one of Elliott's and Elma's classmates at Georgetown, a fellow Tau Theta Kappa member, and business manager of the *Georgetonian*. According to the 1920 yearbook, "He intended to specialize in Math, but ...met with an insoluble feminine problem and gave up the idea. The next we knew of him he was in Europe chasing the Huns."
- Browning, Mr. — Mr. Browning was Elma's supervisor in the business office at Georgetown. She mentions him saying she deserved "a vacation of ten

DRAMATIS PERSONAE

minutes" after working from 1 to 5:30 p.m. one day. She sometimes refers to him as "Wee Willie."

- Bryant, Mary Eliza — Mary Eliza Bryant is described as "a quiet but active member of the class of '20 who has enough A's to teach anywhere she desires but ...does not intend to teach school."
- Bryson, Gladys — Gladys Eugenia Bryson from Carlisle, Kentucky, was two years ahead of Elma. She is described in the 1918 *Georgetonian* as a bright and happy lass who sometimes got in the dumps, but it was said that when she smiled, it surely was contagious.
- Bush — Elma mentions him in connection with Mr. Duvall when she says it's a shame that such pills as he and Bush could get out of military service but Elliott can't.
- Carson, Ruth — A student at Georgetown. Elma mentioned Ruth had an attack of appendicitis and has to be operated on.
- Carter, Governor — Lillard Harvey Carter was a lawyer in Lawrenceburg, Kentucky, for more than 30 years and served as lieutenant governor. According to Elliott, he was acting governor for one day and therefore he was called Governor in his home town.
- Carter, Nolen — One of the new students in 1918 from Lawrenceburg. His father Lillard Harvey Carter was a good friend of Elliott's.
- Chapman — Elliott met a fellow named Chapman while he was at Great Lakes, who attended Berea College the previous year and was a cousin of a Chapman from Georgetown College.
- Coker, Frank — Frank Coker from Salem, class of '20, was described as steady and consistent. He was said to spend most of his time in the chemical laboratory singing solos. Elliott says he would love to see the meeting between Elma and Coker, provided neither of them saw him. Elma says John Conn offered to let his students off a chemistry test if Coker would give an hour's lecture on alcohol.
- Conn, John Ferguson — John Conn, nicknamed "Chinc," was a friend of Elma's from Franklin, Kentucky, and a fellow student at Georgetown College. He and Elliott were once roommates at Georgetown. According to their senior yearbook, John was especially noted for his scientific ability. The 1920 *Belle of the Blue* describes him as "a chemist, physicist, photographer, and musician" and says he was "enthusiastic, full of fun and pep, and an excellent student."

DRAMATIS PERSONAE

- Cook, Mr. — Elliott was at Great Lakes training camp with a Mr. Cook. He was from western Kentucky and a graduate of Vanderbilt. He took some Kodak pictures of Elliott at camp. In earlier letters Elliott refers to him as a friend and he says he likes him quite well, but in a later letter he comments that Cook broke off a two-year engagement with his girl after she lost her health, which Elliott disapproved of. He also commented that Cook pretends to be wealthy.
- Corbin, June — One of Elma's close friends from Franklin. Elma sometimes refers to June as her "first husband," but it is not clear what she means by this.
- Corbin, Miss — Elliott mentions taking a Miss Corbin from the train station in Lawrenceburg to her home in Alton, because no one was there at the station to meet her. Her first name may have been Lot.
- Cranfill, Calvin DeWitt — Calvin DeWitt Cranfill ("Cal"), Elliott's oldest brother, was seven years older than Elliott. By the time of these letters, Cal was married (to Raymie) and running a farm near Taylorsville, Kentucky. According to Elliott, he was exempted from the draft due to weight, but he does not specify whether Cal was considered overweight or underweight.
- Cranfill, George Alfred — Elliott's father George Alfred Cranfill was born October 4, 1854, and died May 16, 1933.
- Cranfill, William Isaac — Isaac Cranfill ("Ike") was five years older than Elliott. Ike registered for the draft during the first registration June 5, 1917. He was single at the time, but he eventually married Elliott's "best girl" from high school, Grace Crossfield.
- Cranfill, Thomas Edgar — Thomas Cranfill ("Tom") was six years older than Elliott. Tom registered for the draft during the first registration June 5, 1917. At first married men with dependents were granted an exemption, but Tom was called to duty in September 1918.
- Crossfield, Grace — Grace was Elliott's girlfriend in high school, but she eventually married Elliott's brother Isaac.
- Dan — Elma mentions a man named Dan who is the only one who knows how to manipulate the furnace in the chapel basement.
- Daniel, Robert Norman — Professor Daniel taught English language and literature at Georgetown College. He was described in the yearbook as a "gentle, happy, smiling, youthful gentleman." They speculated that the

reason he was so happy all of the time was because of the freshman themes. They described him as a dreamer who revels in Browning.

- Daniels, Eula — Elma mentions Eula in her letter of July 16, 1918, about the Chautauqua Academy.
- Daniels — The Secretary of the Navy visited Great Lakes Station twice during the war.
- Delma — *See McClanahan.*
- DeWitt, Louise Frances — Elliott's mother Louise Frances DeWitt was born June 10, 1864, and died December 13, 1916.
- Dickey, J.S. — While in summer school in 1918, Elma worked for Mr. Dickey, President of Bowling Green Business University.
- Doty, Grandma — Elma mentions her as the owner of the pear trees that she and Sophy robbed.
- Duval, H.H. — Herbert Harding Duval, from Glendale, graduated from Georgetown in 1919. His nickname was "Percy," and he was described in the yearbook as "one of the college celebrities." Apparently he was thought to be good looking, because Elliott at one point says that if he just had H.H. Duval's face or bearing, he thinks he could get somewhere in the Navy. Elma refers to Duval in one letter as "the prof puncher." "Punching" abilities apparently meant that he was a good student and was able to finish his course in record time.
- Eberhardt, Dr. — F.W. Eberhardt became pastor of Georgetown Baptist Church in 1917. He was described as a "large man" with a dignified voice. Elma mentioned him preaching a sermon directed to the young ladies describing the kind of girl a young man should seek for a wife.
- Eddings, Mr. — Elliott ran into him at the Anderson County fair, possibly a student from Lawrenceburg. Elma refers to him as one of the "preacher men."
- Fields, Wilbur — Wilbur Owen Fields from Louisville, class of 1920, was a close friend of Elliott's, possibly his roommate during their first years at school. The yearbook described him as a man of few words, save when engaged in an argument over some prominent political issue of the day, one who never said anything he would have to take back. They probably could have said the same about Elliott.
- "Fine Day" — Elma's nickname for one of the boys she knows in Bowling Green.

DRAMATIS PERSONAE

- Flannery or Flannigan, Mr. — One of Elliott's friends at Great Lakes Naval Station (Mr. Cook) said he knew someone at Georgetown named Flannery or Flannigan.
- Fogle, Professor — Professor D.E. Fogle taught in the modern language department. Apparently the relationship between Professor Fogle and Miss Porter was common knowledge. The students wrote in the 1918 *Georgetonian*, "Our 'bachelor prof' frequently goes on long walks, and he always takes the 'porter' with him. The students and the 'porter' will miss him next year," when he leaves to go teach French to officers at Camp Zachary Taylor. Professor Fogle was one of two members of the college faculty who were granted a year's leave of absence to engage in YMCA War Work, the other being Coach Hinton.
- Ford, J.J. — A former student at Georgetown who was accepted to the Officer Materials School and told Mr. Amos that "G.C. is a kindergarten compared with it." Elliott later refers to him as I.Q. Ford.
- Freeman, Arthur — Arthur Clarence Freeman from Nocatee, Florida, class of '20, member of Tau Theta Kappa, nicknamed "Pussyfoot." It was said that he was always ready with one of those big laughs and that he always looked on the bright side of life. Elma reports that he was in charge of training at G.C. in the fall of 1918, along with Brothers Ogden, Siler, Redding, and Professor Martin. Elliott says all those fellows took their training at Fort Sheridan. He sseemed surprised that Freeman had been put in charge, because he thought he was "thoroughly disgusted with G.C. from the way he talked." Elma describes an incident where Arthur Freeman insulted her by patting her on the cheek when she asked him to deliver a message from the office. There is a cocky-looking man named Freeman listed as a junior in the 1919 *Belle of the Blue*. He is wearing an Army hat in his class photo.
- Glenn, Francis — Elma mentions him in a list of Georgetown College boys who were on furlough in November.
- Gosset, Miss — There is an Argene Gossett listed on a 1916 recital program from Franklin Female College.
- Hall, Blanche — Blanche Marie Hall, Elma's college roommate, was from Woodburn, Kentucky, near where Elma grew up, so they probably knew each other before college. Elma mentions numerous incidents in which they collaborated to have some fun. The 1920 *Belle of the Blue* describes Blanche

DRAMATIS PERSONAE

as "an ideal college girl, enthusiastic, industrious, studious, a leader in every college activity, the valedictorian of her class." She was also a laboratory assistant in physics. Blanche Hall and Ira Porter were a couple while in college.

- Harrington, 2nd Lt. Aldis — Lt. Harrington was commanding officer of the Student Army Training Corps at Georgetown College in 1918. Elma was assigned to work for him in the office and do any typing he might need. During the flu outbreak in October 1918, Lt. Harrington detailed certain boys to assist with caring for the sick students in the dormitories.
- Harris, Lelia — Lelia Goode Harris, from Madisonville, class of 1920, was assistant to the registrar. She is described in her college yearbook as "an artist, a poet, an efficient business woman, a good student, and best of all, a loving and sympathetic friend."
- Hart, Miss — Elliott mentioned a Miss Hart riding by in a car in Anderson County.
- Hart, Mrs. — Elma mentions being invited to Mrs. Hart's for dinner, along with Blanche and Lelia Harris.
- Henderson, Ralph — Elliott mentioned meeting a fellow at camp who knew "all the Shelby bunch at G.C.," including Ralph Henderson.
- Hill, John L. — John Leonard Hill was the first dean of Georgetown College and professor of history, economics, and political science. He was said to have a "distinguished physical bearing and his manner commanded respect from all who met him." (*History of Georgetown College* by Robert Snyder, page 88.) The students wrote in the 1918 Georgetonian, "When a student gets homesick, he goes to Prof. Hill. When a student needs advice, he goes to Prof. Hill. When a student wants to pour out his troubles into a sympathetic ear, he goes to Prof. Hill. Prof Hill knows every students almost as well as the student knows himself, and a little better sometimes, we think." During the flu outbreak in October 1918, Dr. Hill and his wife took charge of the students at Old Sem.
- Hinds, Charles — Elma mentions a "Bro Hinds" as one of the "preacher men" at Georgetown. Charles F Hinds graduated in 1919 and returned for his MA degree. He wrote his thesis on "The Economic Aspects of the Bible."
- Hinton, Coach — Professor Hinton was one of two members of the college faculty who were granted a year's leave of absence to engage in YMCA War Work. Professor R. T. Hinton, professor of biology and head of the athletics

department, left June 1 for France to train the "Sammies" in various athletic games while Professor D.E. Fogle of the modern languages department taught French to officers at Camp Zachary Taylor. (1918 *Georgetonian*)

- Holmes, Lillian — In the 1919 yearbook, there is a sophomore with the last name of Holmes, but no first name is given. Elma had a lifelong friend named Lillian, who worked in the business office with her and later married James Moreland. Perhaps this is the same Lillian.
- Hough — Elma mentioned someone named Hough who was on the train ride home after their sophomore year at school.
- Howard, Grace — Miss Howard taught domestic science at Georgetown beginning in 1915. (*Georgetown College Historical Catalogue*, 1907–1917.) Elma and Elliott mention concerns that a Miss Howard might report them for sitting on the swing together one night. She may have also been housemother at Rucker Hall.
- Hughes, Elizabeth Kathryn — The "grass widow" who married Elliott's father. She was known as "Miss Betty." Her name from her previous marriage was Calvert.
- Hughes, Mrs. — Mrs. Hughes may have been the woman who ran the boarding house where Elma stayed in Bowling Green. Elma mentions her in connection with an incident in which she and Sopha stole a peck of pears from the backyard.
- Ichie — Ichie may have been a fellow student. Elma makes several deprecating remarks about him and mentions a "Prof Ichie" who gave an illustrated lecture on France for the Zeta program.
- Jackson, Walter — A lab assistant in chemistry at Georgetown. During the flu outbreak in October 1918, Elma reported that he helped nurse the boys at the Jameson House for four days with only eight hours of sleep until he also came down with a serious case of the flu.
- "Jake" — A friend of Elma's from Franklin who was going to China as a missionary.
- "Jeff" — Elliott and his best friend Ezra Sparrow from Lawrenceburg were nicknamed Mutt and Jeff, after the popular American cartoon of the time. Elliott was the shorter of the two, so he earned the nickname "Jeff," while Ezra was called "Mutt." Elliott and Ezra remained friends for life.
- Jennings, Alan — Alan was apparently a member of the Tau Theta Kappa literary society. In fall 1918, Elma reported that the T.θ.K.s only got 17

DRAMATIS PERSONAE

pledges and Alan was responsible for getting 10 of the 17. Elma also mentions a "Jennings" who scored the only points in a football game with the University of Kentucky.

- Jim — Elma talks about getting Jim to send her suitcase to the station. It is unusual for Elma to refer to people other than very close friends by their first names, so perhaps Jim was an employee at the college?
- Johnson, Alma — A friend of Elma's from Franklin who stayed at the same boarding house with her in Bowling Green. This may be the same "pal" she mentions studying with on Reservoir Park and eating candy.
- Kay, Mr. — Elliott refers to him as a Baptist friend of his at camp from Missouri. He says they have almost the same ideals of life. They spent at least one liberty together.
- Keena, Mr. — Elliott's friend at Great Lakes, an ordained minister from Ohio and a graduate of Princeton. Elliott describes him as smart and a good scout and one of the most popular fellows there. After training, he was put on a freighter bound for France.
- Keller, Wayne H. — Elma mentions riding home on the train with "Keller" in June 1918. The 1920 *Belle of the Blue* lists a Wayne H. Keller from Henderson in the class behind Elliott and Elma.
- Kirton, Professor — Elma refers to him as "prissy little Prof Kirton," who "has an electric iron and presses his suit every day." He apparently was assistant math teacher after Professor Rhoton left and before Professor Richardson arrived.
- Kunkel — A fellow from Elliott's old company from Milwaukee whom people mistake as his brother.
- Lady Mac — See McFerran.
- Learned, Laura — A friend of Elma's who was engaged to "Jake" and also on her way to China as a missionary.
- Lehnard, "Dutch" — George Lehnhard, halfback on the football team, "came to GC in 1917 from Paducah High with a big rep. Everybody thought he would be swell headed, but he got down to practice without advertising himself and, ever since, the Tigers have had the best open field runner and one of the best tacklers in the state." (1919 *Belle of the Blue*)
- Leigh, Dr. — Townes Randolph Leigh was professor of chemistry at Georgetown College. At the end of the school year in 1918, he went to sea to try out a new smoke screen for the Navy. Elma mentions that he came down

DRAMATIS PERSONAE

with the flu in the fall of 1918, and six of the boys in the chemistry department went together to buy him $5 worth of American Beauty roses.

- Lindley, Willie — Willie Lindley was a fellow student in the class of 1920, described as a "good old girl" who met the ups and downs of college life with a smile and made many lasting friends.
- Lovelace, Bro. — Brother Lovelace was the preacher at Elma's church in Franklin and the preacher who married them.
- Lowe, Lillian — A friend of Elma's. According to the 1918 *Georgetonian*, "she is not as low as you would think by her name" but has proved herself of very high qualities. Although some people might think she is shy, "this thought soon disappears when the curly, brown head is tossed to one side, and the brown eyes snap. But don't get scared, she's getting ready for a smile!" She married a man named Patterson.
- Lowe, Mrs. — Elma mentions Mrs. Lowe several times. Presumably she is the mother of Lillian Lowe.
- Lunsford, Sopha — Elma's new pal at the boarding house in Bowling Green, who delights in doing things to shock some people's dignity. Also referred to as Sophia and Sofa.
- Lyons, Mr. — One of Elliott's pals at Great Lakes, from Michigan. Elliott describes him as a gentleman and writes that they share the same ideals. They sometimes go on liberty together.
- Mabley, Miss — Marguerite Dudley Mabley was an instructor in English and French. Elma refers to her as "that red-headed Miss Mabley" and says the class will be trying.
- McClanahan, Delma — Delma was one of Elma's closest friends from Franklin. They had gone to Miss Blair's elementary school and Franklin Female Academy together.
- McFerran, Mrs. — "Lady Mac" seems to have been the conscience of Rucker Hall, and both Elma and Elliott mention several incidents that shocked her. She was apparently responsible for enforcing curfew and rules of behavior at Rucker Hall, though whether she was an instructor, house mother, or student on the self-governance committee is unclear. Elliott suggested that she surely had been in the Navy because they also get "points" for various infractions. Elma and Elliott use variant spellings, including McFerron, McFerson, and Macferan.

DRAMATIS PERSONAE

- McGlothlin, Dr. — Elma mentions Dr. McGlothlin often. In addition to preaching regular sermons at the church in Bowling Green, he also preached the commencement sermon there.
- Mai, Miss — Miss Mai was likely one of the residents at Mrs. Potter's boarding house.
- Macklin — Elliott mentions running into him at Great Lakes. A student named Macklin is listed as a sophomore in the 1919 yearbook.
- Martin, Dean W. — Dr. Martin was professor of physics at Georgetown. Elma mentioned that he was also in charge of military training on campus during the fall of 1918.
- Martin, Gene — Eugene Ray Martin from Toledo, Ohio, president of Tau Theta Kappa and president of the student body, was described as "an excellent student, athlete, and companion." Elma mentions him calling for Mary Anna Beard. She also talks about borrowing his suit to wear when she played "a dude" in a "moving picture show" put on by the Alphas and Zetas. The yearbook says he was nicknamed "Bene" and described him as a clever little backfield man, fast, heady, and with plenty of fight.
- Martin, Robin D. — Robin was from Utica and comes up often in Elma's letters. He was in the class behind Elma and Elliott and seems to have been a good friend. He was a member of the Tau Theta Kappa Society, on the tack team and the college debating team. He represented the college in Prohibition Oratorical. He dated a girl named Jessie Beagle, who died of the flu during the fall of 1918.
- Martin, Roy — William Roy Martin, from Waddy, was an acquaintance of Elliott's whom he ran into at Camp Perry in Great Lakes. He was in the class of '19 and described as an "economical student—never making less than a 75 nor more than 79." It was said that he "cut his teeth on a mule shoe way down in Waddy, Kentucky, and ever since he has continued to cut up."
- Mary Eliza — Mary Eliza was one of the 25 Georgetown College students riding home on the train with Elma at Christmas break, who walked downtown to see a movie during their layover in Louisville.
- May, Mr. — Elma mentions him as going to the seminary.
- Meador, Thomas — Thomas Meador comes up often in these letters. Elma describes him as "the little preacher who has been going to Bethel College" and to whom she wrote a "crazy letter" one time. On several occasions, Elma "keeps company" with Thomas during the summer of 1918 (always as part

of a group of friends), but she worries that Elliott will be angry and think there is more to the relationship than just friends.

- Miller, Fulton — Elliott mentions seeing Elma's "good friend Fulton" in New York and says he is as cute as ever and is going out on the battle cruiser Huntington but expects to be back to Georgetown by mid-year.
- Mitchell, George — One of the Georgetown College men who made good in the Army and went to Princeton University in the paymaster's corps.
- Mitchell, W.E. — Dr. Mitchell was vice president of Georgetown College. He comes up in several of these letters. Elma apparently had much contact with him through her office work. She often mentions his "gum chewing" habit and says he "raves around continually like some wild animal." The 1918 *Georgetonian* describes him as greeting everyone with a smile and a hearty "Good Morning" and says he is present at all of the ball games to cheer the Tigers on to victory. They report that he always kept a cool head "when there was need of some thinking to be done, as in the instance of the Pawling Hall fire, when he had rooming places provided for the boys, even before the fire had been put out." Without him, it was said, things would not move so smoothly. During the flu outbreak in October 1918, Dr. Mitchell was in charge of the boys at the Jameson House.
- Moffet, Capt — According to *The Great Lakes Naval Training Station: A History* by Francis Buzzell, Captain W.A. Moffett had a "policy of refusing to include 'can't' in his vocabulary, or to tolerate its use by his subordinates."
- Moffett, Lou — While telling about driving a woman named Miss Corbin from the train station to her home in Alton, Elliott mentions a man named Ben (also known as Lou) Moffatt.
- Moore, Dr. — Elma mentions being called out to take Dr. Moore's place in nursing students during the flu outbreak in October 1918.
- Moore, Sally Ford — Sallie Ford Moore was in the class of '19. She was described as a conscientious student whose favorite study was The Letters of Paul the Apostle.
- Moreland, Jimmy — Jimmy Moreland was a junior in 1920. He was from Georgetown, a member of Tau Theta Kappa, *Georgetonian* reporter and editor, and vice president of the junior class. He married Elma's friend and office mate Lillian.
- Morris, Jack — Elliott mentioned running into him at the Anderson County fair early in the summer of 1918. Jackson B. Morris from Harrodsburg was a

junior in 1917 but like many of his fellow students, he left school to join the Navy. He was at Great Lakes about the same time as Elliott and graduated from the Officers Material School. In his senior yearbook, he is described as, "Ensign in the U.S. Navy, Judge of Hog Heaven Court, and the possessor of many other such proud titles. ...Jack was really a member of the Class of 1918, but he let his education in the Navy interfere with his mere college learning."

- Mullins, Clyde — Elma mentions taking Mullins' place in the business office, helping keep books. Clyde Vernon Mullins was in their class, an officer in the Ciceronians, and assistant business manager for the *Georgetonian* staff. Elliott refers to him disparagingly as "Miss Mullins." In a different letter he talks about a "Sister Stone Mullins." Elma also refers to him at least once as "Sis."

- Mullins, Dr. E.Y. — Dr. Mullins of Louisville gave the address at Georgetown when the boys in the Student Army Training Corps were inducted into military service.

- Mumford, Mr. — Elma mentions a Mr. Mumford of the Gregg Shorthand School in Chicago who gave an address at the Business School in Bowling Green.

- "Mutt"— Elliott and his best friend Ezra Sparrow from Lawrenceburg were nicknamed Mutt and Jeff, after the popular American cartoon of the time. Elliott was the shorter of the two, so he earned the nickname "Jeff," while Ezra was called "Mutt." Elliott and Ezra remained friends for life.

- Newell, George — Elma mentions that (Miss) George Newell had the flu in late November.

- Nina — Nina comes up several times in these letters, but it is not clear what her relationship with Elliott was. Elliott mentioned Nina asking him to a reception at his old high school and Elma teased him a couple times about her.

- Ogden — Elliott mentioned running into him at Great Lakes. Squire Redmon Ogden from Winchester, class of '20, secretary of the Ciceronians, was described as "an athlete, a scholar, a debater, an editor, a leader and friend." Elma reported that he was put in charge of military training at Georgetown during the fall of 1918, along with Freeman, Siler, Redding, and Professor Martin. Elliott says all those fellows took their training at Fort Sheridan.

DRAMATIS PERSONAE

- Oldham — Elma mentioned Oldham as a boy out in town who had the flu and was not expected to live.
- Oral — Oral was Delma's fiancé.
- Patterson, Lillian — See Lillian Lowe.
- Patty — Patty apparently worked in the administrative office at Georgetown College.
- Payne, Lavinia — One of Elma's friends in the Zeta literary society. Lavinia was from Franklin, Kentucky, and had also attended Franklin Female Academy. She apparently majored in music at Georgetown. (1916 FFC program)
- Porter, Beulah — Beulah was Ira Porter's sister. She was from Caneyville, Kentucky. The 1919 *Belle of the Blue* describes her as "one of the best known and friendliest students of this college" who was "never too busy with her duties to help anyone in trouble or enter into any kind of fun."
- Porter, Ira — Ira Porter was one of Elliott's and Elma's classmates at Georgetown, who later went on to serve on the board of trustees for decades. According to their yearbook, "Tightwad" was an all-around college man. He held numerous offices while in college; played football, basketball, and track; and was president of the student body their senior year. The 1920 *Belle of the Blue* refers to "his enviable athletic record, literary work and scholastic achievements." Ira Porter and Blanche Hall were a couple while in college.
- Potter, Mrs. Charlie — Mrs. Potter ran the boarding house where Elma stayed in Bowling Green during the summer of 1918.
- Powell, Dr. — State Mission Secretary from Louisville, who preached at Bowling Green.
- Powers, P.D. — Elma mentions that he got three ribs broken at a football game with Centre College in November 1918.
- Ragland, Professor — George Ragland was professor of Latin and Greek at Georgetown. The 1918 *Georgetonian* says "When a freshman enters college, he is not usually aware of greenness. Prof. Ragland takes it upon himself to convince him of his lack of knowledge and keeps him from being a fool." Regarding his classes, the *Georgetonian* reports, "A Latin class taught by Prof Ragland is one class in which you do not go to sleep. Though you hear the same jokes almost every day, there is always something interesting about them, and the twinkle in Prof. Ragland's eye makes you smile, even if the joke does not." Elliott says he did not admire the professor very much but he

DRAMATIS PERSONAE

thought his home seemed almost ideal, exhibiting freedom or frankness and devotion among the whole family.

- Rameses — The 1920 *Belle of the Blue* identifies William Richard Miner, from Frankfort, as "Rameses," the modern Rip Van Winkle. He graduated in 1920 after serving as "one of Uncle Sam's guardians of the briny deep." His favorite saying was said to be "Cheer up, Mabel."
- Rankley, Harry — Elliott mentions Harry Rankley as one of several Georgetonians who were at Great Lakes while he was there. Harry Romaine Rankley, from Turners Station, Kentucky, graduated from Georgetown College in 1918. The *Georgetonian* says "his stay has been a delightful one, his specialties being Biology and girls" and says that "no better all-around man can be found in school." He was a year or two ahead of Elliott and Elma.
- Ray, L.C. — An "old G.C. student" whom Elliott got to bunk with at Great Lakes training camp.
- Reagan, Frances — Elma mentions Frances in connection with the YWCA. She reports that Frances Reagan and Miss Porter went to some university in Chicago, and Professor Fogle went up to see Miss Porter.
- Redding, Clarence — Clarence D Redding from Georgetown, class of '19, president of Tau Theta Kappa. He was said to have "endeared himself to the student body by his quiet unassuming manner." Elma mentions him being in charge of training in the fall of 1918, along with Brothers Freeman, Ogden, Siler, and Professor Martin. Elliott says all those fellows took their training at Fort Sheridan.
- Rhoton, Prof. — Alvis L Rhoton was professor of mathematics at Georgetown 1907-1918.
- Richardson, C.H. — C.H. Richardson began teaching math at Georgetown in 1918.
- Roberts, Hayden — Hayden Roberts was one of the students at Georgetown serving in the military during 1918. Elma mentions writing to him in her capacity as an office worker at Georgetown. He is listed in the 1918 Georgetonian Honor Roll as being in Aviation Camp, Waco, Texas.
- Roomie Steve — Elliott's roommate his first year of college, who apparently went into the Army and got a job in radio work.
- Routt, Paul — Paul Routt was a new student in 1918 from Anderson County. He told Elma that Elliott was the only man in school the year he

DRAMATIS PERSONAE

graduated and so took all the honors. Elliott apparently didn't think much of him. He says he was "one of Lawrenceburg's dudes" and a frat man at Transylvania the previous year so Elliott guesses he will make a "typical Ciceronian."

- Rusk, Beulah — Beulah Elizabeth Rusk was in the class ahead of Elma and active in the Young Woman's Christian Association (YW) Cabinet. Elma talks about receiving a long chain letter started by Beulah Rusk from Blue Ridge. The 1919 yearbook described her as "a fine, grand old girl" who helped everyone by her loving and cheerful nature. In the fall of 1918, the YW presented an orange and black battalion flag to the Student Army Training Corps, and Beulah gave the address for that. Beulah was one of several girls, including Elma and Blanche, who took care of those who came down with the flu in October 1918.
- Saunders, Helen — A fellow Georgetonian from Pulaski County, Kentucky.
- Sebastian, Bro. — Elma mentions him as one of the "preacher men" who returned to campus in September 1918.
- Shewmaker, Kate — Kate Shewmaker, a member of the Zeta literary society, was identified as "one of the stars of the class of '20, a leader from the word go" and said that "Pep" was her middle name.
- Siler — Elma mentions him as being in charge of training at G.C., along with Brothers Freeman, Ogden, Redding, and Professor Martin. Elliott says all those fellows took their training at Fort Sheridan.
- Sis Mullins — There is a Clyde Vernon Mullins from Paducah listed in the 1920 yearbook. He may be the one nicknamed "Sis."
- Sisk — Elma mentions a Mr. Sisk and his wife returning to Georgetown in the fall of 1918 and Mr. Sisk asking about Elliott.
- Slaughter — Elliott mentioned running into Slaughter, a student at G.C., while at Great Lakes.
- Snuggs, Faith — Faith Mary Snuggs, a classmate "from far-off China," was said to possess that "stick-to-it-ive-ness" which always spells success—success in her class work, girls' athletics, and in winning the friendship of her schoolmates.
- Snuggs, Harold — Harold Hebinger Snuggs was a fellow student and friend at Georgetown College. He and Elliott were in the same literary society, Tau Theta Kappa. He was born in Pakhoi, South China. He was a lab assistant in

DRAMATIS PERSONAE

chemistry, known for his hard work and varied interests. He attended a chemical school in New Jersey during the war.

- Snuggs, Roland — Roland Edward Snuggs, class of 1920, was described as "another wise man from the East, a chemist by choice, an alchemist by Fate's decree, with a happy heart and a busy brain."
- Snyder, Chocolate — Elma mentions someone named Chocolate Snyder in connection with a "big bunch of folks in the parlor playing and singing" at Old Sem.
- Sofa — See Lunsford, Sopha.
- Sophia — See Lunsford, Sopha.
- Sparrow, Ezra — See Jeff.
- Spillman, Mr. — Elma mentions a Mr. Spillman from New York who gave several patriotic speeches at Bowling Green on the topics of "My Ships," "My Friends," and "My Country."
- Stevenson, Holly — There is a man named Stevenson listed as a junior in the 1919 *Belle of the Blue*. Holly was a man's name until the mid-20th century. This may have been the same Stevenson that Elliott referred to as a "good worker" for Tau Theta Kappa.
- Stone, Sister — Elliott mentioned a "Sister" Stone in connection with John Browning and Luttie Williams from Georgetown College. A fellow he met at camp named Chapman said he knew them. Elliott refers to a Sister Stone Mullins in the same context.
- Stumpy — This name comes up often but not sure who it refers to. The nickname apparently was earned after spraining an ankle.
- Sufferin' Susie — Elma mentions her in connection with the freshman who ate 14 biscuits at supper one night.
- Sullivan, "Doodle" — Elma mentions him in a list of Georgetown College boys who were on furlough in November 1918.
- Summers, Judd — Elma mentions that Judd Summers was at the point of death the last week of October but had some slight chance of recovery.
- Tabor — Elliott describes him as a "sissy sort of fellow" who invited him to see a movie while in New York. He says "he is a musical artist or thinks he is at least."
- Taylor, Slim — Mr. Taylor was one of the students at Georgetown serving in the military during 1918. Elma mentions writing to him in her capacity as an

office worker at Georgetown. J. B. Taylor is listed in the 1918 Georgetonian Honor Roll as being at Naval Electrical School, Brooklyn, New York.

- Theophilus — One of Elliott's nicknames in college. Theophilus is the name or honorary title of the person to whom the Gospel of Luke and the Acts of the Apostles were written.
- Thomasson, Coach — Football coach at Georgetown.
- Thompson, Mary — Mary Beatrice Thompson, from Bagdad, KY, class of '19, was described as "a jolly good sport—an athlete, a student, a chum, a friend, a sure-nuf rollicking romping college girl."
- Thompson, James William — Dr. Thompson was professor of Bible at Georgetown beginning in 1917. Elliott commented that he was fine as a man, but he did not think he was a very good teacher. He thought he was tiresome to listen to. Elma also complained about his classes and expressed disappointment because she expected to enjoy Bible classes.
- Thompson, Paul — Elliott met a fellow at Great Lakes who knew all the Shelby bunch at G.C., including Paul Thompson.
- Tomlinson, Eddy — Elma mentions getting a letter from a Mr. Tomlinson about the Student Mission Board.
- Townsend, Mr. — An employee at the *Louisville Herald* and friend of a friend of Elma's.
- Tupper, Mr. — Elma mentions a Mr. Tupper from some city out West who spoke at the church in Bowling Green, and Elliott thinks this may be the same man who spoke at the women's meeting during commencement at Georgetown College.
- Vaughn — Elma mentions a Mr. Vaughn in one of her "confessions" about walking across campus with a man, who proceeded to "sing [Elliott's] praises during the entire journey." She described him as Elliott's friend and admirer.
- Volmer, Dutch — One of the Georgetown College students who made good in the Army and became a captain. A.M. Vollmer was listed in the 1918 *Georgetonian* as a lieutenant in the 354 Infantry at Camp Funston, Kansas. He apparently did not return to Georgetown College after becoming an officer in the Army.
- Wahn — Elliott mentioned him in connection with another friend from Princeton at Great Lakes but doesn't give any details.
- Washburn, Ava — Ava was a friend of Elma's from Franklin who attended Georgetown College in 1916.

DRAMATIS PERSONAE

- Washburn, Hal — Hal was a friend of Elma's from Franklin who graduated from dental college in Louisville around 1916.
- Watson, Viola — Viola got the flu at the same time as everyone else at Georgetown and got up in time to start back to school when classes reopened, but then she came down with spinal meningitis, with little hope of recovery.
- Willett, Dr. — The man from Chicago University who spoke at Bowling Green Business University for commencement in 1918. There is a Dr. Willett who taught Hebrew listed in the 1918 circular from Chicago University.
- Williams, Luttie —Elliott mentions Luttie Williams in connection with John Browning and Sister Stone from Georgetown College. A fellow he met at camp named Chapman said he knew them. Chapman told Elliott that Luttie was very wealthy and owned eight automobiles, which seemed to surprise Elliott.
- Yager, Arthur — Arthur Yager was born in Campbellsburg, Kentucky. He earned bachelor's and master's degrees from Georgetown College and a doctorate from Johns Hopkins University. Yager was professor of history, economics, and politics at Georgetown College while becoming active in politics. He served as president of Georgetown College from 1908 to 1913. President Wilson appointed him governor of Puerto Rico from 1913 to 1921.
- Yager, Holmes — Son of Arthur Yager. Elma mentions him in connection with a "wild adventure" involving stealing a saucer of gelatin.

Notes

INTRODUCTION

1. Kenneth A. Simon and W. Vance Grant, Digest of Educational Statistics, Office of Education, Bulletin 1965, No. 4 (Washington, D.C., U.S. Government Printing Office, 1965).
2. Georgetown College was well established by then. Elliott lived in Pawling Hall, built in 1844, and Elma lived across the street in Rucker Hall, completed in 1895. There were three other buildings on campus at the time: (1) Giddings Hall, built in 1841; (2) Highbaugh Hall/Academy Building, built in 1861; and (3) the Chapel-Library-Gymnasium building, built in 1894.
3. *A History of Georgetown College* by Robert Snyder, page 84

1. JUNE - AUGUST, 1917

1. "The Sunshine of Your Smile," with lyrics by Leonard Cooke and music by Lilian Ray, 1913
2. Grace Howard taught domestic science at Georgetown beginning in 1915, according to the Georgetown College Historical Catalogue, 1907–1917.
3. Elliott was known as Tot at home, presumably because he was the youngest and smallest of the brothers.
4. Elliott had signed his first letter "Sam the T.ø.K." (His full name was Samuel Elliott Cranfill.) Perhaps "Tham" is Elma's attempt at alliteration, by lisping "Tham," the Tau Theta Kappa."
5. Franklin is the county seat of Simpson County, Kentucky. The population in 1910 was 3,063.
6. Woodburn, KY, is about 10 miles from Franklin. The 1910 census reported a population of 217.
7. *The League of Youth* (1869), Henrik Ibsen's first open venture in realistic comedy, was a slashing attack on political hypocrisy.
8. *The School for Scandal* was produced at Drury Lane Theater, London, May 8, 1777
9. Elliott was the youngest of five brothers: Thomas Edgar (born March 27, 1890), William Isaac (born June 1, 1891), Calvin DeWitt (born March 19, 1889), and Elmo (born July 6, 1886).
10. Tradition suggests that the name "Tin Lizzie" was derived from the most common American name for a horse in the early 1900s — Lizzie, short for Elizabeth.
11. The Selective Service Act of 1917 was enacted May 18, 1917, the first draft held since the Civil War. There were three registrations. The first was held June 5, 1917, for men between the ages of 21 and 31
12. The Baptist Young People's Union trained youth in public speaking, the importance of prayer, daily Bible reading, personal work, giving, and loyalty to all services of the church. Source: *History of Georgetown Baptist Church*
13. Franklin Female Academy

NOTES

14. Blanche Hall lived in Woodburn.
15. Bowling Green is the county seat of Warren County, Kentucky. The population in 1910 was 9,173.
16. William Jennings Bryan, congressman from Nebraska, three-time presidential candidate, and secretary of state under Woodrow Wilson.
17. Friendship Baptist Church is located at 3683 Bardstown Road (US 62), Sinai, Kentucky (Anderson County).
18. International Mission Board of the Southern Baptists
19. In 1838, Kentucky passed the first statewide woman suffrage law allowing female heads of household to vote in elections deciding on taxes and local boards for the new county "common school" system.
20. The first of the famous Brownie Cameras was introduced in 1900. It sold for $1 and used film that sold for 15 cents a roll.
21. The Victorian-style dormitory where Elma lived at Georgetown College
22. The Academy prepared high school students to do college-level work.
23. Two of Elliott's nicknames
24. There is a Jackson Morris from Harrodsburg listed in the 1919 Belle of the Blue.

2. DECEMBER, 1917

1. "Ring Out the Bells for Christmas," attributed to E. A. Washburn and J. S. B. Hodges and published in at least 29 hymnals
2. Perhaps this refers to Ira Porter's girlfriend Blanche Hall.
3. This letter has a few more ink blots than usual.
4. Lawrenceburg is the nearest town and the county seat of Anderson County. The population was 1,723, according to the 1910 census
5. *Bum* was first recorded in 1855, and during the Civil War was used to describe a foraging soldier. It appears to derive from two words: the German *bummer*, "a high-spirited, irresponsible person," and the old English word *bum*, which has for four centuries been slang for both "a drunk" and "buttocks." From *Facts on File Encyclopedia of Word and Phrase Origins* (1997)
6. "There's no place like home," the last line of the 1823 song "Home! Sweet Home!" (words by John Howard Payne and music by Sir Henry Bishop).
7. Kavanaugh High School was a preparatory school for students from all over the United States seeking to enter the Annapolis naval academy and West Point military academy, as well as a high school for day students.
8. Probably refers to Dr. M.B. Adams, president of the college.
9. In later letters she expresses concern about gaining weight. Perhaps she wrote that she was going to be "fat" from all the Christmas dinners.

3. JUNE, 1918

1. "Love's Garden of Roses," with words by Ruth Rutherford and music by Haydn Wood. Published by Chappell & Co, Ltd, copyright 1914.
2. The book *Over the Top* was first published in 1917 and was a best seller at the time. It was written by an American who had joined the British Army as an infantryman and recounts the horrors of trench warfare.

NOTES

3. *The Louisville Herald*, an independent democratic paper, was published from 1903 to 1925.
4. "Before women were admitted to Georgetown College, Georgetown Female Seminary offered an option for further study beyond basic female education. A new building built after the former building burned was later dubbed 'Old Sem' when a co-education program was permanently installed at the college in 1892." Source: Georgetown College by Megan LeMaster, p. 40.
5. Bowling Green had a business school.
6. Transplanting tobacco seedlings into the ground.
7. Grace Crossfield later married Elliott's brother Isaac Cranfill.
8. The nephew was most likely Melwood Cranfill, born 1914, the son of Calvin and Rayme Cranfill.
9. Women were required to sign in and out at Rucker Hall, and callers had to leave by curfew.
10. A total solar eclipse crossed the United States from Washington state to Florida on June 8, 1918.
11. This was a magazine for children published by the Southern Baptist Sunday School Board beginning in 1866.
12. Bethel College was a Baptist college in Logan County, Kentucky founded in 1854 and closed in 1964.
13. This may be intended as a joke. There was a Sallie Ford Moore in their class at Georgetown.
14. The second registration for the draft was held on June 5, 1918, for men who turned 21 after June 5, 1917.
15. Class I included unmarried registrants with no dependents and married registrants with independent spouse and/or one or more dependent children over 16 with sufficient family income if drafted.
16. Elma used to talk about receiving phone calls at a neighbor's house. Before Elma's family got their own phone, the neighbor, who lived across the street, would step out onto her porch and holler, "Elma! Telephone!" and Elma would run to answer it. However, the neighbor also had a parrot, who soon learned to holler "Elma! Telephone!"
17. Elliott was known as "Theophilus" in college. Theophilus is the name or honorary title of the person to whom the Gospel of Luke and the Acts of the Apostles were written.
18. Radio in the U.S. had become a government monopoly, reserved for the war effort. Source: http://earlyradiohistory.us/sec013.htm
19. According to the Bureau of Labor, the average household earned $1,518 in 1918.
20. According to the Bureau of Labor Statistics, the average hourly wage for services in 1918 was 31¢ an hour.
21. Many of the candies we still enjoy were available by 1918, including Hershey's chocolate, peppermint sticks, NECCO wafers and conversation hearts, Brach's caramels, Hershey's kisses, Toblerone, Life Savers, Goo Goo Clusters, Whitman's samplers, Mars bar, Heath bar, Mary Janes, the Turtle. Other candies available at the time included fruit-flavored Charms, Cherry Mash, Goldenberg's Peanut Chews, Peach Blossoms, and Squirrel Nut Zipper. Source: CandyFavorites.com
22. *The History of Pendennis: His Fortunes and Misfortunes, His Friends and His Greatest Enemy* (1848–1850) is a novel by the English author William Makepeace Thackeray. The novel traces the youthful career of Arthur Pendennis: his first love affair, his experiences at "Oxbridge University," his employment as a London journalist, and so on.

NOTES

23. Louisville's *Courier Journal* was created from the merger of several Kentucky newspapers in the nineteenth century.
24. A pike or turnpike is commonly associated with toll roads. Most of the early roads in Kentucky were privately owned and charged tolls, but in 1896 the Kentucky General Assembly voted to provide a free turnpike system.
25. There were several mills along the Elkhorn Creek near Georgetown.
26. In 1918, "to make love" did not mean to have sexual intercourse. Rather, it meant to be loving and attentive, to court or woo, to be a sweetheart.
27. This is an example of Elma's slang or baby talk for "throw away."
28. *Over the Top* was the title of the book about trench warfare that Elma had borrowed from Elliott and was reading on the train ride home in early June.
29. Obviously some kind of inside joke. *Clarissa, or, the History of a Young Lady*, is an epistolary novel by Samuel Richardson, published in 1748. It tells the tragic story of a heroine whose quest for virtue is continually thwarted by her family. In later letters Elma refers to playing the part of Clarissa.

4. JULY, 1918

1. "Au Revoir But Not Goodbye," composed by Albert von Tilzer with lyrics by Lew Brown, 1917.
2. The detention camp is where new arrivals at Great Lakes Naval Station were housed during World War I.
3. The Chautauqua movement, a popular U.S. movement in adult education in the nineteenth and early twentieth centuries, began as a program for training Sunday school teachers and church workers but eventually broadened to include general education, recreation, and popular entertainment. The program included summer lectures, as well as year-round directed readings and correspondence courses. Source: Britannica.com
4. When Great Lakes was established by an act of Congress in 1904, the project was considered a glaring example of congressional "pork." The idea of a Navy training center so far from the coast was laughable. However, it would become the largest naval training station in the world and the Navy's main source of manpower. In 1916 an average of 220 recruits per month arrived at the Great Lakes. In January 1917, the station received 618 recruits. Between April 6, 1917 (when the United States entered the war) and November 11, 1918 (Armistice Day), Great Lakes received 125,000 men for training, sometimes accommodating as many as 50,000 trainees at a time. During the same period, the physical size of the station increased from 33 buildings on 167 acres to 775 buildings on 1200 acres. Source: Buzzell, Francis. *The Great Lakes Naval Training Station: A History*. Boston: Small, Maynard, and Company, 1918.
5. Vaudeville shows were given twice a week for the men in incoming detention. Source: *The Great Lakes Training Center: A History*
6. Camps Decatur and Farragut
7. It should be no surprise that her mother worried over her after she got her vaccination. Elma's sister Mary had died of typhoid 15 years earlier, just before she was to be married.
8. On July 19, an explosion rocked the *San Diego*, an armored cruiser, and it sank just 10 miles off the New York coastline. Six crew members were lost; 1177 crew and officers were able to abandon ship. The exact cause of the explosion is not known.
9. This line is from the spiritual "Standing in the Need of Prayer." Could these singers have been part of the Jubilee Singers from Fisk University (only 58 miles from Bowling

NOTES

Green)?

10. Her use of the term "niggers" here is quite shocking, especially since she used the term "negroes" earlier in the paragraph. Could this be her way of making some sort of cultural distinction based on class or education?
11. Camp Decatur was one of two camps at the Great Lakes Naval Station designed for incoming recruits. Camp Perry was one of the larger training camps.
12. According to Webster's, the term "grass widow" refers to a discarded mistress, a woman who has had an illegitimate child, a woman whose husband is temporarily away from her, or a woman divorced or separated from her husband.
13. Judging by ads for "safety" razors in 1918, women started shaving their underarms and legs around this time.
14. The Pictorial Review was a glossy magazine aimed at women, covering fashion, style, homemaking, and other things the editors thought women needed to know about.
15. President Woodrow Wilson's World Vision led to the eventual establishment of the United Nations.

5. AUGUST, 1918

1. "There's a Long Long Trail A'Winding," with lyrics by Stoddard King and music by Alonzo Elliott, 1913.
2. This is Elma's nickname for a boy she knew in Bowling Green.
3. This seems to be a combination of "baptize" and "souse," indicating that the boy was drenched in water.
4. From stories my grandmother Elma later told about her days in Rucker Hall, the girls loved to play tricks on each other and on their dates. This included throwing ink bottles out the windows if a "gentleman caller" failed to bring enough candy for all the girls on the floor.
5. A documentary on American soldiers in France, released May 1918.
6. A silent film based on the book by Arthur Guy Empey.
7. Written by Reverend Joseph Holt Ingraham (1809-1865), an American born in Maine who was a popular writer in Victorian times. This is the first of his biblical romances, selling more than a million copies in the 19th century, and is an epistolary novel about a young Jewish girl during the life of Christ which was first published in New York in 1855.
8. Camp Ross was a regimental unit used as an outgoing detention camp.
9. This probably was Calvin's wife, Rayme.
10. The men were vaccinated against smallpox and received three injections of antityphoid serum. They also received a Schick test to determine immunity to diphtheria and throat cultures to discover and isolate chronic carriers of cerebrospinal fever.
11. This may have been some sort of candy. In Elma's August 1 letter, she said her new nickname is "Zip," because she eats so much of it.
12. Tent shows were popular in rural America and typically featured a three-act comedy or drama interspersed with "polite" vaudeville.
13. Ira Porter
14. The term Jack refers to the starred blue flag flown at the jackstay of a commissioned ship that is not underway. Judging from this, the term Jackie appears to refer to new sailors or sailors not yet at sea.
15. The Oxford English Dictionary gives this definition from 1915: gen. Something designed to deceive or bamboozle; a fraudulent design or action; a piece of deception or

humbug.
16. Sometimes Elma refers to her new friend as Sopha and sometimes as Sophia.
17. In his letter of June 12, Elliott says Harold Snuggs also called him Clarissa.
18. 1918 American silent Great War propaganda comedy film.
19. Elma used the shorthand symbol for "therefore" here, consisting of three dots.

6. SEPTEMBER, 1918

1. "Keep the Home Fires Burning," with words by Lena Guibert Ford and published in 1914.
2. Two of the four literary societies at Georgetown College. According to the 1920 yearbook, the women's literary society, Zeta, "has always stood for fair play in all contests, high scholarship and lofty ideals." The ideals of the men's society, Tau Theta Kappa, "encourage a spirit of enthusiasm and energy that will surely mean success."
3. Georgetown College was one of many educational institutions in the United States that had a unit of the Students Army Training Corps during the fall of 1918. The company was composed of about 175 men, who were quartered in the "Old Sem" and Pawling Hall dormitories.
4. The Frankfort and Cincinnati Railroad operated between the towns of Paris and Frankfort, KY. It was a 40-mile shortline railroad that had connections on both ends by the Louisville & Nashville. Near the midway point of Georgetown, KY, it crossed the Southern Railroad. The F&C, known as "The Whiskey Route", serviced many distilleries on the line. It had no affiliation with Cincinnati. Source: AbandonedRails.com
5. The Southern station was still in operation when I was a child, in the 1960s, down on Maddox Street. Flem Smith was stationmaster.
6. The story of the training of a racehorse, the Whip, of the amnesiac nobleman who loves the horse, and of the villains who attempt to keep it from racing. "Big race scenes, wonderful hunting scenes, the best train wreck and most thrilling automobile accident ever seen in pictures, startling scenes in the old Eden Musee, filled with wax figures—all these combined with a powerful and attention-riveting story, make this the world's biggest screen play." Source: IMDB
7. The YW Cabinet sent delegates to Blue Ridge.
8. The Chicago Institute of Art held an exhibit of war paintings by soldiers in France on September 2-15, 1918.
9. The World Series Boston Red Socks defeated the Chicago Cubs 4 games to 2.
10. Camp Taylor was located 6 miles southeast of downtown Louisville, KY. It was once America's largest military training camp, housing 47,500 men at one time, and spurred development in an area that was previously dominated by farmland. Most of the camp was dismantled after World War I and a residential neighborhood emerged, composed mostly of small bungalow and Cape Cod homes, many built or purchased by soldiers returning from the war.
11. Georgetown Baptist Church was only a few blocks from campus.
12. From the eighteenth century to the mid-twentieth century, *negro* was considered the correct and proper term for African Americans. Source: https://aaregistry.org/story/negro-the-word-a-history/
13. This shows how much he valued Elma's letters, since he was willing to carry them around while in the Navy.
14. Lillard Harvey Carter practiced law at Lawrenceburg for nearly thirty years and was president pro tem of the Senate and acting lieutenant governor of Kentucky in 1900-

NOTES

02. Source: History of Kentucky by William Elsey Connelley, 1922.
15. This is the third time Elliott has mentioned Jews. His previous comments did not imply any kind of prejudice against them, so I'm not sure what to make of this comment.
16. Both Elma and Elliott have made references to men they consider to be effeminate.
17. Source: https://www.influenzaarchive.org/cities/city-chicago.html
18. reputation
19. At that time one could teach school with an 8th grade education.
20. Source: https://www.influenzaarchive.org/cities/city-louisville.html
21. There is a town called Wilmette on the western shore of Lake Michigan north of Chicago.

7. OCTOBER, 1918

1. "I Don't Know Where I'm Going But I'm On My Way," written and composed by George Fairman and produced by Harry Von Tilzer Music Publishing Company circa 1917.
2. According to the Students Army Training Corps Descriptive Circular dated October 14, 1918, the only institution in Kentucky that had a Naval unit was State University of Kentucky in Lexington (about 12 miles from Georgetown). By contrast, Army units of the SATC were authorized at numerous schools in Kentucky, including both private and public institutions — Berea College, Bethel College, Centre College, Eastern Kentucky State Normal School, Georgetown College, University of Kentucky, Kentucky Wesleyan College, University of Louisville, Ogden College, Transylvania College, and Western Kentucky State Normal School.
3. A dialectical variant of confab.
4. The Vest pocket Kodak camera (VPK) was one of the most popular cameras of its day, especially among soldiers, with 28,000 VPKs sold in 1915. Source: Science and Media Museum
5. During the war, the young ladies of Rucker Hall were actively engaged in Red Cross work, making bandages and compresses and knitting for the soldier boys.
6. A line running up the left side of the page says, "These little spots are apple stains."
7. This is an exact transcription of the sentence, though its meaning is not completely clear.
8. George Herbert Palmer was president of Harvard.
9. Frank H Simonds, "Victory and the Turn of the Tides."
10. The fire, known as the Cloquet-Moose Lake fire, began at rail lines near Sturgeon Lake, north of Duluth. In all, 38 towns and villages were destroyed, 453 deaths were reported, with another 85 people seriously burned. Property damage included 4,000 houses, 6,000 barns, and 40 schools. Hundreds of thousands of farm animals also perished. The total damage was close to $100 million. Source: History.com
11. And yet he kept all her letters.
12. An 1846 novel by George Sand

NOTES

8. NOVEMBER, 1918

1. "I'll Come Back to You When It's All Over," with lyrics by Lew Brown, arranged by Lee Orean Smith, and composed by Kerry Mills. New York, 1917.
2. The U.S. Naval Air Station at Pauillac, France, was established in December 1917 as an assembly and repair station supporting all U.S. Naval Air Stations in France. Source: National Museum of the U.S. Navy
3. In his letter to Elliott dated October 25, 1918, Wilbur Fields also commented on the training camp at GC: "Throughout the S.A.T.C. boys there has been little studying, for with military interest, flu epidemic, which got 2/3 of the boys, and lack of classical interest generally, it has been hardly possible, and then our studying accommodations consist of a sagging old cot."
4. 1918 marked only the fourth year of the self-government association of Rucker Hall. All young ladies entering college as freshmen automatically became self-governed girls at the expiration of ten weeks, that is, provided they showed due respect for rules and regulations. The executive committee was composed of five members: president, vice-president, secretary, and two associate members chosen from the sophomore and junior classes. The committee met once a week and kept records of points and fixed penalties for all disobedience of the rules. Source: Belle of the Blue, 1917
5. Play on words with suffragette
6. This poem by Mary Carolyn Davies appeared in *Good Housekeeping*, Volume 67, Number 3. It was later anthologized in *The Drums in Our Street, A Book of War Poems* by Mary Carolyn Davies, Macmillan, 1918.
7. Interestingly, Elma omitted a couple lines in her transcription. The original poem here says "my heart would be / An opened book filled full with witchery, / Filled, too, with pain, / An opened book that had been left too long upon a dusty shelf."
8. Centre College is a private school in Danville, Kentucky

9. DECEMBER, 1918

1. "Smiles," by Lambert Murphy and released on September 9, 1918.
2. Women's Christian Temperance Union
3. Jennie Benedict's Restaurant, 554 S. 4th St. Louisville, Kentucky, (inventor of the Benedictine Sandwich).

BEFORE TEXTING

1. These are actual quotes from their letters.

Works Cited

"Arthur Yager." 2021. Wikipedia. November 7, 2021. Accessed November 8, 2022. https://en.wikipedia.org/wiki/Arthur_Yager.
Belle of the Blue. 1917. Georgetown, Kentucky: Georgetown College.
Belle of the Blue. 1919. Georgetown, Kentucky: Georgetown College.
Belle of the Blue. 1920. Georgetown, Kentucky: Georgetown College.
"Benedict's Restaurant." 2017. Welcome to "the Little Colonel" Website. January 5, 2017. Accessed November 8, 2022. https://littlecolonel.com/node/392.
"Bethel College (Kentucky)." 2022. Wikipedia. July 19, 2022. Accessed November 8, 2022. https://en.wikipedia.org/wiki/Bethel_College_(Kentucky).
"Bowling Green." 2021. Wikipedia. May 23, 2021. Accessed November 8, 2022. https://en.wikipedia.org/wiki/Bowling_Green,_Kentucky.
Brown, Lew and Albert Von Tilzer. 1917. "Au Revoir but Not Goodbye." Library of Congress, Washington, D.C. 20540 USA. Accessed October 29, 2022. https://www.loc.gov/item/jukebox-817664/.
Brown, Lew and Albert Von Tilzer. 1917. "Au Revoir, but Not Good-Bye (Soldier Boy)." Library of Congress, Washington, D.C. 20540 USA. 1917. Accessed November 8, 2022. https://www.loc.gov/item/2014562659/.
Brown, Lew, and Kerry Mills. 1917. "I'll Come back to You When It's All Over." Digital Collections at the University of Illinois at Urbana-Champaign Library. 1917. Accessed November 8, 2022. https://digital.library.illinois.edu/items/85cbb4d0-c55a-0134-2373-0050569601ca-b#?cv=0&r=0&xywh=-1741%2C-467%2C9896%2C9325.
Brown, Lew and Kerry Mills. 1917b. "I'll Come Back to You When It's Over (Recorded 1917)." Accessed November 8, 2022. Www.youtube.com. 1917. https://www.youtube.com/watch?v=ueMF0mNwYs0.
Bureau of Labor Statistics, 1918-1919. U.S. Bureau of Labor Statistics, Consumer Expenditure Survey, and U.S. Census Bureau, *Statistical Abstract of the United States*
Burns, Adam. 2002. "Kentucky Railroads: Map, History, Abandoned Lines." American-Rails.com. October 9, 2002. Accessed November 8, 2022. https://www.american-rails.com/ky.html.
Buzzell, Francis. 1910. *The Great Lakes Naval Training Station: A History*. Google Books. Small, Maynard. Accessed November 8. 2022. My Book.
Callahan, J., and Lee Roberts. 1918. "Smiles." *Historic Sheet Music Collection*. Accessed November 8, 2022. https://digitalcommons.conncoll.edu/sheetmusic/1270/.
Callahan, J. Will, and Lee S. Roberts. 1917. "Smiles." Library of Congress, Washington, D.C. 20540 USA. 1917. Accessed November 8, 2022. https://www.loc.gov/item/jukebox-659550/.
"Camp Taylor, Louisville." 2022. Wikipedia. January 1, 2022. Accessed November 8, 2022. https://en.wikipedia.org/wiki/Camp_Taylor.
"Chicago, Illinois and the 1918-1919 Influenza Epidemic | the American Influenza

WORKS CITED

Epidemic of 1918: A Digital Encyclopedia." 2021. Influenzaarchive.org. 2021. Accessed November 8, 2022. https://www.influenzaarchive.org/cities/city-chicago.html.

"Clarissa." 2019. Wikipedia. Wikimedia Foundation. October 3, 2019. Accessed November 9, 2022. https://en.wikipedia.org/wiki/Clarissa.

Davies, Mary Carolyn. 1918. *The Drums in Our Street*. New York: The MacMillan Company.

Elliott, Zo, and Stoddard King. 1917. "There's a Long, Long Trail." Library of Congress, Washington, D.C. 20540 USA. 1917. Accessed November 8, 2022. https://www.loc.gov/item/jukebox-817436/.

Empey, Arthur Guy, and Boston University of Massachusetts. 1917. *"Over the Top," by an American Soldier Who Went, Arthur Guy Empey, Machine Gunner, Serving in France; Internet Archive*. New York and London, G. P. Putnam's sons. Accessed November 8, 2022. https://archive.org/details/overtopbyamerica00empe.

Eyler, John M. 2010. "The State of Science, Microbiology, and Vaccines circa 1918." *Public Health Reports* 125 (3_suppl): 27–36. https://doi.org/10.1177/00333549101250s306.

Fairman, George. 1917. "I Don't Know Where I'm Going but I'm on My Way." Library of Congress, Washington, D.C. 20540 USA. 1917. Accessed November 8, 2022. https://www.loc.gov/item/2013563182/.

Fairman, George. 1917. "I Don't Know Where I'm Going, but I'm on My Way." Library of Congress, Washington, D.C. 20540 USA. 1917. Accessed November 8, 2022. https://www.loc.gov/item/jukebox-25045/.

Fields, Wilbur. Letter to Elliott Cranfill. 2018, October 25, 2018.

"Franklin." 2019. Wikipedia. May 1, 2019. Accessed November 8, 2022. https://en.wikipedia.org/wiki/Franklin,_Kentucky.

Georgetown College. *Historical Catalogue of Georgetown College, 1829-1917*. Georgetown News Press.

"Glossary of Nautical Terms (A-L)." 2022. Wikipedia. Accessed October 27, 2022. https://en.wikipedia.org/wiki/Glossary_of_nautical_terms_(A-L)#J.

Grabenstein, J. D. 2006. "Immunization to Protect the US Armed Forces: Heritage, Current Practice, and Prospects." *Epidemiologic Reviews* 28 (1): 3–26. https://doi.org/10.1093/epirev/mxj003.

Hambrick (Ed.), Maribeth, and Stan Dyer (Ed.). 2011. *History of Georgetown Baptist Church 1810-2010*. Lexington, Kentucky: The Clark Group.

Harding, Colin. 2014. "The Vest Pocket Kodak Was the Soldier's Camera - National Science and Media Museum Blog." National Science and Media Museum Blog. Eleanor Mitchell. March 13, 2014. Accessed November 8, 2022. https://blog.scienceandmediamuseum.org.uk/the-vest-pocket-kodak-was-the-soldiers-camera/.

Harper, Douglas. 2015. "Online Etymology Dictionary." Etymonline.com. 2015. Accessed November 8, 2022. https://www.etymonline.com/.

Hendrickson, Robert, and Internet Archive. 1997. *The Facts on File Encyclopedia of Word and Phrase Origins. Internet Archive*. New York: Facts on File. Accessed November 8, 2022. https://archive.org/details/factsonfileencyc00hend.

History.com Editors. 2009. "Fire Rages in Minnesota." History. November 13, 2009. Accessed November 8, 2022. https://www.history.com/this-day-in-history/fire-rages-in-minnesota.

History.com Editors. 2018. "Model T." History. A&E Television Networks. August 21,

WORKS CITED

2018. Accessed November 8, 2022. https://www.history.com/topics/inventions/model-t.

"'Home, Sweet Home': A Civil War Soldier's Favorite Song." 2006. Historynet. June 12, 2006. Accessed November 8, 2022. https://www.historynet.com/home-sweet-home-a-civil-war-soldiers-favorite-song/.

"How to Grow, Harvest and Cure Tobacco." n.d. Victory Seed Company. Accessed October 25, 2022. https://victoryseeds.com/pages/how-to-grow-harvest-and-cure-tobacco.

"Kavanaugh Academy." In *The Kentucky Encyclopedia*. Edited by John E. Kleber. 1992. Kentucky Bicentennial Commission, and Frank And. Lexington, Ky.: University Press Of Kentucky.

Kentucky Secretary of State. n.d. "Kentucky Roads." Accessed October 26, 2022. https://www.sos.ky.gov/land/resources/articles/Documents/Kentuckyroads.pdf.

"La Mare Au Diable." 2022. Wikipedia. August 21, 2022. Accessed November 8, 2022. https://en.wikipedia.org/wiki/La_Mare_au_Diable.

"Lawrenceburg." 2021. Wikipedia. November 30, 2021. Accessed November 8, 2022. https://en.wikipedia.org/wiki/Lawrenceburg,_Kentucky.

"Learn about Woodrow Wilson's Fourteen Points Designed to Sow Peace after World War I." n.d. Encyclopedia Britannica. Accessed November 8, 2022. https://www.britannica.com/video/172722/overview-Woodrow-Wilson.

LeMaster, Megan. 2005. *Georgetown College*. Arcadia Publishing.

"Lillard H. Carter (1867-1923) - Find a Grave..." n.d. Www.findagrave.com. Accessed October 29, 2022. https://www.findagrave.com/memorial/107878197/lillard-h-carter.

"Louisville, Kentucky and the 1918-1919 Influenza Epidemic | the American Influenza Epidemic of 1918: A Digital Encyclopedia." n.d. Www.influenzaarchive.org. Accessed October 25, 2022. https://www.influenzaarchive.org/cities/city-louisville.html#.

Matteo, Virginia. 2022. "When Did Women Start Shaving? The History of Female Hair Removal." Owlcation. July 6, 2022. Accessed November 8, 2022. https://owlcation.com/humanities/When-Did-Women-Start-Shaving-The-Painful-History-of-Female-Depilation.

"Maumee II (Fuel Ship No. 14)." n.d. Public2.Nhhcaws.local. Accessed November 8, 2022. https://www.history.navy.mil/research/histories/ship-histories/danfs/m/maumee-ii.html.

"Memorials in Cranfill Cemetery - Find a Grave." n.d. Www.findagrave.com. Accessed October 25, 2022. https://www.findagrave.com/cemetery/2208968/memorial-search?page=1#sr-18195688.

Muzdakis, Madeleine. 2021. "Learn How the Affordable Kodak Brownie Camera Made Photography Accessible." *My Modern Met*, March 21, 2021. Accessed November 8, 2022. https://mymodernmet.com/kodak-brownie-camera/.

"National Digital Newspaper Program: A History." n.d. Www.uky.edu. Accessed October 27, 2022. https://www.uky.edu/NDNP/kyhistory.html.

"Negro (the Word) a History - African American Registry." 2014. African American Registry. 2014. Accessed November 8, 2022. https://aaregistry.org/story/negro-the-word-a-history/.

Novello, Ivor. 1916. "Keep the Home Fires Burning." Library of Congress, Washington, D.C. 20540 USA. 1916. Accessed November 8, 2022. https://www.loc.gov/item/00694067/.

WORKS CITED

Ogden, William Augustine. 1870. "Ring out the Bells for Christmas." Hymnary.org. 1870. Accessed November 8, 2022. https://hymnary.org/text/ring_out_the_bells_for_christmas.

Olmsted, Larry. 2012. "100 Years of Delicious American Candy History." Forbes. April 12, 2012. https://www.forbes.com/sites/larryolmsted/2012/08/23/100-years-of-delicious-american-candy-history/?sh=3305268f26f3.

"Pendennis." 2022. Wikipedia. September 5, 2022. Accessed November 8, 2022. https://en.wikipedia.org/wiki/Pendennis.

"Pictorial Review." 2022. Wikipedia. July 13, 2022. Accessed November 8, 2022. https://en.wikipedia.org/wiki/Pictorial_Review.

Prince, Jon. 2013. "Retro Candy Timeline." Candyfavorites.com. 2013. Accessed November 8. 2022. https://www.candyfavorites.com/shop/history-american-candy.php.

Ray, Lillian, and Leonard Cooke. 1916. "The Sunshine of Your Smile." Library of Congress, Washington, D.C. 20540 USA. 1916. Accessed November 8, 2022. https://www.loc.gov/item/jukebox-751631/.

———. 2022. "The Sunshine of Your Smile." Wikipedia. June 8, 2022. https://en.wikipedia.org/wiki/The_Sunshine_of_Your_Smile.

Richardson, Samuel. 1748. "Clarissa Harlowe or the History of a Young Lady." Project Gutenberg. 1748. https://www.gutenberg.org/files/9296/9296-h/9296-h.htm.

Rouse, Steve. 2019. "Swing Low, Sweet Chariot by Steve Rouse." Manhattanbeachmusic.com. 2019. https://www.manhattanbeachmusic.com/html/swing_low.html.

"Selective Service Act of 1917." 2018. Wikipedia. Wikimedia Foundation. December 22, 2018. Accessed November 8, 2022. https://en.wikipedia.org/wiki/Selective_Service_Act_of_1917.

Simon, Kenneth A., and W. Vance Grant. 1965. "U.S. High School Graduation Rates: An Historical View." Safe & Civil Schools. Accessed November 8, 2022. https://www.safeandcivilschools.com/research/graduation_rates.php.

Simonds, Frank H. 1918. "The American Review of Reviews." *Review of Reviews* 58 (July-Dec 1918): 256–64. Accessed November 8, 2022. https://babel.hathitrust.org/cgi/pt?id=njp.32101076870524&view=1up&seq=278.

Snyder, Robert. 1979. *A History of Georgetown College.*

"The Courier-Journal." 2022. Wikipedia. September 14, 2022. Accessed November 8, 2022. https://en.wikipedia.org/wiki/The_Courier-Journal.

"The Frankfort and Cincinnati Railroad - Abandoned Rails." n.d. Www.abandonedrails.com. Accessed October 29, 2022. https://www.abandonedrails.com/frankfort-and-cincinnati-railroad.

The Georgetonian. 1916. *Internet Archive.* Georgetown, Ky.: Georgetown College. https://archive.org/details/georgetonian1918geor.

"The League of Youth." 2021. Wikipedia. April 29, 2021. Accessed November 8, 2022. https://en.wikipedia.org/wiki/The_League_of_Youth.

"The School for Scandal." 2019. Wikipedia. October 15, 2019. Accessed November 8, 2022. https://en.wikipedia.org/wiki/The_School_for_Scandal.

"The Students Army Training Corps." n.d. Docslib. Accessed October 25, 2022. https://docslib.org/doc/3791714/the-students-army-training-corps.

WORKS CITED

"The Whip (1917 Film)." 2022. Wikipedia. August 20, 2022. Accessed November 8, 2022. https://en.wikipedia.org/wiki/The_Whip_(1917_film).

US National Archives. n.d. "Pershing's Crusaders." Www.youtube.com. https://www.youtube.com/watch?v=B_Usu_AfAzw.

"What Sank the *USS San Diego*? A WWI Naval Mystery May Be Solved." 2017. San Diego Union-Tribune. September 15, 2017. Accessed November 8, 2022. https://www.sandiegouniontribune.com/military/sd-me-usssandiego-exploration-20170913-story.html.

White, Thomas H. 2019. "Section 13. Radio during World War One (1914-1919)." Earlyradiohistory.us. 2019. Accessed November 8, 2022. https://earlyradiohistory.us/sec013.htm.

William Elsey Connelley, and Ellis Merton Coulter. 1922. *History of Kentucky*.

Wolfson, Andrew. 2018. "For 150 Years, the Courier Journal Has Fought for Justice and Fairness." *The Courier-Journal*. November 8, 2018. Accessed November 8, 2022. https://www.courier-journal.com/story/news/2018/11/08/courier-journal-150-anniversary-justice-fairness/1200347002/.

"Women's Right to Vote in Kentucky. Notable Kentucky African Americans Database." n.d. Accessed November 8, 2022. Nkaa.uky.edu. https://nkaa.uky.edu/nkaa/items/show/1621.

Wood, Haydn, and Ruth Rutherford. 1917. "Love's Garden of Roses." Library of Congress, Washington, D.C. 20540 USA. 1917. Accessed November 8, 2022. https://www.loc.gov/item/jukebox-27372/.

"Woodburn." 2020. Wikipedia. September 30, 2020. Accessed November 8, 2022. https://en.wikipedia.org/wiki/Woodburn,_Kentucky.

"World War I Draft Registration Cards." 2016. National Archives. August 15, 2016. Accessed November 8, 2022. https://www.archives.gov/research/military/ww1/draft-registration.

"WWI: U.S. Naval Air Station: Pauillac, France." n.d. Public1.Nhhcaws.local. Accessed October 30, 2022. https://www.history.navy.mil/content/history/museums/nmusn/explore/photography/wwi/wwi-aviation/u-s--naval-air-stations/us-naval-stations-france/france-pauillac.html.

Bibliography

"100 Years of Population 1910-2010 | Kentucky: By the Numbers." n.d. Kybtn.ca.uky.edu. Accessed October 26, 2022. https://kybtn.ca.uky.edu/content/100-years-population-1910-2010.

"1917 in Film." 2022. Wikipedia. September 25, 2022. https://en.wikipedia.org/wiki/1917_in_film.

"A Retrospect of Words from 1918." n.d. Www.merriam-Webster.com. Accessed October 27, 2022. https://www.merriam-webster.com/words-at-play/1918-word-list.

"A School for Scandal." 2022. Theatrehistory.com. 2022. https://www.theatrehistory.com/british/sheridan002.html.

"About This Collection | World War I Sheet Music | Digital Collections | Library of Congress." n.d. Library of Congress, Washington, D.C. 20540 USA. Accessed October 25, 2022. https://www.loc.gov/collections/world-war-i-sheet-music/about-this-collection/.

"Al Alberts - Love Here Is My Heart." n.d. Www.youtube.com. Accessed October 25, 2022. https://www.youtube.com/watch?v=YYD-L7dalCw.

"Arthur Yager." 2021. Wikipedia. November 7, 2021. https://en.wikipedia.org/wiki/Arthur_Yager.

Baker, Chuck. 2015. "The 1st Brownie Camera." 2015. https://www.brownie-camera.com/blog/the-1st-kodak-brownie-camera/.

Belle of the Blue. 1917. Georgetown, Kentucky: Georgetown College.

Belle of the Blue. 1919. Georgetown, Kentucky: Georgetown College.

Belle of the Blue. 1920. Georgetown, Kentucky: Georgetown College.

"Benedict's Restaurant." 2017. Welcome to "the Little Colonel" Website. January 5, 2017. https://littlecolonel.com/node/392.

"Bethel College (Kentucky)." 2022. Wikipedia. July 19, 2022. https://en.wikipedia.org/wiki/Bethel_College_(Kentucky).

Bettez, David J. 2016. *Kentucky and the Great War*. University Press of Kentucky.

Boles, John B. 1976. *Religion in Antebellum Kentucky*. Lexington, Kentucky: The University Press of Kentucky.

"Bowling Green." 2021. Wikipedia. May 23, 2021. https://en.wikipedia.org/wiki/Bowling_Green.

"Bowling Green Kentucky Vintage Postcards & Images." n.d. CardCow.com. Accessed October 25, 2022. https://www.cardcow.com/viewall/64974/.

Britannica. 2022. "Encyclopedia Britannica." In *Encyclopædia Britannica*. https://www.britannica.com/.

Brown, Lew, and Kerry Mills. 1917a. "I'll Come back to You When It's All Over." Digital Collections at the University of Illinois at Urbana-Champaign Library. 1917. https://digital.library.illinois.edu/items/85cbb4d0-c55a-0134-2373-0050569601ca-b#?cv=0&r=0&xywh=-1741%2C-467%2C9896%2C9325.

BIBLIOGRAPHY

———. 1917b. "I'll Come back to You When It's Over." Www.youtube.com. 1917. https://www.youtube.com/watch?v=ueMF0mNwYs0.

Brown, Lew, and Albert Von Tilzer. 1917a. "Au Revoir but Not Goodbye." Www.youtube.com. 1917. https://www.youtube.com/watch?v=rnWiBirpW9k.

———. 1917b. "Au Revoir but Not Goodbye." Library of Congress, Washington, D.C. 20540 USA. 1917. https://www.loc.gov/item/jukebox-817664/.

———. 1917c. "Au Revoir, but Not Good Bye, (Soldier Boy) by Albert von Tilzer - 1917 Sheet Music." Www.ggarchives.com. 1917. https://www.ggarchives.com/SpCol/SheetMusic/AuRevoirButNotGoodbye-VonTilzer-1917.html#gsc.tab=0.

———. 1917d. "Au Revoir, but Not Good-Bye (Soldier Boy)." Library of Congress, Washington, D.C. 20540 USA. 1917. https://www.loc.gov/item/2014562659/.

———. 1917e. "Au Revoir, but Not Goodbye, Soldier Boy (1917)." Www.youtube.com. 1917. https://www.youtube.com/watch?v=JG4IbjBQlpQ.

Bureau, US Census. n.d. "Statistical Abstract of the United States: 1918." Census.gov. https://www.census.gov/library/publications/1919/compendia/statab/41ed.html.

Burns, Adam. 2002. "Kentucky Railroads: Map, History, Abandoned Lines." American-Rails.com. October 9, 2002. https://www.american-rails.com/ky.html.

Buzzell, Francis. 1910. *The Great Lakes Naval Training Station: A History*. Google Books. Small, Maynard. My Book.

Byerly, Carol R. 2010. "The U.S. Military and the Influenza Pandemic of 1918-1919." *Public Health Reports (Washington, D.C. : 1974)* 125 Suppl 3 (Suppl 3): 82–91. https://www.ncbi.nlm.nih.gov/pmc/articles/PMC2862337/.

Callahan, J Will, and Lee S Roberts. 1918. "Smiles." Library of Congress, Washington, D.C. 20540 USA. 1918. https://www.loc.gov/item/jukebox-30166/.

Callahan, J. Will, and Lee S. Roberts. 1917. "Smiles." Library of Congress, Washington, D.C. 20540 USA. 1917. https://www.loc.gov/item/jukebox-659550/.

Callahan, J., and Lee Roberts. 1918. "Smiles." *Historic Sheet Music Collection*, January. https://digitalcommons.conncoll.edu/sheetmusic/1270/.

"Camp Taylor, Louisville." 2022. Wikipedia. January 1, 2022. https://en.wikipedia.org/wiki/Camp_Taylor.

Carina. 2011. "An Annotated History of the Vaudeville Theater." TheaterSeatStore Blog. October 11, 2011. https://www.theaterseatstore.com/blog/vaudeville-theater.

Centers for Disease Control and Prevention. 2018. "History of 1918 Flu Pandemic." Centers for Disease Control and Prevention. CDC. March 21, 2018. https://www.cdc.gov/flu/pandemic-resources/1918-commemoration/1918-pandemic-history.htm.

"Chicago, Illinois and the 1918-1919 Influenza Epidemic | the American Influenza Epidemic of 1918: A Digital Encyclopedia." 2021. Influenzaarchive.org. 2021. https://www.influenzaarchive.org/cities/city-chicago.html.

"Clarissa." 2019. Wikipedia. Wikimedia Foundation. October 3, 2019. https://en.wikipedia.org/wiki/Clarissa.

Clark, Thomas Dionysius. 1977. *Agrarian Kentucky*. Lexington, Kentucky: The University Press of Kentucky.

Conley, John Wesley, and William Carey University Libraries. 1913. *History of the Baptist Young People's Union of America*. Internet Archive. Griffith. https://archive.org/details/historyofbaptist00conl.

BIBLIOGRAPHY

Davies, Mary Carolyn. 1918. *The Drums in Our Street*. New York: The MacMillan Company.

"Detroit, Michigan and the 1918-1919 Influenza Epidemic | the American Influenza Epidemic of 1918: A Digital Encyclopedia." n.d. Www.influenzaarchive.org. Accessed October 25, 2022. https://www.influenzaarchive.org/cities/city-detroit.html#.

Dirks, Tim. n.d. "Film History Milestones - 1917." Www.filmsite.org. Accessed October 25, 2022. https://www.filmsite.org/1917-filmhistory.html.

Duffy, Michael. 2009. "First World War.com - Who's Who - Sir David Beatty." Www.firstworldwar.com. August 22, 2009. https://www.firstworldwar.com/bio/beatty.htm.

Elliott, Zo, and Stoddard King. 1917. "There's a Long, Long Trail." Library of Congress, Washington, D.C. 20540 USA. 1917. https://www.loc.gov/item/jukebox-817436/.

Empey, Arthur Guy, and Boston University of Massachusetts. 1917. *"Over the Top," by an American Soldier Who Went, Arthur Guy Empey, Machine Gunner, Serving in France; Internet Archive*. New York and London, G. P. Putnam's sons. https://archive.org/details/overtopbyamerica00empe.

Eyler, John M. 2010. "The State of Science, Microbiology, and Vaccines circa 1918." *Public Health Reports* 125 (3_suppl): 27–36. https://doi.org/10.1177/00333549101250s306.

Fairman, George. 1917a. "I Don't Know Where I'm Going but I'm on My Way." Www.youtube.com. 1917. https://www.youtube.com/watch?v=HkIv6J6Vyu0.

———. 1917b. "I Don't Know Where I'm Going but I'm on My Way." Library of Congress, Washington, D.C. 20540 USA. 1917. https://www.loc.gov/item/2013563182/.

———. 1917c. "I Don't Know Where I'm Going, but I'm on My Way." Library of Congress, Washington, D.C. 20540 USA. 1917. https://www.loc.gov/item/jukebox-25045/.

Fields, Carl R. *A Sesquicentennial History of Georgetown College*.

Fields, Wilbur. Letter to Elliott Cranfill. 2018, October 25, 2018.

"Franklin." 2019. Wikipedia. May 1, 2019. https://en.wikipedia.org/wiki/Franklin,_Kentucky.

Georgetown College. 1894. *Historical Catalogue of Georgetown College, 1829-1917*. Georgetown News Press.

"Glossary of Nautical Terms (A-L)." 2022. Wikipedia. October 27, 2022. https://en.wikipedia.org/wiki/Glossary_of_nautical_terms_(A-L)#J.

"'Good Morning Mr. Zip-Zip-Zip' (1918) - Eugene Buckley & Peerless Quartette." n.d. Www.youtube.com. Accessed October 25, 2022. https://www.youtube.com/watch?v=_8kNpGTPbvk&list=PL9-qGPmFEWNMXw57S_q3TZNZg-f99GUMC.

Grabenstein, J. D. 2006. "Immunization to Protect the US Armed Forces: Heritage, Current Practice, and Prospects." *Epidemiologic Reviews* 28 (1): 3–26. https://doi.org/10.1093/epirev/mxj003.

Grossman, Ron. 2014. "Flashback: 1918 Influenza Epidemic Struck Hard, Fast." Chicago Tribune. October 18, 2014. https://www.chicagotribune.com/news/ct-epidemic-scare-flashback-1019-2-20141018-story.html.

"Guide to Writing Love Letters. British Library." n.d. Www.bl.uk. Accessed October 25, 2022. https://www.bl.uk/collection-items/guide-to-writing-love-letters.

Hambrick (Ed.), Maribeth, and Stan Dyer (Ed.). 2011. *History of Georgetown Baptist Church 1810-2010*. Lexington, Kentucky: The Clark Group.

BIBLIOGRAPHY

Hammond, Trevor. 2018. "Early Household Appliances - the Official Blog of Newspapers.com." July 12, 2018. https://blog.newspapers.com/early-household-appliances/.

Harding, Colin. 2014. "The Vest Pocket Kodak Was the Soldier's Camera - National Science and Media Museum Blog." National Science and Media Museum Blog. Eleanor Mitchell. March 13, 2014. https://blog.scienceandmediamuseum.org.uk/the-vest-pocket-kodak-was-the-soldiers-camera/.

Harman, J. 1948. "UA1A Brief Historical Sketch of the Bowling Green Business University." *WKU Archives Records*, January. https://digitalcommons.wku.edu/dlsc_ua_records/589.

Harper, Douglas. 2015. "Online Etymology Dictionary." Etymonline.com. 2015. https://www.etymonline.com/.

Harrison, Lowell H. 2021. *Western Kentucky University*. University Press of Kentucky.

Hartford, Ellis F. 1977. *The Little White Schoolhouse*. Lexington, Kentucky: The University Press of Kentucky.

Heller, Otto. 1912. *Henrik Ibsen; Plays and Problems*. New York: Houghton Mifflin.

Hendrickson, Robert, and Internet Archive. 1997. *The Facts on File Encyclopedia of Word and Phrase Origins*. Internet Archive. New York : Facts on File. https://archive.org/details/factsonfileencyc00hend.

"Historical Photos of the 1918 Fires." 2018. Duluth News Tribune. October 12, 2018. https://www.duluthnewstribune.com/news/historical-photos-of-the-1918-fires.

"History of Kentucky Utilities Company – FundingUniverse." n.d. Www.fundinguniverse.com. Accessed October 25, 2022. http://www.fundinguniverse.com/company-histories/kentucky-utilities-company-history/.

History.com Editors. 2009. "Fire Rages in Minnesota." History. November 13, 2009. https://www.history.com/this-day-in-history/fire-rages-in-minnesota.

———. 2018. "Model T." History. A&E Television Networks. August 21, 2018. https://www.history.com/topics/inventions/model-t.

Hixson, Kenneth R. 2007. *Forty Miles, Forty Bridges*. Henry Clay Press.

Hollingsworth, Jana. 2018. "1918 Fires Remain State's Worst Natural Disaster." Duluth News Tribune. October 12, 2018. https://www.duluthnewstribune.com/news/1918-fires-remain-states-worst-natural-disaster.

Hollingsworth, Randolph. 2018. "History of Kentucky Women's Suffrage: An Overview | H-Kentucky | H-Net." Networks.h-Net.org. February 3, 2018. https://networks.h-net.org/node/2289/blog/ky-woman-suffrage/1324424/history-kentucky-womens-suffrage-overview.

"Home." 2019. Wikipedia. November 8, 2019. https://en.wikipedia.org/wiki/Home.

"Home Sweet Home (1823)." n.d. Www.youtube.com. https://www.youtube.com/watch?v=OqjjfF1Wn-s.

"'Home, Sweet Home': A Civil War Soldier's Favorite Song." 2006. Historynet. June 12, 2006. https://www.historynet.com/home-sweet-home-a-civil-war-soldiers-favorite-song/.

"Household Appliances Timeline - Greatest Engineering Achievements of the Twentieth Century." 2019. Greatachievements.org. 2019. http://www.greatachievements.org/?id=3768.

"How to Grow, Harvest and Cure Tobacco." n.d. Victory Seed Company. Accessed October 25, 2022. https://victoryseeds.com/pages/how-to-grow-harvest-and-cure-tobacco.

BIBLIOGRAPHY

Howell, Carl. 2015. *Kentucky in the Early 1900s: A Postcard Tribute*. Louisville, Kentucky: Butler Books.

Hulme, David. 2001. "Biography: Woodrow Wilson: Making the World Safe for Democracy | Vision." Www.vision.org. 2001. https://www.vision.org/biography-woodrow-wilson-making-world-safe-democracy-451.

Humanities, National Endowment for the. n.d. "The Louisville Herald. [Volume]." *Chroniclingamerica.loc.gov*. Accessed October 26, 2022. https://chroniclingamerica.loc.gov/lccn/sn82016284/.

Ingraham, J. H. (Joseph Holt), and University of California Libraries. 1858. *The Prince of the House of David; Or, Three Years in the Holy City. Being a Series of the Letters of Adina, a Jewess of Alexandria, Sojourning in Jerusalem in the Days of Herod, Addressed to Her Father, a Wealthy Jew in Egypt; and Relating, as If by an Eye-Witness, All the Scenes and Wonderful Incidents in the Life of Jesus of Nazareth, from His Baptism in Jordan to His Crucifixion on Calvary. Internet Archive*. New York : Pudney & Russell. https://archive.org/details/princehousedav00ingrrich/mode/2up?ref=ol&view=theater.

Irvin, Helen D. 1979. *Women in Kentucky*. Lexington, Kentucky: The University Press of Kentucky.

Ivor, Novello. n.d. "Keep the Home Fires Burning." Library of Congress, Washington, D.C. 20540 USA. Accessed October 29, 2022. https://www.loc.gov/item/00694067/.

Jeffrey, Jonathan. 2002. *Bowling Green in Vintage Postcards*. Arcadia Publishing.

John McCormack. n.d. "Theres a Long Long Trail a Winding Sung by John McCormack." *YouTube*. Accessed July 26, 2022. https://www.youtube.com/watch?v=DczcPkogrZU.

"John McCormack - Love's Garden of Roses (1918)." n.d. Www.youtube.com. Accessed October 26, 2022. https://www.youtube.com/watch?v=CfFw9sFATPc.

"John McCormack - the Sunshine of Your Smile (1916)." n.d. Www.youtube.com. Accessed October 27, 2022. https://www.youtube.com/watch?v=VMDs1sJ3PMI.

"John McCormack Keep the Home Fires Burning." 2008. *YouTube*. https://www.youtube.com/watch?v=5P8UokgVqWs.

Kentucky Secretary of State. n.d. "Kentucky Roads." Accessed October 26, 2022. https://www.sos.ky.gov/land/resources/articles/Documents/Kentuckyroads.pdf.

Kleber, John E, Kentucky Bicentennial Commission, and Frank And. 1992. *The Kentucky Encyclopedia*. Lexington, Ky.: University Press Of Kentucky.

Klotter, James C. 1996. *Kentucky : Portrait in Paradox, 1900-1950*. Frankfort, Ky: Kentucky Historical Society.

"La Mare Au Diable." 2022. Wikipedia. August 21, 2022. https://en.wikipedia.org/wiki/La_Mare_au_Diable.

"Lambert Murphy - Smiles (1917 Music Video) | #24 Song." n.d. Playback.fm. Accessed October 25, 2022. https://playback.fm/charts/top-100-songs/video/1917/Lambert-Murphy-Smiles.

"Lambert Murphy 'Smiles' (1918)." n.d. Www.youtube.com. Accessed October 26, 2022. https://www.youtube.com/watch?v=Yh9CC-6CmWs.

"Lawrenceburg." 2021. Wikipedia. November 30, 2021. https://en.wikipedia.org/wiki/Lawrenceburg,_Kentucky.

"Learn about Woodrow Wilson's Fourteen Points Designed to Sow Peace after World War

BIBLIOGRAPHY

I." n.d. Encyclopedia Britannica. https://www.britannica.com/video/172722/overview-Woodrow-Wilson.

LeMaster, Megan. 2005. *Georgetown College*. Arcadia Publishing.

"Lillard H. Carter (1867-1923) - Find a Grave..." n.d. Www.findagrave.com. Accessed October 29, 2022. https://www.findagrave.com/memorial/107878197/lillard-h-carter.

Logan, S. 2020. "The 1918 'Spanish' Influenza Pandemic." Kentucky Historic Institutions. January 30, 2020. https://kyhi.org/2020/01/30/the-1918-spanish-influenza-pandemic/.

"Louisville, Kentucky and the 1918-1919 Influenza Epidemic | the American Influenza Epidemic of 1918: A Digital Encyclopedia." n.d. Www.influenzaarchive.org. Accessed October 25, 2022. https://www.influenzaarchive.org/cities/city-louisville.html#.

Matteo, Virginia. 2022. "When Did Women Start Shaving? The History of Female Hair Removal." Owlcation. July 6, 2022. https://owlcation.com/humanities/When-Did-Women-Start-Shaving-The-Painful-History-of-Female-Depilation.

"Maumee II (Fuel Ship No. 14)." n.d. Public2.Nhhcaws.local. https://www.history.navy.mil/research/histories/ship-histories/danfs/m/maumee-ii.html.

"Memorials in Cranfill Cemetery - Find a Grave." n.d. Www.findagrave.com. Accessed October 25, 2022. https://www.findagrave.com/cemetery/2208968/memorial-search?page=1#sr-18195688.

Merriam-Webster. 2022. "Merriam-Webster Dictionary." Merriam-Webster.com. Merriam-Webster. 2022. https://www.merriam-webster.com/.

Muzdakis, Madeleine. 2021. "Learn How the Affordable Kodak Brownie Camera Made Photography Accessible." *My Modern Met*, March 21, 2021. https://mymodernmet.com/kodak-brownie-camera/.

"National Digital Newspaper Program: A History." n.d. Www.uky.edu. Accessed October 27, 2022. https://www.uky.edu/NDNP/kyhistory.html.

"Negro (the Word) a History - African American Registry." 2014. African American Registry. 2014. https://aaregistry.org/story/negro-the-word-a-history/.

Novello, Ivor. 1916a. "Keep the Home Fires Burning." Library of Congress, Washington, D.C. 20540 USA. 1916. https://www.loc.gov/item/00694067/.

———. 1916b. "Keep the Home Fires Burning...a WW1 Song (with Lyrics)." Www.youtube.com. 1916. https://www.youtube.com/watch?v=NrvMUEyXLSg.

Ogden, William Augustine. 1870. "Ring out the Bells for Christmas." Hymnary.org. 1870. https://hymnary.org/text/ring_out_the_bells_for_christmas.

Olmsted, Larry. 2012. "100 Years of Delicious American Candy History." Forbes. April 12, 2012. https://www.forbes.com/sites/larryolmsted/2012/08/23/100-years-of-delicious-american-candy-history/?sh=3305268f26f3.

Palmer, A. N. 1894. *Business Writing*. Cedar Rapids, Iowa: Western Penman Publishing Company.

Palmer, George Herbert. 1908. *The Life of Alice Freeman Palmer*. Boston: Riverside Press.

Party, New York State Woman Suffrage. 1917. "Broadside : What Every Woman Knows. New York State Woman Suffrage Party. [1917]." New York : National Woman Suffrage Publishing Company, Inc. 1917. https://lewissuffragecollection.omeka.net/items/show/1628.

"Peerless Quartet - the Lights of My Home Town (1916 Music Video) | #7 Song." n.d. Playback.fm. Accessed October 25, 2022. https://playback.fm/charts/top-100-songs/video/1916/Peerless-Quartet-The-Lights-of-My-Home-Town.

"Pendennis." 2022. Wikipedia. September 5, 2022. https://en.wikipedia.org/wiki/Pendennis.

Phillips, Judith J. 1985. *Enlightenment, Education and Entertainment*. University of Louisville.

"Pictorial Review." 2022. Wikipedia. July 13, 2022. https://en.wikipedia.org/wiki/Pictorial_Review.

Prince, Jon. 2013. "Retro Candy Timeline." Candyfavorites.com. 2013. https://www.candyfavorites.com/shop/history-american-candy.php.

Ray, Lillian, and Leonard Cooke. 1916. "The Sunshine of Your Smile." Library of Congress, Washington, D.C. 20540 USA. 1916. https://www.loc.gov/item/jukebox-751631/.

———. 2022. "The Sunshine of Your Smile." Wikipedia. June 8, 2022. https://en.wikipedia.org/wiki/The_Sunshine_of_Your_Smile.

"Records of the Bureau of Labor Statistics [BLS]." 2016. National Archives. August 15, 2016. https://www.archives.gov/research/guide-fed-records/groups/257.html.

Richard Shawn Faulkner. 2017. *Pershing's Crusaders : The American Soldier in World War I*. Lawrence: University Press Of Kansas.

Richardson, Samuel. 1748. "Clarissa Harlowe or the History of a Young Lady." Project Gutenberg. 1748. https://www.gutenberg.org/files/9296/9296-h/9296-h.htm.

Rouse, Steve. 2019. "Swing Low, Sweet Chariot by Steve Rouse." Manhattanbeachmusic.com. 2019. https://www.manhattanbeachmusic.com/html/swing_low.html.

Sebakijje, Lena. n.d. "Research Guides: World War I Draft: Topics in Chronicling America: Introduction." Guides.loc.gov. https://guides.loc.gov/chronicling-america-wwi-draft.

"Selective Service Act of 1917." 2018. Wikipedia. Wikimedia Foundation. December 22, 2018. https://en.wikipedia.org/wiki/Selective_Service_Act_of_1917.

Share, Allen J. 1982. *Cities in the Commonwealth*. Lexington, Kentucky: The University Press of Kentucky.

Simon, Kenneth A., and W. Vance Grant. 1965. "U.S. High School Graduation Rates: An Historical View." Safe and Civil Schools. 1965. https://www.safeandcivilschools.com/research/graduation_rates.php.

Simonds, Frank H. 1918. "The American Review of Reviews." *Review of Reviews* 58 (July-Dec 1918): 256–64. https://babel.hathitrust.org/cgi/pt?id=njp.32101076870524&view=1up&seq=278.

Slout, William L. 2008. *Theatre in a Tent*. Wildside Press LLC.

Snyder, Robert. 1979. *A History of Georgetown College*.

Songs the Soldiers and Sailors Sing! 1918. Leo Feist.

Stapler, Martha G. 1917. *The Woman Suffrage Year Book, 1917*. *Google Books*. National Woman Suffrage Publishing Company. https://books.google.com/books?id=YH4EAAAAYAAJ&printsec=frontcover#v=onepage&q&f=false.

States., United. 1920. *Census of Electrical Industries: 1917- Telephones and Telegraphs*. Government Printing Office.

Taylor, Richard. 2018. *Elkhorn*. Lexington, Kentucky: The University Press of Kentucky.

"The Courier-Journal." 2022. Wikipedia. September 14, 2022. https://en.wikipedia.org/wiki/The_Courier-Journal.

"The Frankfort and Cincinnati Railroad - Abandoned Rails." n.d. Www.abandonedrails.-

com. Accessed October 29, 2022. https://www.abandonedrails.com/frankfort-and-cincinnati-railroad.

The Georgetonian. 1918. *Internet Archive.* Georgetown, Ky. : Georgetown College. https://archive.org/details/georgetonian1918geor.

"The League of Youth." 2021. Wikipedia. April 29, 2021. https://en.wikipedia.org/wiki/The_League_of_Youth.

"The SAVEUR Candy Timeline: 150 Years in American Sweets." 2019. Saveur. March 18, 2019. https://www.saveur.com/gallery/Classic-Candy-Time-Line/.

"The School for Scandal." 2019. Wikipedia. October 15, 2019. https://en.wikipedia.org/wiki/The_School_for_Scandal.

"The Students Army Training Corps." 1918. Docslib. 1918. https://docslib.org/doc/3791714/the-students-army-training-corps.

"The Victor-Victrola Page." 2022. Victor-Victrola.com. 2022. http://www.victor-victrola.com/History%20of%20the%20Victor%20Phonograph.htm.

"The Whip (1917 Film)." 2022. Wikipedia. August 20, 2022. https://en.wikipedia.org/wiki/The_Whip_(1917_film).

"There's a Long Long Trail A-Winding." 2021. Wikipedia. July 19, 2021. https://en.wikipedia.org/wiki/There%27s_a_Long_Long_Trail_A-Winding.

"To Hell with the Kaiser!" 2013. Wikipedia. September 13, 2013. https://en.wikipedia.org/wiki/To_Hell_with_the_Kaiser!.

United States. Office of Naval Records and Library. Historical Section., and State Library of Pennsylvania. n.d. *American Ship Casualties of the World War Including Naval Vessels, Merchant Ships, Sailing Vessels, and Fishing Craft / Compiled by Historical Section. Internet Archive.* G.P.O.,. Accessed October 25, 2022. https://archive.org/stream/americanshipcasu00unit/americanshipcasu00unit_djvu.txt.

US National Archives. n.d. "Pershing's Crusaders." Www.youtube.com. https://www.youtube.com/watch?v=B_Usu_AfAzw.

"Walter Glynne - I Passed by Your Window (1917 Music Video) | #12 Song." n.d. Playback.fm. Accessed October 25, 2022. https://playback.fm/charts/top-100-songs/video/1917/Walter-Glynne-I-Passed-By-Your-Window.

"What Sank the USS San Diego? A WWI Naval Mystery May Be Solved." 2017. San Diego Union-Tribune. September 15, 2017. https://www.sandiegouniontribune.com/military/sd-me-usssandiego-exploration-20170913-story.html.

White, Thomas H. 2019. "Section 13. Radio during World War One (1914-1919)." Earlyradiohistory.us. 2019. https://earlyradiohistory.us/sec013.htm.

William Elsey Connelley, and Ellis Merton Coulter. 1922. *History of Kentucky.*

Williams, Michael. 2014. "The Story behind World War I's Greatest Anthem, 100 Years On." The Conversation. October 8, 2014. https://theconversation.com/the-story-behind-world-war-is-greatest-anthem-100-years-on-31601.

Wolfson, Andrew. 2018. "For 150 Years, the Courier Journal Has Fought for Justice and Fairness." The Courier-Journal. November 8, 2018. https://www.courier-journal.com/story/news/2018/11/08/courier-journal-150-anniversary-justice-fairness/1200347002/.

"Women's Right to Vote in Kentucky · Notable Kentucky African Americans Database." n.d. Nkaa.uky.edu. https://nkaa.uky.edu/nkaa/items/show/1621.

Wood, Haydn, and Ruth Rutherford. 1917. "Love's Garden of Roses." Library of Congress, Washington, D.C. 20540 USA. 1917. https://www.loc.gov/item/jukebox-27372/.

BIBLIOGRAPHY

"Woodburn." 2020. Wikipedia. September 30, 2020. https://en.wikipedia.org/wiki/Woodburn.

"World War I Draft Registration Cards." 2016. National Archives. August 15, 2016. https://www.archives.gov/research/military/ww1/draft-registration.

"WWI: U.S. Naval Air Station: Pauillac, France." n.d. Public1.Nhhcaws.local. Accessed October 30, 2022. https://www.history.navy.mil/content/history/museums/nmusn/explore/photography/wwi/wwi-aviation/u-s--naval-air-stations/us-naval-stations-france/france-pauillac.html.

Zo, Elliott, and Stoddard King. 1917. "There's a Long, Long Trail." Library of Congress, Washington, D.C. 20540 USA. 1917. https://www.loc.gov/item/jukebox-817436/.

Marcie McGuire

Marcie McGuire is an award-winning poet, English professor, librarian, editor, and instructional designer—now enjoying retirement with a lifetime of projects. She is passionate about genealogy and blends decades of experience in various fields to create heart-warming memoirs from her own family history.

Marcie lives in beautiful Columbia, Missouri with her husband. She spends her days volunteering—either harvesting vegetables for the local food bank or scanning documents for the State Historical Society. When she's not giving time to others, Marcie enjoys dancing, gardening...and collecting honey from her backyard beehives.

www.ingramcontent.com/pod-product-compliance
Lightning Source LLC
Chambersburg PA
CBHW072000150426
43194CB00008B/942